Edited by Catherine A. Cavanaugh
and Randi R. Warne

Telling Tales

ESSAYS IN WESTERN WOMEN'S HISTORY

UBC Press · Vancouver · Toronto

Printed in Canada on acid-free paper ∞

ISBN 0-7748-0794-6 (hardcover)
ISBN 0-7748-0795-4 (paperback)

Canadian Cataloguing in Publication Data

Main entry under title:

Telling tales

Includes bibliographical references and index.
ISBN 0-7748-0794-6 (bound)
ISBN 0-7748-0795-4 (pbk.)

1. Women–Canada, Western–History. 2. Women pioneers–Canada, Western–History. 3. Canada, Western–History. I. Cavanaugh, Catherine Anne, 1945- II. Warne, R. R. (Randi Ruth), 1952-
HG1459.W4T44 2000 305.4′09712′09 C00-910652-9

This book has been published with the help of a grant from the Humanities and Social Sciences Federation of Canada, using funds provided by the Social Sciences and Humanities Research Council of Canada.

UBC Press acknowledges the financial support of the Government of Canada through the Book Publishing Industry Development Program (BPIDP) for our publishing activities.

Canadä

We also gratefully acknowledge the support of the Canada Council for the Arts for our publishing program, as well as the support of the British Columbia Arts Council.

UBC Press
University of British Columbia
2029 West Mall, Vancouver, BC V6T 1Z2
(604) 822-5959
Fax: (604) 822-6083
E-mail: info@ubcpress.ubc.ca
www.ubcpress.ubc.ca

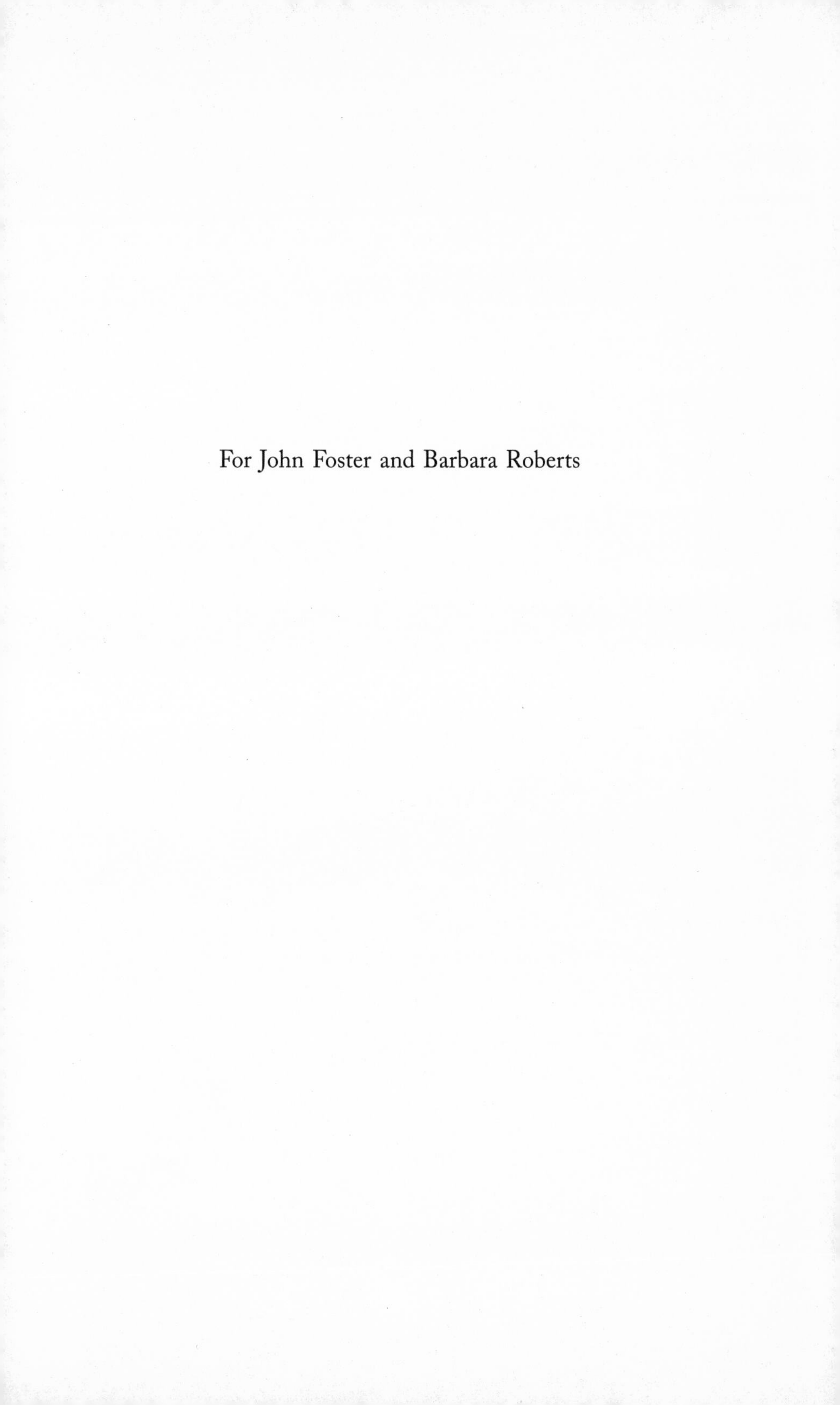

For John Foster and Barbara Roberts

Contents

Illustrations

Acknowledgments

This volume owes much to John Foster, who first brought us together as editors in the *Alberta Nature and Culture Series* for which he was General Editor, with Dick Harrison. The result was *Standing on New Ground* (1993), an interdisciplinary collection of essays on women in Alberta. Dr. Foster was a gifted teacher and mentor. He inspired many people who are currently researching and writing western history. His premature death in 1996 was a great loss to the University of Alberta's Department of History and Classics, the community of provincial historians generally, and those of us who gained so much from his thoughtfulness, care, and attention.

We also dedicate this volume to a dear friend and colleague, Barbara Roberts, who was a constant source of support and encouragement during the early stages of this project. Barbara was part of a generation of feminist historians who redefined how we think and write about Canadian history. Her article, "'They Drove Him to Drink': Donald Creighton's Macdonald and His Wives," in *Canada: An Historical Magazine* (December 1975), is a revisionist classic – provocative, humorous and insightful. She is greatly missed.

We thank the contributors to this volume for remaining with the project through many interruptions as life repeatedly intervened with births, deaths, illnesses, job changes, migrations out of the country and back again, and technological developments that facilitated working at a distance but also created unanticipated difficulties. The contributors' faith in the project was essential to its successful completion. Working on the book has only reinforced for us the theme at the heart of this volume. That is, for women, working and living in a man-made world is a dicey business. It is risky, challenging, and complex. Understanding that complexity is essential to making a future in which historical work by and about women will be viewed as normal and celebrated regularly.

We are a small cohort of scholars researching and writing in western women's history, but not everyone is represented here. There are others whose work we would have liked to have included in this book. Some of their work is referred to in the introduction. Western women's history is still an area of Canadian history that is, institutionally, relatively weak. As a result, individual support for projects such as this is especially important. We thank the anonymous readers for their time and thoughtful comments that helped to improve the essays overall. We are especially grateful to our editors at UBC Press: Laura Macleod, who first had the idea, and Ann Macklem and Jean Wilson, for so ably shepherding the book through its final stages. Thanks too to Lloydene Eherer and Kathy Ponto at Athabasca University who rescued us from technological nightmares on several occasions, converting and otherwise adapting copy to make it accessible. We are grateful to Margot Young for her timely assistance assembling the bibliography. We also appreciate the journals that agreed to allow us to reprint several articles, and the archives that gave permission to reproduce photographs. Finally, we wish to thank family and friends who have provided loving care through good times and bad and the many colleagues who encouraged us (you know who you are.) Cathy particularly wants to thank her partner, John Beckingham, for his constant support, Pat, Frances, and Jennifer for the great takeout dinners, and "the girls" for sticking together. Randi wishes to acknowledge her grandmother, Ruth Dahl Warne, Prairie immigrant, speed skater, telephone pioneer, and example. She also thanks Manitoba winters, for teaching endurance.

Telling Tales

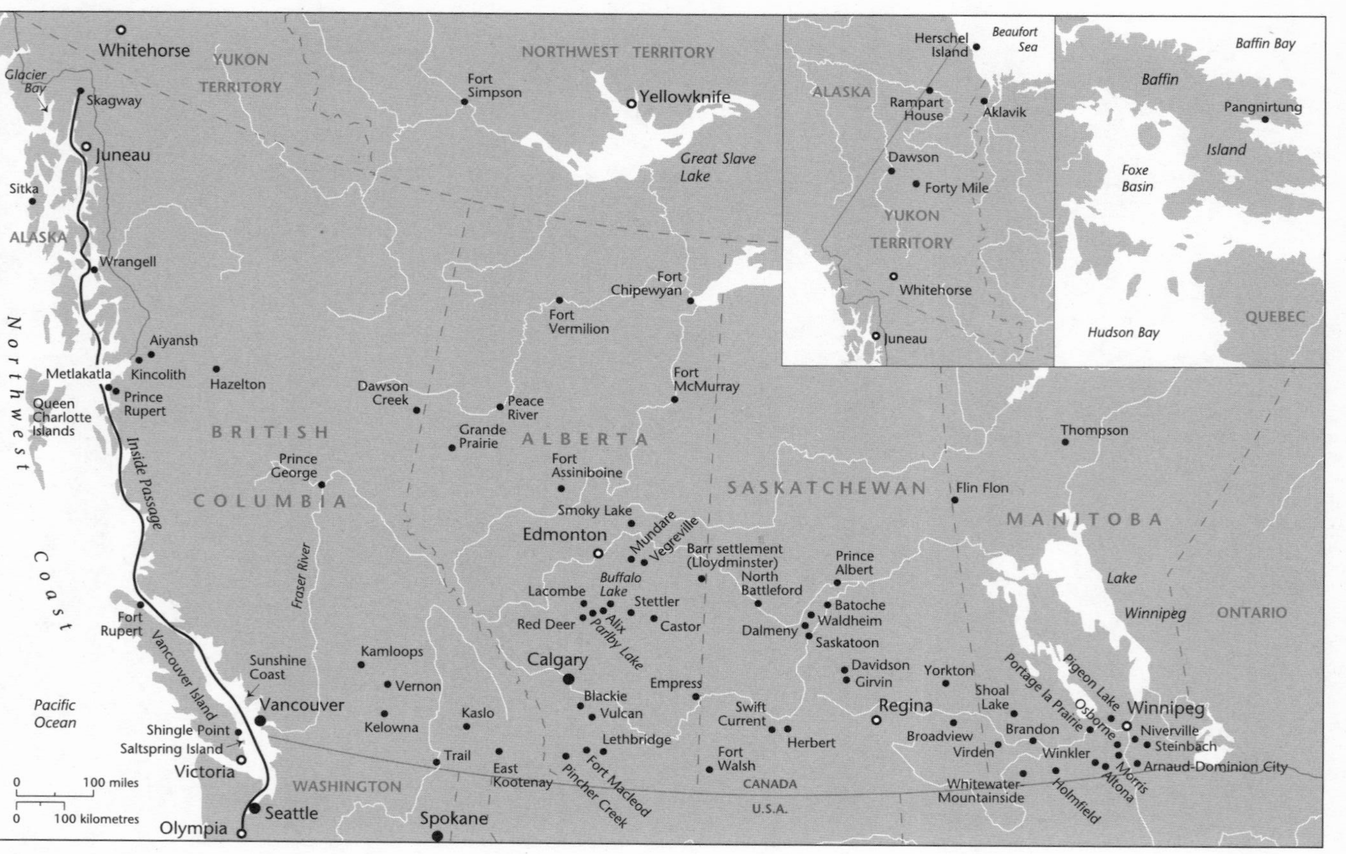

Place names referred to in the book

Introduction

CATHERINE A. CAVANAUGH AND
RANDI R. WARNE

Human beings are incurable storytellers. We weave narratives like cloth, creating multipatterned garments that we inhabit as memory. Whether real or imagined, the stories matter; they shape our understanding of what has gone before, and provide both basis and direction for what might happen in the future. They give us our identities, casting the horizon of our possibilities, what we imagine our lives might be. The nature of the story – and the authority of the storyteller – is therefore of the utmost importance. Changing who tells the story can change the tale itself and, with it, the whole way the world is seen. Storytelling is thus a weighty business and not to be taken lightly.

History writing is one form of storytelling, and at the turn of the twenty-first century in Canada its terrain resembles nothing so much as a pitched battle.[1] The nature of that battle has its own history, though that narrative would be told differently by the various contestants. Nevertheless, some broad outlines can be sketched with which most would agree. Canadian history writing in the first half of the twentieth century focused on nation building. It sought to create a strong, unified narrative that would provide a comprehensive sense of identity for an emerging nation. Consensus was the dominant theme of this early history, and politicians, explorers, and other "great men" were its primary agents. While not identified as such, its narrative centred on Euro-North American colonial hegemony – in lay terms, the story of the "conquest" of an "empty" land and its transformation into an industrial, urbanized civilization on the model of the European nation state. The authors of this history were typically professionals who were employed by universities to generate and disseminate a common understanding of the country's past through their publication and teaching and, more than occasionally, through their advice to the Canadian government. This was nation building in its most practical form. They were also, by and large, members of a relatively homogeneous cultural elite, men of European, often Anglo-Saxon, ancestry who understood their story as the universal story, the binding narrative for the Canadian nation. Beginning in the later half of the twentieth century that relatively stable structure has been seriously challenged.

Every story has its own themes and actors. The increasing prosperity of post-Second World War North America combined with the baby boom and social change movements to produce a new, much more diverse cohort of historians. Some (not all, and fewer as the century reached its end) secured academic employment and set about the business of rethinking the past, informed by their own assumptions, questions, and political concerns. A prodigious array of new "subspecialties" was generated, including social history, labour history, women's history, immigrant history, Native history, and gender history, each with its own theoretical (and political) investments and critical analyses. In contrast to "consensus," the underlying assumption of these diverse approaches to historical narrative was "difference." Various forms of difference, whether of social class, occupation, race, sex, gender, or ethnicity, became the interpretive lens through which these history writers gazed. In each case, what emerged was a remarkable diversity in both the actors identified and the stories told.

The range of narratives available to readers and writers of Canadian history at the beginning of the twenty-first century is the product of an invigorated theorization of the field of history.[2] When the cohort telling the story is relatively homogeneous, inspired by similar questions and ultimate goals, it is easy to naturalize those questions and goals, to assume that they, and they alone, "logically" follow from the evidence. It is relatively easy, for example, to answer the question "where are the women in your histories?" with the reply "women haven't done anything worth noting historically" when the prior, unexamined assumption is that, by definition, it is what men (especially "men like us") do that is important. If you work from the assumption that women are domestic and maternal by nature, then it is unlikely that you will question the construction and maintenance of social and economic arrangements that confine women's human possibilities to marriage and childrearing. Similarly, if you assume that indigenous peoples are "poor savages" in need of "civilizing," then you will have a considerably different understanding of residential schools than you will if you see White settlement of North America as a European colonial invasion that included, as part of its logic of domination, the marginalization and control of Native inhabitants.

When many stories are being told the key question of how each narrative is put together can no longer be avoided. As new voices enter the conversation, we begin to see the ways in which each narrative is limited or partial; that is, we begin to see the way it is *located* in specific social and cultural contexts. The illusion of neutrality, of the "god's eye view" (or the view from nowhere), that marks early histories must be given up. Each narrative is a result of a series of choices, conscious and unconscious, about what one puts in the centre of the study and what questions one seeks to answer. When these multiple narratives are placed alongside one another, what each takes for granted – their "blind spots," as it were – ultimately become visible. Seen in this light, the current multiplicity of perspectives being contested in Canadian history writing signals a vigorous engagement in the generation of more reliable knowledge about Canada, past and present.

In practice, however, the battle lines are drawn. Generally, there are roughly three main configurations of historians. The first, consisting of the so-called traditional historian, advances the cause of an integrated national narrative that emphasizes the institutions, dynamics, and agendas of the "public sphere." That those spheres of government, industry, and intellectual life have been dominated by men of European descent is treated simply as an unremarkable fact. The second configuration of historians advances the perspectives and agendas of those who have generally been either subordinated by or left out of the dominant narrative. Its focus is particularity (e.g., "Ukrainians," "the working class," "women," "the Chinese," and so on), often with a specific focus on the experiences that are deemed characteristic of the group being studied. Unlike traditionalists, who take the particular narrative of a specific segment of the population and treat it as a normative, generic story for everyone, historians of the "particularity" camp emphasize that "traditional" history is but one narrative amongst many. They maintain that other identities and experiences are equally important and that we need to ask the questions and gather the data that will bring them into focus.

The third configuration of historians is suspicious of the homogeneity assumed in both the traditional "consensus" model and the "particularity" model. Postmodernist writers question the existence of reliable, unitary identities and point out that social identity is a tricky question. We all occupy multiple subject positions consisting of shifting identities of race, gender, class, sexuality, ethnicity, age, abilities, and other markers of social difference. No single one of these can be given priority or be set as the base upon which all other identifying features may be grafted. This group sees itself doing "gender" history rather than "women's" history.[3] This distinction is important, although not absolute. Women's history arose as a corrective to the androcentric bias of so-called mainstream history. Rather than emphasizing (a particular cohort of) men as the human norm and ideal, assuming that their actions and concerns are representative of "human" actions and concerns in general, writers of women's history placed women at the centre of their inquiry.[4] This approach implied that a certain universality pertained to "women's experience," or, if not universality, then a kind of stability of identity that allowed for discussions and analysis of, for example, "women's experience under patriarchy." Early critics of this approach noted a replication of the same error that had impaired mainstream history writing, namely, the tendency to assume that one's own cohort represents the general case. Race was a particularly significant issue here, given the overrepresentation, within the ranks of academic historians, of White women of relative economic privilege. (However, women, irrespective of race, are significantly *under*-represented when compared to men.)

Rather than positing "women" as a unitary or fixed category and then investigating those within it, "gender" historians turned their attention to the processes and power relations in and through which gender – sex difference socially reconstructed as masculinity and femininity – is created and made operational.[5] In gender history, experience is often replaced by "discourse" (i.e., the linguistic strategies that create and maintain identities and through which power is deployed in particular settings) as a central focus. The theoretical debates attached to what has been called "the linguistic turn" in history are intricate and have, on occasion, become quite heated.[6] But by pushing the boundaries of our approaches to the past, women's history and gender history have proven useful for challenging androcentric narratives and generating more adequate and reliable knowledge of the past.

The debates within and amongst these various approaches to Canadian history writing at the turn of the twenty-first century underscores the crying need for all kinds of stories to be told and for many kinds of analyses to be conducted. If a single clarity exists, it is that history writing in Canada cannot be conducted in isolation or in one voice. Diversity – in approaches, in subject matter – is essential, as is the reconfiguration of old narrative frameworks. Similarly, the strategies employed to elicit new understandings are necessarily multiple, drawing on the techniques of a range of theoretical commitments. We have endeavoured to reflect that range of exploration here.

Telling Tales introduces readers to recent scholarship in women's history in the Canadian West. While customary mapping places "the West" in the Prairie provinces, we include British Columbia. Under the influence of regional history in Canada, scholars have tended to treat these geographical areas as separate, emphasizing in particular the economic differences between the Prairies' wheat-based economy and British Columbia's mineral and forest economy.[7] But women rarely neatly fit into these categories (which reflect men's experience), and their economic activity tends to straddle the domestic and public. Considering women's experience across western Canada allows for commonalities (as well as differences) to become visible. This approach can prompt a different set of questions and concerns – questions, for example, of relations between women of different social, racial, and ethnic groups.

Also, there are historiographical reasons for combining the Prairies and British Columbia. Most significant is the dominant role played by Britain and central Canada in the economic and political development of the entire western Canadian region. Both the Prairies and British Columbia entered Confederation at about the same time, and the region as a whole depended upon immigration as the primary source of population growth. In much of the West, strong institutional attachments to Anglo Canada existed uneasily with ethnic and cultural diversity. Combining the Prairies and British Columbia captures the social and cultural tensions of a heterogeneous population and opens investigation to a broader range of experiences than does focusing on either alone.

The Ontario border provides the usual eastern line of demarcation, but there is some crossing there as well, as the ideals and ideas of central Canada inflected the experiences of western women. The chapters are arranged to reflect this understanding, disrupting the conventional east-to-west notion of migration and settlement by beginning on the Pacific coast and moving in roughly chronological order from "encounter," to settlement, to the construction of diverse communities.

Telling Tales focuses primarily on newcomer women of dominant and minority cultures during the turbulent, sometimes violent, decades from the 1880s to roughly the 1940s. A cross-cultural/multicultural approach to western women's history has a number of advantages. It reflects the West's characteristically mixed population – British Columbia remained predominantly Anglo-Canadian but, by 1940, about half of Prairie inhabitants were non-British in origin – and underscores the significance of settler communities as places of social and cultural exchange.[8] By exploring their relationships within and across diverse communities we are better able to evaluate women's unequal relations of race, ethnicity, class, religion, and other social factors. At the same time, we can identify common themes in the construction and reshaping of gender relations and social power in new environments. Newcomers brought cultural conventions with them to the West, but migration and resettlement also disrupted established social practices and made new ones possible. The movements of new peoples into western Canada could revive old contests for power and authority or stimulate new ones. A multicultural approach highlights the variety of ways women negotiated these changes as they engaged in cross-cultural encounters, colonization, settlement, and community building. It presents opportunities to explore change and continuity at the intersection of communities or where people of different social backgrounds met, whether in opposition or for mutual benefit and support. The portrait that emerges when this part of Canada's past is viewed from the perspectives of women of diverse social and cultural backgrounds is varied, complex, and often contradictory. It invites writers and readers to rethink our collective heritage.

Of course, women's history in western Canada predates the arrival of Europeans. It includes the many different Aboriginal women who already lived in the territory occupied by newcomers. But, from about the 1880s, Euro-Canadian expansion marked a sharp divide in the history of the West.[9] Underwritten by government policy aimed at consolidating the continental boundaries of Confederation and establishing new investment frontiers by extending Canada's industrial and agricultural base north-westward, large-scale settlement signalled a shift in favour of White institutions, severely restricting the interracial mixing of the fur trade period. Expansionists wanted the West to be the special preserve of British Canada. Their purposes were backed up by official segregation and the control of indigenous peoples, along with aggressive campaigns to attract new (White) populations that would "make the land productive." Between 1896 and 1914, more than 1 million people came to western Canada, laying the foundations of society as we know it today. By 1929 the non-Native population had increased almost tenfold, while the Native population declined by almost one-third. In 1930 Native populations in the region represented about 3 percent of the total, whereas fifty years earlier they were the majority.[10]

Compared with what occurred in other "new" countries of settlement, western immigration fell short of central Canada's colonial dreams. In national terms, however, growth was striking. During the first decade of the twentieth century, the height of the western "boom years," the Prairies alone witnessed nearly a threefold population increase – from 419,000 in 1901 to 1,328,000 in 1911.[11] Western agriculture registered a similarly dramatic increase in the number of acres of wheat, from 300,000 in the 1890s – almost entirely in Manitoba – to 20 million by the 1920s. At this time Canada provided almost half of the world's trade in wheat, and wheat accounted for between 25 percent and 30 percent of the nation's total export trade.[12] The rush to "open the West" was also spurred by a search for new industrial staples, particularly forest and mineral products. Gold sparked the most frenzied rushes, beginning in 1858 when deposits were discovered in the Fraser River. By 1910, the Klondike was exhausted and production had all but ceased. During this period, British Columbia took the lead in silver production in Canada, and in both British Columbia and Alberta coal benefited from the opening of San Francisco markets. West Coast forestry also registered spectacular growth during the early decades of the twentieth century. By 1911, 80 percent of Crown timberland was under lease, and six years later British Columbia led the country in lumber production, much of it absorbed by burgeoning Prairie markets.[13]

Western settlement is often associated with the movement to fill up the continental interior with farmers, but population growth and economic development also fuelled rapid urban expansion. While the rural population on the Prairies rose 2.7 times between 1901 and 1911, the urban population increased 4.6 times, from 103,000 to 500,000.[14] During this period, British Columbia became the most urbanized province in Canada, outstripping Ontario by 1911, when 51 percent of the coastal population was identified as urban dwellers.[15] Whether urban or rural, as noted above the western provinces were culturally and ethnically more diverse than was the rest of the country. By 1940, half of Prairie residents identified themselves as other than British in origin.[16] And non-British Europeans also represented a growing portion of the "foreign"-born in British Columbia where, by 1911, Asian immigrants made up about 6 percent of the total population.[17]

Women were a vital part of these dramatic changes that were shaping the new West. Behind patterns of migration and resettlement, behind wheat and mineral production, and behind the success or failure of businesses, towns, and cities were the actions and behaviours of women and men going about their day-to-day and night-to-night lives. They were often constrained by harsh or exploitative conditions, but newcomers made strategic choices. They pooled resources, adapted Old World skills to New World circumstances, greased the palms of immigration officials and land agents, renegotiated the division of labour within the home, decided who went out to work and to what jobs, selected appropriate marriage partners, determined family size, and made educational and training choices for their sons and daughters.[18]

Immigration literature points to the crucial importance of family, kin, and community in the processes of migration, settlement, and community building in new, often hostile, Canadian environments, yet we know surprisingly little about women's contributions or the differences sex and gender made to the opportunities and obstacles women encountered in the West. Recently, Gillian Creese, Veronica Strong-Boag, and Jean Barman have contributed good work on women in British Columbia, but historical writing on the Prairie West has proven especially resistant to including sex and gender as analytical frameworks.[19] Writing about the "limited identities" of region over and against the homogenizing narrative of central Canada, particularly Ontario, these scholars did not challenge the androcentric frame that undergirded their own analyses and that of the narratives they contested.[20] If women appear at all, it is within categories and stories that assumed the primacy of White male agency and agendas. In this telling of the West the invisibility of White women, indigenous peoples, and minority cultures was further reinforced by the identification of the region as a masculine terrain, a space that was presumed "empty" until filled with White men.[21]

Scholars (and activists) have challenged these distortions, pointing out that any approach to the past that marginalizes the majority of the population is not only incomplete, it also ultimately fails as a guide to the development it seeks to explain. History is shaped by all participants – people whose lives are linked by an intricate web of shifting social relationships formed in and across family, community, and society in ways that weave a collective past. Re-imaging western Canada's past from the perspective of the women who lived it requires us to rethink the ways in which social relationships are constructed and contested within the multiple social locations of daily life.

Feminist scholarship has provided important insights into the ways in which sex and gender have shaped social power. Recently, as part of the broad postmodern shift in historical writing noted above, their investigations have led some historians to question the very notion of "women" as a distinctly boundaried body. While this approach opens investigation to a plurality of experience, critics charge that it threatens to fatally fracture the women's history project and evacuate its political force. Moreover, historical debate has developed unevenly. Where some would consider the concept of women's history as an outdated intellectual construct – a remnant of an earlier, simpler era of binary opposition and familiar borders that must either be breached or maintained – there are those who still resist acknowledging the legitimacy of the questions that led to its creation in the first place. As Joy Parr has deftly outlined, older Canadian historians still offer considerable opposition to gender history, cultural history, and the "new" social history, arguing that they are agents of fragmentation and uncertainty.[22] Those wishing to place women at the centre of historical inquiry thus find themselves in a curious position, interrogating a subject rejected by conventional scholars for being too fragmentary and rejected by postmodernist/postcolonialist scholars for not being fragmentary enough.

Given the contested terrain of the current theoretical debate, it is important to provide a brief explanation of the position presented in this book. We take seriously the issues and problems that attend the use of the analytical category "women." The chapters that appear here amply illustrate the multiple positions and diverse experience of western women. At the same time, we note Denise Riley's point, as expertly taken up by Judith Allen, that so long as women are *treated* as a stable category (and, for example, prohibited from owning homesteads or voting on the basis of their sex), there is merit to examining that conceptual moment reconstructively as well as deconstructively.[23] The contributors to this book position themselves differently on this issue, exploring the ways in which the women at the centre of their studies engage, challenge, and renegotiate the gendered, raced, and classed boundaries encountered in their specific contexts. They show the diversity of newcomer women's experience while highlighting common themes in the construction and reshaping of gender relationships during the colonization and settlement of western Canada. We hope that they will provide an incentive to further explorations.

In the context of the richness and liveliness of international debates, the relative neglect of western Canadian women's history presents a paradox. We welcome the massive developments in the field generally but often face the basic task of recovering women's stories. Because we know so little about western women's lives and experiences, researching and writing must proceed on a number of levels. We need to continue to search for new or unused sources that are scattered or buried in archives and rarely organized according to topics related to women. Addressing new questions to traditional sources (such as official documents, newspapers, and government records) has yielded many overlooked stories. Women's history has also relied on broadening its search to include women's diaries, letters, memoirs, arts and crafts, and oral histories. But recovering women's stories is only the first step towards making women visible as people who actively shape their own lives. Women's history long ago recognized that women's lives rarely fit into models that reflect men's experiences. A full understanding of the significance of women's cultural, social, political, and economic contributions requires that we re-imagine the past in ways that reflect women's perspectives – what women thought, felt, and did, and how their experience was mediated by culture and society.

Telling Canadian history from the point of view of the women who lived it promises a more complex and complete portrait of the past than has hitherto been offered. It challenges the deeply rooted founding myths of region and Empire. In the colony-to-nation narratives told by conventional historians, the West appears as virgin territory, ripe for exploitation and offering seemingly boundless opportunities in the form of "free" land and untapped natural resources. It is dominated by adventuring fur traders, railroad tycoons, freewheeling entrepreneurs, and land speculators. In the wake of their relentless drive westward and northward in pursuit of wealth and profits, civilization triumphs over savagery, order replaces chaos, and chronological time begins. In this narrative western development is cast as an exclusively male enterprise in which indigenous peoples, immigrants of minority cultures, workers, and women play supporting roles at best. The image of elite White men as agents of progress works to construct Euro-North American male dominance as inevitable. Events seem to unfold as they should, part of the natural order of things. Seen from the perspective of women's stories of migration and resettlement, these conventions of western history not only appear hollow and self-serving, they lose all explanatory force.

Moving beyond Eurocentric/androcentric western Canadian history requires a rethinking of women's relationships to Anglo-Canadian imperialism and colonization. But integrating women into western colonization and settlement is complicated by Anglo women's status as both colonizer (members of the dominant culture) and colonized (by patriarchy) within a country that was both colony and colonizer.[24] Initially, European expansion westward and northward was dominated by central Canada (Ottawa) and Britain – popularly known as the Empire upon which the sun never set. By the 1920s the international balance of power had shifted, and Canada fell under the increasing economic and political clout of the United States. But, in Canada, historiographical conventions that emphasize the movement from colony to nation tend to obscure colonial contests in the West. Even when scholars focus on cultural competitions and violent confrontations, these events are represented as struggles between competing groups of men (e.g., the Riel-led uprisings against the Canadian government and its colonial police force; or the farmers' movement of the 1910s and 1920s, which was opposed to eastern-based capitalists). Generally, historians of the Canadian West have been slow to take up the postcolonial challenge, favouring, instead, a narrative of relatively peaceful race relations that were developed during the fur trade and were followed by an orderly transition to nation building. However, as one critic has pointedly remarked, "one cannot excuse a robbery by describing it as orderly."[25]

Once Ottawa and London turned their attention from fur trade to settlement and resource extraction, there was a rapid shift in favour of White institutions. The annexation of Rupert's Land in 1870, coupled with the series of treaties put in place between 1871 and 1877, secured land for non-Native occupation and exploitation. The completion of the Canadian Pacific Railway eight years later provided the means of placing a large number of immigrants onto the Prairies and into the British Columbia interior. But recent work also shows that colonial control and profits depended upon much more than legal and technological change. Colonialism also relied upon a complex social system that worked to secure the hegemony of a small group of elite men by constructing and deploying social categories of race, class, and gender in ways that delineated access to wealth and privilege. As Sarah Carter demonstrates in Chapter 2, within colonial systems representations of Aboriginals as racially inferior and as a threat to social order served to underwrite legal interventions and to enforce race-based segregation. This is graphically illustrated by, within several generations, the relegation of the once powerful Métis to non-status "road allowance" people. The fate of the "mixed-blood" Métis underscores the important point that colonialism affected indigenous peoples differently, although racialization – the processes by which race difference is made operational, enshrining "Whiteness" as a dominant value – worked broadly to subordinate all non-Whites. (In Chapter 10 Sherry Edmunds-Flett discusses the implications of this for Black newcomers on Vancouver Island.) Racialization was also intimately bound up with dominant sex and gender codes. For example, Carter illustrates how representations of Indian women as sexually promiscuous or unfit mothers reinforced notions of them as racially inferior.[26]

Within colonial social hierarchies, Anglo-Canadian women (particularly educated, middle-class women) occupied a position of race privilege. Indeed, a common theme in histories of colonial women is the extent to which colonies offered middle-class European women, like Myra Rutherdale's missionaries (see Chapter 1), greater freedom and opportunity than they were allowed in their home countries. Certainly, the success of settler societies relied upon women reproducing the White race. However, assuming that women's functional domestic role worked in unison with imperial and patriarchal goals reinforces gender stereotypes by subordinating women's experiences to men's agendas.[27] Making homes on the prairie or in remote lumber and mining camps often challenged imperial ideology and the aesthetic of racial superiority, particularly where newcomers relied upon Native knowledge and skills to survive. Moreover, as scholars have pointed out, within colonial systems race privilege was hedged around by notions of ideal femininity. Even the most privileged elite women remained secondary as a result of their sex. Women rarely exercised authority independently, and they did not hold official positions as decision makers. Canadian expansionists recognized the importance of attracting White women to settlement frontiers, but, in the West, land – and therefore wealth – was not only delimited to non-Aboriginal populations, it was also designated an exclusively male preserve. Women were specifically barred by their sex from acquiring the "free" homesteads that were available to any man over eighteen years of age. But, as chapters in this book demonstrate, even within colonial systems gender was not firmly fixed and frontier conditions could disrupt the concept of separate spheres. British women – particularly single, middle-class women who entered colonial service as missionaries, teachers, nurses, and philanthropists – were able to expand their spheres of influence and to exercise great personal autonomy. In some cases close contact with indigenous peoples altered women's perceptions of Natives as the "exotic" Other and/or raised for them personal questions about an assumed racial order. (For example, in Chapter 3, Nancy Pagh examines the changing face of cultural "encounter" from the perspective of women travellers, while, in Chapter 4, Catherine Cavanaugh explores race privilege in the life of one British gentlewoman.)

The majority of newcomers in western Canada were working-class women who emigrated as daughters, sisters, wives, and mothers. Many were non-British in origin and, for them, "ethnicity" was a product of migration that worked in a double fashion, operating simultaneously as a site of subordination and resistance. Constructed by the dominant culture as a category of social exclusion, ethnicity also worked to solidify identity and to strengthen the bonds of minority communities. Early work on immigrant communities pointed to the ways in which dominant constructions reconfigured ethnicity as class, designating non-English-speaking women as a category of worker.[28] This was clearly the case for the Mennonite women in Frieda Klippenstein's study (Chapter 8). Klippenstein shows that, regardless of their social background, Mennonite women found themselves employed as domestic servants in the homes of middle-class Winnipeggers. But, as these women tell their stories, we see that exploitation was not the entire picture. From the perspective of Klippenstein's informants, domestic service also operated as a site of adaptation and as a means of regaining economic stability. This example shows that a thorough understanding of the past requires that we integrate women into the shifting power matrix of class, race, and gender that undergirded colonization and settlement. Highlighting women's resistance, accommodation, and adaptation to the imperial project draws attention to western Canada's colonial past as being man-made rather than being an inevitable transformation from wilderness to civilization. It also brings women's unequal relationships into fuller analytical focus.

Women's relationship to settlement and community building is similarly far from straightforward.[29] In part, contradiction and complexity arise out of the processes of migration and resettlement. But the necessary change affected men and women differently. For example, the boom-and-bust economic cycles associated with resource-dependent western economies created unstable and transient communities. The instability and disorder of "bonanza frontiers" increased women's domestic responsibilities, particularly when they were forced to relocate or to re-establish the family home. At the same time, women's work in establishing community-based institutions such as schools, hospitals, hostels, and clubs was crucial to ameliorating the harsh circumstances of settler communities. (In Chapter 7, Beverly Boutilier examines an underdeveloped aspect of women's efforts to establish nursing care in western Canada.) Moreover, development did not proceed at an even pace, and the circumstances confronting newcomers varied. In some areas the subsistence economies associated with "frontier" conditions persisted long after the initial stages of settlement, while other areas were rapidly transformed by industrialization and urbanization. In either case, newcomers often traded one form of uncertainty for another and were forced to negotiate the vagaries of geography and climate under the highly competitive conditions created by eastern-based speculators and profiteers.

While industrial sectors of western economies worked to reinforce a sharp division of labour along sex lines, agricultural production based on the family farm relied heavily on the work of women and children. But here, too, the story is complex. Farm families frequently redeployed labour within the household, but the sexual division of the land grant reinforced women's economic dependence on marriage and men. (In Chapter 8, Klippenstein examines the implications of these contradictions for Mennonite women, and in Chapter 5, Sheila McManus explores the impact on the politics of organized farm women.) Territorial legislation also severed the widow's long-standing right to a portion of family property. Should a homesteader die or desert his family, his wife and children faced losing their home and farm livelihood. Western migration and resettlement meant that women, often separated from the protection of family and kin networks, also lost the legal rights they had had in their country or province of origin.[30] These legal disabilities could be exacerbated by cultural practices that dictated the designation of resources within the household. As Marjorie Cohen shows in her study of women in the Canadian dairy industry, the devaluation of their work deprived farm women of necessary resources. Sectors of the farm economy associated with women remained undercapitalized and, as a result, were slow to develop, thus reinforcing the economic marginalization of women's farm production.[31] Sara Brooks Sundberg also points to the unequal application of new technologies to explain women's prolonged frontier experience. She concludes that the "domestic frontier" occupied by women persisted long after non-domestic production (dominated by men) was mechanized and integrated into the market economy.[32]

Defined by law and custom that reflected middle-class, Victorian gender conventions, the "women's West" was also demographically shaped by age and sex. Immigrant populations were typically younger than the general population. A preponderance of newcomer women were in their childbearing years and were at high risk, particularly during pregnancy and childbirth. Mothers with young children also carried a double load, working inside and outside the farm home. Equally striking in this population is the fact that there were fewer women than men. Although this demographic imbalance between the sexes varied geographically, according to the local economy of the area, initially, at least, men outnumbered women among newcomer communities. The records are scattered and incomplete, but estimates suggest a ratio of about ten men to each woman on early resource frontiers. On agricultural frontiers, where production was primarily organized on the basis of the family farm, this ratio declined sharply to fewer than two men to one woman.[33]

The implications of these demographic patterns for women have yet to be fully explored, but, as one scholar has observed, "nothing in the memoir literature suggests that men and women often braved the hardships of pioneer life alone."[34] Migration often relied on family and kin networks. In some cases young men preceded other family members, who followed a year or two later; in other cases, entire families migrated on their own or in groups.[35] Of course, not all women who came to the West were married. Single women emigrated in search of adventure and employment. Rapidly growing communities called out for women workers in areas that were beginning to emerge as new female occupations. In western Canada, women worked as nurses, teachers, and telegraph and telephone operators, in offices and factories, and in newspapers. They ran their own businesses and worked as domestic servants, waitresses, cooks, and store clerks. Women's employment often consisted of low-paid, short-term work that provided only a temporary alternative to marriage or relief from family economic crisis. Western economies, particularly primary resource economies that relied almost exclusively on male labour, combined with cultural expectations in ways that limited women's public paid employment opportunities. But in subsistence economies, or where cash was short, women's paid labour often bridged sharp distinctions between home-based and public work, their "indoor" and "outdoor" work following a continuum of opportunity. In short, women tended to make their own economic opportunities by selling their domestic skills to bachelors or other women's families.[36] Still, the difficulties of securing an independent living meant that the majority of newcomer women married within a year or two of their arrival in the West. Others came as intended brides and concubines.[37]

As a number of essays show, marriage and family often improved the material conditions of newcomer men; their effect on women was more ambiguous. Rough frontier domesticity meant that birthing and raising children and making a home on Prairie farms and in isolated mining and lumbering camps increased the physical and emotional demands on women[38] (see in particular Nanci Langford's Chapter 6). On western homesteads married women carried a double load, working outdoors but also assuming the primary responsibility for "indoor" work.[39] The high rate of homestead failure, which reached 80 percent and 90 percent in some districts, also added to women's domestic labour as families were forced to relocate, sometimes repeatedly. Moving a home, a farm, or a family business presented an additional burden for mothers with young children, and for older women in particular. Studies also suggest that the economic and social instability that characterized late nineteenth- and early twentieth-century migrations could place additional strain on family relationships, endangering women's lives even further. For example, although the causes of domestic violence and wife assault among newcomer families can be traced to broad cultural practices, domestic tensions could be heightened by harsh frontier conditions and a husband's frustrated ambition. (In Chapter 9, Frances Swyripa explores Ukrainian women's responses to sexual violence in one particular community.)[40]

In the early-twentieth-century West, newcomer women confronted an additional contradiction based on their sex. While fledgling resource-based economies tended to reinforce a traditional gender division of labour, women's roles in Western society were changing. In Canada, as elsewhere, women gained wider access to education, entered work and professions previously closed to them, won the right to vote, and gained official recognition as persons under the Constitution. Organized women pushed for laws to improve their working conditions, to grant the mother child custody, and to recognize the value of women's domestic labour. Moreover, English Canadians' ideas about respectable domesticity were changing, and family life became increasingly home- and child-centred. These developments are usually associated with urban life in the early decades of the twentieth century, when consumerism and mass culture began to make itself felt. Their effects on rural women have yet to be examined. What we do know is that all women did not participate equally in reform campaigns and that change did not benefit women as a group. During the decades under review here, only a tiny minority of women ever held public office or exercised decision-making authority. But, as women sought to expand their horizons or improve their life chances, these broader social changes redefined what was possible or acceptable. (In Chapter 11, Ann Leger-Anderson traces these developments in the lives of Gertrude and John Telford.)

The essays in this book show that western women employed a range of strategies as they negotiated their new lives: they married, had children, went to court and out to work, and a few entered public office. They made do, got by, changed local custom and social practice, pushed the boundaries of inequality, and redefined their own possibilities as women. In the process, even the least advantaged made important contributions to their communities.

Telling Tales begins with the question of British women's relationship to imperialism and gender construction within the colonial context. In Chapter 1, taking the Canadian North-West mission field as her interrogatory site, Myra Rutherdale allows readers to see the particularities of newcomers' gendered experience against a backdrop of rigid stereotyping transformed by necessity. She begins by laying out the dominant discourse of masculinity, which is constructed around ideals of "Muscular Christianity." Missionaries, no less than hunters and explorers, were constructed as thoroughgoing embodiments of masculine culture. Yet the mission field demanded more than men; most prized was the male missionary who was married or who had a fiancée willing to travel and work at his side. Unremitting masculinism was fittingly offset by a woman able to bring "feminine virtues" – and hard work – to the mission field.

Rutherdale shows that, however much the received cultural gender script might be touted, the practical demands of the mission field forced greater fluidity in gendered behaviour than convention suggests. She contends that, while the mission field released both single and married women from certain expectations around gender, married women were more constrained due to their symbolic function as role models to Native women. Carrying the burden of "true womanhood," missionary wives were expected to "civilize" Native women, to teach them to adopt imperial women's domestic ways. As Rutherdale observes, male missionaries had no parallel obligation to transform Native men; indeed, such a venture would have significantly undermined the raced and gendered infrastructures of imperial dominance. Women, White or Native, being inherent inferiors, could be "trained" to the home. Masculine competence on the part of Native men, on the other hand, would have directly challenged White male dominance. "Conversion to the faith" thus played out differently for women and men on both sides of the Native/White experience.

Unmarried women had far greater freedom in renegotiating gender roles. By necessity required to do more "men's work" (such as hunting) in order to survive, single women missionaries were seen to transcend their gendered role through their "higher calling": service to Christ. The notion of "high calling" intersected with the notion of class. One missionary remarked that the "refined" ladies in the mission field were far more likely than were their lower-class sisters to undertake the more repulsive tasks associated with their work, their obedience to the demands of duty having been inculcated through years of genteel training. Ultimately, Rutherdale concludes, the mission field provided both women and men with opportunities to move beyond the expectations associated with their gender identities. Their roles as agents of Empire, however, remained intact.

Restoring the history of racialization and ethnicization to our imaginative reconstructions of the West and its terrain is continued in Chapters 2 and 3, which examine shifting European representations of Native peoples. Sarah Carter reminds us that the land occupied by newcomers was contested terrain. She documents the changing images of Native women during the early settlement period to show how notions of race, class, and gender were deployed to underwrite imperialism and to reinforce White male privilege. Using both formal and informal examples, she demonstrates that racialized and gendered representations of Native women as dissolute and dangerous served to solidify social boundaries and to justify the use of force against indigenous peoples. A generation earlier, Native women were prized as wives and daughters by European fur traders. Targeted by segregationist policies at the end of the nineteenth century, women faced the increasingly severe political and economic consequences of a new racial order. In Chapter 3, Nancy Pagh approaches the "imperial gaze" through the accounts of female tourists. She finds that imperial literary conventions paralleled official policy but that the authors' stances became increasingly ambiguous. This difference may reflect the distinction between settlers and travellers, as the latter were assumed to be primarily responsible for maintaining a sense of cultural identity in the colonies by guarding social boundaries. As a result, settler women were often much more constrained by class and hierarchy than were travellers, who could move through their environments in more "eccentric" ways.[41]

"Feminine" discourse in travel writing is a rapidly expanding area of study, but, as Pagh points out, the focus of these inquiries is typically that of British travellers to colonial Africa and Asia. Women travellers to settler colonies have received less attention but promise fertile ground for future investigation. Pagh's analysis of four women travel writers (two from the 1880s and 1890s, and two from the 1920s and 1930s) highlights the complexities of Victorian women's positionalities and how their contexts shift through time. As representatives of Empire and "high civilization," pressures were in place to ensure that these women either "adopt[ed] a pose of certain and steady femininity in their writing" or risked being discredited as cranks or liars. Just as masculine imperialist literature was gendered, replete with tropes of "mastery" and "penetration," so "feminine" discourse was required to reveal a delicate tentativeness and to focus on appearances, particularly the appearance of the "Other," against whom the colonizer's superiority might be judged.

Pagh documents shifts in the parameters of this discourse, noting that, over time, ambiguity replaced condescension in the authors' representations of Native culture. By the 1920s, writers were able to relegate the "disappearing Indian" to a romantic "Past," thus keeping the conditions of contemporary Native peoples at a safe distance from White privilege. Yet, interestingly, later writers were able to reflexively construct their subjects in a way that their Victorian antecedents could not, thus coming to see themselves and their perceptions as alien. If only momentarily, these writers were able to relinquish their imperial gaze as they reflected on their connection with, and their distance from, the Indian women they were describing.

As previous chapters show, the imperial project proceeded both consciously and unconsciously, acted out by intentional agents of its propagation and embodied in the visions, perceptions, and narratives of individuals enmeshed within it. In Chapter 4, Catherine Cavanaugh writes about Irene Marryat Parlby, sole woman member of Alberta's United Farmers' government (1921 to 1935), and unfolds the layers of her transition from "imperial daughter" to "western Canadian." Cavanaugh's study challenges a number of key assumptions surrounding Anglo-Canadian women and western settlement. First and foremost, she questions previously static constructions of immigrant British women as single-minded and unrelenting advocates of racist imperialism. Likewise, in her assessment of one British gentlewoman's life, Cavanaugh scrutinizes notions of the West as "inherently" liberating.

Parlby's appointment as minister without portfolio in 1921 only underscored the ambiguity of the unearned advantages she carried as a female representative of Ango-Canadian cultural hegemony in western Canada. Cavanaugh convincingly argues that, in public office, Parlby moved significantly from her newcomer's view of the West as "properly" British to a more nuanced view that welcomed a diversity of ethnicities on the western plains. Yet her supporters valued her precisely because of her aura of British gentility. Her "plummy" diction and impeccable dress were seen to represent the civilizing influence of both Woman and Empire. As representative of Empire, Parlby was accepted as a rightful member of the ruling class, the conferred dominance of her Britishness being seen as natural. As Woman, however, she was constrained by convention and expectation to exercise only that political authority extended to her primarily through "feminine" means. As Cavanaugh notes, she was invited to a place at the table but denied the resources that would make her position in government a meaningful one. Significantly, the minister without portfolio was also without either budget or staff. At the same time, Parlby was widely considered the "woman's minister," with primary responsibility for all matters concerning women in the province. The disparity between expectation and support acutely highlights the gendered construction of her position.

Cavanaugh teases out the implications of the contradictions inhering in Parlby's race, class, and gender positioning, illustrating the inadequacy of the static "imperial daughter." The West, for Parlby, was a shaping context, not simply an empty terrain upon which to inscribe imperial dreams. Yet the West was not an uncomplicated liberator. The architects of its new social possibilities remained enmeshed in the values and visions of the past, playing with these sedimentations in their attempts to determine the region's future. Neither simply dominant nor absolutely unfettered, Cavanaugh concludes that British women were "both bound and free as they adapted to their new circumstances in Canada."

Not only do women's identities change through time, they are multiply configured in relation to class, ethnicity, occupation, race, sexuality, and other factors. In Chapter 5, Sheila McManus explores the tensions in the lives of English-speaking women in rural Alberta. Although McManus's argument takes a number of different turns, she concludes, as does Cavanaugh, that Alberta women were "both bound and free" as they played out their roles of farming women who were also members of a hegemonic Anglo-Canadian cultural elite.

As members of the United Farm Women of Alberta (UFWA), English-speaking farm women were able to advocate for a number of important reforms that would improve their lives. However, as McManus asserts, they were most successful with those reforms associated with women in their domestic, "feminine" roles. Health care is a prime example. Maternal and infant mortality was a serious concern of isolated farming women. Largely due to the lobbying of such women's groups as the UFWA, the Alberta government created a Department of Health in 1918. Several hospitals were subsequently built in more remote areas to serve the farming populations. In contrast, the UFWA campaign for married women's property rights was both more conflicted and protracted – a fact McManus attributes to the gendered tensions of women's farm work.

As women, farm wives were responsible for domestic, indoor labour; in asking for an equal share of the farms upon which they laboured they were entering the "masculine" world of commerce and the "market." Caught in the contradiction of wanting both to show solidarity with their farmer husbands and to contest their material disenfranchisement as women, farm women resisted any analysis that would see their husbands as recipients of an unearned advantage. Those women who did challenge the situation in the public press (e.g., the *Grain Growers' Guide*) did so, McManus tells us, within the idiom of domestic and familial responsibility. Adherence to the notions and tropes of femininity was thus double-edged. It provided a specific identity and a place from which to advance particular interests, but it also circumscribed the boundaries within which such expression was acceptable. McManus concludes that a "separate-but-equal configuration of women's labour had considerable social utility in structuring respectable femininity ... and maintaining [a] position of racial and ethnic privilege," but it was much less powerful as a radical political tool.

We know that women went West as travellers, adventurers, economic migrants, and settlers. But we know surprisingly little about their daily lives on settlement frontiers. In Chapter 6, Nanci Langford explores the question of women's reproduction under rough frontier conditions. As mentioned above, female populations in western Canada were younger than the national average, predominantly of marriageable age, and in their childbearing years. As Langford points out, pregnancy and childbirth focus our attention on the social cost of settlement, challenging western myths of heroic individualism and (manly) triumph over nature.

Drawing upon women's own accounts, Langford shows how the masculine frontier ethic – which expressed itself in central government planning, economic organization, and the division of the Prairies into large quarter sections – cut off parturient women and new mothers from crucial supports and resources. Isolated on remote homesteads, separated from family and kin, without ready access to medical aid, the expectant mother and her infant were rendered more vulnerable to the usual risks of childbirth. Langford's study reminds us that, in the West, newcomer women frequently experienced a sharp decline in their standard of living. Her study also underscores the importance of women's friendships. Like Myra Rutherdale's missionary women, the women in Langford's study relied significantly on their friendships with other women, finding in that connection a means to survive the rigorous demands of an isolated life.

Given the risks involved, it is not surprising that maternity and infant health care became a central concern for organized women who sought to win the same standards of treatment for rural women that were already widely available to many urban women. As McManus points out, these campaigns would appear to have been on firm ground, as they sought to provide adequate care to the nation's mothers. However, in Chapter 7, Beverly Boutilier demonstrates that, initially at least, the politicization of maternity aid worked against early efforts to extend medical care to western women. She closely reconstructs the debate that took place within the ranks of the National Council of Women of Canada (NCWC) (dubbed the women's parliament) – a debate that floundered when the expressed needs of westerners ran up against the nation-building aims of central Canadians. Indeed, according to Boutilier, the campaign to bring medical care to western mothers was most successful when local and national interests coincided. Her study adds an important chapter to women's campaign for health care in Canada while raising crucial questions about the ways in which metropolitan and regional influences divided women from each other, thus weakening them politically.

Significantly, many of the western reformers in Boutilier's study were Ontario transplants whose efforts were aimed at restoring services that had been lost to them through resettlement. The next two chapters consider continuity and change in the lives of women in ethnic minority communities. They show that Anglo women were not alone in renegotiating sex and gender in the West. Indeed, because ethnic minority women typically had access to fewer resources than did their Anglo-Canadian counterparts, they were often much more vulnerable to the economic, social, and cultural disruptions that accompanied migration and resettlement. This was certainly true of the Mennonite women whom Frieda Klippenstein discusses in Chapter 8. Forced into domestic service in the homes of Winnipeg's elite families, the daughters of newcomer Mennonite families found themselves in a world turned upside down. Raised to an agricultural life, they were rapidly converted into urban workers whose wages went to support fathers and brothers who were formerly their providers. But the exploitation of some women's labour gave other women their life's work, as, for example, in the case of Anna Thiessen, founder of the Mennonite Girls' Homes, and her contemporary, Helen Epp.

By reminding us that many of the Mennonite servants were employed by elite women who were at the forefront of social reform in western Canada, Klippenstein highlights the ways in which class and ethnicity divided women. At the same time, her account of the transition of Mennonite Girl's Homes, or *Maedchenheim*e, "from refuge to hiring hall," parallels the experience of middle-class Anglo-Canadian women who repeatedly established local services in response to specific needs only to have them taken over by the men of their community. In the process, women's contributions were often lost to history.[42] In Klippenstein's study it is male church leaders who prevail over the refuge homes. Their influence ensured that, while breaking long-standing cultural codes, Mennonite girls' domestic work was seen by the community as conforming to religious traditions. Klippenstein asserts that the Mennonite community's acceptance of women's domestic service as part of a Christian "mission" enabled the authority of church fathers to be extended and community and family bonds to be preserved. In contrast to the Anglican women missionaries in Rutherdale's study, the "mission" work of young Mennonite girls was configured so as to reinforce rather than to weaken gender roles. Still, going out to work facilitated adaptation to a new environment. Mennonite domestic servants learned the language and culture of their employer families, thus becoming interpreters of the dominant culture within their communities.

While Klippenstein relies on oral history to uncover a previously hidden aspect of immigration, in Chapter 9, Frances Swyripa turns to criminal court records for her exploration of sex and gender in Alberta's Ukrainian Bloc Settlement. Again, the result is complex. As with Mennonite immigration, Ukrainian group settlement worked to ensure cultural vitality and to strengthen community boundaries. But Swyripa's study also challenges the deeply rooted notion of women as essentially conservative and resistant to change. Stimulus to change was often beyond the control of individuals, but women were not passive victims of external forces. Klippenstein's and Swyripa's studies reveal ways in which women acted to influence both the nature and direction of change, thus shaping cultural transition. They also alert us to the complex nature of women's interventions. Sometimes they conformed to cultural expectations – whether of the dominant or minority culture – thus maximizing their opportunities, as in the case of Klippenstein's Mennonite women. At other times, they rebelled. As Swyripa shows, the forms of women's rebellions are equally provocative. When long-established community sanctions failed to protect them, the women in her study used Canadian courts to enforce traditional cultural standards and expectations. They also invoked middle-class Anglo-Canadian gender conventions to shift those standards in ways that were intended to enhance Ukrainian women's freedoms.

In Chapter 10, Sherry Edmunds-Flett takes us into virtually unexplored territory – African-American settlement on Vancouver Island. Her careful reconstruction of the lives of Black emigrants to Victoria and Saltspring Island in the mid- to late nineteenth century challenges long-standing images of Canada's most British colony. Wishing to escape the racial persecution they experienced in California, Black settlers created a distinct community on the West Coast. Long overlooked by historians, African Canadians made a range of economic contributions to early Victoria. Men worked as merchants, tailors, blacksmiths, bookkeepers, contractors, and restaurant owners, amongst other occupations, while women ran boarding houses and worked as teachers, nurses, seamstresses, laundresses, domestic servants, and cooks. Government rules concerning land ownership meant that it was often more difficult for Blacks to qualify than for Whites, and their island communities tended to be urban. Although some African-Canadian settlers operated small farms, they were few in number.

In contrast to Victoria's Native and Métis founding families, who are the subject of Sylvia Van Kirk's recent work, Black settlers were not readily absorbed into the "genteel" culture of their colonial milieu.[43] They remained a dynamic part of British Columbia's working class but had strong and stable community boundaries. Such solidarity was essential for a small and vulnerable group. The racism they sought to escape by moving to the Pacific Northwest followed them. Racial prejudice, even threats of violent reprisals, were a consequence of attempts to enter the social and cultural life of early Victoria. African Canadians survived, but

Vancouver Island did not become the hoped-for haven they had sought when they moved north.

Many themes of this book – continuity, change, identity, agency, family, and culture – come together in the final chapter in Ann Leger-Anderson's exploration of the domestic lives of Gertrude and John Telford. The Telfords were prominent, both individually and as a couple, in the cooperative movement that flourished in Saskatchewan during the early decades of this century. Like the first leader of the Co-operative Commonwealth Federation (CCF), Tommy Douglas, they were also Baptists, and their religious convictions fuelled their commitment to the cooperative ideal. Leger-Anderson asks how the Telfords' political and religious commitments to cooperation played out within the context of their marriage and family life. What she finds is suggestive of the other explorations in this book.

As husband and wife the Telfords appeared to others to be the model of cooperation, with Gertrude free to take the public stage whenever she desired. But, as Leger-Anderson shows, in reality her ambition was profoundly constrained by the forces of convention within herself, her marriage, and the political culture of the CCF. Though she advanced her arguments for women's inclusion in politics on the double rhetorical ground of "common justice" and maternal and domestic expertise, neither was sufficient to overcome the blanket rejection of "Woman" outside her designated sphere. Leger-Anderson's study highlights the complexity of power relations in the intersection of race, class, and gender. Having a White skin, an advanced education, and a respected social place as a minister's and then a lawyer's wife, Gertrude Telford was still bound by gender conventions both inside and outside herself. Her attempts to redefine her possibilities foundered on entrenched structures and the expectations of women's subordination, some of which, judging by her behaviour, she had internalized. While by the end of her life Gertrude Telford successfully achieved some of the independence and prominence she had long sought, this study of the Telford marriage illustrates the ways in which even those with relative social privilege were bound by prevailing cultural scripts.

Viewed from the perspective of the lives of newcomer women, it is far from clear whether or not the West itself altered the possibilities for changing relationships between men and women.[44] More likely, the social, political, and economic instability associated with late nineteenth-century and early twentieth-century settlement opened spaces for women to intervene to alter the circumstances of their own lives. But the ideas that informed their push to maximize freedom and opportunity within their specific contexts also influenced change. The contradictions between Old World traditions and their perceptions of a free Canada underwrote Ukrainian women's bid for safety and respectability. Economic crisis pushed Gertrude Telford into a career outside the home, but renegotiating her domestic relationship depended upon her conception of marriage as an economic partnership based on cooperation. In both cases, the old coexisted with the new, thus circumscribing the possibilities of liberation. These studies caution against simple dichotomies. Rather than asking if the West was liberating or oppressive for women, we need to explore the diversity of their experience against the broader processes of colonization, settlement, cultural engagement, and social, economic, and political change. As observers, settlers, missionaries, politicians, workers, domestic labourers, and mothers, women were both actors and acted upon in complex ways. The interdynamics of privilege and power, played out on terrains of race, class, ethnicity, and gender, created both the multiple contradictions and possibilities facing them. Only by attending to the details of women's lives can we begin to see the ways in which they actively shaped and reshaped the political, cultural, economic, and social development of western Canada.

Notes

1 Jack Granatstein, *Who Killed Canadian History?* (Toronto: Harper Collins, 1998); Michael Bliss, "Privatizing the Mind: The Sundering of Canada," *Journal of Canadian Studies* 26 (1991): 5-17; Veronica Strong-Boag, "Contested Space: The Politics of Canadian Memory," *Journal of the Canadian Historical Association* (1994): 3-17; Joy Parr, "Gender History and Historical Practice," *Canadian Historical Review* 76, 3 (September 1995): 354-76.

2 Ruth Roach Pierson, "Experience, Difference, Dominance and Voice in the Writing of Canadian Women's History," in *Writing Women's History: International Perspectives*, ed. Karen Offen, Ruth Roach Pierson, and Jane Rendall (Bloomington: Indiana University Press, 1991), 79-106.

3 Gail Cuthbert Brandt, "Postmodern Patchwork: Some Recent Trends in the Writing of Women's History in Canada," *Canadian Historical Review* 72, 4 (1991): 441-70. Historians are also debating the usefulness of differentiating between "women's" history and "gender" history. See Joan Sangster, "Beyond Dichotomies: Re-Assessing Gender History and Women's History in Canada," *Left History* 3, 1 (Spring/Summer 1995): 109-12; Karen Dubinsky and Lynn Marks, "Beyond Purity: A Response to Sangster," *Left History* 3, 4 (Fall/Spring 1995/6): 205-20; Franca Iacovetta and Linda Kealey, "Women's History, Gender History and Debating Dichotomies," *Left History* 3, 4 (Fall/Spring 1995/6): 221-37; Joan Sangster, "Reconsidering Dichotomies," *Left History* 3, 4 (Fall/Spring 1995/6): 239-48.

4 Early influential examples are Gerta Lerner, *The Majority Finds its Past: Placing Women in History* (Oxford: Oxford University Press, 1979); and Sheila Rowbotham, *Hidden from History* (London: Pluto, 1973).

5 For a succinct overview of gender as an analytical category, see Randi R. Warne, "Gender," in *Guide to the Study of Religion*, ed. Willi Braun and Russell T. McCutcheon (London and New York: Cassell, 2000), 140-54.

6 See, for example, Kathleen Canning, "Feminist History after the Linguistic Turn: Historicizing Discourse and Experience," *Signs* 19 (1994): 368-404; Laura Lee Downs, "If 'Woman'

Is Just an Empty Category, Then Why Am I Afraid to Walk Alone at Night? Identity Politics Meets the Postmodern Subject," *Comparative Studies in History and Society* 35, 2 (1993): 414-37; Joan Hoff, "Gender as Postmodern Category of Paralysis," *Women's History Review* 3, 2 (1994): 149-68; Peggy Pascoe, "Ideologies of Women's Distinctiveness in Victorian and Postmodern Contexts," *Journal of Women's History* 7, 3 (Fall 1995): 137-45; Mary Poovey, "Feminism and Deconstruction," *Feminist Studies* 14, 1 (1988): 51-65; June Purvis, "Women's History and Poststructuralism," *Women's History Review* 5, 1 (1996): 5-7; Mariana Valverde, "Poststructural Gender Historians," *Labour/Le Travail* 25 (Spring 1990): 227-36.

7 On the idea of region, see John Herd Thompson, "Introduction; Imag(in)ing a Region," in *Forging the Prairie West: The Illustrated History of Canada* (Toronto and London: Oxford University Press, 1998), ix-xii; John G. Reid, "Writing about Regions," in *Writing About Canada: A Handbook for Modern Canadian History*, ed. John Schultz (Scarborough: Prentice-Hall Canada, 1990), 71-96; and Peter McCormick, "Regionalism in Canada: Disentangling the Threads," *Journal of Canadian Studies* 24, 2 (Summer 1989): 5-21. For a recent discussion of regionalism and women's history, see Deborah Gorham, "From Bonavista to Vancouver Island: Canadian Women's History as Regional History in the 1990s," *Acadiensis* 28, 2 (Spring 1999): 119-25.

8 An intercultural approach has proven especially useful for fur trade history. See Jennifer S.H. Brown, *Strangers in Blood: Fur Trade Company Families in Indian Country* (Vancouver: UBC Press, 1980); and Sylvia Van Kirk, *"Many Tender Ties": Women in Fur Trade Society in Western Canada, 1670-1870* (Winnipeg: Watson and Dwyer, 1980). Diversity is the central theme of David DeBrou and Aileen Moffatt, eds., *"Other" Voices: Historical Essays on Saskatchewan Women* (Regina: Canadian Plains Research Centre, University of Regina, 1995). See also Elizabeth Jameson and Susan Armitage, eds., *Writing the Range: Race, Class and Culture in the Women's West* (Norman: University of Oklahoma Press, 1997).

9 For a discussion of some of the problems of recovering a reliable record of First Nations women's pasts, see Diana Pedersen, *Changing Women Changing History* (Ottawa: Carleton University Press, 1996), 81. Moreover, the idea of a western region is itself a product of European colonialism. See John Herd Thompson, *Forging the Prairie West: The Illustrated History of Canada* (Toronto and New York: Oxford University Press, 1998), ix.

10 Alvin Finkel and Margaret Conrad with Veronica Strong-Boag, *History of the Canadian Peoples: 1867 to the Present*, vol. 2 (Toronto: Copp Clark Pitman, 1993), 217. The impact of contact on Native populations varied from place to place. For example, Olive Dickason, in *Canada's First Nations: A History of Founding Peoples from the Earliest Times* (Toronto: McClelland and Stewart, 1992), 206, notes that within a century of the arrival of Europeans, Native populations along the West coast declined by 80 percent.

11 Lewis H. Thomas, "A History of Agriculture on the Prairies to 1914," in *The Prairie West*, ed. Douglas Francis and Howard Palmer (Edmonton: Pica Pica, 1985), 231.

12 Donald Kerr and Deryck W. Holdsworth, eds., *Historical Atlas of Canada*, vol. 3 (Toronto: University of Toronto Press, 1990), 30. See also Kenneth Norrie and Douglas Owram, *A History of the Canadian Economy* (Toronto: Harcourt Brace Jovanovich, 1991), 321-6, 418-25.

13 Jean Barman, *The West beyond the West: A History of British Columbia*, 3rd ed. (Toronto: University of Toronto Press, 1995), 283-4.

14 Paul Voisey, "The Urbanization of the Canadian Prairies, 1871-1916," *Histoire Sociale/Social History* 8 (May 1975): 77-101.

15 Barman, *West beyond*, 198.

16 Gerald Friesen, *The Canadian Prairies: A History* (Toronto and London: University of Toronto Press, 1984), 272.

17 Finkel et al., *History of the Canadian Peoples*, 217.

18 Franca Iacovetta, *The Writing of English Canadian Immigrant History*, The Canadian Historical Association, Canada's Ethnic Group Series, Booklet No. 22 (1997), provides a good summary of historiographical issues in immigrant history. See also Franca Iacovetta, "Manly Militants, Cohesive Communities, and Defiant Domestics: Writing about Immigrants in Canadian Historical Scholarship," *Labour/Le Travail* 36 (Fall 1995): 217-52.

19 Gillian Creese and Veronica Strong-Boag, eds., *British Columbia Reconsidered* (Vancouver:

Press Gang, 1992). See also, *BC Studies*, "Women's History and Gender History" (special issue, Spring/Summer 1995).

20 For example, Paul Voisey, *Vulcan: The Making of a Prairie Community* (Toronto: University of Toronto Press, 1988), esp. 27, sees women as a beachhead of cultural tradition and resistance to change. Similarly, Cole Harris, "Making an Immigrant Society," in *The Resettlement of BC: Essays on Colonialism and Geographical Change* (Vancouver: UBC Press, 1997), esp. 261-2, points to a sharp division of labour along sex lines, along with confinement within domesticity, to explain immigrant women's "conservative" tendencies and their exclusion from modernizing forces. Friesen, *The Canadian Prairies*, mentions a number of prominent majority culture women but within an androcentric narrative framework. More recently, John Herd Thompson, *Forging the Prairie West*, adds gender, race, and ethnicity to his illustrated history. However, the broad narrative framework remains unchanged.

21 Catherine A. Cavanaugh, "'No Place for a Woman': Engendering Western Canadian Settlement," *Western Historical Quarterly* 28 (Winter 1997): 493-518; and Karen Dubinsky, *Improper Advances: Rape and Heterosexual Conflict in Ontario, 1880-1929* (Chicago and London: University of Chicago Press, 1993). For a further discussion of the sexual politics of space, see Alison Blunt and Gillian Rose, eds., *Writing Women and Space: Colonial and Postcolonial Geographies* (New York and London: Guilford, 1994).

22 Joy Parr and Mark Rosenfeld, *Gender and History in Canada* (Toronto: Copp Clark, 1996), 8-27. See also Lynne Segal, *Why Feminism? Gender, Psychology, Politics* (New York: Columbia University Press, 1999).

23 On this point, Allen pointedly asks, "how open and unfixed were the meanings of the terms 'women' and 'men' in the frontier regions of [new settlement countries?] Surely the distinct population patterns and features common to Anglophone frontiers in the eighteenth and nineteenth centuries justify some advance hypotheses on the part of feminist historians concerned with the dynamics of sex in history? ... Will men be found primarily assigned to housework and childcare on the late-nineteenth-century Canadian prairies or New Zealand highlands? Will a double-standard of sexual morality be discovered in the Dakota wild west or Queensland outback ... ?" Judith A. Allen, *Rose Scott: Vision and Revision in Feminism* (Oxford, Auckland, and New York: Oxford University Press, 1994), 22.

24 For a further discussion of sex and gender in Prairie history, see Ann Leger-Anderson, "Canadian Prairie Women's History: An Uncertain Enterprise," *Journal of the West* 37, 1 (January 1998): 47-59.

25 Martin Robin, *The Rush for Spoils: The Company Province, 1871-1933* (Toronto: McClelland and Stewart, 1972), 44.

26 On race and gender in western settlement, see Sarah Carter, *Capturing Women: The Manipulation of Cultural Imagery in Canada's Prairie West* (Montreal and Kingston: McGill-Queen's University Press, 1997); and Sheila McManus, "'Their Own Country': Race, Gender, Landscape, and Colonization around the 49th Parallel, 1896-1900," *Agricultural History* 73, 2 (Spring 1999): 168-82. Also suggestive is Erica Smith, "'Gentlemen, This Is No Ordinary Trial': Sexual Narratives in the Trial of the Reverend Corbett, Red River, 1863," in *Reading Beyond Words: Contexts for Native History*, ed. Jennifer S.H. Brown and Elizabeth Vibert (Peterborough, ON: Broadview Press, 1996): 364-80. On *métissage* and a racialized colonial order see, in particular, Ann Laura Stoler, *Race and the Education of Desire* (Durham and London: Duke University Press, 1995); and Robert J.C. Young, *Colonial Desire: Hybridity in Theory, Culture and Race* (London and New York: Routledge, 1995). For British Columbia useful studies include Peter Ward, *White Canada Forever: Popular Attitudes and Public Policies Toward Orientals in British Columbia*, 2nd ed. (Montreal and Kingston: McGill-Queen's University Press, 1990); Kay J. Anderson, *Vancouver's Chinatown: Racial Discourse in Canada, 1875-1980* (Montreal and Kingston: McGill-Queen's University Press, 1991); Patricia E. Roy, *A White Man's Province: British Columbia Politicians and Chinese and Japanese Immigrants, 1858-1914* (Vancouver: UBC Press, 1989).

27 Studies of European women in colonial settings focus on Asia and Africa but are suggestive for colonies of settlement. See, in particular, Jane Hunter, *The Gospel of Gentility: American Women Missionaries in Turn-of-the-Century China* (New Haven and London: Yale University

Press, 1984); Ann Laura Stoler, "Carnal Knowledge and Imperial Power: Gender, Race, and Morality in Colonial Asia," in *Gender at the Crossroads of Knowledge: Feminist Anthropology in the Postmodern Era*, ed. Micaela di Leonardo (Berkeley: University of California Press, 1991), 51-101; Ann Laura Stoler, "Rethinking Colonial Categories: European Communities and the Boundaries of Rule," in *Colonialism and Culture*, ed. Nicholas B. Dirks (Ann Arbor: University of Michigan Press, 1992), 319-52; Margaret Strobel, *European Women and the Second British Empire* (Bloomington and Indianapolis: Indiana University Press, 1991); and Nupur Chaudhuri and Margaret Strobel, eds., *Western Women and Imperialism: Complicity and Resistance* (Bloomington: Indiana University Press, 1992). For thoughtful critiques of recent works on women and imperialism, see Jane Haggis, "Gendering Colonialism or Colonising Gender?" *Women's Studies International Forum* 13, 1 and 2 (1990): 105-15; and Thomas J. Prasch, "Orientalism's Other, Other Orientalisms: Women in the Scheme of Empire," *Journal of Women's History* 7, 4 (Winter 1995): 174-88.

28 See especially Roxana Ng, "Immigrant Women: The Construction of a Labour Market Category," *Canadian Journal of Women and the Law* 4, 1 (1990): 96-112. Also useful is Patricia M. Daenzer, *Regulating Class Privilege: Immigrant Servants in Canada, 1940-1990s* (Toronto: Canadian Scholar's Press, 1993).

29 Carl A. Dawson and Eva R. Younge, *Pioneering in the Prairie Provinces: The Social Side of the Settlement Process* (Toronto: Macmillan, 1940), takes a conventional approach but is still the most comprehensive treatment of Prairie settlement. John W. Bennett and Seena B. Kohl, *Settling the Canadian-American West, 1890-1915* (Lincoln: University of Nebraska Press, 1995), updates settlement history in the northern Great Plains region but emphasizes western exceptionalism. For women and mining frontiers, see Jeremy Mouat, *Roaring Days: Rossland's Mines and the History of British Columbia* (Vancouver: UBC Press, 1995), especially 109-21; and Sylvia Van Kirk, "A Vital Presence: Women in the Cariboo Gold Rush, 1862-1875," in Creese and Strong-Boag, *British Columbia Reconsidered*, 21-37. For an excellent study that integrates gender and class in an analysis of a US mining community, see Elizabeth Jameson, *All That Glitters: Class, Conflict, and Community in Cripple Creek* (Urbana: University of Illinois, 1998).

30 On married women's property rights in western Canada, see Margaret McCallum, "Prairie Women and the Struggle for Dower Law, 1905-1920," *Prairie Forum* 18 (Spring 1993): 19-34; and Catherine Cavanaugh, "The Limitations of the Pioneering Partnership: The Alberta Campaign for Homestead Dower, 1909-25," *Canadian Historical Review* 74 (June 1993): 198-225.

31 Marjorie Griffin Cohen, *Women's Work, Markets, and Economic Development in Nineteenth-Century Ontario* (Toronto: University of Toronto Press, 1988).

32 Sara Brooks Sundberg, "A Female Frontier: Manitoba Farm Women in 1922," *Prairie Forum* 16 (Fall 1991): 185-204.

33 W. Peter Ward, "Population Growth in Western Canada, 1901-71," in *The Developing West*, ed. John Foster (Edmonton: University of Alberta Press, 1983), 155-77.

34 Ibid., n. 8, p. 176. The sex-based division of the land grant in Canada is in marked distinction to the large number of women homesteaders in western states in the United States, where similar legislation included women. See, for example, Paula Bauman, "Single Women Homesteaders in Wyoming, 1880-1930," *Annals of Wyoming* 58 (Spring 1986): 39-53; Paula Nelson, *After the West Was Won: Homesteaders and Town-Builders in Western South Dakota, 1900-1917* (Iowa City: University of Iowa Press, 1986); Barbara Allen, *Homesteading the High Desert* (Salt Lake City: University of Utah Press, 1987); H. Elaine Lindgren, "Ethnic Women Homesteading on the Plains of North Dakota," *Great Plains Quarterly* 9 (Summer 1989): 157-73; and Sherry L. Smith, "Single Women Homesteaders: The Perplexing Case of Elinore Pruitt Stewart," *Western Historical Quarterly* 22 (May 1991): 163-83. A Canadian exception is Georgina Binnie-Clark, *Wheat and Woman*, reprinted with an introduction by Susan Jackel (Toronto: University of Toronto Press, 1979 [1914]).

35 For a good account of this settlement process on the Prairies, see the first volume of prairie activist and feminist Nellie L. McClung's autobiography, *Clearing in the West* (Toronto: Thomas Allen, 1935).

36 For further discussion on this point, see Van Kirk, "A Vital Presence," and on the continuum of women's work, see Susan Morton, *Ideal Surroundings: Domestic Life in a Working-Class Suburb in the 1920s* (Toronto: University of Toronto Press, 1995), esp. 78-81.

37 For a moving portrait of one family's experience, see Denise Chong, *The Concubine's Children* (New York: Viking, 1995). See also Midge Ayukawa, "Good Wives and Wise Mothers: Japanese Picture Brides in Early Twentieth-Century British Columbia," *BC Studies* 105/6 (Spring/Summer 1995): 103-18.

38 For a further discussion, see Nanci Langford, *First Generation and Lasting Impressions: The Gendered Identities of Prairie Homestead Women*" (PhD thesis, University of Alberta, 1994); and Elliott West, "Beyond Baby Doe: Child Rearing on the Mining Frontier," in *The Women's West*, ed. Susan Armitage and Elizabeth Jameson (Norman: University of Oklahoma Press, 1987), 179-92.

39 Veronica Strong-Boag, "Pulling in Double Harness or Hauling a Double Load: Women, Work and Feminism on the Canadian Prairie," *Journal of Canadian Studies* 1, 3 (Fall 1986): 32-52.

40 Betsy Downey, "Battered Pioneers," *Great Plains Quarterly*, 12 (Winter 1992): 31-49. See also Terry L. Chapman, "'Till Death Do Us Part:' Wife Beating in Alberta, 1905-1920," *Alberta History* 36 (Autumn 1988): 13-22.

41 Sara Mills, *Discourses of Difference: An Analysis of Women's Travel Writing and Colonialism* (London and New York: Routledge, 1991).

42 The deeding of Regina's cottage hospital to the town discussed by Beverly Boutilier is one example.

43 Sylvia Van Kirk, "Tracing the Fortunes of Five Founding Families of Victoria," 115/6, *BC Studies* (Autumn/Winter 1997/8): 148-79.

44 On this point, see Kathryn McPherson, "Was the 'Frontier' Good for Women? Historical Approaches to Women and Agricultural Settlement in the Prairie West, 1870–1900," *Atlantis: A Women's Studies Journal* 25, 1 (Fall/Winter 2000); special issue entitled "Feminism and History" guest edited by Margaret Conrad and Linda Kealey.

CHAPTER 1

"I Wish the Men Were Half as Good"

Gender Constructions in the Canadian North-Western Mission Field, 1860–1940

MYRA RUTHERDALE

New opportunities for women's mission work in the late nineteenth and early twentieth centuries were inextricably linked to the expansion of the British Empire. The Empire, upon which the sun was said never to set, provided what British, American, and Canadian evangelicals saw as an infinite opportunity to spread the Christian gospel. Women's mission work began in India's *zenanas*, where Muslim and high-caste Hindu women lived in seclusion and were permitted to socialize only with other women. Male missionaries were not permitted to attempt to convert these women and were forced to hand the work over to female missionaries.[1] Throughout the nineteenth century religious work in North America and Britain became increasingly feminized. Clergy relied on women to fill the pews, organize church groups, and raise funds.

This involvement notwithstanding, women's entrance into mission work still met resistance. In fact, Ann Douglas has argued that women entered the mission field despite "repeated widespread clerical objection."[2] They were clearly able to overcome clerical hostility since, by the end of the century, foreign and domestic mission work had become the preserve of women. According to the Church of England's *Church Missionary Intelligencer*, by 1895 women outnumbered men in the mission field: "The latest statistics of all Protestant Missionary Societies, British, Continental, American &c., give no less than 2,576 unmarried women missionaries. The male missionaries are given as 5,233, and as these have 3,641 wives, the total number of women, married and unmarried, exceeds that of men by just a thousand."[3]

Mission work allowed women to leave both the "private sphere" and their home towns to travel to new environments where they encountered unfamiliar conditions. Historian Ruth Compton Brouwer, who has written on Canadian Presbyterian women in India at the turn of the century, argues that mission work was indeed a liberating experience for women. Brouwer contends that the missionary movement was presented to critics of women's rights as a "'less injurious' sphere to true Western womanhood than others being contemplated or pursued by the era's restless 'new woman.'"[4] While mission work could be and often was strategically constructed to appear to be an extension of the domestic sphere, women in the mission field went well beyond that realm.

The study of missionaries who came to northwestern Canada to Christianize Aboriginals has focused on men.[5] There are several popular and scholarly histories on "wilderness saints" like William Bompas, William Duncan, and William Ridley. Like other denominations, the Anglican Church began to recruit unmarried women in the late nineteenth century while at the same time encouraging missionary wives to work as unpaid missionaries. The Church's first male missionary was sent to northern British Columbia, the future Diocese of Caledonia, in 1856, and throughout the 1860s and 1870s the number of mission stations expanded throughout the Yukon and North-West Territories.

One of the largest Anglican missionary societies during this period in northern Canada was the Church Missionary Society (CMS), which was based in London, England. Between 1860 and 1945, the dates focused on in this chapter, the CMS and, later, the Canadian-based Missionary Society of the Church of England in Canada (MSCC) sent nearly 150 women to work in the North. These women were from both Britain and Canada, and most had spent from one to two years training at deaconess houses either in Toronto or in England.

Despite the growing numbers of women enrolling as missionaries, the mission calling was still thought of as a male occupation. This misconception seemed to be reinforced in both popular and church literature. In 1904 Norman Tucker, the first secretary of the MSCC, suggested that, since it was becoming more difficult to find new male recruits for the North, women should be sent there: "Owing to the great lack of men for the ministry and the unlimited field for workers in the territories and western provinces, it is necessary that trained, God fearing women should stand in the gap." Tucker typically overlooked the fact that women had been working in the North for years. In fact, especially at the turn of the century, the majority of Anglican missionaries in the North were women. Their experiences in many respects should direct us to consider social responses to sexual difference. In other words, where were gender boundaries drawn?

This chapter examines constructions of gender within the context of the Anglican missionary experience in Canada's North-West in the late nineteenth and early twentieth centuries. It considers gender from a relational perspective by approaching interactions among male and female missionaries as well as friendships among women missionaries.

Images of masculine and feminine conduct were well ingrained in those who ventured into the mission field. Despite society's intent to impose gender identities, there were occasional slippages in behaviour. As Denise Riley argues in *Am I That Name?*, it is obvious that "any attention to the life of a woman, if traced out carefully, must admit the degree to which the effects of lived gender are at least sometimes unpredictable and fleeting."[6] "Can anyone," Riley asks, "fully inhabit a gender without a degree of horror? How could someone 'be a woman' through and through, make a final home in that classification without suffering claustrophobia?"[7]

This chapter shows that, despite an attempt to maintain the feminine ideal in the mission field, there were moments when women fleetingly and unpredictably escaped its confines. Normative gender constructions were based on a "separate sphere" ideology, in which masculinity and femininity were thought to be dichotomous. Women were to be the moral guardians of society, with their influence centred on the domestic sphere, whereas men were to be arbitrators over matters deemed to be public, including business and government.[8] In the mission field, however, conventional gender identities were disrupted, and both women and men were required to transcend boundaries that were fixed in their home settings. I will present the contradictions between women's images and the work they actually did as missionaries. First, however, I will discuss popular masculine images.

Although the numbers of missionary women were growing, in fact, the image of missionaries was still closely tied to masculinity. Late nineteenth-century writers like George Alfred Henty and Rider Haggard romanticized and popularized the masculine character of Empire in their so-called epic tales of adventure. Using such literature, scholars have recently turned critical attention to the construction of masculinity in the late Victorian and early Edwardian periods. According to historian Patrick A. Dunae, boys' literature "reflected the missionary zeal and the pragmatic materialism associated with empire during the last decades of the nineteenth century."[9]

The middle- and upper-class discourse of masculinity employed terms like "virile," "manly," "muscular," and "forceful." In describing the mythical portrait of a colonizer, Albert Memmi states: "We sometimes enjoy picturing the colonizer as a tall man, bronzed by the sun, wearing Wellington boots, proudly leaning on a shovel as he rivets his gaze far away on the land. When not engaged in battles against nature, we think of him labouring selflessly for mankind, attending the sick, and spreading culture to the non-literate. In other words his pose is one of the noble adventurer, a righteous pioneer."[10] Typically, colonizers were portrayed in boyhood adventure texts as "gentlemen" who were loyal to the queen, patriotic, and both physically and morally superior. Muscular Christianity and boys' leisure movements (e.g., the Boy Scouts) fused to produce an image of masculinity associated with Empire – a masculinist culture of which missionaries, too, were a part.

Similarities between male missionary correspondence/memoirs and the texts of late nineteenth-century adventure writers are quite striking. The language of masculine adventure was especially evident in the writing of at least two Caledonia-based missionaries, both of whom served in northern British Columbia for over twenty years. Bishop William Ridley's diaries and letters and Archdeacon William Henry Collison's evocatively entitled *In the Wake of the War Canoe* epitomized muscular Christianity and masculinity. Bold undertakings often involved long canoe trips with risky portages and harrowing weather conditions. Strength and endurance were exhibited by hunting or building log houses, churches, and schools. Manful leadership was called upon when crews were organized for extended travel.[11]

Missionary societies appealed to masculinity to attract recruits, and, at the same time, images of missionary men continued to be reinforced by those already in the field. Whether shooting rapids or being heralded as great hunters, male missionaries appeared, at least from the correspondence, to revel in the glories of the outdoor life of muscular Christianity. As we shall see, however, men also had to learn some small measure of women's traditional work in order to survive in the mission field. In the same way that images of masculinity were a social-cultural construct, so too were images of femininity.

Constructs of Womanhood and Missionary Marriages

Prevailing representations of missionary women were tied closely to Victorian constructs of womanhood. Though it was true that numerically women dominated mission work, shadows of separate sphere ideology were cast as far as the mission field in northern Canada. Just as male missionaries were constructed as masculine and responsible for the public sphere, women missionaries were portrayed as feminine and responsible for the private sphere. One dominant metaphor applied to missionary wives in particular was that of helpmate. Within this role, White missionary women were to function primarily as role models for Native women, displaying to them proper womanly and domestic conduct. Beneath the performance of womanly rituals rested an assumption that the British (and Anglo-Canadian) way was the only way and that Native women were lacking the skills necessary to maintain households and raise children. However, for White women the mission field also provided an opportunity to transcend the boundaries of gender that, ironically, they were attempting to impose on Native women.[12]

Women were simultaneously trapped by tradition and liberated by their unique positions as missionary wives. This juxtaposition is clearly shown in Lois Boyd's insightful article, which outlines the various duties and responsibilities that befell Presbyterian ministers' wives in the nineteenth-century United States. She claims that even the title "minister's wife" signified a certain category that implied specific obligations. Yet, despite the great and at times unachievable expectations, she argues that to be a minister's wife also gave a woman the potential to step outside the boundaries of womanhood: "Although the denomination expected women to remain silent in public, in actuality a number of ministers' wives addressed groups of men and women, assumed leadership positions in church and community organizations, became active in social concerns, and at times taught and prayed in front of some public gatherings."[13] It was still true, though, that they were expected to keep a perfect household, control the family economy, and counsel their husbands. In an ironic mode, one Presbyterian periodical suggested that the dilemma of ministers' wives was that they should be "always at home and always abroad, always serving God and always serving tables."[14]

Wives on the northern mission "frontier" were not as vulnerable to public scrutiny as were those located elsewhere – at least in the late nineteenth and early twentieth centuries, prior to permanent White settlement. This fact alone provided for some relief from prescribed roles. There were still clear expectations that were associated more with gendered perceptions than with women's individual personalities. Expectations about the duties of missionary women were especially apparent to male missionaries and their wives in the early years of contact. Charlotte Selina Bompas was quite conscious of the role that White Christian women in the North should play. Bompas was the daughter of Charlotte and Joseph Cox, MD, of Montague Square in London, England. She spent most of her youth in Italy due to her father's asthma. She had her coming out party in Italy and read and spoke Italian fluently. Bompas arrived at Fort Simpson at the confluence of the Liard and MacKenzie Rivers in September 1874 to join her husband, the Reverend William Carpenter Bompas, the first bishop of Athabasca.

In November 1907, after many years of living in the North, Charlotte Bompas wrote an article for the *Canadian Churchman* concerning the type of White women needed there. She insisted that White women were to act as role models for Native women: "Dear sister-settlers amongst the Indians, there is power given you from on high which is intended you should use among them or any other race with whom you may be placed – it is the power of *influence* ... In your Christian households, in your modest demeanour, in your fair dealings with all let them see what they should seek to copy more than the jewels and costly attire which in their eyes are all that is needed to constitute a lady."[15] The implication was that Native women needed White role models to learn how to behave like so-called "proper ladies." As Nancy Pagh argues in Chapter 3, Native women's own cultural traditions regarding care-giving and domesticity were rarely acknowledged. The White women in her study found little in common with the so-called "counterfeit women" of the Northwest Coast.[16]

Charlotte Selina Bompas

Other missionaries were equally explicit in their views that Native women needed to be taught feminine rituals and etiquette. The first married woman missionary in the Diocese of Caledonia sent by the CMS came out from England in 1860. The Reverend Lewin S. Tugwell and Mrs. Tugwell arrived at Victoria in August 1860 and were greeted by William Duncan who, at that time, was one of only two Anglican missionaries serving in northern British Columbia. Duncan quickly grew resentful of the recently married Tugwells and claimed early on to be doubtful of their commitment to the work: "I see that wives after all may be a great hindrance to a man in diverting his mind from the work before him."[17] Upon their arrival at Port Simpson, the Tugwells began to unpack their possessions. It was at this time Duncan apparently told Mrs. Tugwell that he and the Reverend Tugwell could manage the baggage but that she should prepare biscuits. To Duncan's surprise she replied that she had never made bread in her life. Many years later, Duncan recounted this anecdote to one of his co-workers, adding, "What do you think of that? The C.M.S. had sent more than five thousand miles, somebody to help me teach the Indians Christian home life, and here I was obliged to make bread for her myself."[18] Note Duncan's assumption of a gendered division of labour, despite the fact that he was able to make bread himself.

When Reverend J.B. McCullagh's second wife, Mary Webster McCullagh, joined him in his work in northern British Columbia's Nass River Valley, he wrote to the Nishga Missionary Union to report on her success. He boasted of her capable management of the daily chores, which included "cooking, washing up, brushing and dusting rooms, washing, starching and ironing, and every other thing that has to be done in a house." He claimed that this routine tested her strength, and he wrote in glowing terms of her "missionary spirit": "Looking at her amongst a crowd of Indian women, teaching them to cut and make up articles of wearing apparel, my wife is a source of intense joy and astonishment to me. When one considers how difficult it is to 'handle' Indians, the tact, patience and self-forgetting spirit it requires, to say nothing of the demand on one's physical energy, it is a wonder to me to find her put in two solid hours of this work, and then come away as fresh as the proverbial daisy."[19] Clearly, the rhetoric of the "Angel in the Home" was easily transferred to the mission field. Orientalist discourse and separate sphere ideology were intricately connected in a seamless web of relationships that connected the colonizers and the colonized.

Attempts to export Christian domesticity were characteristic of the global mission movement. According to historian Jane Hunter, women missionaries defined themselves within the context of an "expansive domesticity, endeavouring to embody traditional notions of nurturance, gentility, and affection which distinguished them from men."[20] Ultimately, their purpose was to aid in the conversion process, but, as in other settings, Native women did not necessarily convert because of their new knowledge of Western housekeeping.

While modelling domesticity was standard for women, very little was said in the official correspondence about teaching Native men how to be "proper gentlemen." The act of consciously modelling gentlemanly behaviour was not a common feature in the discourse of male missionaries. There was not the same concern for teaching men manners as there was for teaching women manners. According to the newcomers, Native men had to be civilized but not to the same extent as did women. Male missionaries were more concerned with conversion statistics, linguistic translations, and itinerant schedules. They sought Native knowledge from their guides and translators, hoping to learn skills that would make them more adept at travelling and living in the outdoors.

Despite the seemingly rigid categories of femininity and masculinity, when we look at the relationship between missionary men and missionary women in the field the boundaries of gender often appear to be shifting. At times men had to do what might be traditionally considered women's work and women often had to do what might be traditionally considered men's work. At times, too, it was necessary to overlook the rhetoric, if not the practice, of true womanhood altogether. When Isaac Stringer wrote back to his future bride, Sarah Alexander, then training to be a nurse at Grace Hospital in Toronto, he suggested some areas of medicine to which she should pay particular attention: "I must just mention that syphilis is one of the common diseases amongst the Eskimos. It may seem out of place to mention this to a lady but in our circumstances we must be practical and the mention of this may lead you to study up the different forms of the disease."[21] Stringer thought that it would be impractical to shield his future partner in the mission field from the reality of what would soon face her, even if society might sanction any discussion of sexuality. Separate-spheres ideology was not always practical in the mission field, where husbands and wives had to eschew tensions between masculinity and femininity and face the day-to-day realities of their work. Dealing with prolonged absences stands out as a particular problem, perhaps because of the extended period of experimentation that was required. At times Selina Bompas complained bitterly about being alone. Luckily, she was spirited enough to overcome these periods of loneliness. So, too, was Jane Ridley of the Diocese of

Caledonia. In 1884, Bishop Ridley went to Ottawa to present his interpretation of the Duncan uprising. He found himself in an awkward position with regard to Hazelton, where the CMS had just established a station. The missionary there was forced to return to England due to his wife's ill health, and Bishop Ridley did not want to leave the station unattended. So Jane Ridley volunteered to stay behind while Ridley went to Ottawa and then on to England. As the *Church Missionary Intelligencer and Record* reported in March 1884:

> Mrs. Ridley can have no idea of his having come on to England. He had left her at Hazelton, the interior station at the Skeena Forks, vacated by the return to England of the Rev. W.J. Faulconer on account of his wife's illness; and there she is spending the winter and carrying on the work of the station entirely alone. We cannot but be too thankful for the self-denying courage with which she has thrown herself into the breach, and for the happy influence she evidently exercises upon the Indians.[22]

After her death Jane Ridley was described by the *Canadian Church Magazine* as a "Missionary Heroine" because she had so successfully maintained the Hazelton station in the winter of 1880-1.[23] At her deathbed her husband wrote a very melodramatic testimony to the CMS: "crowds of Indians hung round her bed and she was delighted ... In her death she, by her beautiful and tender words, and patient endurance of agony at times through choking, drew more souls to Jesus than ever. It was victory on victory, triumph on triumph. Quite two hundred souls shared in the blessing."[24] In the end he claimed to have given her body over to the Tsimshian.

Ridley was using the hyperbole commonly adopted in missionary obituaries, but it appears that he believed that in the theatre of Jane Ridley's death, souls were saved. William Collison attended her funeral, and he too was swept up in the emotion: "She bade farewell to all the Zimshian [sic] native Christians individually and gave to each a parting charge. She was thus enabled by the divine grace to set a seal on the teachings of a life consecrated & devoted to the service of the master amongst the Zimshians [sic]."[25] In the fashion of missionary eulogies, Jane Ridley was constructed as a heroine.

While traditional gender roles reflected in the discourse applied either to men or women in the mission field, descriptions of certain religious identities could blur gender distinctions. In the case of Jane Ridley an apparent freedom from gendered constraints was implied in her "higher calling." Within the context of a calling, Ridley's gender identity could at times appear to be subsumed. In a subsequent tribute to women missionaries Bishop Ridley stated that women in the mission field "work hardest and by their example fire the men with emulation. There is not one married woman among us who would think she was free to devote nearly all her time to domestic economy. The wife is as much called of God to be his instrument in soul-winning as the husband."[26] From Ridley's perspective the Christian calling was not gender-specific. This is not to say that Ridley would necessarily have supported equal political or legal rights for women, but with respect to religious work, or "soul-winning," he tended to cast men and women as equals.

As much as Christianity could serve as a strategic force for women, in terms of the day-to-day realities of mission life, it was important for both men and women to go beyond their traditional spheres if for no other reason than to ensure survival. Men certainly had to know how to cook and do other household chores in the mission field. The Reverend G. Neilson attracted the compliments of Pangnirtung missionaries Florence Hirst and Prudence Hockin because of his capable shortbread cookies and doughnuts, although both agreed that "men don't look right cooking doughnuts somehow."[27] In this case Hirst and Hockin found it

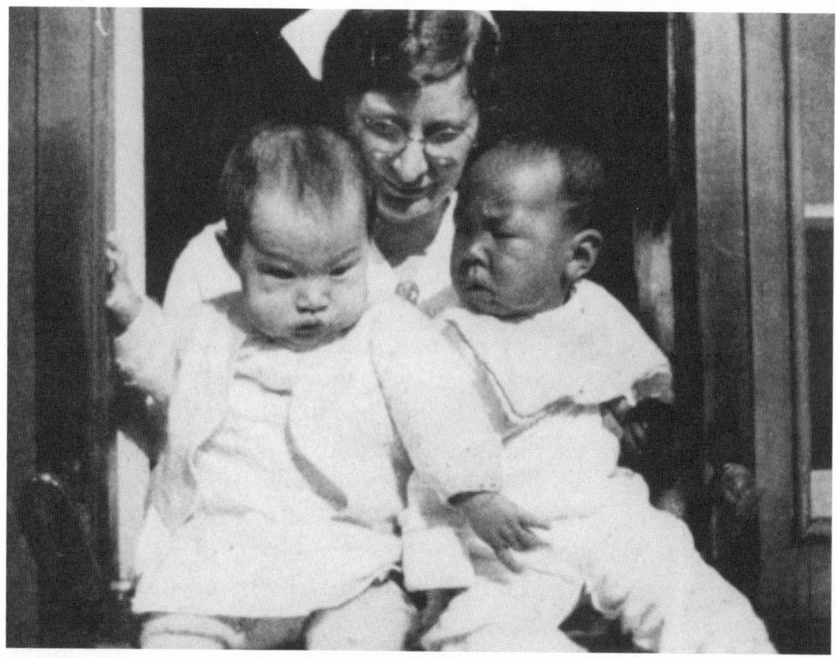

Nurse Prudence Hockin at St. Luke's Hospital, Pangnirtung, NWT

odd to see a man do what was traditionally defined as women's work. The Reverend Alfred Price, stationed at Kitwanga, wrote back to the CMS complaining that the Native woman they had hired to help his wife in the delivery of their child had abandoned them as the date became imminent: "there was no one to do the washing. I had to do everything even to delivering the child."[28]

Childbirth in the mission field posed new challenges for missionary couples. Alice Woods, who had been raised in Victoria, married Robert Tomlinson, originally from Ireland, when she was seventeen. In the summer of 1871, while stationed at Kincolith, Alice Tomlinson, who was expecting her first child, contracted typhoid fever. Fortunately, her husband had some medical training and was with her throughout the crisis of the fever. She gave birth, but their first-born survived only a few hours. Tomlinson expressed his feeling of isolation in his report back to the parent committee: "It is hard for those living among sympathizing friends to realize the trials of those more isolated. On this day I had to fill the place of Father, Husband, Mourner, Doctor, Nurse, Clergyman."[29] All of these roles required a sympathetic individual rather unlike the one portrayed by the rugged frontiersman or masculine stereotype. The trials of marriage and childbirth often recast the boundaries of gender.

Sarah Stringer had her first two children when she and her husband were stationed at Herschel Island, a coastal island off the northwest tip of the North-West Territories. In her diary she recorded the birth of her first-born, Rowena, on 14 December 1896. Up until the baby's birth Stringer had kept active, claiming that she had taught school, gone for walks, and held choir practice until just days before the birth. From the tone of her diary it seems that she was very calm about the arrival of their child. Ten days after the delivery she wrote that she had been "an invalid for the past few days Mr. Stringer being my physician he was also my nurse also Mr. Whittaker helping and cooking me many dainty dishes. He excelled in this much to my pleasure."[30] The Reverend Whittaker had been at Wycliffe College in Toronto with the Reverend Stringer and was sent to the North in 1896. Whittaker and the Reverend Stringer both cared for Sarah Stringer and were able to manage the household while she was recovering from childbirth. They not only coped, but they actually cooked fancy dishes. One month after Rowena was born Sarah Stringer was teaching again.[31]

Her apparent calm during childbirth may be traced to her medical experience as a nurse and, perhaps, to her personality. Her letters and diaries give the impression that she rarely complained about feeling lonely or isolated. However, she could be critical of women in the field who

Bishop and Mrs. Stringer, London, England, 1929

did. Emma Hatley, born and raised in London, England, arrived in July 1898 to marry the Reverend C. Whittaker and to work with him at Peel River. Sarah Stringer gave away the bride, and Reverend I.O. Stringer performed the service. The next summer the Stringers visited Peel River again, just after the delivery of the Whittakers' first child. Apparently, Emma Whittaker felt nervous and was reluctant to return to Herschel Island with the Stringers for a visit. In a letter to her friend back in Ontario, Sarah Stringer recorded her impression of Whittaker: "Mrs. Whittaker does not know whether she will go or not. She fears this that and the other so I do not know if she will go ... She is rather delicate."[32] The challenges of adapting to a new environment, married life, and a new baby all at the same time were great, as the Reverend Whittaker himself acknowledged. In a letter back to the Toronto's Women's Auxiliary he boasted of having a new companion but cast some doubt on her adaptability: "Personally, you will be glad to know that I have now some one of my own to get a lunch for me if I come in late. My wife enjoys life here very much, although it is rather hard for one delicately reared."[33] Indeed, in describing his marriage proposal, he spoke of the practicality of the arrangement. Emma Hatley had, according to the Reverend Whittaker, "responded to my invitation to be co-helper in the mission."[34]

Many years later Archibald Fleming, the first bishop of the Arctic, recalled the trials of the Whittakers and other pioneer missionaries when he visited a church in Fort McPherson: "Memorial brasses in the Arctic are somehow much more poignant than those in the south. I suppose it is because they represent suffering remote from the comfort of friends. Here in St. Matthew's church this experience is told so eloquently and yet so briefly on three small brass plates each bearing the name of a child born to Archdeacon and Mrs. Whittaker. Two had died at Herschel Island and their bodies were carried two hundred and fifty miles by sledge and dog team to Fort McPherson for burial; the third died up the river."[35]

Life in the North presented unique sets of challenges. For some mission couples these challenges were unbearable, forcing early resignation from the field. As it turned out, the Whittakers were in the North until 1921, but not everyone could adapt to such new conditions. The Tugwells stayed for only two years. The next couple sent out to help Duncan, the Gribbells, lasted only six weeks.[36] In both cases it was claimed that the women's health was too delicate to prolong their stay – a common explanation when couples chose to leave their assigned station earlier than anticipated by the CMS. Women missionaries had to be physically and emotionally equipped to adapt to life in the northern mission field. Many challenges, particularly in areas thought to be isolated, may have been impossible for some women as well as for some men.[37] Many may have found it impossible to adjust to such a different way of life.

Newcomers, both men and women, especially complained about the lack of privacy that suddenly faced them in isolated communities. When the Collisons moved to the Queen Charlotte Islands they were immediately faced with this issue. As a cultural construct, privacy, according to the Reverend Collison, was not important to the Haida. In his memoirs he confessed that it often was difficult to insist that his family be left alone in its hut:

> The Haida, many of whom had not seen a white woman, crowded into our little shanty in their paint and feathers, and squatted down on the floor, so closely packed together that there was no room to move ... Not knowing their language, I could not convey to them our desire, or had I attempted to drive them out, I might have been ejected in turn, or subjected to even rougher treatment. I concluded therefore that what could not be helped must be endured. Day after day this continued, so that it was impossible to get near the stove to prepare any food. Any article of wearing apparel within reach was freely made use of. Hats, coats, and boots were passed from one another, each one trying them on and inviting the opinions of the others as to the appearance or otherwise.[38]

From Collison's recollections we can see that his mission was so tenuous that he feared causing offence to visitors by asking them to leave. His acceptance of the visitors meant that it would be difficult to spend any private time with his family. Writing to Bishop Stringer in 1922, Catherine Hoare, originally from Ottawa, Ontario, who was stationed at Aklavik with her husband, expressed similar concerns: "I often wonder how you people managed about eating etc. We had quite a time of it. They even sat in the bedroom and watched us dress. One hates to offend them for they mean no harm."[39] Stringer replied to Hoare that it was most important that they treat their unwanted visitors delicately, but in his view they should not sit in the bedroom to watch the Hoares dress. He suggested a few words they could use to encourage them to leave without offence.[40]

Mission houses were never private homes; rather, they were places where visitors, wanted and unwanted, often crossed family thresholds. Some missionaries encouraged Natives who were leaving the villages for winter to leave their children behind at the mission so that the missionaries' wives could teach them English. Mission homes were often converted into schools during the day. The issue of privacy had an impact on both men and women, but one could argue that, because the running of the household was deemed a woman's responsibility, the lack of privacy affected women more than it did men. As well, because male missionaries tended to travel more than their wives, the mission household developed into a gendered space. In negotiating the living space, as well as in determining other duties related to mission work, marriages had to be partnerships or a couple's failure in the mission field would be certain.

The lack of privacy should not have been surprising, as the problem was often raised during training and preparation. Parent societies invariably warned that women who married missionaries would themselves become missionaries and, more particularly, share their challenges. The *Canadian Church Magazine* of January 1897 commented that the work done by missionary wives was not always mentioned in reports back to the parent society but that their contributions were, nonetheless, "valuable items of solid missionary usefulness."[41] In another article, which originally appeared in the *Missionary Herald*, Dr. Herrick boasted about the value of missionary wives: "I never yet saw a missionary's wife whose companionship did not double her husband's usefulness. One of the choicest things of missionary work is the unwritten heroism of missionary homes. It is the missionary's wife, who by years of endurance and acquired experience in the foreign field, has made it possible in these later years – the years of Women's Missionary Societies – for unmarried ladies to go abroad and live and work among the people of Eastern lands."[42]

Mission societies were also likely to comment on the appropriateness of certain marriages. When William Collison went out to Metlakatla after completing his education at the CMS's Islington College in London, England, he was accompanied by his wife, Marion M. Goodwin. He was told that, since there was no female missionary at Metlakatla, he should marry, and he did so three weeks prior to sailing in September 1873. The CMS applauded his choice and expressed its sincere satisfaction that he was about to marry a nurse and a woman that, it was convinced, would be a wonderful help in the mission field.[43] Marion Goodwin was herself a deaconess. She had a wealth of nursing experience, from assisting the wounded soldiers on the battlefields of the Franco-Prussian War to establishing a hospital for incurables at Cork.[44] In its instructions to Collison, the CMS demonstrated that it saw the value of sending married men into the field.

The bishops in the field also recognized the importance of missionary wives. Writing back to the parent committee in 1895, the Yukon's Bishop Bompas described the type of man he wanted in the North: "I may say that I prefer a married Missionary or if not thus, then one engaged to be married to whom his wife may be sent without his returning to fetch her."[45] He was quite delighted when Reverend J. Naylor, a McGill University graduate, was on his way to the Yukon with his wife, Ada Esther (Mount) Naylor. In the summer of 1896 he wrote to Naylor to tell him how anxious he was about their arrival: "I cannot tell you how earnestly I have longed for additional help and I still cannot but hope that you are bringing with you a second recruit for our work besides Mrs. Naylor to whom please to offer our best respects, and who will I doubt not be an important acquisition in our Mission field."[46] Bompas viewed Ada Naylor as an acquisition, but, in his strained circumstances, this is perhaps understandable. He was continually calling out for more recruits.

The Reverend Isaac Stringer, who became the bishop of the Yukon in 1906, also saw the value of married couples in the mission field. In a letter of recommendation for Reverend W.H. Fry, a graduate of Wycliffe College who had worked on Herschel Island for four years, Stringer found himself boasting about both Fry and his wife: "Mrs. Fry is an excellent helpmeet possessing all the qualities that a clergyman's wife should possess – tactful and judicious, a good housekeeper and interested in the work of the church. She was formerly a school teacher, and did good work as teacher at the school at Herschel Island."[47] Underlying such praise was the fact that the mission society was getting two workers for the price of one.

For women, missionary work offered both work and the possibility of marriage. Women like Mrs. Fry could, at the same time, work as schoolteachers and be considered exemplary missionary wives. Stringer's letter also indicated that, at least in the case of Mrs. Fry, and undoubtedly in the case of other missionary wives, these women did double duty. They were expected to teach school, nurse, hold choir practices, start women's auxiliaries, and do other similar work as well as all of the household chores. Many of these tasks were categorized as traditional women's work, but when women, as was often the case, were left alone to maintain the mission station, they took on public roles, thus transcending gender barriers. Men had to know how to cook and perform other domestic and nurturing tasks, while women had to be physically active and able to perform roles that demanded strength and endurance.

Unmarried Women Missionaries

Like their married sisters, unmarried women missionaries were also expected to participate in all aspects of mission work. In 1896 Ridley wrote back to the CMS to describe the exact type of woman missionary he wanted. Interestingly, he insisted on "ladies accustomed to refined environments." "Refined women," Ridley had found, were more willing to agree to perform undesirable tasks. Scrubbing and cleaning children with "crawling things" were listed as two jobs that "servants or unrefined women" would not perform. "I want ladies," Ridley concluded, "who for Christ's sake will undertake anything in the path of duty." He also argued that women who "are not refined in thought and behavior ... would not meet with the same unreservedness socially as others who are refined."[48] Ridley clearly had a type in mind, and although he employed the rhetoric of traditional womanhood, when he turned to practical issues his definition of the ideal woman changed dramatically. Ridley expected "ladies" to be something quite different from "proverbial daisies." He demanded that they be prepared to do absolutely any work that was "in the path of duty." If that meant work that appeared undesirable, than so be it. Women who would respond to "higher claims" despite gendered expectations were considered essential.

Ridley was pleased with the first unmarried missionary women in his diocese, writing back to the CMS in October 1898: "We do get splendid lady workers for this place. I wish the men were half as good."[49] Eleanor Dickenson of the Isle of Wight arrived in June 1890 and was instantly in demand. According to Ridley she was the "maid of all work." Her duties, listed by Ridley in a letter back to the CMS, were extensive: "She is secretary to the ladies prayer union and Bible reading union ...

she is always ready to go to the rescue when trained nursing is required at the hospital. This is her forte. She would have taken charge of it but that I feared her energy (which is great) would have brought her into collision with our doctor who though much improved of late is not and never will be energetic. She attends to the sick at their homes and so has won the hearts of all the mothers in the place. Her chief work is the girls home. She has nine girls with her."[50] Her hard work had earned her much respect among the other missionaries, and, because she would never rest, Ridley said that he had to insist that she submit to the "curb." In other words, in Ridley's estimation, Eleanor Dickinson was an excellent worker but had to be warned not to overdo it. He also seemed to be afraid that Dickinson's energy would show up the doctor's lassitude.

While there is ample evidence to suggest that women missionaries spent much of their time, as the CMS described it, in "the performance of everyday common place duties," it is also apparent that they were not perpetually trapped in the category of "women."[51] In fact, they often did almost the same work as their male counterparts, and they experienced similar moments of adventure in the outdoors. In *Discourses of Difference: An Analysis of Women's Travel Writing and Colonialism*, Sara Mills argues that women travel writers of the eighteenth and nineteenth centuries "were restricted as to the type of language they might use and the sort of 'experience' they might depict, and thus their work was judged to be limited compared to the relative freedom of male novelists."[52] Mills focuses on travel writers, but the same can be said for women missionaries. Their letters and diaries do not contain the masculine discourse of Haggard or Henty. Women were not conditioned, like their male counterparts, to glory in the adventure of tipping canoes or chopping wood, or to romanticize the general hardships of life in the North. Yet their experiences indicate that they shared, thrived, and suffered equally with men in the experience offered by missionary work.

An incident that illustrates this point was reported in the official CMS history, ironically entitled *History of the Church Missionary Society, Its Environment, Its Men and Its Work*, chronicled by Eugene Stock. Bishop Ridley reported back to the CMS that, during the summer months, missionaries were stationed at coastal fish canneries. In the summer of 1893, Margaret West taught school and held meetings at Sunnyside and Inverness – two coastal canneries located about twelve miles from Metlakatla. West rowed her own boat between the canneries despite the treacherous tidal currents and rough landings. Ridley claimed that "she pursued her steady course, so that she has become an expert sailor, handling her 16 foot boat all alone as well as any man on our staff. She had it all to learn to her cost. Once she got into serious difficulties, being capsized in deep and rough water, and was half drowned before she could climb back into the boat. It was a risk to appoint a lady to such a station single-handed where there are some hundreds of Indians, Chinese, Japanese and a band of white men unaccustomed to social or religious restraints."[53]

According to Ridley, by the end of the summer West had proven the effectiveness of what he called "true womanliness" combined with "self sacrificing service for Christ." It is striking that, while she could handle a boat "as well as any man" in the mission, she was still characterized by Ridley according to the distinctive features of "true womanliness." Her accomplishments were described in the language of work for Christ, and little reflection was given to the fact that she had crossed traditional gender boundaries.[54]

Women working in the Diocese of Caledonia both taught school and conducted services. However, the list did not end there. Bessie Quirt's diary reveals the range of activities experienced by missionary women. Originally from Orillia, Ontario, Quirt was the first schoolteacher at the first Anglican school for Inuit children at Shingle Point. In a four-month period she spoke of the joy of "taking the new canoe out for a wonderful paddle," the excitement of having the bishop come to visit (at which time she commented that she had "acted as a scullery maid at the mission house"), and the pride of the first day of school: "I couldn't help feeling thrilled as I walked over to school that morning feeling what a privilege was mine being the first teacher."[55] She also recorded humorous moments: "Flossie and I will never forget Christmas eve and Christmas morning hacking, sewing and cutting at that Cariboo to make it into Christmas dinner ... We certainly could see the funny side of it and stopped to enjoy the novelty of it quite often."

From piling wood to canoeing to experiencing her first Arctic winter, Quirt was apparently thrilled to be in the North: "I can scarcely realize at times yet that it is actually the Arctic ocean over which I am looking and that I am here working among the Eskimo. The glamour certainly has not entirely worn off yet."[56] There was never a shortage of work or adventure for women missionaries. Unmarried women often travelled considerable distances from their stations. In the spring of 1896 the *Canadian Church Magazine* recorded that Caledonia's "lady" missionaries "have sometimes pretty trying times of it, for they go up and down the rivers in small boats, teaching and nursing at their various stopping places, which are not always of the smoothest as regards either water or land."[57] Women experienced the multifaceted demands of mission work and enjoyed freedoms that went well beyond normative gender constructs.

Through their religious work they also developed long-lasting and close friendships with other women missionaries, and it is to these that I will now turn.

Female Friendships

The community of Anglican missionary women in the North was small. Distance may have divided these women, but a spirit of neighbourliness and sometimes even intimacy was part of their mutual experience. In order to overcome the feeling of isolation, most women kept up a regular correspondence with their friends and relatives at home and struck up friendships with other women in the field.[58] These ties were valuable and important, especially at times of crisis or loneliness. In her *Independent Women: Work and Community for Single Women, 1850-1920* Martha Vicinus explores relationships among unmarried Victorian professional women. Her focus is entirely on single women who worked in specific institutions, like deaconess houses, boarding schools, or convents. Vicinus argues that, publicly, many of the women in her study were typical "upper-class ladies of severe manners and distinct demeanour. But privately their society permitted, and they experienced, a wide range of emotional behavior with intimate friends. The very distance and self-control demanded of them in public rebounded to make moments of intimacy more precious; friendships bore the entire weight of the emotions."[59]

This pattern certainly applies to single women missionaries in the North, and it could apply to married women as well. Husbands were often away for months at a time, and the intensity of the work and the isolation frequently led to close friendships amongst women. Because of Charlotte Selina Bompas's long tenure in the Yukon she came to know many of the missionary wives very well.[60] For example, when Bompas was visiting Britain in 1885 she corresponded with Sarah French, who was planning to leave for the Yukon to marry the Reverend T.H. Canham, the Anglican missionary at Fort McPherson. French was from Monivea, Galway County, Ireland, and at the age of forty agreed to marry Canham. Bompas wrote to her sister-in-law to tell her about French: "Miss French (Mr. C's fiancee) seems a very sweet girl I have had several letters from her & had to tell her about all her outfit and advise her about many things."[61] She and Bompas travelled back to Canada together in the spring of 1885. Apparently, they were detained in Winnipeg for one year because of the second Riel Rebellion. Their friendship began with Bompas offering advice on life in the North and lasted through travelling and living together in Winnipeg for one year, until the Canhams' retirement.

Another woman she befriended was Susan Mellett, the first unmarried woman missionary sent to the Yukon by the Anglican Church. Mellett, like French, was originally from Ireland, where she had taught in the Ragged Schools. In 1893 she signed up as a missionary at the age of twenty-three and was met at Forty Mile, her first station, by Bishop Bompas.[62] She lived with the Bompas family and taught school at Forty Mile and later at Rampart House. According to her diary Charlotte Selina Bompas appreciated Mellett from the outset: "Our household goes on very peacefully and happily. Miss Millett [sic] is a real blessing to us. She is a thorough Irish girl and a good churchwoman. She gets on well with everybody. The children are devoted to her, and she keeps them in first-rate order. One comfort is that she has good health and is not troubled with nerves. She bears the cold manfully, and was only a little startled lately when her blanket at night was fringed with icicles from her breath freezing."[63] Interestingly, Bompas chose the term "manfully" to describe Mellett's endurance of the cold, implying that it took the kind of grit that may not be associated with "proverbial daisies." Bompas and Mellett spent many hours together learning the Tukudah language.

In 1898 Bishop Bompas performed the marriage of Mellett and the Reverend R.J. Bowen, who had arrived in the Yukon in 1895. The Bowens moved to Dawson and then to Whitehorse, where Charlotte Selina Bompas became a regular houseguest and their friendship continued.[64] In May 1901, when Bompas became ill with pneumonia, she noted in her diary that she had "been most tenderly and lovingly nursed and cared for. Mrs. Bowen came from Whitehorse and stayed a fortnight."[65] When a missionary wife became ill or was about to deliver a child it was not uncommon for her co-workers to go and nurse her if they were within travelling distance.

Women could also count on each other during stressful times. At one point in 1909, when Bishop Stringer was on circuit in the Mackenzie River area and had not been in contact with Sarah Stringer, Bompas wrote a letter of reassurance: "I think you have good reason for anxiety but not for alarm, his long absence can all be explained." She ended by advising her to "keep up yr. character" and suggesting that if she had not already, then she must try to get a copy of *Anne of Green Gables* and "read it at once."[66] Bompas was no doubt speaking from experience. She remembered waiting for Bishop Bompas to return from his many long travels. Whether offering support during pregnancies, comforting one another, or simply catching up on news, missionary wives often relied on each other. Furthermore, even after the women left Canada's North it appears that many of their friendships continued.

Unmarried missionary women often turned to each other for comfort. At Shingle Point Bessie Quirt recognized that other workers in the mission field looked up to her. Flossie Hirst, who worked as an assistant nurse at Pangnirtung after an eight-year tenure at Shingle Point, became very close to Quirt. Quirt related to her diary that she felt an intense loyalty towards, and spiritual responsibility for, Hirst:

> Last week she was feeling all right physically but got a depressed and lonesome streak on. However she's been quite herself since I went and slept with her on Wednesday night. She seemed to enjoy so much having me back to cuddle her up again. My Flossie darlin she has caused me a lot of worry and unhappiness but I am glad my love for her has cost me something. I feel almost frightened knowing upon what a pinnacle she places me and how she looks to me for her example and tries to live to please me. Oh that I may never lead her even a step off the path her master would have her tread.[67]

Florence Hirst and Bessie Quirt skating, 1932

The demands of missionary life often shifted boundaries of gender, yet women missionaries did not cease to respond to one another as women. The evidence suggests that these relationships exhibited emotional and physical bonding. The isolation and strain of missionary work encouraged this closeness. Female closeness provided important emotional security that was expressed by many women in the language of joy and contentment. Rarely, however, was this same intensity expressed between men. Men travelled and worked together in the mission field, but they did not discuss their friendships in intimate language.[68]

Monica Storrs, who became well known in the Peace River region of northern British Columbia in the late 1920s, shared a similarly intimate friendship with Adeline Harmer, who joined her in 1931. Storrs worked in the region as a Sunday school teacher and scout and guide leader for two years before she returned to England to retrieve her lifelong friend. In her diary Storrs reflected upon how she felt to be with Harmer: "It was almost a joy being at Peace Coupe again, the place where I had been so anxious last September and was now so perfectly hopeful and happy with Adeline."[69] She and Harmer immediately began building a home in which they intended to share a bedroom. Although much of the building was contracted, Harmer and Storrs found themselves doing some of the physical labour. "On Sunday as usual," Harmer quipped in her diary "we became perfect ladies in cotton dresses, shaking off the crysalis [sic] of filthy dark blue overalls."[70] Interestingly, Harmer, for a fleeting and perhaps unconscious moment, had adopted a new gendered space for herself and Storrs.

At Metlakatla an equally intense friendship developed between Jane Ridley and Margaret West. Bishop Ridley often commented in his letters back to the CMS on how close they were. They often spent as much as two hours a day reading Tsimshian together, and when Jane Ridley was forced to return to England for one year Margaret West accompanied her as her nurse. When Jane died one year after their return in December 1896, Margaret expressed her grief: "What her loss is to me I cannot tell. She was more than guide and friend and I do trust that her loving words and example may fit me for the work our master has set out here. It is difficult to write much more now."[71]

Despite the loss of her close friend, Margaret West continued with her work and developed other similar friendships. Bishop Ridley observed that "Miss West mothers the young fellow workers and the new ones already have given their love and trust to her as she did to her who has just died."[72]

Like Quirt, West was placed on the pedestal of the feminine ideal, but it was not a place that either inhabited permanently. They did not, to return to Denise Riley's characterization, "make a final home in that classification."[73] The boundaries of gender were more fluid than that. While West "mothered" the young workers, she simultaneously endured physical challenges that went beyond those associated with traditional images of womanhood. Years later, in 1931, when West died at Metlakatla, it was noted that she and Rose Davies, who went to Metlakatla in 1896, had worked in "harmonious and loving agreement."[74] West and Davies were partners in supervising the Ridley House for Métis children, and, so boasted the *North British Columbia News,* they would be "inscribed on the Roll of Honour, of the Pioneer Missionaries of Caledonia."

The network of female companionship was often tight and long-lasting. The women in the Yukon and the Arctic kept in close contact with one another and appeared to have a strong sense of comradeship and, later, social memory. During the 1930s it was common for missionary women in the Arctic to refer back to the early twentieth century and the origins of the Anglican Church in the region. In fact, on her way to Shingle Point in 1932, Adelaide Butler stopped at Winnipeg to visit with the Stringers. She described her visit as follows: "[I] was in *society* and I enjoyed myself."[75] She thought Sarah Stringer was "very motherly" because she insisted that Butler should take a long rest before leaving on her journey.[76] Like Bompas, well into the 1930s Stringer kept up a correspondence with the women who went to the North. The Anglican community in the North was small, and the women who entered it shared experiences that bound them together. The unique setting and conditions of their work heightened the intensity of their friendships and produced a certain camaraderie that has too often been overlooked or attributed only to male experience.

Conclusion

It becomes clear, with respect to missionary women in the North, that the boundaries of gender were fluid. Masculine stereotypes broke down with the demands of mission work. Despite the fact that the image of missionary women was closely tied to Victorian domesticity, in reality women exercised freedoms in the mission field that they could not have exercised at home. And after leaving the North, Selina Bompas, Sarah Stringer, and others were frequently invited to give public lectures on their missionary experiences. More than "proverbial daisies," or auxiliary members of a mission team, women were often critical to the survival of missions in the North.

By the middle of the twentieth century the description of the type of women wanted in the North had changed to reflect the reality of mission work. In his memoirs the first bishop of the Arctic, Archibald L. Fleming, praised Prue Hockin, a Canadian missionary nurse who had been in the Arctic for twenty-five years: "In my opinion it is not too much to say that she is the epitome of what a white woman in the Arctic ought to be – efficient, self reliant, generous of nature, good humoured and with an ever increasing devotion to the Lord."[77] Women in the mission field went beyond the private sphere. In the context of a "higher calling" they challenged traditional images and could both enjoy, and be appreciated for, their self-reliance. The demands of the mission field were equally great for women and men, requiring similar strengths and skills.

Acknowledgments

I wish to thank Randi Warne and Catherine Cavanaugh for their helpful advice on earlier versions of this chapter, and Robert Rutherdale, William Westfall, and Kate McPherson for useful commentaries. I also wish to acknowledge Dorothy Kealey from the General Synod Archives in Toronto for her enthusiastic support.

Notes

1 An excellent collection of essays that looks at the origins and impact of women's mission work in Asia is Leslie A. Flemming, ed., *Women's Work for Women: Missionaries and Social Change in Asia* (Boulder: Westview, 1989).

2 Ann Douglas, *The Feminization of American Culture* (New York: Knopf, 1977), 110. See also Barbara Welter, "The Feminization of American Religion: 1800-1860," in *Dimity Convictions: The American Woman in the Nineteenth Century* (Athens, OH: Ohio University Press, 1976), 83-102.

3 Eugene Stock, "Women Missionaries in C.M.S. Fields," *Church Missionary Intelligencer* (May 1894): 343.

4 Ruth Compton Brouwer, *New Women for God: Canadian Presbyterian Women and India Missions, 1876-1914* (Toronto: University of Toronto Press, 1990), 188-96.

5 One noteworthy exception to this is the welcome contribution of Margaret Whitehead. See, for example, Margaret Whitehead, "Women Were Made for Such Things: Women Missionaries in British Columbia, 1850s to 1940s," *Atlantis* 14 (Fall 1988): 141-50; Margaret Whitehead, "'A Useful Christian Woman': First Nations Women and Protestant Missionary Work in British Columbia," *Atlantis* 18 (Fall/Summer 1992/3): 142-68. Ruth Compton Brouwer and Rosemary Gagan have provided a significant corrective to a gender imbalance in the historiography, but their focus has largely been on international mission fields. See Brouwer, as well as Rosemary Gagan, *A Sensitive Independence: Canadian Methodist Women Missionaries in Canada and the Orient, 1881-1925* (Montreal and Kingston: McGill-Queen's University

Press, 1992). See also Peter Murray, *The Devil and Mr. Duncan: The Tale of the Two Metlakatlas* (Victoria: Sono Nis, 1985); Jean Usher-Friesen, *William Duncan of Metlakatla: A Victorian Missionary in British Columbia* (Ottawa: National Museum of Man Publications in History No. 5, 1974); Ken Coates, "Send Only Those Who Rise a Peg: Anglican Clergy in the Yukon, 1858-1932," *Journal of the Canadian Church Historical Society* 28, 1 (1986): 3-17. In this case the North refers to northern British Columbia, the Yukon, and the North-West Territories. In the late nineteenth century the borders of the northern dioceses of the Anglican Church were often shifting. The Church Missionary Society of the Church of England was the first Anglican Church Society in Canada's North, and many of the notorious missionaries, including Duncan, Bompas, and Ridley, were sent out under its auspices.

6 Denise Riley, *"Am I That Name?": Feminism and the Category of Women in History* (Minneapolis: University of Minnesota Press, 1988), 6.

7 Ibid.

8 Separate sphere ideology has received the attention of many scholars who have studied Victorian culture and society. See, for example, Linda K. Kerber, "Separate Spheres, Female Worlds, Woman's Place: The Rhetoric of Women's History," *Journal of American History* 75 (1988): 9-39; Leonore Davidoff and Catherine Hall, *Family Fortunes: Men and Women of the English Middle Class, 1780-1850* (London: Hutchinson, 1987) esp. 149-93.

9 See Patrick A. Dunae, "Boys' Literature and the Idea of Empire, 1870-1914," *Victorian Studies* 24 (Autumn 1980): 120. See also Louis James, "Tom Brown's Imperialist Sons," *Victorian Studies* 18 (September 1973): 89-99.

10 Albert Memmi, *The Colonizer and the Colonized* (Boston: Beacon, 1965), 3.

11 For an example of Ridley's writing, see Charles Lillard, ed., *Warriors of the North Pacific* (Victoria: Sono Nis, 1984), 186-271. See also William Henry Collison, *In the Wake of the War Canoe*, ed. Charles Lillard (Victoria: Sono Nis, 1981).

12 This was not always the pattern for mission wives. In her study of American missionary wives Patricia Grimshaw argues that the eighty Congregationalist women she examined frequently felt disappointed with their experiences as missionaries: "The demands on women for American-style housekeeping," Grimshaw asserts, "and the responsibility mothers were forced to assume for childrearing, however, were experienced as oppressive, though few could attribute blame to anything other than the novel circumstances of their situation. The assumption of a domestic burden first prevented as active a participation as the men's in the public mission work. Further, however, the notion of the sex-specific nature and role of women was used deliberately to restrain mission wives from extending the boundaries of female participation in a direction which conflicted with male dominance." Missionary wives in the context of early nineteenth-century Hawaii were trapped by separate sphere ideology and could not transcend its boundaries. See Patricia Grimshaw, *Paths of Duty: American Missionary Wives in Nineteenth-Century Hawaii* (Honolulu: University of Hawaii Press, 1989), 194.

13 Lois Boyd, "Presbyterian Ministers' Wives: A Nineteenth-Century Portrait," *Journal of Presbyterian History* 59, 1 (Spring 1981): 3-4.

14 Cited in Boyd, "Presbyterian Ministers' Wives," 7.

15 Selina Bompas, "Our Women of the North," *Canadian Churchman*, 14, November 1907.

16 Nancy Pagh, "Imagining Native Women: Feminine Discourse and Four Women Travelling the Northwest Coast," this volume.

17 Murray, *Devil and Mr. Duncan*, 62.

18 Collison, *In the Wake of the War Canoe*, 16.

19 Reverend. J.B. McCullagh, "Aiyansh," *Aiyansh Notes*, April 1908. The Reverend J.B. McCullagh, originally from Newry, Ireland, was a CMS veteran, having served in the north British Columbian field since 1883. His first wife died of typhoid fever in Aiyansh.

20 Jane Hunter, "The Home and the World: The Missionary Message of U.S. Domesticity," in *Women's Work for Women: Missionaries and Social Change in Asia*, ed. Leslie A. Flemming (Boulder: Westview, 1989), 160.

21 General Synod Archives (hereafter GSA) M74-3, Stringer Series 1-A-1, correspondence outward, 1888-92. Isaac Stringer to Sadie Alexander, 6 July 1893.

22 "Bishop Ridley and the North Pacific Mission," *Church Missionary Intelligencer and Record*,

vol. 9, no. 99, March 1884, 166. Jane Ridley was a trained nurse and was decorated for her nursing service during the Franco-Prussian War.

23 "Caledonia," *Canadian Church Magazine*, May 1899, 120.

24 Eugene Stock, *History of the Church Missionary Society, Its Environment, Its Men and Its Work* (London: Church Missionary Society, 1899), 639.

25 Church Missionary Society Papers (hereafter CMS Papers) C.2 British Columbia, C.2./o, original letters to 1900 North Pacific Mission G.1 C2/03 1897. Collison to parent committee, 6 January 1897.

26 Stock, *History of the Church Missionary Society*, 638.

27 GSA, M71-4, box 12, Diocese of the Arctic Collection, St. Luke's Mission, Pangnirtung, Florence Hirst Journals, 17 July 1937. Florence (Flossie) Hirst came to the North from Yorkshire, England, in 1928 and stayed until 1955. In the late 1930s she married the Reverend George Nicholson. Prudence Hockin was originally from Oak Lake, Manitoba. She graduated in nursing from Winnipeg Children's Hospital and started her northern missionary career in 1931. Between 1931 and 1962 she worked as head nurse and hospital supervisor in both Aklavik and Pangnirtung.

28 CMS Papers, reel A 125, Price to parent committee, 3 September 1889.

29 Books and letters of the Church Missionary Society, London Public Archives of Canada, class C C.2, North Pacific Mission C.2, original letters, etc., correspondence inward, 1857-80. Tomlinson to parent committee, 15 June 1872. Tomlinson's father was a clergyman in Ireland. Robert Tomlinson was educated at Trinity College in Dublin, and he served in northern British Columbia and Alaska until his death in 1912.

30 GSA, Stringer Papers, series 2, Sarah Ann Stringer, diaries 1-17, 97, 2-C, diary, 24 December 1896. Sarah (Alexander) Stringer was born and raised in Biddolph Township in Ontario. Her father was a farmer, and after completing high school she took a secretarial course and then entered Grace Hospital for nurse's training. She also attended classes at Toronto's Anglican Women's Training College.

31 Ibid., Stringer Diary, July 1898.

32 Ibid., Stringer to Mrs. Newton, 16 July 1899.

33 *Letter Leaflet*, September 1899.

34 Archdeacon C.E. Whittaker, *Recollections of an Arctic Parson*, n.d. GSA, 24.

35 Archibald Lang Fleming, *Archibald the Arctic: The Flying Bishop* (New York: Appleton-Century Crofts, 1956), 287.

36 CMS Papers, reel 105, Doolan to parent committee, 8 September 1866 and 20 October 1866.

37 V.C. Sim, for example, neglected his health to such an extent that he died in service. See Coates, "Send Only Those," 8.

38 Collison, *In the Wake of the War Canoe*, 81.

39 Yukon Territorial Archives (hereafter YTA), Anglican Church Series 1-1A, box 4, folder 3, cor. 252, C. Hoare to Bishop Stringer, 11 January 1922.

40 Ibid., Stringer to Hoare, 2 June 1922.

41 "Missionary Wives," *Canadian Church Magazine and Mission News*, January 1897, 18.

42 Dr. Herrick, "Missionaries' Wives," *Canadian Church Magazine and Mission News*, October 1889, 226.

43 Collison, *In the Wake of the War Canoe*, 18-9.

44 Ibid., 19. Patients deemed to be incurable were sent to these hospitals for extended care until death.

45 Coates, "Send Only Those," 7. See also Sarah Carter, "Categories and Terrains of Exclusion," this volume, 66.

46 Bompas/Naylor correspondence, 14 July 1896.

47 YTA, Anglican Church Series 1-1A, box 3, folder 16, cor. 251, Stringer to Venn. Arch. Warren, 15 January 1920.

48 CMS Papers, correspondence outward, reel A 123, 16 June 1896, Ridley to parent committee.

49 Ibid., reel A 125, 28 October 1898.

50 CMS Papers, correspondence outward, Ridley to parent committee, 17 August 1891. Dickenson trained at the Mildmay Deaconess House in England. There she would have had a daily routine that consisted of morning prayers, Bible study classes, and mission work

practice in nearby neighbourhoods. One hour a day would have been dedicated to meditating or reading religious material. At the age of twenty-seven she departed for northern British Columbia. She retired five years later in 1895.

51 CMS Papers, A 122, parent committee to Bertha Davies, 30 March 1900. Bertha Davies started her mission/nursing career in 1897. In 1900 she retired due to her marriage to the Reverend W.E. Collison, the son of Archdeacon and Mrs. W.H. Collison. She continued to live and work in northern British Columbia after her marriage.

52 Sara Mills, *Discourses of Difference: An Analysis of Women's Travel Writing and Colonialism* (London: Routledge, 1991), 42.

53 Quoted in Stock, *History of the Church Missionary Society*, 638.

54 Edith Beeching had similar experiences in her work at the mission stations near Alert Bay. Originally from Dover, England, Beeching arrived at Alert Bay in the summer of 1894 after a stint at the Highbury Deaconess Home. The following year she was sent for three weeks to a fishing station at River Inlet, fifty miles north of Alert Bay. While there she visited two canneries separated by a river described as a mile in breadth. She met with girls and women in the fields where they prayed and sang together, and she held services with community members in a small Methodist Church. In her physical freedom and in leading meetings Beeching had temporarily achieved a freedom from the specific gendered constraints of women in mission stations. See CMS Papers, A 123, Beeching to parent committee, 14 July 1895; diary, 14 July 1895.

55 GSA, Bessie Quirt Papers, diary, 27 August 1929, 26 September 1929, and 16 September 1929. Quirt was likely encouraged to take up mission work by her Orillia clergyman, the Reverend J.R.S. Boyd, a former China missionary. Quirt graduated from the North Bay Normal School and worked as a teacher for four years in Ontario before entering the Anglican Women's Training College in 1928.

56 Ibid., 15 January 1930.

57 "Caledonia," *Canadian Church Magazine and Mission News*, April 1896, 83.

58 In her discussion on female friendships in nineteenth-century United States, Carroll Smith-Rosenberg emphasizes the prevalence of intimate relations between women. She concludes that, within the confines of family and close friends, a woman's world developed, and this world was characterized by what she calls a "generic and unself-conscious pattern of single-sex or homosocial networks. These supportive networks were institutionalized in social conventions or rituals that accompanied virtually every important event in a woman's life, from birth to death. Within such a world of emotional richness and complexity, devotion to and love of other women became a plausible and socially accepted form of human interaction." See Carroll Smith-Rosenberg, *Disorderly Conduct: Visions of Gender in Victorian America* (New York: Oxford University Press, 1985), 60.

59 Martha Vicinus, *Independent Women: Work and Community for Single Women, 1850-1920* (Chicago: University of Chicago Press, 1985), 202.

60 Bompas arrived in the North in 1874, and, except for the years that she went on furlough, she stayed until 1906.

61 GSA, M89-3-N4, Bompas Papers. Bompas to Bompas, n.d. The Reverend T.H. Canham started his northern career in 1881 and stayed until 1915.

62 YTA, Anglican Church of Canada, Yukon Synod, Bowen Biography File.

63 S.A. Archer, ed., *Heroine of the North Pacific: Memoirs of Charlotte Selina Bompas, 1830-1917* (London: Macmillan, 1929), 144-5.

64 For example, in a letter to her sister-in-law, Bompas told her about visiting the "kind and hospitable" Bowens in Whitehorse and staying with them for one week. GSA, M89-3-N4, Bompas Papers, Bompas to Bompas, October 1900. The Bowens were sponsored by the London-based Society for the Propagation of the Gospel.

65 Archer, *Heroine of the North*, 167.

66 Ibid., Bompas to Stringer, n.d.

67 Quirt Diary, 21 December 1930.

68 This is not to say, however, that men did not have similar intimate relations. For an illuminating study of male friendships in Victorian society, see, Jeffrey Richards, "'Passing the

Love of Women': Manly Love and Victorian Society," in *Manliness and Morality: Middle-Class Masculinity in Britain and America, 1800-1940*, ed. J.A. Mangan and James Walvin (Manchester: Manchester University Press, 1987), 92-122.

69 W.L. Morton, ed., *God's Galloping Girl: The Peace River Diaries of Monica Storrs, 1929-1931* (Vancouver: UBC Press, 1979), 180. Storrs was originally from London, England, and had attended the Francis Holland Church of England School for Girls and St. Christopher's College. Her father was an Anglican clergyman and the dean of Rochester, England. Harmer's father was the bishop of Rochester. Storrs worked under the auspices of the Fellowship of the Maple Leaf (FML), a missionary society determined to promote assimilation (especially amongst new Canadian immigrants). For more on the FML, see Marilyn Barber, "The Fellowship of the Maple Leaf Teachers," in *The Anglican Church and the World of Western Canada*, ed. Barry Ferguson (Regina: University of Regina Press, 1991), 154-66.

70 Ibid., 229.

71 CMS Papers, C.2 British Columbia, C2/original letters to 1900, North Pacific Mission, G.1 C2/03 1897, reel A 125, West to parent committee, 11 December 1896.

72 Ibid., Ridley to parent committee, 7 December 1896.

73 Riley, *"Am I That Name?"*, 6.

74 "The Late Miss Margaret West," *North British Columbia News*, July 1931. Excluding furloughs, West stayed in northern British Columbia for forty years. Rose Margaret Davies, a nursing graduate of Mildmay Hospital, started her career at Metlakatla in 1896 and retired in 1942.

75 GSA, M88-4, Adelaide Jane Butler Papers. Butler to Dollie, 7 January 1933. Butler was a schoolteacher from England, and she worked as a missionary at Shingle Point for five years.

76 Ibid.

77 Fleming, *Archibald the Arctic*, 321. Hockin was presented with the Order of Canada in 1961 in appreciation of her service in northern Canada. She retired in 1962 after thirty-one years of work.

CHAPTER 2

Categories and Terrains of Exclusion

Constructing the "Indian Woman" in the Early Settlement Era in Western Canada

SARAH CARTER

In 1884 Mary E. Inderwick wrote to her Ontario family from the ranch near Pincher Creek, Alberta, where she had lived with her new husband for six months.[1] The letter provides a perspective on the stratifications of race, gender, and class that were forming as the Euro-Canadian enclave grew in the district of Alberta. Mary Inderwick lamented that it was a lonely life, as she was twenty-two miles from any other women, and she even offered to help some of the men near them to "get their shacks done up if only they will go east and marry some really nice girls." She did not consider the companionship of women such as "the squaw who is the nominal wife of a white man near us," and she had dismissed her maid, who had become discontented with her position as a servant. Inderwick had disapproved of a ball at the North West Mounted Police (NWMP) barracks at Fort Macleod, despite the fact that it was "the first Ball to which the squaws were not allowed to go, but there were several half breeds." Commenting on the Aboriginal population that still greatly outnumbered the new arrivals, Inderwick wrote that they should have been "isolated in the mountains" rather than settled on nearby reserves and that the sooner they became extinct the better for themselves and the country.

At the time of Mary Inderwick's arrival in the West the consolidation of Canada's rule was not yet secure. The Métis resistance of 1885 fed fears of a larger uprising, and an uncertain economic climate threatened the promise of a prosperous West. There was a sharpening of racial boundaries and categories in the 1880s and an intensification of discrimination in the Canadian West. The arrival of women immigrants like Mary

Inderwick after the Canadian Pacific Railway (CPR) was completed through Alberta in 1883 coincided with other developments – such as the railway itself, the treaties, and the development of ranching and farming – that were to stabilize the new order and allow the recreation of Euro-Canadian institutions and society. The women did not introduce notions of spatial and social segregation, but their presence helped to justify policies already in motion – policies that segregated the new community from indigenous contacts.[2] The Canadian state adopted increasingly segregationist policies towards the Aboriginal people of the West. Central to these policies were images of Aboriginal women as dissolute, dangerous, and sinister.

From the earliest years that people were settled on reserves in western Canada, Canadian government administrators and statesmen, as well as the national press, promoted a cluster of negative images of Aboriginal women. Those in power used these images to explain conditions of poverty and ill health on reserves. The failure of agriculture on reserves was attributed to the incapacity of Aboriginal men to become other than hunters, warriors, and nomads.[3] Responsibility for a host of other problems, including the deplorable state of housing on reserves, the lack of clothing and footwear, and the high mortality rate, was placed upon the supposed cultural traits and temperament of Aboriginal women. The depiction of these women as lewd and licentious, particularly after 1885, was used to deflect criticism from the behaviour of government officials and the NWMP and to legitimize the constraints placed on the activities and movements of Aboriginal women in the world off the reserve. These negative images became deeply embedded in the consciousness of the most powerful socio-economic groups on the Prairies and have resisted revision.

The images were neither new nor unique to the Canadian West. In "The Pocahontas Perplex" Rayna Green explores the complex, many-faceted dimensions of the image of the Indian woman in American folklore and literature. The beautiful "Indian Princess" who saved or aided White men while remaining aloof and virtuous in a woodland paradise was the positive side of the image. Her opposite, the squalid and immoral "Squaw," lived in a shack at the edge of town, and her "physical removal or destruction can be understood as necessary to the progress of civilization."[4] The "Squaw" was pressed into service, and her image predominated in the Canadian West in the late nineteenth century as boundaries were clarified and social and geographic space marked out. The either/or binary left newcomers little room to consider the diversity of the Aboriginal people of the West or the complex identities and roles of Aboriginal women. Not all Euro-Canadians shared in these sentiments and perceptions. Methodist missionary John McDougall, for example, in 1895 chastised a fellow missionary author for his use of the term "squaw": "In the name of decency and civilization and Christianity, why call one person a woman and another a squaw?"[5] While it would be a mistake to assume a unified mentality among all Euro-Canadians, it is nonetheless clear that the negative stereotype not only prevailed but was deliberately propagated by officials of the state.

Euro-Canadian Settlement of the West

Following the transfer of the Hudson's Bay Company territories to the Dominion of Canada in 1870, the policy of the federal government was to clear the land of the Aboriginal inhabitants and open the West to Euro-Canadian agricultural settlement. To regulate settlement the North West Mounted Police (later the Royal North West Mounted Police and then the Royal Canadian Mounted Police) was created, and 300 officers were dispatched west in 1874. A "free" homestead system was modelled on the American example, and a transcontinental railway was completed in 1885. To open up the West to "actual settlers," seven treaties with Aboriginal peoples were negotiated between 1871 and 1877, and through these the Government of Canada acquired legal control of most of the land of the West. In exchange, Aboriginal peoples received land reserves; annuities; and, as a result of hard bargaining by Aboriginal spokespeople, commitments to assist them to take up agriculture as their buffalo-based economy collapsed. A Department of Indian Affairs, with its headquarters in Ottawa, was established in 1880, and in the field an ever-expanding team of Indian agents, farm instructors, and inspectors was assigned to implement the reserve system and to enforce the Indian Act, 1876. The people who had entered into treaties were wards of the government and did not have the privileges of full citizenship; they were subject to a wide variety of controls and regulations.

Much to the disappointment of the federal government, the West did not begin rapid development until the later 1890s. There were small pockets of Euro-Canadian settlement, but in 1885, in the district of Alberta, for example, the Aboriginal and Métis population was more than 9,500, while the recent arrivals numbered only 4,900.[6] All seemed hopeless, especially by the mid-1880s, when immigration was at a near standstill. Years of drought and frost and problems finding suitable techniques for farming the northern Plains account in part for the lack of settlers, and the 1885 resistance of the Métis in present-day Saskatchewan did little to enhance the image the government wished to project of the West as a suitable and safe home for newcomers.

Resistance to Settlement

The Métis were people of mixed Aboriginal and European ancestry who regarded the Red River settlement (Winnipeg) as the heartland of their nation. It was here, in 1869-70, under the leadership of Louis Riel, that the Métis first resisted Canadian imperialism, effectively blocking Ottawa's takeover of the West until they had been guaranteed their land rights, their French language, and their Roman Catholic religion. But the victory negotiated into the Manitoba Act, 1870, soon proved hollow, as the Canadian government adopted a variety of strategies to ensure that the Métis did not receive the lands promised them. As a result of this, many Métis moved farther west.[7] In their new territories the Métis again demanded land guarantees; when the Canadian government largely ignored their requests, they asked Louis Riel to lead another protest in 1884. The Canadian government dispatched troops west and defeated the Métis at Batoche in May 1885. Riel was found guilty of treason and was hanged, as were eight Aboriginal men who were convicted of murder.

Despite desperate economic circumstances and deep resentment over government mistreatment, few of the treaty people of the West joined the Métis resistance, although at a settlement called Frog Lake, in present-day Alberta, some young Cree men killed an Indian agent, a farm instructor, and seven others; and in the Battleford District two farm instructors were killed. This limited participation in the events of 1885 became a rationale for the increasingly authoritarian regime that governed the lives of the treaty people. Anxious to see western development succeed in the face of all of the setbacks of the 1880s, the Canadian government restricted the Aboriginal population in order to protect and enrich recent and prospective immigrants.

Development of Stereotypes

Particularly irksome to many of the recently arrived "actual settlers" was the Aboriginal competition they faced in the hay, grain, and vegetable markets. Despite obstacles, many Aboriginal farmers had produced a surplus for sale. Settlers' particularly vocal and strident complaints led the government to curtail farming on reserves. To explain why underused reserves had become pockets of rural poverty, Indian Affairs officials claimed that Aboriginal culture and temperament rendered the men unwilling and unable to farm.

Plains women were also responsible: according to government pronouncements they were idle and gossipy, preferring tents to proper housing because the former required less work to maintain and could be clustered in groups that allowed visiting. Reports of the superintendent general of Indian Affairs claimed that Indians raised dust with their dancing and that the women's failure to clean it up spread diseases such as tuberculosis. Administrators blamed the high infant mortality rate upon the indifferent care of the mothers. The neglected children of these mothers grew up "rebellious, sullen, disobedient and unthankful."[8] While men were blamed for the failure of agriculture, women were portrayed as resisting, resenting, and preventing any progress towards modernization. As an inspector of Indian agencies lamented in 1908, "The women, here, as on nearly every reserve, are a hindrance to the advancement of the men. No sooner do the men earn some money than the women want to go and visit their relations on some other reserve, or else give a feast or dance to their friends ... The majority of [the women] are discontented, dirty, lazy and slovenly."[9]

But unofficial and unpublished reports of reserve life show that officials recognized that problems with reserve housing and health had little to do with women's preferences, temperaments, or poor housekeeping abilities. Because of their poverty, in winter the people were confined in large numbers to what were little better than one-room and one-story huts, or shacks, that were poorly ventilated and impossible to keep clean, as they had dirt floors and were plastered with mud and hay. Tents and tipis might well have been more sanitary and more comfortable. One inspector of agencies noted in 1891 that women had neither soap, towels, wash basins, nor wash pails and that they had no means by which to acquire these.[10] Officials frequently noted that women were short of basic clothing and had no textiles or yarn with which to work. Yet, in official public statements, the tendency was to ascribe blame to the women rather than to draw attention to conditions that would injure the reputation of government administrators.

"Licentiousness" and Government Officials

In order to deflect criticism from government agents and policies, officials propagated an image of Aboriginal women as dissolute, as the bearers of sinister influences. This image was evoked with particular strength in the wake of an 1886 controversy that focused upon the alleged "brutal, heartless and ostentatious licentiousness" of government officials resident in western Canada.[11] The remarks of Samuel Trivett, a Church of England missionary on the Blood reserve in present-day southern Alberta, became the focus of the controversy. To a special correspondent for the *Mail* of Toronto, Trivett said that Indian women were being bought and sold by White men who lived with them without legally marrying them and then abandoned the offspring to life on the reserve.[12]

Trivett strongly hinted that some government agents were involved in licentious behaviour, an accusation seized upon by critics of the administration of Indian Affairs in western Canada. In the aftermath of the Métis resistance of 1885, opponents of John A. Macdonald's Conservatives amassed evidence of neglect, injustice, and incompetence and were delighted to add immorality to this list. In the House of Commons in April 1886, Malcolm Cameron, Liberal MP, delivered a lengthy indictment of Indian Affairs in the West, focusing upon the unprincipled and unscrupulous behaviour of officials of the Indian department. Cameron quoted Trivett and further charged that agents of the government, sent to elevate and educate, had instead acted to "humiliate, to lower, to degrade and debase the virgin daughters of the wards of the nation." He knew of one young Indian agent from England, "unfit to do anything there, who was living on a reserve in open adultery with two young squaws ... revelling in the sensual enjoyments of a western harem, plentifully supplied with select cullings from the western prairie flowers."[13]

Cameron implicated members of the NWMP in this behaviour, wondering why it was that over 45 percent of them were reported to have been under medical treatment for venereal disease. Cameron was not the first to raise the matter of police propriety in the House. Concern about possible improper relations between the police and Aboriginal women long predated the Trivett scandal and was one aspect of a larger debate in the press and in the House in the late 1870s over charges of inefficiency, lack of discipline, high desertion rates, and low morale in the Force. In 1878 the lieutenant-governor of the North-West Territories, David Laird, alerted NWMP commissioner James Macleod that reports about immoral conduct were in circulation: "I fear from what reports are brought me, that some of your officers at Fort Walsh are making rather free with the women around there. It is to be hoped that the good name of the Force will not be hurt through too open indulgence of that kind. And I sincerely hope that Indian women will not be treated in a way that hereafter may give trouble."[14]

Although Macleod and Assistant Commissioner A.G. Irvine denied that there was "anything like 'a regular brothel'" about the police posts, such reports persisted. In the House of Commons in 1880 Joseph Royal, a Manitoba MP, claimed that the NWMP was accused of "disgraceful immorality" all over the West. Royal had evidence that at one of the police posts that winter there had been "an open quarrel between an officer and one of the constables for the possession of a squaw" and that one officer slapped another "in the face on account of a squaw." Royal had been informed that "many members of the force were living in concubinage with Indian women, whom they had purchased from their parents and friends."[15] In 1886 public attention was once again drawn to police behaviour. The *Mail* informed its readers that between 1874 and 1881 the police had "lived openly with Indian girls purchased from their parents" and that only the arrival of settlers had compelled them to abandon or at least to be "more discreet in the pursuit of their profligacy."[16]

There is little doubt that Trivett and other critics based their accusations concerning both the police and government officials on some foundation, but remaining evidence is scanty and scattered. Missionaries depended to a large extent on the good will of government and were rarely as outspoken as Trivett or John Maclean, a Methodist missionary on the Blood reserve near Fort Macleod, who, in 1885, characterized many reserve employees as utterly incompetent and urged the government to employ only married men "of sterling Christian character."[17] But in 1886 missionaries were instructed by Edgar Dewdney, lieutenant-governor of the North-West Territories, not to voice their accusations to the newspapers "even if allegations against public officials were true," as this would do more harm than good, would affect mission work, and could be used to stir up political strife.[18] Government officials generally investigated reports of government misconduct themselves, and this functioned to cover up or to mitigate such allegations. Similarly, members of the NWMP themselves looked into any complaints about the Force's behaviour.

Marriages of Aboriginal Women and NWMP Members

There were members of the NWMP, especially among the earliest recruits of the 1870s and early 1880s, who formed relationships with Aboriginal women, as did a great many other male immigrants of these years. Some of these were marriages of long-standing, sanctioned by Christian ceremony or customary law. Lakota author/historian John O'Kute-sica noted that, in the early 1880s, six "Red Coats" of the Wood Mountain Detachment married Lakota women from Sitting Bull's band, and most of the couples, such as Mary Blackmoon and Thomas Aspdin, lived together to old age and death. One couple, Archie LeCaine and Emma Loves War, separated because the woman did not wish to move to eastern Canada.[19]

Other relationships were of a more temporary nature. Of course there were children. Cecil Denny, for example, while a sub-inspector at Fort Macleod, had a daughter with Victoria Mckay, a part-Piegan woman who was the wife of another policeman, constable Percy Robinson.[20] Denny was forced to resign from the force in 1881 as a result of his involvement in a series of court cases that Robinson brought against him for "having induced his wife to desert him and also having criminal connections with her."[21] The child was raised by her mother on the American Blackfoot reservation. Assistant Surgeon Henry Dodd of the NWMP had a daughter who lived on one of the Crooked Lake reserves in the Qu'Appelle Valley. There is a record of this in the police files only because Dodd was granted leave to attend to her when she was very ill in 1889.[22]

D.J. Grier, who served three years with the NWMP beginning in 1877 at Fort Macleod, married Molly Tailfeathers, a Piegan woman, and together they had three children.[23] By 1887, however, Grier had remarried to a White woman. For a short time the children from his first marriage lived with their mother on the Piegan reserve, but the two eldest were taken from her and placed in the care of Grier's parents, who had also settled in Fort Macleod. Grier was one of the most prominent men of the West. Renowned as the first commercial wheat grower in Alberta, he also served as mayor of Fort Macleod for twelve years from 1901 to 1913.

Abuse of Aboriginal Women

John O'Kute-sica wrote at length about one unsuccessful Wood Mountain customary marriage, that of his aunt Iteskawin and Superintendent William D. Jarvis, who had been with the original contingent and who was dismissed from the Force in 1881. According to O'Kute-sica his aunt consented to marry Jarvis (who hailed from a prominent Ontario family) because he promised that her brothers and sisters would have something to eat twice a day (all of her people were in want and suffering). After only a few weeks of marriage Jarvis, in a jealous rage, publicly assaulted Iteskawin at a Lakota "Night Dance," an incident that strained relations between the two communities, and she immediately left him.[24] On most of the few occasions that Aboriginal women laid charges against policemen for assault or rape, their claims were hastily dismissed as defamation or blackmail.[25]

Some government employees residing on reserves clearly abused their positions of authority. In 1882, for example, Blackfoot Chief Crowfoot and his wife complained that the farm instructor on their reserve demanded sexual favours from a young girl in return for rations, and when an investigation proved this to be the case the man was dismissed.[26] Both the documentary and oral records suggest that several of the government employees that the Crees killed at Frog Lake and Battleford in the spring of 1885 were resented intensely because of their callous and at times brutal treatment of Aboriginal women. The farm instructor on the Mosquito reserve near Battleford, James Payne, was known for his violent temper: he once beat a young woman and threw her out of his house when he found her visiting his young Aboriginal wife. The terrified and shaken woman, who was found by her father, died soon after, and her grieving father blamed Payne, whom he killed in 1885.[27] Farm instructor John Delaney, who was killed at Frog Lake in 1885, laid charges against a man by the name of Sand Fly in 1881 so he could cohabit with Sand Fly's wife. Delaney first claimed that Sand Fly had struck him with a whip, and when this charge did not result in the desired jail sentence, Delaney claimed that the man had beaten his wife. The farm instructor then lived with Sand Fly's wife, and the general feeling in the district, shared by the local NWMP, was that "Mr. Delaney had the man arrested in order to accomplish his designs."[28] As a Touchwood Hills farm instructor told a visiting newspaper correspondent in 1885, the charges of immorality among farm instructors on reserves were in many instances too true, as "the greatest facilities are afforded the Indian instructor for the seduction of Indian girls. The instructor holds the grub. The agent gives him the supplies and he issues them to the Indians. Now you have a good idea of what semi-starvation is."[29]

Blaming Aboriginal Women

The most vocal response to the accusations of Trivett and other critics was not to deny that there had been "immorality" in the West, but to exonerate the men and blame the Aboriginal women, who were said to have behaved in an abandoned and wanton manner and were supposedly accustomed to being treated with contempt, to being bought and sold as commodities, within their own societies. In defending the NWMP in 1880, the Toronto *Globe* emphasized that Aboriginal women had "loose morals" that were "notorious the world over" and that "no men in the world are so good as to teach them better, or to try to reform them in this respect." These sentiments were echoed again and again in the wake of the 1886 controversy. The editor of the *Macleod Gazette,* a former

NWMP member, argued that whatever immorality there might have been came from the women themselves and from the customs of their society. They were prostitutes before they went to live with White men, who did not encourage this behaviour but were simply "taking advantage of an Indian's offer." The *Mail* told readers that Aboriginal males had sold their wives and children in the thousands to soldiers and settlers since the time of the French fur trade in exchange for alcohol and that, with the arrival of the police, a great deal had been done to end this situation.[30]

The *Gazette* stressed, incorrectly, that there was no marriage in Plains societies: a little lively bartering with the father, and a woman could be purchased for a horse or two. The argument that Aboriginal women were virtual slaves, first to their fathers and then to their husbands, was called upon by all who wished to deflect criticism from government officials and the NWMP. In the House of Commons in April 1886 Sir Hector Langevin defended the record of the government against Cameron's charges of immorality. Langevin claimed that to Indians marriage was simply a bargain and a sale and that immorality among them long predated the arrival of government agents in the North-West.[31]

The government published its official response to the criticisms of Indian Affairs in the North-West in an 1886 pamphlet entitled "The Facts Respecting Indian Administration in the North-West." A government official had again inquired into accusations about the misconduct of employees of the Indian department and, predictably, had found no evidence. The investigator, Hayter Reed, assistant commissioner of Indian Affairs, was one of those unmarried officials who had been accused of having Aboriginal "mistresses" as well as a child from one of these relationships.[32] The pamphlet boldly asserted that Trivett was unable to come up with a shred of actual evidence, although the missionary vehemently denied this.[33] The pamphlet writer admitted that some men had acquired their wives by purchase but claimed that this was the Indian custom and that "no father ever dreams of letting his daughter leave his wigwam till he has received a valuable consideration for her." If the government stopped this custom, there would be loud protests, over and above the Indians' "chronic habit of grumbling." "The Facts" insisted that it was not fair to criticize the behaviour of the dead, such as Delaney and Payne, who had "passed from the bar of human judgment."[34]

Endangered White Women

Settlement discourse, as illustrated in captivity narratives, constructed "danger" not to Indian women but to White women, who might again be dragged into horrible captivity if critics encouraged Indians in their exaggerated, misled notions. Two White women, Theresa Delaney and Theresa Gowanlock, had been taken hostage by Big Bear's band following the events at Frog Lake. There were a great number of Aboriginal women (and men) hostages as well, but outrage and indignation did not focus upon them. Although Delaney and Gowanlock were fed and housed as well as their captors and released unharmed, the government publication played up the perils, hazards, and threat to the safety of these women and others who might move west. The women's account of their two months of captivity stressed the "savagery" of their captors and the ever-present danger of "the fate worse than death."[35]

Following the period of heightened tensions within the Euro-Canadian community after the events of 1885 there was an increased emphasis upon the supposed vulnerability of White women in the West. Rumours circulated through the press that one of Big Bear's wives was a White woman being held against her will.[36] In 1899, after a girl of about nine, with fair hair and blue eyes, was spotted on the Blackfoot reserve by an English artist accompanying Canada's governor general on a tour across the continent, the story of a "captive" White child attracted international attention and calls for a rescue mission. Indignant outrage was expressed, especially in the Fort Macleod newspaper, which called for prompt action to rescue the girl from "the horrible fate that is surely in store for her." The NWMP and Indian Affairs officials assigned to look into the case knew all along that the child was not a captive at all but resided with her mother on the reserve. The captivity story functioned, however, to reaffirm the vulnerability of White women in the West and to provide a rationale for those who wished to secure greater control over the Aboriginal population.[37]

The Image of the "Squaw Man"

The use of the term "squaw man" to denote men of the lowest social class became increasingly frequent during the later 1880s. There was disdain for those within the community who did not conform to the new demands to clarify boundaries. Police reports blamed "squaw men" for many crimes, such as liquor offences or the killing of cattle. S.B. Steele of the NWMP wrote from the Fort Macleod District in 1890 that the wives of these men "readily act as agents, and speaking the language, and being closely connected with the various tribes, their houses soon become a rendezvous for idle and dissolute Indians and half breeds, and being themselves in that debatable land between savagery and civilization possibly do not realize the heinousness and danger to the community."[38] The

Moosomin Courier of March 1890 blamed the "squaw-men" for stirring up trouble with the Indians in 1885 and prejudicing them against policies that were for their own good.[39]

Lives of Aboriginal Women

The overwhelming image that emerged from the 1886 "immorality" controversy was that of dissolute Aboriginal women. They, and the traditions of the society from which they came, were identified as the cause of vice and corruption in the new settlements of the Prairie West. This was not an image shared or accepted by all Euro-Canadians in the West at all times, nor did it bear resemblance to the lives of the vast majority of Aboriginal women. Women were not commodities that were bought, sold, or exchanged at will by men. Plains marriage practices entailed mutual obligations between the families of the couple and an ongoing exchange of marriage-validating gifts.

Aboriginal oral and documentary sources suggest that in the early reserve years, particularly in the aftermath of the events of 1885, women provided essential security and stability in communities that had experienced great upheaval. In these years of low resources and shattered morale, the work of women in their own new settlements was vital, materially as well as spiritually. Cree author Joe Dion wrote that when spirits and resources were low on his reserve in the late 1880s "much of the inspiration for the Crees came from the old ladies, for they set to work with a will that impressed everybody."[40] Aboriginal women also provided considerable assistance to new immigrants, particularly women. They were important as midwives to some early immigrants, and they helped instruct newcomers in the use of edible prairie plants and other native materials.[41] Aboriginal women formed what was described as a "protective society" around the women and children hostages in Big Bear's camp in 1885, keeping them out of harm's way, but this aspect of the drama was absent from the headlines of the day.[42]

Constraints on Aboriginal Women

It was the image of Aboriginal women as immoral and corrupting influences that predominated in the non-Aboriginal society that was taking shape. Authorities used this characterization to define and treat Aboriginal women, increasingly narrowing their options and opportunities. Both informal and formal constraints served to keep Aboriginal people from the towns and settled areas of the Prairies, and their presence there became more and more marginal. While they may not have wished to live in the towns, their land-use patterns for a time intersected with the new order and they might have taken advantage of markets and other economic opportunities, but townspeople believed that Aboriginal people did not belong within the new settlements that were replacing and expelling "savagery."[43] Their presence was seen as incongruous, corrupting, and demoralizing. Classified as prostitutes, Aboriginal women were seen as particular threats to morality and health. An 1886 pamphlet ("What Canadian Women Say of the Canadian North-West") that offered advice for emigrants was quick to reassure newcomers that Aboriginal people were seldom seen. The 320 women who responded to the question "Do you experience any dread of the Indians?" overwhelmingly replied that they rarely saw any. S. Lumsden, for example, thought they were "hundreds of miles away with sufficient force to keep them quiet."[44]

Following the events of 1885, government officials as well as the NWMP made strenuous efforts to keep Aboriginal people on their reserves. A pass system required all who wished to leave to acquire a pass from the farm instructor or agent, declaring the length of and reason for absence. A central rationale for the pass system was to keep towns and villages safe from Aboriginal women "of abandoned character who were there for the worst purposes."[45] There is evidence that some Aboriginal women worked as prostitutes.[46] Cree chiefs of the Edmonton District complained to the prime minister in 1883 that their young women were reduced by starvation to prostitution, something unheard of among their people before.[47] Officials attributed prostitution not to economic conditions but to what they insisted was the personal disposition or inherent immorality of Aboriginal women.[48] Classified as prostitutes, Aboriginal women could be restricted by a new disciplinary regime. Separate legislation under the Indian Act, and, after 1892, under the Criminal Code, governed Aboriginal prostitution, making it easier to convict Aboriginal women than other women. As legal historian Constance Backhouse has observed, this separate criminal legislation, "with its attendant emphasis on the activities of Indians rather than whites, revealed that racial discrimination ran deep through the veins of nineteenth century Canadian society."[49]

The pass system was also used to bar Aboriginal women from the towns, where it was assumed they would only go for "immoral purposes." Women who were found by the NWMP to be without passes and without means of support were arrested and ordered back to their reserves.[50] In March 1886 the Battleford police dealt with one woman who refused to leave the town by taking her to the barracks and cutting off locks of her hair. Two years later the Battleford paper reported that "during the early part of the week the Mounted Police ordered out of town a number of squaws who had come in from time to time and settled here. The promise to take them to the barracks and cut off their hair had a wonderful effect in hastening their movements."[51]

Accustomed to a high degree of mobility about the landscape, Aboriginal women found that the pass system not only restricted their traditional subsistence strategies but also hampered their pursuit of new jobs and resources. Government officials further limited the women's employment and marketing opportunities through advice such as that given by one Indian agent, who, in 1885, urged the citizens of Calgary not to purchase anything from or hire Aboriginal people. The reason for this was to keep them out of the town.[52] The periodic sale of produce, art, and craftwork in urban or tourist areas could have provided income to women and their families, as it did for Aboriginal women in eastern Canada. Studies of rural women in western Canada suggest that, in the Prairie boom-and-bust cycle, the numerous strategies of women, including the marketing of country provisions and farm products, provided the buffer against farm failure.[53] Aboriginal women were not allowed the same opportunities to market these resources.

The mechanisms and attitudes that excluded Aboriginal women from the new settlements also hampered their access to some of the services these places offered. Jane Livingston, the wife of one of the earliest farmers in the Calgary District, found that whenever there was a new policeman in Calgary, he would ask her and her children for passes and make trouble because of their appearance. On one occasion, when a child was sick and she needed medicines from downtown Calgary, she rubbed flour into her face and "hoped [she] looked like a white Calgary housewife" so that the new police constable would not bother her about a pass.[54]

Murders of Aboriginal Women

Community reactions to the poisoning of one Aboriginal woman and the brutal murder of another in the late 1880s in southern Alberta reflect the racial prejudices of many of the recent immigrants. In 1888 Constable Alfred Symonds of the NWMP detachment of Stand Off was accused of feloniously killing a Blood woman by the name of Only Kill by giving her a fatal dose of iodine. The woman had swallowed the contents of a bottle given to her by Symonds; the bottle had apparently held iodine and she died the next morning. The same day she had also eaten a quantity of beans that had turned sour in the heat. Although Only Kill died Wednesday morning, the matter was not reported to the coroner until late Friday night. The coroner claimed that by this time the body was too decomposed for post mortem examination, and the coroner's jury decided that the deceased had come to her death either from eating sour beans or from drinking the fluid given to her by Symonds, who was committed to trial and charged with having administered the poison.[55] Constable Symonds was a popular and jocular cricketeer and boxer, the son of a professor from Galt, Ontario.[56] In his report on the case, Superintendent P.R. Neale of the NWMP wrote to his superior, "I do not think any Western jury will convict him." Symonds appeared before Judge James F. Macleod, former commissioner of the NWMP, in August 1888, but the Crown prosecutor made application for "Nolle Prosequi," which was granted, and the prisoner was released.[57]

During the 1889 trials of the murderer of a Cree woman identified only as "Rosalie," who had been working as a prostitute, it became clear that there were many in Calgary who felt that "Rosalie was only a squaw and that her death did not matter much";[58] instead, the murderer gained the sympathy and support of much of the town. The murder was a particularly brutal one, and even though the accused, William "Jumbo" Fisk, had confessed and given himself up to authorities, there were problems finding any citizens willing to serve on a jury that might convict a White man for such a crime. The Crown prosecutor stated that he regretted having to conduct the case, as he had known the accused for several years as a "genial, accommodating and upright young man."[59] Fisk was a popular veteran of 1885, and he was from a well-established eastern Canadian family. At the end of the first of the Rosalie trials the jury – astoundingly – found the accused "Not Guilty." Judge Charles Rouleau refused to accept this verdict, and he ordered a re-trial, at the end of which he told the jury to "forget the woman's race and to consider only the evidence at hand," that "it made no difference whether Rosalie was white or black, an Indian or a negro. In the eyes of the law, every British subject is equal."[60] It was only after the second trial that Fisk was convicted of manslaughter and sent to prison for fourteen years of hard labour. The judge intended to sentence him for life, but letters written by MPs and other influential persons (who had made representations to the Court as to his good character), combined with a petition from the most respectable people of Calgary, persuaded him to impose the lesser sentence.

The people of Calgary tried to show that they were not callous and indifferent towards Rosalie. They did this by giving her "as respectable a burial as if she had been a white woman," although several months later the town council squabbled with the Indian department over the costs incurred, as the department did not think it necessary to go beyond the costs of a pauper's funeral. As a final indignity, the priests would not allow Rosalie to be buried in the mission graveyard, even though she had been baptized into the Roman Catholic Church, because they regarded her as a prostitute who had died in sin. The lesson to be learned from the tragedy, according to a Calgary newspaper, was "keep the Indians out of town."[61]

Aboriginal Women and Anglo-Saxon Moral Reformers

There was an intensification of racial discrimination and a stiffening of boundaries between Aboriginal and newcomer in the late 1880s in western Canada. In part this may have been because the immigrants exemplified the increasingly racist ideas and assumptions of the British towards "primitive" peoples.[62] Like the Jamaica Revolt and the India Mutiny, the events of 1885 in western Canada sanctioned perceptions of Aboriginal people as dangerous and ungrateful and justified increased control and segregation.[63] Aboriginal women presented particular perils and hazards. The Métis of the Canadian West had fomented two "rebellions" in western Canada, so authorities wanted to discourage such miscegenation, which could potentially produce great numbers of "malcontents" who might demand that their rights and interests be recognized.[64]

A fervour for moral reform in Protestant English Canada also began to take shape in the later 1880s. Sexual immorality was a main target, and racial purity was one of the goals of the reformers.[65] There were fears that Anglo-Saxons might well be overrun by more fertile, darker, and lower people who were believed not to be in control of their sexual desires. Attitudes of the moral reformers towards the inhabitants of the cities' slums were in keeping with categorizations of "savages" as improvident, filthy, impure, and morally depraved. The 1886 accusations of Malcolm Cameron concerning the extent of venereal disease among the NWMP had led to an internal investigation of the matter, and although this proved that Cameron's claims were exaggerated, they were not entirely incorrect.[66] The concerns of the moral reformers, however, justified policies segregating Aboriginal and newcomer communities.

The Invalidation of Mixed Marriages

Also at issue in the West at this time was the question of who was to control property and capital, who was to have privilege and respectability, and who was not. The possibility that the progeny of interracial marriages might be recognized as legitimate heirs to the sometimes considerable wealth of their fathers posed problems and acted as a powerful incentive for the immigrants to view Aboriginal women as immoral and as accustomed to a great number of partners. With the arrival of Euro-Canadian women, Aboriginal wives became fewer, and there is evidence, just as Trivett had suggested, that in the 1880s husbands and fathers were leaving their Aboriginal wives and children for non-Aboriginal wives. D.W. Davis, for example, began his career in Alberta as a whisky trader at the infamous Fort Whoop-Up, but by 1887 he was elected as the first MP for the Alberta District. He had a family of four children with a Blood woman by the name of Revenge Walker, but in 1887 he married an Ontario woman, Lillie Grier (sister of D.J. Grier), with whom he had a second family. Although Davis, like Grier, acknowledged the children of the earlier marriage and provided for their education, they were excluded from the economic and social elite in the non-Aboriginal community.[67]

While the validity of mixed marriages that were conducted according to "the custom of the country" had been upheld in Canadian courts earlier in the nineteenth century, this changed with the influential 1886 ruling in *Jones* v. *Fraser*. The judge ruled that the court would not accept that "the cohabitation of a civilized man and a savage woman, even for a long period of time, gives rise to the presumption that they consented to be married in our sense of marriage."[68] In 1899 the Supreme Court for the North-West Territories decided that the two sons of Mary Brown, a Piegan woman, and Nicholas Sheran, a founder of a lucrative coal mine near Lethbridge, were not entitled, as next of kin, to a share of their father's estate. The judge found that Sheran could have but did not legally marry Brown while they lived together from 1878 until Sheran's death in 1882.[69]

Haunted by an Image

Negative images of Aboriginal women proved extraordinarily persistent. Their morality was questioned in a number of sections of the Indian Act. If a woman was not of "good moral character," for example, then she lost her one-third interest in her husband's estate. A male government official was the sole and final judge of moral character. As late as 1921 the House of Commons debated a Criminal Code amendment that would have made it an offence for any White man to have "illicit connection" with an Indian woman. Part of the rationale advanced was that "the Indian women are, perhaps, not as alive as women of other races in the country to the importance of maintaining their chastity." The amendment was not passed, as it was argued that this could make unsuspecting White men the "victims" of Indian women who would blackmail them.[70] By contrast, any critical reflections upon the behaviour of early government officials and the police in western Canada did not survive beyond the controversy of the 1880s. Ideological constraints, combined with more formal mechanisms of control (such as the pass system), succeeded in marginalizing Aboriginal women and in limiting the alternatives and opportunities available to them.

Local histories of the Prairies suggest that by the turn of the century many of the settlements of the West had their "local Indian" who was tolerated on the fringes of society and whose behaviour and appearance was the subject of local anecdotes. "Old Dewdney," for example, an ancient, often flamboyantly dressed man, was a familiar sight in Fort Macleod. Local people exchanged stories about the exotic past of the old man and of their generosity and kindness towards him.[71] "Nikamoos," or the Singer, camped each summer by herself on the trail to the Onion Lake reserve agency in Saskatchewan. Among the White community it was reputed that as a girl Nikamoos had run away with a policeman but that he had been compelled to leave her. The child she bore died and Nikamoos went insane.[72]

A solitary Indian woman known only as Liza camped on the outskirts of Virden, Manitoba, for many years until her disappearance sometime in the 1940s. By then Liza was thought to have been well over 100 years old. She lived winter and summer in an unheated tent by the railroad tracks, although she spent the long winter days huddled in the livery stable and also at times crept into the Nu-Art Beauty Parlour, where she sat on the floor in front of the window, warming herself in the sun. Liza smoked a corncob pipe as she shuffled about the streets and lanes of Virden, rummaging in garbage tins. She bathed under the overflow pipe at the water tower, sometimes clothed and sometimes not, and dried off by standing over the huge heat register in Scales and Rothnie's General Store. To an extent she was tolerated and even assisted; town employees shovelled out a path for her when she was buried under snow, and it was thought that the town fathers supplied her with food from time to time. Children were half fascinated and half frightened by this ancient woman. Old-timers believed that Liza was there well before the first settlers, that she was among the Lakota (Sioux) who had escaped the pursuing American army in 1876, that she received regular cheques from the United States, and that she was capable of fine handwriting (where she had learned this, no one knew).[73]

The presence of Liza, and the stories told about her, served to sharpen the boundaries of community membership and to articulate what was and what was not considered acceptable and respectable.[74] Liza was the object of both fascination and repugnance, as she violated norms of conventional behaviour, dress, and cleanliness, representing the antithesis of "civilized" Prairie society. Although economically and socially marginal, Liza was symbolically important. Her role attests to the recurrent pattern through which the new society of the West gained in strength and identity and sought to legitimate its own authority by defining itself against the people who were there before them. Liza was a real person, but what she represented was a Euro-Canadian artefact, created by the settlement. The narratives circulated about Liza were not those she might have told herself – of the disasters that had stripped her of family and community or perhaps of her strategies in adopting the character role – and this folklore reflected less about Liza than it did about the community itself. Her solitary life was unique and in contrast to the lives of Aboriginal women: Liza was not representative of a Lakota woman within Lakota society. Yet her presence on the margins of the settlement was tolerated and encouraged because she appeared to fit into the well-established category of the "Squaw" – a category that still served to confirm the Euro-Canadian newcomers in their belief that their cultural and moral superiority entitled them to the land that had become their home.

Acknowledgments

Thanks to Hugh Dempsey and Donald Smith for kindly sharing their research material with me. This chapter is reprinted courtesy of *Great Plains Quarterly* 13 (Summer 1993): 147-61.

Notes

1 Mary E. Inderwick, "A Lady and Her Ranch," in *The Best from Alberta History,* ed. Hugh Dempsey (Saskatoon: Western Producer Prairie Books, 1981), 65-77. In 1882 the North-West Territories were divided into four provisional districts: Assiniboia, Saskatchewan, Alberta, and Athabasca.

2 For an examination and critique of the argument that European women introduced segregation, see Margaret Strobel, *European Women and the Second British Empire* (Bloomington: Indiana University Press, 1991). See also essays by Ann Laura Stoler, "Carnal Knowledge and Imperial Power: Gender, Race and Morality in Colonial Asia," in *Gender at the Crossroads of Knowledge: Feminist Anthropology in the Postmodern Era,* ed. Micaela di Leonardo (Berkeley: University of California Press, 1991), 51-101; and Ann Laura Stoler, "Rethinking Colonial Categories: European Communities and the Boundaries of Rule," in *Colonialism and Culture,* ed. Nicholas B. Dirks (Ann Arbor: University of Michigan Press, 1992), 319-52.

3 See Sarah Carter, *Lost Harvests: Prairie Indian Reserve Farmers and Government Policy* (Montreal: McGill-Queen's University Press, 1990).

4 Rayna Green, "The Pocahontas Perplex: The Image of Indian Women in American Culture,"

in *Unequal Sisters: A Multicultural Reader in U.S. Women's History,* ed. Ellen Carol DuBois and Vicki L. Ruiz (New York: Routledge, 1990), 15-21.

5 John McDougall, "A Criticism of 'Indian Wigwams and Northern Camp-Fires'" (n.p.: 1895), 12-3.

6 P.B. Waite, *Canada, 1874-1896: Arduous Destiny* (Toronto: McClelland and Stewart, 1971), 149.

7 D.N. Sprague, *Canada and the Métis, 1869-1885* (Waterloo, ON: Wilfrid Laurier University Press, 1988).

8 Canada, *Sessional Papers,* Annual Report of the Superintendent General of Indian Affairs for the year ending 30 June 1898, xix; for the year ending 31 December 1899, xxiii, xxviii, 166; the *Mail* (Toronto), 2 March 1889; Pamela Margaret White, "Restructuring the Domestic Sphere: Prairie Indian Women on Reserves: Image, Ideology and State Policy, 1880-1930" (PhD thesis, McGill University, 1987); W.H. Withrow, *Native Races of North America* (Toronto: Methodist Mission Rooms, 1895), 114.

9 Canada, *Sessional Papers,* Annual Report of the Superintendent General of Indian Affairs for the year ending March 1908, 110.

10 Inspector Alex McGibbon's report on Onion Lake, October 1891, National Archives of Canada (NAC), Record Group (RG) 10, records relating to Indian Affairs, Black Series, vol. 3860, file 82, 319-6.

11 The *Globe* (Toronto), 1 February 1886.

12 The *Mail* (Toronto), 23 January 1886.

13 Canada, House of Commons *Debates,* Malcolm Cameron, Session 1886, vol. 1, 720-1.

14 As quoted in E.C. Morgan, "The North-West Mounted Police: Internal Problems and Public Criticism, 1874-1883," *Saskatchewan History* 26, 2 (Spring 1973): 56.

15 Canada, House of Commons *Debates,* 21 April 1880, Joseph Royal, 4th Parliament, 2nd session, 1638.

16 The *Mail,* 2 February 1886.

17 John Maclean, "The Half-breed and Indian Insurrection," *Canadian Methodist Magazine* 22, 1 (July 1885): 173-4.

18 Edgar Dewdney to the Bishop of Saskatchewan, 31 May 1886, NAC, RG 10, vol. 3753, file 30613.

19 John O'Kute-sica Correspondence, collection no. R-834, file 17(b), 15, Saskatchewan Archives Board (SAB).

20 *Blackfeet Heritage: 1907-08* (Browning: Blackfeet Heritage Program, n.d.), 171.

21 A.B. McCullough, "Papers Relating to the North West Mounted Police and Fort Walsh," Manuscript Report Series no. 213 (Ottawa: Parks Canada, Department of Indian and Northern Affairs, 1977): 132-3.

22 L. Herchmer to Comptroller, 23 May 1889, NAC, RG 18, vol. 35, file 499-1889.

23 Personal Interview with Kirsten Grier, great-granddaughter of D.J. Grier, Calgary, 19 May 1993. See also *Fort Macleod – Our Colourful Past: A History of the Town of Fort Macleod from 1874 to 1924* (Fort Macleod, AB: Fort Macleod History Committee, 1977), 268-9.

24 O'Kute-sica Correspondence, 3.

25 See, for example, S.B. Steele to Commissioner, Fort Macleod, 20 July 1895, NAC, RG 18, vol. 2182, file RCMP 1895, pt. 2; Gilbert E. Sanders Diaries, 20 October 1885, Edward Sanders Family Papers, M1093, file 38, Glenbow Archives.

26 F. Laurie Barron, "Indian Agents and the North-West Rebellion," in *1885 and After: Native Society in Transition,* ed. F. Laurie Barron and James B. Waldram (Regina: Canadian Plains Research Centre, 1986), 36.

27 Norma Sluman and Jean Goodwill, *John Tootoosis: A Biography of a Cree Leader* (Ottawa: Golden Dog, 1982), 37.

28 Hugh A. Dempsey, *Big Bear: The End of Freedom* (Vancouver: Douglas and McIntyre, 1984), 117. See also *Saskatchewan Herald* (Battleford), 14 and 28 February 1881.

29 Newspaper clipping, "Through the Saskatchewan," n.p., n.d., n.a., William Henry Cotton Collection, SAB.

30 The *Globe,* 4 June 1880; *Macleod Gazette* (Fort Macleod, AB), 23 March 1886; the *Mail,* 2 February 1886.

31 Canada, House of Commons *Debates,* session 1886, vol. 1, 730.

32 William Donovan to L. Vankoughnet, 31 October 1886, NAC, RG 10, vol. 3772, file 34983.
33 The *Globe*, 4 June 1886.
34 *The Facts Respecting Indian Administration in the North-West* (Ottawa: Department of Indian Affairs, 1886), 9, 12.
35 Theresa Gowanlock and Theresa Delaney, *Two Months in the Camp of Big Bear* (Parkdale: Parkdale Times, 1885).
36 *Manitoba Sun* (Winnipeg), 7 December 1886.
37 Sarah Carter, *Capturing Women: The Manipulation of Cultural Imagery in Canada's Prairie West* (Montreal: McGill-Queen's University Press, 1997).
38 Canada, *Sessional Papers*, Annual Report of the Commissioner of the North West Mounted Police for 1890, vol. 24, no. 9, 62.
39 *Moosomin Courier*, 13 March 1890.
40 Joe Dion, *My Tribe the Crees* (Calgary: Glenbow-Alberta Institute, 1979), 114.
41 See Sarah Carter, "Relations Between Native and Non-Native Women in the Prairie West, 1870-1920," paper presented to the Women and History Association of Manitoba, Winnipeg, February 1992.
42 Elizabeth M. McLean, "Prisoners of the Indians," *Beaver*, Outfit 278 (June 1947): 15-6.
43 David Hamer, *New Towns in the New World: Images and Perceptions of the Nineteenth Century Urban Frontier* (New York: Columbia University Press, 1990), 17, 213.
44 "What Canadian Women Say of the Canadian North-West" (Montreal: Canadian Pacific Railway, 1886), 44.
45 L. Vankoughnet to John A. Macdonald, 15 November 1883, NAC, RG 10, vol. 1009, file 628, no. 596-635.
46 S.W. Horrall, "The (Royal) North-West Mounted Police and Prostitution on the Canadian Prairies," *Prairie Forum* 10, 1 (Spring 1985): 105-27.
47 Clipping from the *Bulletin* (Edmonton), 7 January 1883, NAC, RG 10, vol. 3673, file 10986.
48 Canada, *Sessional Papers*, Annual Report of the superintendent general of Indian affairs for the year ending 1906, 82.
49 Constance B. Backhouse, "Nineteenth Century Canadian Prostitution Law: Reflection of a Discriminatory Society," *Histoire sociale/Social History* 18, 36 (November 1985): 422.
50 Canada, *Sessional Papers*, Annual Report of the Commissioner of the North West Mounted Police Force for the year 1889, reprinted in *The New West* (Toronto: Coles, 1973), 101.
51 *Saskatchewan Herald* (Battleford), 15 March 1886, 13 March 1888 (quoted).
52 *Calgary Herald*, 5 March 1885.
53 See, for example, Carolina Antoinetta J.A. Van de Vorst, "A History of Farm Women's Work in Manitoba" (MA thesis, University of Manitoba, 1988).
54 Lyn Hancock with Marion Dowler, *Tell Me Grandmother* (Toronto: McClelland and Stewart, 1985), 139.
55 *Macleod Gazette*, 18 July 1888.
56 John D. Higinbotham, *When the West Was Young: Historical Reminiscences of the Early Canadian West* (Toronto: Ryerson, 1933), 260-1.
57 R.C. Macleod, *The North-West Mounted Police and Law Enforcement, 1873-1905* (Toronto: University of Toronto Press, 1976), 145. See also NAC, RG 18, vol. 24, file 667–1888.
58 Donald Smith, "Bloody Murder Almost Became Miscarriage of Justice," *Herald Sunday Magazine*, 23 July 1989, 13. Thanks to Donald Smith, Department of History, University of Calgary for allowing me to draw upon his sources on this case.
59 James Gray, *Talk to My Lawyer: Great Stories of Southern Alberta's Bar and Bench* (Edmonton: Hurtig, 1987), 7.
60 Rouleau, quoted in Smith, "Bloody Murder," 15.
61 *Calgary Herald*, 24 July, 10 September (quoted), 27 February, and 8 March (quoted) 1889.
62 See Christine Bolt, *Victorian Attitudes to Race* (Toronto: University of Toronto Press, 1971); Philip D. Curtin, *The Image of Africa: British Ideas and Action, 1780-1850* (Madison: University of Wisconsin Press, 1964); V.G. Kieman, *The Lords of Human Kind: European Attitudes Toward the Outside World in the Imperial Age* (Middlesex: Penguin, 1972); Douglas A. Lorimer, *Colour, Class and the Victorians* (Leicester: Leicester University Press 1978); and Philip Mason, *Patterns of Dominance* (London: Oxford University Press, 1971).

63 Walter Hildebrandt, "Official Images of 1885," *Prairie Fire* 6, 4 (1985): 31-40.
64 This is suggested by Backhouse, "Nineteenth-Century Canadian Prostitution Law," 422.
65 Mariana Valverde, *The Age of Light, Soap, and Water: Moral Reform in English Canada, 1885-1925* (Toronto: McClelland and Stewart, 1991).
66 NAC, RG 18, vol. 1039, file 87–1886, pt. 1.
67 Beverley A. Stacey, "D.W. Davis: Whiskey Trader to Politician," *Alberta History* 38, 3 (Summer 1990): 1-11.
68 Sylvia Van Kirk, *"Many Tender Ties": Women in Fur Trade Society in Western Canada, 1670-1870* (Winnipeg: Watson and Dwyer, 1980), 241; and Constance Backhouse, *Petticoats and Prejudice: Women and the Law in Nineteenth-Century Canada* (Toronto: University of Toronto Press and Osgoode Society, 1991), chap. 1; judge quoted in Van Kirk, *Many Tender Ties*, 241.
69 Brian Slattery and Linda Charlton, eds., *Canadian Native Law Cases 1891-1910* (Saskatoon: Native Law Centre, 1985): 636-44.
70 Canada, House of Commons, *Debates*, session 1921, vol. 4, 26 May 1921, 3908.
71 *Fort Macleod – Our Colourful Past*, 217-8.
72 Ruth Matheson Buck, "Wives and Daughters," *Folklore* 9, 4 (Autumn 1988): 14-5.
73 "Talk About Stories," *Anecdotes and Updates: Virden Centennial, 1982* (Virden: Empire Publishing Company, 1982): 57-9.
74 Diane Tye, "Local Character Anecdotes: A Nova Scotia Case Study," *Western Folklore* 48 (July 1989): 196.

CHAPTER 3

Imagining Native Women

Feminine Discourse and Four Women Travelling the Northwest Coast

NANCY PAGH

This essay took root from my interest in accounts of women travelling the Northwest Coast by boat and in the work of feminist theorists who explore the relationships between colonial discourse and feminine discourse in British women's travel writing.[1] In this chapter I look at women boat travellers' constructions of Northwest Coast Native women between 1885 and 1960 in the context of what Sara Mills defines as a feminine discourse of travel writing. Although travel writing generally, and women's travel writing particularly, has been perceived as lightweight (unprofessional, unscholarly) material, accounts by women boaters seem significant to me because they are written from a position not often considered in studies of the Northwest Coast; that is, these accounts were generated neither by traders nor missionaries nor settlers nor novelists, but by women who were mobile and who had the leisure to observe and record the world and people around them. My work does not address questions of Native cultural history; my focus is on the images that women boat travellers of the late nineteenth and early twentieth centuries imagined, recycled, and passed along to their readers as well as on the ways that the discursive pressures of feminine discourse shaped these images. I am interested in how these constructions of Native women changed over time, and I explore how, in the more recent accounts, feminine discourse allows White women the space to question their own constructions of Natives and to reconsider their own position in a Native world.

In "First Impressions: Rhetorical Strategies in Travel Writing by Victorian Women," Eva-Marie Kröller identifies ways in which the tropes women writers share with their male peers can be "used with different intentions and to different effect." This rhetorical complexity, she writes, leads to the multiple personae and multiple voices of Victorian women travellers; these are frustrating to critics who see evidence of strength, independence, and sensuality in the same accounts that demonstrate "the women's insistence on propriety, their conservative politics and sense of racial superiority, and ... their apparent lack of pride in their own achievements."[2] The same year, Shirley Foster published similar ideas in *Across New Worlds: Nineteenth-Century Women Travellers and Their Writings*. She identifies the ambiguous position of female travellers who must adopt "the 'masculine' virtues of strength, initiative and decisiveness while retaining the less aggressive qualities considered appropriate for their own sex."[3] One common result of this ambiguity is that "women travel writers have to substitute self-effacement or self-mockery for more aggressive or positive assertiveness in order to demonstrate a true femininity."[4] This self-deprecatory tone is frequently established when a female travel writer begins her text with an apology or appeal for leniency regarding the deficiencies in her work. This stands "in contrast to the prefaces appended to the works of most male travellers which positively burst with confident self-assertion."[5] Foster concludes that it is possible to detect "a distinctive and overtly feminine voice" in women's travel accounts of the century, recognizable by the self-effacing tone and by the treatment of topics not generally explored in depth in male travel writing: the costume and manners of women, details of domestic management, marriage customs and female status, and the representation of Natives as "individuals with whom she tries to identify rather than as symbols of an alien 'otherness.'"[6]

With *Discourses of Difference*, Sara Mills furthers this discussion by theorizing a discourse of femininity within a specifically colonial context: "There are various discursive pressures on women writers which encourage them to write in particular ways. That is not to say that all women write in the same way, but rather that there are pressures which they either resist, negotiate or simply give in to."[7]

These discursive constraints on both the production and reception of women's texts, Mills tells us, produce a feminine discourse in travel writing of the high imperial period (1850-1930) that is identifiable by its ambivalent position. Female narrators of this time draw on the dominant writing techniques of colonialism (for example, "othering" a race to assert the superiority of one's own), yet at the same time they are excluded from fully adopting them because of their disadvantaged position. Colonial British women travel writers use humour, self-deprecation, and an emphasis on personal relationships in their writing. The result is that their texts can then both operate within colonial discourse and serve to critique it from its own margins. These women are not exempt from racism nor from participation in imperialism, Mills writes, but feminine discourse additionally creates the opportunity for women to be "affiliated" with Natives. That is, their accounts draw attention to interaction with Natives not as representatives of their race (as in male-authored accounts), but as individuals. Mills writes that this form of writing then constitutes a challenge to male Orientalism.[8]

Mills points out that there are many discourses at work in the whole of the colonial situation: "Each colonial relation develops narrative and descriptive techniques particular to its setting and history."[9] What I want to do here is to look at the accounts of women travellers in order to explore the use of feminine discourse in a Northwest Coast setting. Although the narratives of women travelling to Asia and Africa have enjoyed a great deal of recent critical attention, virtually nothing has been written about gender and tourism along the Northwest Coast. I have selected four representative texts; however, there is a great deal more material. By the 1888 season, more than 2,000 people were travelling by steamship from Puget Sound to the newly purchased Alaska;[10] many of them published their diaries of the voyages. Steamship companies, advertising the region as "the Lover's Lane of the Seven Seas," succeeded in recruiting large numbers of female passengers after the turn of the century. Since that time, marine tourism has only grown in popularity; literally millions of people now enjoy pleasure boating and cruise-ship travel along the coast.

In this chapter, I specifically focus on the effects of feminine discourse on tourists' constructions of Native women; I hypothesize that White women did not articulate an "affiliation" with Native peoples (as, Foster and Mills argue, did women travelling to other sites in the nineteenth century) until well into the twentieth century. Such an "affiliation" proves to be problematic and is linked to the myth of "the disappearing Indian," popularized by the photographer Edward S. Curtis and others.[11]

Native Women on the Northwest Coast

In his study of Native labour in British Columbia between 1858 and 1930, Rolf Knight suggests that the roles of Native women changed less than did those of men after contact. He depicts women comprising the bulk of BC cannery labour in the 1870s, 1880s, and 1890s, working in cottage industries (e.g., knitting the Cowichan sweaters introduced at missions in the 1860s) and domestic labour, tending potato gardens, backpacking eighty pounds of freight (standard weight for Native women to carry "over narrow trails, up hills and down, over roots, muck and rock"),[12] migrating with their husbands and families from the BC coast to work in Washington Territory sawmills in the 1870s, working as boat-pullers in the gill net fishery, and "paddl[ing] canoes for their husbands or relatives in seal hunting."[13]

Pre-contact activities of women in Northwest Coast First Nations appear to focus upon the preparation, storage, and distribution of food, although some oral histories indicate grandmothers or other female ancestors who were skilled at fishing and hunting, even though taboos associated with menstruation could prohibit women from hunting or handling fish nets.[14] Carol Cooper writes that, because women controlled the production and distribution of food and other economic resources among the Nisga'a and Tsimshian, they "received recognition for the skilled management of resources, because the surplus they produced became the basis of trade and generated wealth for distribution in the potlatch."[15] The presence of White fur traders, she argues, did not have a negative impact on the status of these Native women but offered further opportunities for women to create wealth and enhance their status: "On the northern Pacific coast, amassing wealth through successful exploitation of resources and trade was an equally if not more important means to prestige and public power than warfare. Significantly, these were activities in which Nishga [sic] and Tsimshian women could readily engage."[16]

Women participated in trade by controlling resources, by setting the prices, and by getting into canoes and engaging in trade themselves. Nisga'a, Tsimshian, and Haida women were known as excellent canoeists, commonly receiving instruction from the age of six;[17] it was not uncommon for women to paddle hundreds of miles to trade.

Regardless of the Sacajewea, or Pocahontas, stereotype for Native women in North America, constructions of coastal Native women by European men do not focus on their beauty or strength. Sylvia Van Kirk and Jennifer Brown have shown how valuable Native women were in the lives of overland fur traders in early Canadian history.[18] However, men visiting the coast in ships to trade for furs were less interested in domestic companions or guides. Their depictions of Native women draw attention to the "filthy" look of their painted faces and oily hair, and to their sexual availability, and these constructions seeped beyond fur trade rhetoric. Marcia Crosby, in "Construction of the Imaginary Indian," comments on the stereotype of the Native woman as bad-smelling, promiscuous, and drunken.[19] Some White men were attracted to "exotic" young Indian women: after describing a mixed-blood girl's blushing face,

Theodore Winthrop, a traveller to Washington Territory in 1853, says simply: "Indian maids are pretty; Indian dames are hags. Only high civilization keeps its women beautiful to the last."[20] Such a construction draws attention to the writer's own power, masculinity, and "good taste," and it is one that many women boat travellers on the Northwest Coast would share, although not for the same reasons. Winthrop's comment that high civilization *keeps* women beautiful to the last hints at the difference. Nineteenth-century women travellers who were not kept beautiful, who did not adopt a pose of certain and steady femininity in their writing, were commonly received as either liars or discreditable eccentrics.[21] Both men and women were aware of the precarious position of women travellers of the nineteenth century and were aware that something must be amiss with a woman if she did not adopt a particular pose and discourse.

Eliza Scidmore and Septima Collis

Eliza Scidmore's *Alaska, Its Southern Coast and the Sitkan Archipelago* is the product of an American woman travelling the coast as a passenger on working steamships in 1883, 1884, and 1885.[22] Generally, her account is that of a woman clearly resisting the expectations for Victorian feminine discourse. She never apologizes for herself, and she writes primarily about history – the names of explorers and pioneers, the process of Alaska changing hands from Russia to the United States, the development of canneries, the educational system, and rules of navigation. She rarely writes about herself as a woman, except to note that she is the "first woman" to visit some of these places and to downplay any attention drawn by her sex. When a male passenger comments on her presence, she depicts herself and another female passenger as taking danger lightly – definitely not the "shrinking lady":

> "You ladies are very brave to venture up in such a place. If you only knew the risks you are running – the dangers you are in!" And the pioneer's voice had a tone of the deepest concern as he said it.
>
> We received this with some laughter, and expressed entire confidence in the captain and pilot, who had penetrated glacial fastnesses and unknown waters before.[23]

Using penetration – the typical trope of male colonial discourse – Scidmore acknowledges the capability of a professional without feigning helplessness. An early writer and editor for the *National Geographic*, Scidmore was the first woman on the National Geographic Society's board of managers.[24] Her confident and factual style would have been more acceptable than would feminine discourse to the quasi-scientific magazine.

Scidmore's construction of Native women is highly concerned with social position. She is interested in the status of coastal Native women compared to those on the Plains, recording that the former "[have] a good many rights up here that [their] sisters of the western plains know not."[25] She connects the coastal woman's status with water travel and trade:

> Woman's rights, and her sphere and influence, have reached a development among the Sitkans, that would astonish the suffrage leaders of Wyoming and Washington Territory. They are all keen, sharp traders, and if the women object to the final price offered for their furs at the Sitka stores, they get into their canoes, and paddle up to Juneau, or down to Wrangell, and even across the border to the British trading posts. They take no account of time or travel, and a journey of a thousand miles is justified to them, if they only get another yard of calico in exchange for their furs.[26]

In her text generally, Scidmore resists the sentimentalizing, self-deprecatory, and overtly moralizing tone that can characterize feminine discourse of the nineteenth century, and she adopts the language of the masculine imperial adventurer when she tells us she "feels quite like an explorer penetrating unknown lands."[27] But although she resists feminine discourse throughout most of her travelogue, she adopts it when writing about Native women. Her construction of one particular Native woman illustrates this point. Mrs. Tom, she tells her reader, "is the reputed possessor of $10,000, accumulated by her own energy and shrewdness" in trading. "Even savage people bow down to wealth," she writes. When Scidmore visits Mrs. Tom she has this to report: "She is a plump matron, fat, fair, and forty in fact, and her house is a model of neatness and order. On gala occasions she arrays herself in her best velvet dress, her bonnet with the red feather, a prodigious necktie and breastpin, and then, with two silver rings on every finger, and nine silver bracelets on each arm, she is the envy of all the other ladies of Siwash town."[28]

Scidmore's use of feminine discourse here – focusing on Mrs. Tom's neat home and velvet dress, and on the envy of the other Native women whom she mockingly calls "ladies" – creates an ambiguous and absurd portrait of the Native women of Sitka. It is absurd because Scidmore makes it pointedly clear in her text that Natives are held back from "upward progress" because of "their want of all moral sense or instincts."[29] Mrs. Tom is caricatured as a woman who does not know the difference between formal and gaudy: she is wealthy, but too crude to understand that two silver rings on each finger is unladylike. Scidmore enhances this construction of the coarseness of Mrs. Tom by reporting unconfirmed gossip that Mrs. Tom bought a young male slave and then married him. When shown the respected trader known as Mrs. Tom, the Victorian reader is left vaguely admiring a Native woman decked out in Western apparel yet being aware that her lack of morality and feminine subtlety makes her only a facsimile of a "real" woman.

With *A Woman's Trip to Alaska*, eastern American Septima Collis consciously employs feminine discourse to construct her voyage generally and Native women specifically.[30] Her work – the record of a twelve-day voyage in May and June 1890 – is addressed to "my country-women" and begins with the characteristically feminine apology: "I have not made even a pretence of writing a scientific or historical work ... All this has been done better than I could ever hope to do it."[31] Her text takes the form of letters or journal entries to her daughter, Amelia, and is highly concerned with "explain[ing] how this delightful excursion can be enjoyed without the slightest fatigue or discomfort."[32] She tries to capture the

Septima Collis, as shown in *A Woman's Trip to Alaska* (1890). Her traveller's pose – with notebook and pen in hand, field glasses draped carefully across her torso, and fitted dress – suggests her attention to appearances.

romantic imagination of her daughter and of all female readers by confiding: "*Entre nous*, I have heard of and seen more than one friendship, commencing on an Alaskan trip, which has ripened into mutual pledges 'for good or for bad, for better, for worse,' and especially of one wealthy and much-travelled Benedict who ... fell a victim in Alaskan waters to female charms, in furs and ulster."[33]

Collis's construction of Natives focuses upon their "poor souls whose darkness may never be dispelled by the enlightenment of education and civilization."[34] Like many upper- and middle-class women of her time, Collis gains a sense of power by directing help toward those she perceives as beneath herself. Interestingly, Collis, a Jew ("I am not a Christian woman; my faith is that of the chosen people"),[35] vehemently praises the work of the Presbyterian missions: "hereafter no man, nor woman either, shall outdo me in words of praise and thanks for the glorious Godlike work which is being performed by the good people who are rescuing the lives, the bodies, and the souls of these poor creatures from the physical and moral deaths they are dying."[36]

Christian charity was a cornerstone of Victorian feminine discourse; it was, of course, also a significant element in imperialist discourse. It is not surprising, then, that many nineteenth-century women travellers (sometimes called "maternal imperialists")[37] describe colonialism through metaphors of motherhood and care-giving, and legitimize their presence in the colonial project by their sex. That Collis redirects attention from

PRINCESS THOM.
(*Kodak'd by Miss M. D. Beach.*)

"Princess Thom," as illustrated in Collis's *A Woman's Trip to Alaska* (1890). The caption clearly is meant to be ironic, as the "princess" is depicted as a lumpish beggar. Baskets such as those shown in the foreground were a valued commodity by steamship tourists, who collected them from Native women as "curios" and proof of a brush with the authentically primitive.

her own otherness (as a Jew) to praise the Christianization of Alaska intimates the power and appeal of both imperialist and feminine discourses, and it underscores the dominance of Christian ideology in both colonial and patriarchal world views. To criticize the Christian missionary enterprise would have amplified Collis's own position as a "heathen" in anti-Semitic times.

As a result of one of the pressures of nineteenth-century feminine discourse, Collis cannot depict Native women without judging their manners against her own feminine habits. Native women are "stretched upon the ground like as many seals" and "repulsive" because of the way they smell.[38] She describes a group of Sitkan women squatting in the shadow of a house as "counterfeiting with their olive skins, bright black eyes, and showy colors the Italian peasants."[39] Mrs. Tom – the same Native woman who appeared in Scidmore's popular account – is exposed here as a counterfeit as well: "her Royal Highness," as Collis dubs her, "is said to be worth $100,000 (though we saw little evidence of any such luxurious wealth)."[40] In apparent reference and contradiction to Scidmore's description of Mrs. Tom as "fat, fair, and forty in fact," Collis mimics the alliteration and points out "she is very fat, of course not very fair, and much over forty."[41] I think in doing this Collis is not so much updating the reader on Mrs. Tom five years later as she is drawing attention to what she perceives to be Scidmore's lack of feminine discourse, her lack of attention to the unfemininity of Native women.

Although Collis and Scidmore are very different writers, I would like to consider what their constructions of Native women have in common and how the pressure of feminine discourse affected these constructions. In essence, both authors construct and, to some extent, applaud Native women as counterfeit White women. Collis openly embraces nineteenth-century feminine discourse to construct Native women as interesting, odd, and laughable in their manners – thus drawing attention to her own normalcy as a woman. For Scidmore, the Native woman is admirable in her social freedoms, yet her "want of all moral sense" makes her something less than a real woman. These constructions of Native women are not simply the result of a general Eurocentricity among nineteenth-century travellers along the coast; they are also the result of the discursive pressures of the Victorian "cult of the home" on women travellers. Victorian ideals of womanhood were based upon the relatively new assumption of the biological weakness of women and spread far beyond the geographical boundaries of Victorian England through etiquette books, manuals on domestic economy, educational tracts, sermons, popular literature, and travel accounts. This "cult" conceived of sexual difference in terms of strict opposites (e.g., men were intellectual, active, and strong; women were emotional, passive, and fragile) and was visible in a widespread system of symbols, as Cunnington shows:

> Symbolism is an unconscious way of expressing hidden thoughts, and is most used, of course, when conventions forbid more outspoken methods … all through the Victorian era, symbols were abundantly employed by women. The small hand, and therefore the tight glove, indicated that the owner was above having to do manual work; the huge crinoline signified that the wearer occupied a large space in the social world; the trailing skirt that she did not belong to the "walking classes," and the stiff corset proved that she was a woman of unbending rectitude.
>
> May we not also read in the small waist a mute appeal for the support of the masculine arm?[42]

Lest we think Cunnington was exaggerating, much more recently, Joan Perkins, in her book *Victorian Women*, writes:

> Women spent their leisure time in a variety of pursuits, depending on the kind of person each was, but women of all social classes were preoccupied with dress. In the upper and middle classes the variety and complexity of their clothes showed rank and position. Every cap, bow, streamer, ruffle, fringe, bustle, glove and other elaboration signalled some difference in status. It was said that jewellery was "a badge that women wore like a sergeant-major's stripes or field marshal's baton."[43]

Given this widely acknowledged system of symbols, it is not, therefore, unreasonable to assume that Collis's depiction of Native women as "seals" and Scidmore's portrait of Mrs. Tom wearing inappropriate jewellery are meant to give very precise indications of the failure of Native women to meet the standards of "true womanhood." Such descriptions of the exteriors of Native women have explicit implications for their status and morality. Given that this system was so widespread and thoroughly absorbed by women in Victorian society, it seems nearly impossible for Collis or Scidmore to have conceived of or to have constructed "other" women in any other way.

Robin Sheets explains the location of the Victorian ideal of womanhood:

> Woman's mission was to begin the moral regeneration of society by displaying the principles of Christianity in all her daily activities; her sphere was the

> home, a shelter for her own innocence and a sanctuary for her husband when he returned from the brutally competitive world of commerce. Within the domestic sphere, she could exercise her influence, a moral and spiritual force so strong that it was said to obviate the need for political power.[44]

This mission and emphasis on the home is commonly referred to in the United States as "the cult of true womanhood." When she travelled, the Victorian woman packed her Christian charity – "the most popular alternative to vacuity"[45] for middle-class Victorian women – and her moral and spiritual force and brought them with her from home. Mills writes that British women of the high imperial period were expected to concern themselves with "the spiritual and moral well-being" of others;[46] this would involve extending their role at home with their children to Native populations. This pressure appears to have extended to the Northwest Coast and was an important factor in leading Eliza Scidmore and Septima Collis to construct Native women as counterfeit women. However, neither Collis nor Scidmore "affiliate" themselves with Native women nor seriously challenge the "othering" aspect of colonial discourse. This affiliation and challenge would not begin until nearly half a century later, with the accounts of Kathrene Pinkerton and Muriel Blanchet.

Kathrene Pinkerton and Muriel Blanchet

Passengers aboard nineteenth-century sailing ships and steamers spent most of their time in their staterooms or on the high decks of vessels. On the Northwest Coast, cloud cover, rain, and fog frequently hid the landscape and the presence of Native people. If local scenery and local inhabitants could be seen clearly, they were viewed from a physical perspective that led to a rhetorical distancing. By the 1920s, when the American writer Kathrene Pinkerton was travelling the coast, as described in her book *Three's a Crew*, the experience of boat travel was dramatically changing for women.[47] Women were no longer limited to travelling as passengers aboard large steamships; some were "cruising" by small boat with their families. This form of transportation allowed White women to get beyond the commercial routes and into the more remote Native villages along the coast.

In his foreword to Pinkerton's reissued *Three's a Crew*, Charles Lillard acknowledges that the book "remains our first cruiser's-eye view of the Northwest Coast."[48] Her account of learning how to live "at home afloat" between 1924 and 1931 – first aboard the thirty-six-foot cruiser *Yakima*, then remodelling and living aboard the larger *Triton* – is made up of "impressions which had no place" either in the collaborative research and writing she did with her husband "or in the ship's log."[49] Although her husband Robert jeers at her for keeping a "personal log," Pinkerton values memories that cannot be categorized under the headings "fishing," "logging," or "boats." A Native woman near Fort Rupert – Mrs. Hunt[50] – described as very large and very friendly and unable to speak a word of English, is one of these memories:

> She motioned me to sit beside her while she wove clams on three long sticks. The two outer sticks were thrust through the bodies or pillows of the clams, while the necks were interlaced around the center stick. One clam was strung on top of another. The plaiting was so beautifully regular that the finished product, a braid of clams two feet long and six inches wide, looked like an elaborate piece of knitting.
>
> I tried it but my plaited clams had great holes where I'd dropped clam stitches. We squatted there together, plaiting, smoking and stopping occasionally to eat a roasted clam. Talk was not necessary to establish a feeling of friendship and of understanding.[51]

What Pinkerton describes as an "understanding" between herself and Mrs. Hunt is probably largely the imagining of a tourist, made all the more romantic by Pinkerton's frequent warning that "soon all this [culture] will be forgotten."[52] Pinkerton's regular use of adjectives such as "sad," "lost," "decrepit," "torn," and "broken," which she applies to the Native villages they visit as they journey between Puget Sound and Glacier Bay, plays neatly into the myth of the disappearing Indian.[53] As Marcia Crosby and Gordon Johnston argue, we should look back at this kind of construction and resist the myth it supports – for indeed, Native people are "our" contemporaries, not symbols of "The Past."[54] However, within my study of feminine discourse and the colonialism of women boat travellers, Pinkerton's account marks an important shift. In the passage above, she is using discourse in a way that seeks to braid the experiences of White and Native women together rather than to reveal the unfemininity or inadequacy of Native women. Pinkerton constructs connecting with specific Native women as experiences that challenge her complacency and cause her to rethink assumptions; in her account, this effect is described through the use of typically feminine domestic scenes such as "weaving" smoked clams (above) or discussing the most delicious recipe for crab (below). Here, she and her daughter Bobs eat hot boiled crab with Mrs. Cadwallader and her children. Mr. Cadwallader, who is White, refuses to join them:

> "He eats only at a table at regular meals," his wife said, as though explaining a quaint custom. "White men cool their crabs to lose the flavor and then put on mayonnaise to make up for the flavor they have lost. He says it's civilized to do it that way." I felt as sorry for him as she did. Elaborations had never seemed quite so idiotic. As I started on the second crab of my morning snack I seemed to remember some other self in a comment on the native's irregular meal hours. "It's either a feast or a famine, and they eat when game is caught." Now having sloughed layers of [White] tradition, I wondered vaguely why this had seemed so reprehensible.[55]

Pinkerton oversimplifies and misrepresents Native women when she weaves them tidily into a narrative about White and Native common understanding. Her account is not free of racism, and quite possibly she would be less interested in Native women if she did not perceive them as the last of a dying race and unthreatening to herself and her family. She values traditional Native culture; when she hears that missionaries had tried to stop George Hunt from visiting elder Native women and writing a cookbook of Native recipes, she protests: "But this is valuable!" and "Don't let anyone stop you."[56] But she is confused about "the strange mingling of two cultures" on the coast.[57] She admits, "There is a difference of opinion as to what the white man has accomplished for the coast Indian. We heard both sides."[58] Regardless of this ambiguity, Pinkerton's *Three's a Crew* marks a point in the accounts of women travelling the Northwest Coast by boat at which narrators *did* affiliate themselves with Native women and challenge the jeers of men who had no discursive category for such impressions.

Muriel "Capi" Blanchet's *The Curve of Time* uses feminine discourse to explore Native culture and to expose herself as the other within that world. In her preface she emphasizes that she has not written a story or a logbook: "it is just an account" of the summer cruises that she and her five children took from their home in Victoria up the Sunshine Coast in the 1920s and 1930s.[59] Her insistence that this is "just an account" seems less an apology than an appeal for the reader to take this book on its own terms – to drop our expectations for history or logbook-style accuracy and accept the teasing fantasy she introduces among her family's memories. Because she does not write her account until the 1950s, there are fewer, or more subtle, limitations placed upon women's travel discourse; we are no longer as apt to question her identity or honesty if she is less than preoccupied with morals and manners.

The Curve of Time is, however, concerned with motherhood and being a mother at sea, and, as the title suggests, it is also a rambling exploration into time. As she describes the family's travels aboard the twenty-five-foot cruiser the *Caprice*, Blanchet recycles the myth of the vanishing Native. She writes: "we had made up our minds to spend part of the summer among the old villages with the big community houses, and try to recapture something of a Past [sic] that will soon be gone forever."[60] As she and her children near the villages, "we felt we were living in a different age – had perhaps lived there before … perhaps dimly remembered it all."[61] Playing the role of the adventurer, she ignores notices and padlocks and invades winter villages while the Native inhabitants are away. "We played with their old boxes-for-the-dead," she writes, "trying to see if we could fit in."[62] Blanchet wants to believe she can be Indian or, at one point in time, was Indian.

Throughout her account Blanchet refers back to the logbooks of male explorers, drawing attention to how she and they are exploring the same places but with different priorities. For instance, Captain Vancouver was primarily concerned with charting and claiming the Northwest Coast so as to increase England's power in trade, while Blanchet's main project is the health and happiness of her children. Unlike Vancouver, Blanchet and her children play and dream, and her account challenges the format of the traditional exploration log by consciously including fantasy. Here she tries to imagine Native women on a hill beyond an uninhabited village:

> It was harder to imagine the women. Perhaps they were shyer. I could only catch glimpses of them; they would never let me get very close. But later, on a sunny knoll on a bluff beyond the village, I surprised a group of the old ones. They were sitting there teasing wool with their crooked old fingers, their grey heads bent as they worked and gossiped – warming their old bones in the last hours of the sun. Then a squirrel scolded above my head; I started, and it was all spoiled … And all around me, perhaps, the old women held their breath until this strange woman had gone.[63]

Unlike Pinkerton's construction, which plaits together the White and Native women's common understanding, Blanchet's construction recognizes that she is a stranger, an outsider who is, perhaps, to be scolded. Through her imagination and/or intuition, she eventually faces the knowledge that "I did not understand … or never knew" Native culture and that her White family members "were just visitors" in this place.[64]

Blanchet, like Pinkerton, is ambiguous when constructing Native culture and her affiliation with it. She portrays that world as romantic and gentle, and as dangerous and horrifying. Native people, in her account, are less than real both because she visits only their uninhabited villages and because she constructs Aboriginal people as limited to the past. This latter element is not especially unique in ethnography or literature. In *Time and the Other: How Anthropology Makes Its Object*, Johannes Fabian critiques the persistent and systematic tendency of ethnographers to place their referents in a time other than that of the producer of the discourse.[65] One assigns conquered populations a different space (a reserve) and a different time (the past), and this ideology has political consequences:

> Neither political Space nor political Time are natural resources. They are ideologically construed instruments of power. Most critics of imperialism are prepared to admit this with regard to Space. It has long been recognized that imperialist claims to the right of occupying "empty," under-used, underdeveloped space for the common good of mankind should be taken for what they really are: a monstrous lie perpetuated for the benefit of one part of humanity, for a few societies of that part, and, in the end, for one part of these societies, its dominant classes. But by and large, we remain under the spell of an equally mendacious fiction: that interpersonal, intergroup, indeed, international Time is "public Time" – there to be occupied, measured, and allotted by the powers that be.[66]

When Blanchet constructs Native people as the embodiment of "the Past," she refuses to allow that these very real people are her contemporaries, alive and working in the summer fishery while she is fantasizing about them from their winter villages.

Margery Fee writes that, in Canadian literature, White narrators are often gripped by a strong desire to know more about the past, and they rely on identification with Natives to pursue this desire. Fee shows that Euro-Canadians typically appropriate Native culture to move from outsider to insider, from observer to participant, from immigrant to "Native."[67] I think that Blanchet's account is remarkable because it stops and questions this easy movement from outsider to insider and because it demonstrates how the effects of a feminine discourse had changed since the turn of the century. While Scidmore and Collis use feminine discourse to construct Native women who are counterfeit women, Blanchet uses it to expose the possibility that *she* is the fake, the counterfeit in this particular world. The space for this realization is opened up for her partly because forms of boat transportation had changed by the 1920s (allowing some women closer access to Native culture), partly because the myth of the disappearing Indian made it safe for her and others to value that culture, and partly because feminine discourse itself had evolved away from a limited focus on morals, manners, and self-mockery.

Looking at women boat travellers' constructions of Native women in the context of feminine discourse is a slippery project. A great deal has been written about Victorian ideals of womanhood and about the specific discursive pressures working upon women at that time. But since the turn of the century, it has become – many of us would argue, fortunately – more and more difficult to define "feminine" and hence "feminine discourse."

In *Gender Trouble: Feminism and the Subversion of Identity*, Judith Butler shows that "the very subject of woman is no longer understood in stable or abiding terms. There is a great deal of material that not only questions the viability of 'the subject' as the ultimate candidate for representation or, indeed, liberation, but there is very little agreement after all on what it is that constitutes, or ought to constitute, the category of women."[68] In *Sea Changes*, Cora Kaplan credits feminism with developing a political language about gender that "refuses the fixed and transhistorical definitions of masculinity and femininity."[69] It becomes, then, difficult for me as a feminist to essentialize what makes twentieth-century women's travel accounts clearly "feminine" in their discourse. However, to look at these constructions of Native women and *not* understand that they are the result of gendered perceptions and gendered language is to miss a significant level of their meaning. While critics of the Victorian travel accounts of British women in Africa and Asia have found that feminine discourse afforded writers a means to transcend racism (by allowing women to connect with Natives as individuals), my reading suggests that, in the nineteenth century, this was not the case along the Northwest Coast. Here, the feminine discourse of travellers, combined with the distancing effect of local steamship travel, led to the othering of Native women as "counterfeit" ladies. Not until well into the twentieth century, as forms of marine tourism evolved (allowing longer, closer contact) and feminine discourse moved away from its limited focus on Christian morals and the cult of the home, would such connections be explored in a Northwest Coast setting.

Notes

1 The term "feminine discourse" refers not simply to women's writing but to writing that specifically illustrates the awareness or internalization of contemporaneous definitions of the "feminine."

2 Eva-Marie Kröller, "First Impressions: Rhetorical Strategies in Travel Writing by Victorian Women," *Ariel* 21, 4 (1990): 88.

3 Shirley Foster, *Across New Worlds: Nineteenth-Century Women Travellers and Their Writings* (New York: Harvester Wheatsheaf, 1990), 11.
4 Ibid., 19.
5 Ibid., 20.
6 Foster, 24. To "other" a race is to assert the superiority of one's own race by relegating "them" to a position of fixed difference. The "other" is frequently perceived as living in "the past." Travel writers can "other" a race by concentrating on "strange" smells, "filthy" villages, or "mysterious" customs; the result of such narrative strategies can be the legitimization of authoritarian and discriminatory forms of government.
7 Sara Mills, *Discourses of Difference: An Analysis of Women's Travel Writing and Colonialism* (London: Routledge, 1991), 99.
8 Mills, 98-9. Mills is certainly not alone; many feminist critics explore how gender features in the discourses of imperialism. See, for example, Deborah Gordon, "Feminism and the Critique of Colonial Discourse," *Inscriptions* 3, 4 (1988): 1-5; Nupur Chaudhuri and Margaret Strobel, eds., *Western Women and Imperialism: Complicity and Resistance* (Bloomington: Indiana University Press, 1992); and Alison Blunt, *Travel, Gender, and Imperialism: Mary Kingsley and West Africa* (New York: Guilford, 1994).
9 Mills, 87.
10 Earl Pomeroy, *In Search of the Golden West: The Tourist in Western America* (Lincoln: University of Nebraska Press, 1957), 57.
11 Significant discussions on the myth of the disappearing Indian in British Columbia include Marcia Crosby, "Construction of the Imaginary Indian," in *Vancouver Anthology: The Institutional Politics of Art*, ed. Stan Douglas (Vancouver: Talon, 1991); Robert Fulford, "The Trouble with Emily," *Canadian Art* 10, 4 (1993): 32-9; and Daniel Francis, *The Imaginary Indian: The Image of the Indian in Canadian Culture* (Vancouver: Arsenal Pulp Press, 1992).
12 Rolf Knight, *Indians at Work: An Informal History of Native Indian Labour in British Columbia, 1858-1930* (Vancouver: New Star, 1978), 143.
13 Knight, 216. In his history, Knight does not consider the significant labour of post-contact prostitution.
14 See Laura F. Klein, "Contending with Colonization: Tlingit Men and Women in Change," in *Women and Colonization: Anthropological Perspectives*, ed. Mona Etienne and Eleanor Leacock (New York: Praeger, 1980), 88-108; and Carol Cooper, "Native Women of the Northern Pacific Coast: An Historical Perspective, 1830-1900," *Journal of Canadian Studies* 27, 4 (Winter 1992/3): 44-75.
15 Cooper, 45.
16 Ibid., 49.
17 Ibid., 47.
18 Sylvia Van Kirk, *"Many Tender Ties": Women in Fur Trade Society in Western Canada, 1670-1870* (Winnipeg: Watson and Dwyer, 1980), and Jennifer Brown, *Strangers in Blood: Fur-Trade Company Families in Indian Country* (Vancouver: UBC Press, 1980).
19 See Crosby.
20 Theodore Winthrop, *The Canoe and the Saddle* (New York: Dodd, Mead and Company, 1862).
21 See Mills, 121. Mills also writes (p. 83): "women's texts are not supposed to be 'scientific' and authoritative, but rather, supposed to be amateurish. This problematic positioning of these texts often leads to the writing being prefaced with a disclaimer which denies any scientific, academic, literary or other merit; this occurs frequently with women's travel writing in the nineteenth century."
22 E. Ruhamah Scidmore, *Alaska, Its Southern Coast and the Sitkan Archipelago* (Boston: D. Lothrop and Company, 1885).
23 Scidmore, 132-3.
24 Charles Lillard, "Afterword: Listening to the Voices of the Coast," in *The Call of the Coast* (Victoria: Horsdal and Schubart, 1992), 158.
25 Scidmore, 37.
26 Ibid., 182.
27 Ibid., 3.
28 Ibid., 176-7.

29 Ibid., 233.
30 Septima Collis, *A Woman's Trip to Alaska* (New York: Cassell, 1890).
31 Collis preface (unpaginated).
32 Ibid.
33 Ibid., 193.
34 Ibid., 127.
35 Ibid., 119.
36 Ibid.
37 Chaudhuri and Strobel, 9.
38 Collis, 185 and 170, respectively.
39 Ibid., 100.
40 Ibid., 104-5. Note that her attributed worth has been increased tenfold for this portrait.
41 Scidmore, 176, and Collis, 105.
42 C. Willett Cunnington, *Feminine Attitudes in the Nineteenth Century* (London: William Heinemann, 1935), 20-1.
43 Joan Perkins, *Victorian Women* (London: Murray, 1993), 93.
44 Robin Sheets, "Womanhood," in *Victorian Britain: An Encyclopedia,* ed. Sally Mitchell (New York: Garland, 1988), 864.
45 Martha Vicinus, "Introduction: The Perfect Victorian Lady," in *Suffer and Be Still: Women in the Victorian Age* (Bloomington: Indiana University Press, 1972), xi.
46 Mills, 94.
47 Kathrene Pinkerton, *Three's a Crew* (Ganges, BC: Horsdal and Schubart, 1991 [1940]).
48 Charles Lillard, "Foreword: What the Pinks Saw," Pinkerton, *Three's a Crew*, 12.
49 Pinkerton, 150.
50 A significant woman in West Coast history, Mrs. Hunt taught Franz Boas about Native culture. Her image is still used in constructions of Native life, appearing, for example, in the recent "Chiefly Feasts" exhibit of Kwakiutl culture at the Seattle Art Museum.
51 Pinkerton, 172-3.
52 Ibid., 175.
53 Ibid., 131.
54 See Crosby and also Gordon Johnston, "An Intolerable Burden of Meaning: Native Peoples in White Fiction," in *The Native in Literature*, ed. Thomas King, Cheryl Calver, and Helen Hoy (Oakville, ON: ECW Press, 1987), 52.
55 Pinkerton, 176.
56 Ibid., 175.
57 Ibid., 136.
58 Ibid., 131.
59 M. Wylie Blanchet, *The Curve of Time* (Sidney, BC: Gray's, 1980 [1961]), 7.
60 Ibid., 66.
61 Ibid.
62 Ibid., 77.
63 Ibid., 78.
64 Ibid., 79 and 103.
65 Johannes Fabian, *Time and the Other: How Anthropology Makes Its Object* (New York: Columbia University Press, 1983), 31.
66 Ibid., 144.
67 Margery Fee, "Romantic Nationalism and the Image of Native People in Contemporary English-Canadian Literature," in *The Native in Literature*, ed. King et al., 16.
68 Judith Butler, *Gender Trouble: Feminism and the Subversion of Identity* (New York: Routledge, 1990), 1.
69 Cora Kaplan, *Sea Changes: Essays on Culture and Feminism* (London: Verso, 1986), 6.

CHAPTER 4

Irene Marryat Parlby

An "Imperial Daughter" in the Canadian West, 1896-1934

CATHERINE A. CAVANAUGH

In 1910 the English journalist Marion Dudley Cran called British womanhood to the "work of Empire" in the Canadian West, asserting that "Canada needs the woman of breed and endurance who will settle on the prairie homesteads and rear their children in the best tradition of Britain (and) ... Britain greatly needs ... a loyal leaven in her greatest colony."[1] Cran was one of many writers promoting immigration to the colonies as a solution to Britain's "surplus," or "redundant," women.[2] The number of women who responded to immigrationists' calls to populate the Canadian West remained small, but, as Susan Jackel has pointed out, middle-class British women's influence on the Prairies far exceeded what their numbers alone would allow.[3] On the nature of their influence, historians have assumed an unambiguous "imperial daughter" dedicated to reproducing the Anglo-Saxon race and preserving colonial ties to the mother country. For example, in their study of British perceptions of colonial Canada, R.G. Moyles and Doug Owram conclude that "the perpetuation of British values [in Canada] ... was in no small way attributable to ... women who emigrated as an imperial duty."[4] Barbara Roberts elaborates on this point, arguing that "as founders of British homes in Canada, as daughters of the empire and mothers of the race in social as well as in personal terms 'philanthropic emigrationists' were the real imperialists. For these women, imperialism was based on a fine enthusiasm for what is known as the English way of life."[5] Certainly by the last decades of the nineteenth century female emigration was an integral part of Britain's imperial expansion overseas. But to make the case for imperial womanhood on reductionist assumptions about women's biological and social reproduction obscures the diversity of motives and ambitions expressed by British women immigrants and forecloses the possibility that their allegiances shifted in response to their new circumstances in Canada.

This chapter examines imperial sentiment and national identity in the life of Irene Marryat Parlby – a British gentlewoman turned Prairie rancher, agrarian reformer, and Alberta legislator. It argues that, although loyalty to Empire animated Parlby's early view of herself as a woman in the West, over time she came to see herself as Canadian, and western Canadian in particular. As this study focuses on the experience of one upper-middle-class Englishwoman, the conclusions it offers are necessarily speculative. There is much more to be done in order to understand the various experiences of gentlewomen immigrants and the way class divisions interacted with nationality in shaping British women's identities as Canadians. Still, Parlby's social position and public career in politics make her an especially useful case study of British womanhood in Canada. Advantaged by race and class, she had ready access to the opportunities the West offered newcomer women as well as influence within her developing community. But in Britain's "greatest colony," race and class privilege were hedged around by gender codes.

Parlby is also a salutary example for exploring imperial sentiment. By social background and family ties she belonged to that group of nineteenth-century English men and women who colonized British possessions overseas. She was born in London on 9 January 1868, the eldest of the eight children of Ernest Marryat, an officer in the Royal Engineers, and his Anglo-Irish wife, Elizabeth Lynch Marryat. Irene spent six of her first sixteen years in Rawalpindi, a large military station in the Punjab region of northern India, where her father worked in railroad construction and, later, as manager of the Bengal and North-West Railway.[6] In 1884 Ernest Marryat retired from colonial service, returning with his family to England, where he became London manager of Egypt's Delta Light Railway and member and chairman of the board of the Bengal and North-West Railway.

In India and in England, Parlby grew up with a strong sense of connection to a far-flung community of British overseas. "Our branch of the Marryat Clan," she explained, "seemed to have been born with an inner urge to leave the Homeland, and pursue their lives in ... far off places."[7] But Marryat migrations were not sustained by a sense of adventure alone. Well established as merchant bankers in eighteenth-century London, the family enjoyed a privileged position among England's business and military ranks. But without landed wealth, Marryat sons and daughters turned to the opportunities afforded by an expanding British Empire as a means of seeking a livelihood.[8] Ernest Marryat's brother Joseph was a career officer in the Royal Navy, retiring with the rank of admiral. A third Marryat son, Arthur, entered the family's banking business to become a successful merchant trader in the British West Indies. Ernest Marryat's eldest sister, Augusta, married Henry E. Fox-Young, one-time lieutenant-governor of South Australia. A younger sister immigrated to the United States, settling in Virginia.[9] Another relative was Anglican dean of Adelaide, Australia. The most well-known family member was Captain Frederick Marryat (1702-1848), a writer of popular fiction that was based on his experiences as a career officer in the Royal Navy and his travels in North America.[10] As a young girl, Parlby was introduced to Canada through her uncle's romantic tale of the fictitious Campbell family's struggles to establish a farm in Upper Canada in the 1790s.[11] The captain's daughter, Florence Marryat, also enjoyed literary success and performed on stage in Britain and in the United States. Among her early published works is *"Gup:" Sketches of Indian Life and Character* (1868), an account of Anglo-Indian life drawn from her experiences as the young wife of an army officer.[12]

Ernest Marryat's social status and professional success provided the family with a comfortable life. Irene and her siblings grew up protected

Irene Marryat Parlby

from the harsh realities of the Indian subcontinent and industrial Britain. She recalled her childhood as "entirely happy," explaining that "we young people in our sheltered lives did not realise ... [the] evil conditions that existed in England."[13] Like other daughters of well-to-do English families, Irene was taught by governesses at home. Her education was intended above all to prepare her for marriage and respectable domesticity.[14] When she was barely out of the home classroom herself, Irene was placed in charge of her younger sisters and expected to assist her mother in the management of the large Marryat household.[15] Parlby later regretted the limited education available to her, but at the time she accepted it as normal, part of the natural order of things. "In my young days," she wrote, "girls were supposed to be content ... with ... social life and were not trained for any job or profession."[16]

In 1896, Parlby was twenty-eight years old, single, unemployed, and living with her parents at their home in suburban Limpsfield outside of London. That year a family friend, Alice Westhead, visited the Marryats on her way home to the Buffalo Lake District in the Canadian North-West.[17] During her stay, Westhead suggested that Irene join her and her companions on their return journey. The alacrity with which Irene accepted Westhead's invitation underscores her growing discontent with life as the daughter-at-home. English country life was "pleasant enough," she recalled, but offered little meaningful occupation for a young, unmarried woman.[18] Parlby's memories of her first encounter with the Canadian Prairies are coloured by a sense of adventure coupled with relief at having been released from the "aimless sort of life" she was living in England.[19] "What a wonderful land it seemed," she wrote, "and what a lucky girl I thought myself to be given the opportunity to see it."[20]

Parlby did not immigrate to Canada; rather, "the idea," as she explained it, was that she would travel and at the same time "be useful ... in helping [her] hostess on [the Westhead] ranch."[21] But in many ways she appears to be the model of the "girl of a high stamp" that imperial writers like Cran deemed ideally suited to the civilizing mission of Empire. By the standards of the day she was relatively well educated, raised to middle-class conventions of ideal femininity, and, as the daughter of a professional man with experience in colonial service, she was well versed in the imperatives of Empire. In Canada, she married a son of Devonshire gentry, Walter Parlby, and settled among a small but prominent community of Anglo-Canadians in central Alberta.[22] She assisted her husband in operating a mid-size ranch, raised a son, and gained a reputation for her English perennial borders.[23] In 1916, at age forty-eight, Parlby became president of the newly formed United Farm Women of

Alberta. Five years later she was elected to the provincial legislature as member for the Lacombe constituency when the United Farmers of Alberta (UFA) was swept into office in 1921. Her unstinting service to the agrarian reform movement earned Parlby a Cabinet position as minister without portfolio, with special responsibility to advise the new government on issues of particular concern to women. Popularly known as the "Woman's Minister," Parlby was twice re-elected and remained in the Cabinet until her retirement from public life in 1934.[24] As one of very few women to assume office in the immediate post-suffrage period, Parlby's career in government gave her influence far beyond her immediate family and community.[25] In addition to her role in government, she wrote for the western farm presses, was a popular radio personality, and, in 1930, was one of the Canadian delegates to the League of Nations in Geneva.

Parlby brought allegiances to Empire with her when she came to Canada. In 1910 she joined other loyal voices of English women overseas, urging British settlers to take up homesteads in Canada. Writing in the pages of the Calgary *Daily Herald*, she warned that by failing to heed the settlement call, the "unbounded prosperity" and economic opportunities of the West would "fall into the hands of every nationality but ours."[26] As a newcomer, Parlby clearly saw the destiny of western Canada as properly British. Moreover, in 1916 she offered the wartime example of "British motherhood" as the ideal for Canadian women to follow. Addressing the question of women's place in the nation, she urged moral motherhood, explaining that "biologically the woman not only typifies the race … she is the race … as its women are, so will the nation be. The finer, the nobler, the more spiritual our mothers, the greater our nation in the generations to come."[27] Parlby's cultural context gave her an understanding of her sex as moral guardian of the home and the state, but her view of feminine influence did not inevitably follow nationality or social background.[28] In 1928, she was equally ready to offer Canadian farm women as a worthy example for their British sisters.[29] Addressing a group of women in Inverkeilor, Scotland, she explained that, politically, "we are very advanced in Canada … [where] women as a whole … take a very great interest in political matters … and have got a great deal of good legislation passed."[30]

Parlby attributed Canadian women's political achievements to their settlement work. "In Alberta," she told her Scottish audience, "women were given equal suffrage … because men recognised that women had played a large part in opening up the country. They had … suffered all the hardships and privations of the pioneers, and ... share[d] the loneliness and the difficulties."[31] As an elected politician and government member, Parlby experienced first hand the limits of a pioneering partnership between the sexes. Indeed, she believed that the central impediment to effective cooperation was men's selfishness and "drive to dominate."[32] But their productive contribution to settlement – to the "building up" of the West – was for her proof of women's "unalterable right by eternal justice to be placed on an equality with men."[33]

Promoted by the immigration literature of the day, the perception that Canada offered unique opportunities to British women seeking independence was at least as important as was imperial sentiment as an incentive to emigration.[34] When Parlby cast emigration as a patriotic duty in 1910, she also emphasized the economic opportunities available to women in the West. She reported that, although women were barred from the "free" homesteads available to men, the West needed farmers, and, with "a comparatively small sum" of money, it was possible for a woman on her own to "set up a small poultry farm."[35] Her assessment was not unrealistic. When Parlby's parents settled in Alberta in 1905, her youngest sister, Sheila, established a poultry business. She operated the business for several years with her partner, Jean Reed, before entering Olds Agricultural College.[36] But just as seeing women as unambiguous agents of Empire is problematic, it is equally mistaken to assume that the frontier acted invariably as a liberating force in the lives of newcomer women. The West was not a priori a place where established cultural practices and beliefs were easily or readily abandoned; rather, middle-class British women measured the freedom of the West by contrast to the social and economic constraints imposed on them in England. As one contemporary expressed it, in Victorian society women were "netted by invisible rules."[37]

Although Parlby grew up in a large, closely knit family, coming to Canada freed her from parental authority and loosened the restrictions of middle-class life. Recalling her first months in the North-West she explained that "first of all I think came the exhilarating feeling of living where the world was really young, where there were no people crowding in on you with their miserable, silly little conventions and pettinesses and prejudices, and all the other barnacles people grow when they congregate together in community."[38] What she most remembered was the country's "freshness, the spaciousness, the extraordinary quietness."[39] Much of her initial enthusiasm for the West persisted throughout her life. While visiting her sisters who were living in Victoria, British Columbia, in 1918, she wrote to a friend saying that her husband Walter worried that she might want to move to the coast. But she found the life too much "like living in a little English village … moss grown and hide bound," and she longed for a "whiff of invigorating Alberta air."[40] For Parlby, migration and resettlement on the Prairie frontier seemed to disrupt old conventions, making new ones possible. As her friend and counterpart in the Women Grain Growers of Saskatchewan, Violet McNaughton, put it, on the Prairies there was "breathing space" and "work to be done."[41] In Nellie McClung's "Land of the Second Chance," Parlby learned that women were "useful and important," by which she meant economically productive and politically influential.[42]

The impact of migration and settlement was also shaped by the late Victorian debate on the changing role of women. In addition to traditional ideas about women's place in society, middle-class British women immigrants to western Canada at the turn of the twentieth century also brought a competing vision of the new "emancipated" woman.[43] Indeed, female emigration literature was written against a backdrop of mounting anxiety over the future of the British Empire, labour unrest, and the

Irene Marryat Parlby at the ranch with her son Humphrey (Hum), c. 1900

revolt of a small but influential group of women who challenged dominant conventions of marriage, work, and the family.[44] As Sandra Gilbert and Susan Gubar have pointed out, "both women and 'natives' simultaneously began to manifest frightening drives toward independence just as England's great century of empire drew to its uneasy close."[45] One contemporary observer summed up the views of many Victorians when he stated that "the two great problems of modern social life are the problem of women and the problem of labour."[46] The "woman question" was never far from Parlby's young adulthood. As an unmarried daughter living with her parents at home well beyond the age when she was expected to marry and establish a household of her own, and being without employment or prospects, her future was deeply uncertain. Confronted with this dilemma, she negotiated the disabilities imposed on her sex by coming to Canada and remaining in the West.

In contrast to England, Canada did offer Parlby new beginnings. In the West she married and managed her ranch home and family on her own – the first woman in her family to do so. She was recruited to the agrarian reform movement and, as president of the United Farm Women of Alberta, guided the organization through its critical early years, dedicating much of her time to establishing new locals, recruiting members, and promoting debate on the conditions of farm women and their children.[47] That experience taught her that "women are ... an important section of our population ... and should take a larger place in public affairs," and it pushed her into politics in the years immediately following the extension of the franchise to Alberta women in 1916.[48] One of only two women members of the Alberta legislature in 1921, she was the second woman in the British Empire to be appointed to a Cabinet position.[49] Although she "[did] not feel confident in any way," she remained in office until ill health forced her return to private life.[50]

In politics Parlby used her "influence with the [farm] men" to advance rural women's reform agenda.[51] She supported votes-for-women but did not actively participate in the provincial campaign. She was a reluctant politician, openly doubting her qualifications for public office, and in her first speech in the legislature she repudiated the usual "battledore and shuttlecock game of political debating."[52] Throughout her political career Parlby emphasized cooperation and education as the means of achieving social improvement. Partly for partisan reasons, but also out of a firm commitment to cooperation with farm men, Parlby criticized Nellie McClung, a member of the Liberal Opposition, for going too far in her attacks on the UFA government. Male newspaper reporters delighted in the occasional disputes between the "Lady Members," exaggerating their political differences. The rules of Cabinet solidarity further constrained the public relationship between Parlby and McClung. As the only woman on the government side of the house, Parlby was expected to reply to her counterpart in the Opposition benches. But their shared interest in improving the conditions of women meant that during the five years that they spent together in the provincial legislature the two were more often allies than they were opponents. Parlby explained that "Mrs. McClung and I are agreed on the same principles but we approach the principles in a different manner."[53] By character and temperament, Parlby was the more reserved, and her efforts to build up the farm women's organization convinced her that a political alliance with "socially minded" men was crucial to gaining the reforms women sought.

In western Canada, where the progressive movement was linked to the farmers' political revolt, activists combined the women's reform agenda with a new, more broadly based vision of citizenship. The idea of citizenship based on unallied cooperation as a necessary guard against narrow political self-interest underpinned the organized farmers' challenge to the political status quo.[54] The new woman voter could readily be seen as conforming to a civic ideal that transcended petty party interests on the double ground of her historical political neutrality, or disassociation from formal party politics, and her contribution to the settlement enterprise. Certainly this is how Parlby saw it, and she pressed for an authentic female authority based on this agrarian civic ideal. Explaining the difference between the relatively peaceful campaign for woman's suffrage in Canada and the more militant struggle in Britain, she asserted that social change occurred more rapidly and less violently in a country where women had shouldered the burdens of settlement equally with men. By their labour, Parlby argued, women had demonstrated their ability to take up the responsibilities of citizenship. Women's work entitled them to share in determining the future direction of the country they had helped to build. Moreover, homesteading women had learned "how to serve and work with others in a hard school." Making family and community life under the harsh conditions of the Prairie West had especially equipped farm women for leadership in the new "cooperative community" agrarian reformers envisioned.[55]

In Chapter 5, Sheila McManus points out that women's alliance with farm men gave them greater political clout, while preserving the appearance of a united farm community in the skirmishes with corporate interests in the East. It also presented risks, particularly where the aims of the two organizations conflicted, as they inevitably did. To shore up women's institutional weakness Parlby led a drive to gain constitutional independence from the men's organization and attempted to carve out an autonomous role for women on the question of social reform. With the First World War drawing to a bloody close in 1917, she asserted that women were "better co-operators" and, therefore, a necessary meliorating influence in politics. Men, she argued, had forfeited the moral authority to govern by their "fighting nature" and allegiance to the "law of force." Women represented the moral "ideal," but men "despise the emotion of the ideal ... [and] all the institutions they created carried the spirit of war and the belief in force as the ultimate principle." Her belief that "male selfishness" and "drive to dominate" was the central obstacle to social and political progress was tempered only by an equally firm conviction that prejudice and ignorance could be overcome by education.[56]

Her experience in government taught Parlby that the West was not as socially progressive on the question of women's rights as she so often argued that it was. But in advocating reforms for women she promoted the possibilities that the wide-open spaces of the Prairies seemed to represent. Like other Progressives she maintained that a new accommodation between the sexes and the classes was possible in the West, where "we set no limits to our imaginings, to our ambitions."[57] She claimed that had she settled in the East she never would have remained in Canada. It was the West that won her. Speaking to the Ottawa Women's Canadian Club in 1930 she told her audience that the difference between Westerners and Easterners was that the Prairies people's "faces are turned more to the future than to the past ... they believe ... in the God of things as they ought to be, rather than in the God of things as they are.

Members of the United Farmers' Government, with Irene Marryat Parlby centre front

Their chief interest is not in the traditions and conventions of the past so much as in a wise development of the future."[58]

The idea of the West as free, not bound by convention, underpinned popular notions of western exceptionalism and was widely adopted as a founding myth of the region. As Gerald Friesen has pointed out, such optimism was crucial to sustaining faith in the pioneering enterprise and the work of settlement.[59] It was equally important to women imagining themselves as full participants in the life of the new western provinces. It led Parlby to question arbitrary male authority and an uncritical acceptance of Victorian social conventions. Ultimately, it led her to take up the challenge of public life. Despite her reluctance to stand as a candidate for elected office she did so, in part at least, in order to resist women's exclusion from the councils of government. Once in office she used her influence to advance the social reforms farm women sought. As she was one woman among forty-eight government men, this proved to be an uphill fight. Nevertheless, Parlby continued to believe that change was possible and sought to use her influence as a representative of a Prairie government to promote tolerance and understanding not only between the sexes but also among people of widely differing cultural and ethnic backgrounds. At a time when nativism was on the rise both nationally and internationally, she criticized intolerance and opposed what she described as the "standardization of human material." Not only should Anglo-Canadians be taught to appreciate the "problems, characteristics and aspirations" of others, Canadians of all nationalities should be encouraged to value and preserve their unique heritages. She argued that "Canadianization" should not mean conforming to "what we [Anglo-Canadians] in our wisdom or lack of wisdom may consider the right pattern for everybody." Pride in her own English heritage did not make her "any worse of a Canadian" but strengthened her loyalty to her new home and, she asserted, "the same thing applies to those other nationalities."[60]

Western settlement relied on immigration, giving the Prairie provinces greater cultural diversity than the rest of the country. For western Canadians, the question of how to build social cohesion among a heterogeneous immigrant population was especially pressing. Parlby advocated education and the use of public radio to encourage respect for ethnic and cultural differences. She was not alone in promoting a vision of western Canada as more tolerant than eastern Canada. Tolerance was widely seen by Progressives as essential to mediating social differences through understanding and cooperation, and this was believed to be the basis of successful community. Just as Parlby argued that women's full inclusion in public life was necessary for the "wise development of the future," so she believed that all newcomers, regardless of social background, contributed to national well-being. She welcomed cultural diversity and the "variety … [it] bring[s] in the things of the spirit, in the genius of … different races … to enrich our national life."[61]

As progressive as Parlby's social vision was, it was not without limits. Two areas warrant particular attention: her role in the eugenics debate in Alberta in the 1920s and her silence on the status of Native peoples in the new West. The former is important because Parlby has been described as a leading advocate of the eugenics legislation introduced by the UFA government in 1928.[62] A full exploration of the eugenics debate in Alberta is beyond the scope of this chapter; however, it is important to point out that Parlby never personally endorsed the legislation.[63] Indeed, in a speech that has been cited as evidence of her support for a sterilization law, she deliberately avoided "offering any personal opinions or recommendations"; instead, responding to a request to speak to the UFA's annual meeting in 1924 on the "Mental Hygiene" debate, she presented a summary of current medical and scientific opinion, urging that delegates "draw [their] own conclusions." She seems to have been persuaded by the medical experts that "mental deficiency" presented a serious social threat, but she rejected sterilization as a practical solution; rather, she argued that reproduction was an individual responsibility and advocated public education as the most effective intervention. She also recognized that women had a special interest in the debate, since they were expected to assume primary responsibility for caring for affected children.[64]

Parlby continued to believe that as "mothers of the race" women represented the first line of defence in guaranteeing the future, but her concern centred on questions of moral uplift and mental well-being rather than on any notion of a master race. Still, as Mariana Valverde has pointed out, notions of women's personal and social "moral mothering" worked to reinforce social hierarchies by privileging some women over others on a wide-ranging basis, including race, ethnicity, social background, and physical and mental ability.[65] Parlby was convinced that most social inequality could be overcome through education, but her vision of an inclusive West remained circumscribed by race. She never contemplated full citizenship for Aboriginals as she did, in principle, for all newcomer women. In part, this reflected her position within British imperialism, what Margaret Strobel describes as European women's "double-edged position" between "complicity and resistance."[66] The contradictions implicit in Parlby's position as a member of the "superior race" and the "inferior sex" were further complicated by her status as a member of a provincial government. Even if the idea of racial equality had enjoyed wide currency at the time, it is entirely unlikely that, as a provincial minister, she would have spoken publicly on the matter, as the status of Native peoples was under federal jurisdiction. Nevertheless, her silence is significant, particularly because there was a large Native and Métis population in her home district of Buffalo Lake, which was an important winter hunting camp prior to White settlement. The Parlbys employed Natives as farm labourers and, when her legislative career took her away from home for long periods of time, Mrs. Archie Whitford, a local Métis woman, worked for the family as a home help.[67] Like the majority of non-Native Canadians at the time, Parlby accepted the assumption of White rule uncritically and benefited from the privileges that flowed from it.

The conventions that bound Parlby by race also underwrote her staunch defence of British liberal democratic institutions, which, she argued, "generations of British people have fought to develop and through which they have demanded and protected the rights of free people."[68] As a member of the UFA government she defended Henry Wise Wood's controversial theory of group government (which was based on representation by occupation) but, by 1952, she explained UFA actions by invoking the conventional view that "legislators are representatives of all the people."[69] Although she had been out of office for eighteen years, she seemed eager to explain the farmers' failure to achieve radical political reform when she went on to say that governments must "survey the good of the whole, as well as the interests of any particular group."[70] As the "woman's minister" she often felt caught between her responsibility to represent all of her constituents – men as well as women – and her equally firm belief that sex-based inequality weakened democratic institutions. In her view, the persistence of women's exclusion from the citizenship rights available to men distorted British democratic ideals, undermining those liberal institutions that continued to resist the call for justice and fairness for women. These contradictions exposed the limits of British legal models, leading Parlby to seek solutions in the example of other nations. In the debate over married women's property rights outlined by McManus, for example, she recommended that Alberta adopt the Swedish principle of joint ownership in husband and wife – legislation that she tried, but failed, to have passed by her male colleagues.[71]

It could, of course, be argued that for an English woman in Canada during the early decades of this century, the question of national identity was readily negotiated. In particular, Parlby's domestic life reflected an "English way of life." One early visitor, the Anglican missionary

Burgon Bickersteth, saw her home as a welcome sign of civilization in an otherwise untamed wilderness.[72] Locally, she was known for her English perennial gardens, which she carefully tended throughout the long drought of the 1920s and 1930s. Her Alberta homes were named "Dartmoor" and "Manadon" after her husband's family estate in Devonshire. By her own account she remained emotionally attached to England long after settling in Canada. In May 1935, while listening to George the Fifth's Empire Day radio broadcast, the geographical distance seemed, to her, to melt away. The program, "London Calling," ended with a celebration service at St. Paul's Cathedral in honour of the king's jubilee. And, Parlby wrote, "as the last fanfare of the trumpets and wild cheering of the crowds died away the radio was shut off." In the ensuing silence, she felt the "strong emotional pull of English soil, irresistible apparently, as the pull of the tides."[73] Forty years in Canada had not dulled her affection for her homeland. Rather than reflecting an uncritical acceptance of a British way of life, Parlby identified these lasting attachments as a common bond between immigrants, and thought that pride of heritage was crucial to forging new attachments to an adopted country.

But national identity was more than a simple matter of transferring old loyalties to new communities. For Parlby, western Canada, with its diverse population, represented the possibility of reinventing society as more tolerant, equitable, and fair. She believed that the political necessity of negotiating cultural and ethnic differences would produce "a democracy of hope, justice and happiness for all."[74] She did not always live up to her own ideals, but in the process of adapting to her new environment she actively promoted a view of society that was more egalitarian than either the one she had known in England or the strict hierarchy that was colonial India. As a newcomer, she believed that the future of the Dominion was inevitably linked to that of the British Empire. But in 1916 she strenuously endorsed "an international court of justice & a strong combination of peace loving powers" as "the only hope for world peace."[75] Her experience as a Canadian delegate to the League of Nations in 1930 strengthened this conviction. Upon her return to Canada, she campaigned to preserve "collective security" through international cooperation even as the concept came under increased criticism within the Western alliance.

Parlby was not a pacifist but neither was she a booster of Canadian wartime involvement. During the First World War she worried privately about her relatives and friends fighting overseas. She resisted wartime jingoism and objected to "this draping up of kids in Khaki." The thought of boy soldiers "makes me sick," she protested to Violet McNaughton, "if children have to know anything about war, they should certainly be told its horrors and responsibilities."[76] When hostilities again broke out in Europe in 1939, she tried unsuccessfully to dissuade her son Humphrey from enlisting. Like other Canadians she viewed war as a regrettable evil, largely brought about, in her opinion, by unrestrained male aggression.

During the 1930s Parlby publicly advocated severing Canada's colonial ties to Britain. Speaking to a national radio audience in 1934, she urged an independent position in international affairs. Critical of those she called "sentimental imperialists," she asserted that the time had come for Canada to chart its own course as a sovereign nation.[77] As the world drifted towards deepening confrontation at the end of the decade, she continued to champion international cooperation under the League of Nations as the best hope for peace. In the event that this should fail, she advised that Canada seek alliances with the United States and the countries of the Pacific. Just as her experience in government enabled her to appreciate the diversity of Prairie society, so her participation in the councils of Geneva enabled her to rethink Canada's national interests. She also felt especially equipped to address the question of the country's future because, she wrote, Canada was the home of her choice. "English by birth and education," she claimed Canadian citizenship "by virtue of 36 years spent on her soil and affection for her people and institutions."[78]

While Parlby came to see herself and her adopted country in new ways, the same cannot be said for her Canadian supporters and admirers. For many of them she continued to represent ideal British womanhood. For example, Alberta premier John Brownlee described her as the "best of the best that the British have to offer."[79] For R.M. Edmanson, a Calgary lawyer, her English accent alone carried the full weight of British authority. After listening to one of Parlby's radio broadcasts, he wrote complimenting her diction and the "quality of her voice."[80] Another correspondent, Harold W. Riley, welcomed the example she set for those who "look upon the pioneers as a 'bunch of mossbacks' devoid of culture and appreciation of the finer things of life."[81] Zella Spencer recalled that as head of the farm women's organization "the gracious, dignified Mrs. Parlby" commanded "a greater respect" for rural women and that, as a result, "we [felt] an added respect for ourselves."[82] These comments suggest that public office was, in part at least, a social reward for being British and, more, a British gentlewoman. It is ironic that, as a result of her political activism and career in government, Parlby achieved a broader, more comprehensive sense of herself as a woman but that her Canadian public never did, imposing on her the stereotypical image of "imperial daughter." From this perspective, her public persona is more revealing of the country, or a segment of it, than it is of the woman herself.

This is not to suggest that Parlby can be seen as outside of the imperial processes that ensured a minority of Anglo-Canadians hegemony in western Canada. Indeed, by ethnicity, class, and social background she was so thoroughly included in colonialism as to be seen as the embodiment of Anglo Canada's highest moral standard. The extent to which her nationality and loyalty to Empire were transformable was inextricably linked to dominant cultural stereotypes of respectable femininity, making her sex inescapable. Bound by these conventions, her own view of women's place in society changed remarkably little despite her long career in public life and the challenge to male authority that it inevitably represented. Parlby advocated a "real" equality for women, but her understanding of the terms of that equality continued to be constrained by what Denise Riley has described as "the weight of characterisation" of the category "women."[83] The idea of a *human* equality lay in the future, and in 1952 she cautioned the women of Alberta to remember that they were the "guardians of the intangibles of life[;] they may not be called upon to play any spectacular part, but their quiet influence in maintaining the finer attitudes toward life can, and does, influence human society."[84] Her faith in women's moral influence prevented Parlby from directly confronting the question of power in her own life. When "feminine influence" failed, as it inevitably did, she turned doubt inward, admitting that she often felt uncertain about herself as a politician, as though she was "on trial" in a man's world.[85] And so she was. The social conventions that privileged her by class and race, giving her entry into male councils, also insisted on her position as a "woman," with the result that her being minister without portfolio was more symbolic than real. As a minister of the Crown, she had influence at the table but was denied the power to determine government policy or programs.

Parlby fits the image of a loyal daughter of Empire only if we assume that she faithfully conformed to a male-defined ideal. The evidence presented here suggests a much more ambiguous reality. The problem is that the image itself is a distorted one. Officially, imperialism was deemed to be an exclusively male enterprise. Early colonial administrators saw women as destructive of men's aims.[86] When women were grafted onto the imperial enterprise in the 1880s they were included on a basis similar to that of patriotic British manhood but were assigned to the cultural, or social, side of conquest.[87] Advocates of female emigration, both men and women, argued that the colonies needed women of high moral character and cultural refinement to maintain racial and cultural purity in the colonies. But women's "civilizing mission" was rarely seen as active. Whether in colonies of occupation or of settlement, "civilizing femininity" was remarkable for its assumed passivity. As Susan Armitage has pointed out for the American West, as civilizing agents, "women did not have to *do* anything, their presence alone was seen as sufficient to tame men, to make them think of polite behaviours and building civilized institutions."[88] By combining the idea of Empire and Victorian gender imperatives, the concept of civilizing womanhood served both imperial and patriarchal goals.

Nor can we rely on women's emigration as a measure of their commitment to imperial duty. The need for women to emigrate arose out of a perception of a demographic imbalance between the sexes in Britain and the real limits of employment opportunities available to single women. Fuelled by imperial enthusiasm and alarm over the social threat of an "excess" number of women in Britain, female emigration societies urged resettlement in the colonies as both a social duty and a guard against female impoverishment at home.[89] The demographic crisis in England was never as serious as contemporaries thought, nor did single middle-class women respond to the call of Empire in the large numbers emigration societies hoped to attract. Even at the height of imperial fervour at the end of the nineteenth century, women who did emigrate were most likely to do so for economic reasons. The majority who came to Canada were daughters of working-class families in search of employment. But the economic and social upheavals that marked late nineteenth- and early twentieth-century Britain meant that they were joined by a growing number of upper- and middle-class women who also faced the urgent necessity of earning a living. As was the case in other colonial settings, structural sex-based inequalities in the Prairie economy worked against emigrationists' attempts to square the circle of middle-class women's employment. With few exceptions, in Canada economic opportunities for women fell far short of the dream of independence.[90] Still, emigrators persisted. Aware of the dilemma that confronted unemployed, unmarried women in Britain, Marion Cran's advice from Canada echoed Parlby's view of the economic opportunities available to women in the West. Cran was unequivocal: "if I had to earn my living," she concluded, "I would go to Canada ... [t]here is money to be made there, at farming and horticulture; at domestic service ... [and] at maternity nursing; and there are happy homes ahead for many."[91]

This chapter suggests that middle-class British women did not migrate, marry, or take up new occupations in western Canada out of loyalty to the imperatives of patriarchal imperialism; rather, they used the opportunities of Empire to negotiate the disabilities imposed on their sex in Britain. In the process, the fortunate created new possibilities for themselves as ranchers, farmers, telegraph and telephone operators, newspaper reporters, secretaries, doctors, nurses, home-helps, midwives, schoolteachers, community leaders, and politicians. What remains to be understood is the ways in which their identities as women were limited and broadened under their changed circumstances. For example, Parlby's "genteel" reputation – one Edmonton newspaper described her as "aristocratic" – was doubtless created in part to attract people and investment capital by countering the view of the West as wild and uncivilized.[92] Her much promoted status as the second woman in the British Empire to be appointed to a Cabinet post did more to advance the image of the UFA as politically progressive than it did to give her political power or advance women's freedoms in general. To the extent that Parlby conformed to her public image, she gained influence but was barred from the full measure of authority for her sex that she sought in public life. Only by moving beyond the stereotypical image of "imperial daughter" can historians begin to accurately assess the role of British women in promoting, maintaining, and resisting imperialism. The image itself prevents us from understanding the ways in which British women immigrants were both bound and free as they adapted to their new circumstances in Canada.

Notes

1 Marion Cran, *A Woman in Canada* (Toronto: Musson, 1910), 14-5.

2 For a good summary of this debate see Judith Worsnop, "A Reevaluation of the Problem of Surplus Women in Nineteenth-Century England," *Women's Studies International Forum* 13, 1-2 (1990): 21-31. On the unmarried, or "odd," woman as a social problem, see Elaine Showalter, *Sexual Anarchy: Gender and Culture at the Fin de Siècle* (London: Penguin, 1990), 19-37. On female emigration, see James Hammerton, *Emigrant Gentlewomen: Genteel and Female Emigration, 1861-1914* (London: Croom Helm, 1979); and James Hammerton, "Feminism and Female Emigration, 1861-1886," in *A Widening Sphere*, ed. Martha Vicinus (Bloomington: Indiana University Press, 1977), 3-71. For a discussion of emigrationists' contradictory aims, see Julia Bush, "'The Right Sort of Woman': Female Emigrators and Emigration to the British Empire, 1890-1910," *Women's History Review* 3, 3 (1994): 385-409.

3 Susan Jackel, ed., *A Flannel Shirt and Liberty: British Emigrant Gentlewomen in the Canadian West, 1880-1914* (Vancouver: UBC Press, 1982).

4 R.G. Moyles and Doug Owram, *Imperial Dreams and Colonial Realities* (Toronto: University of Toronto Press, 1988): 210-1.

5 Barbara Roberts, "A Work of Empire: Canadian Reformers and British Female Emigration," in *A Not Unreasonable Claim*, ed. Linda Kealey (Toronto: Women's Press, 1979), 200.

6 Portions of this chapter appear in my PhD dissertation, "'In Search of a Useful Life': Irene Marryat Parlby, 1868-1965" (University of Alberta, 1994). The details of Parlby's early life that appear here rely on two earlier biographies: Clare Mary McKinlay's "The Honourable Irene Parlby" (MA thesis, University of Alberta, 1953); and Barbara Villy Cormack's *Perennials and Politics* (Sherwood Park, AB: n.p., c. 1968). They also rely on the diary of Parlby's

grandfather, Charles Marryat, and Parlby's own autobiographical notes, "My Experience" (c. 1953) and "Rambling Memories" (c. 1963), which appear in her personal papers (in possession of the family at the time of writing and currently on deposit at the Glenbow Museum and Archives in Calgary, Alberta). My quotes from Parlby's letters to Violet McNaughton are from McNaughton's Personal Papers, which are on deposit at the Saskatchewan Archives Board (SAB) in Saskatoon, file numbers A1. McNaughton, Violet, and D.54, Parlby, Irene.

7 Irene Marryat Parlby, "Rambling Memories," Parlby's personal papers.

8 Joseph Marryat (1757-1824) was head of the family bank and sat in the British House of Commons as the independent member for Horsham from 1808 to 1810 and for Sandwich from 1812 to 1824. Parlby's paternal grandfather was a member of Marryat, Kaye, Price and Company (a bank) until it failed in 1866, two years before Irene was born.

9 A member of the Virginia Marryats, Nora Trench visited the Parlby ranch in 1901. Her diary, which is among Parlby's personal papers, provides an intimate look at the family's life in Alberta, detailing the women's domestic work and family entertainments, including regular polo matches, gymkhanas, and, Parlby's personal favourite, "amateur theatricals."

10 Marryat's most popular books were *Peter Simple* (1833-4) and *Mr. Midshipman Easy* (1836). For further details, see Ira B. Nadel and William E. Fredeman, eds., *Dictionary of Literary Biography*, vol. 21 (Detroit: Bruccoli Clark, 1983): 222-7.

11 Captain Frederick Marryat, *The Settlers in Canada* (London and Glasgow: Collins, 1844).

12 Florence Marryat was the youngest of eleven children. She wrote her first novel, *Love's Conflict* (1865), while nursing her children who were sick with scarlet fever. She was a prolific writer, and her novels were translated into several languages. She also performed on stage as an operatic singer, lecturer, and light entertainer in Britain and in the United States. Her performances included a comic lecture entitled "Women of the Future or What Shall We do Without Men." Towards the end of her career Marryat managed a school of journalism. She was married twice and had eight children. See Janet Todd, ed., *British Women Writers* (New York: Unger, 1989).

13 Irene Marryat Parlby, "My Experiences," Parlby's personal papers.

14 On Victorian girlhood, see Joan N. Burstyn, *Victorian Education and the Ideal of Womanhood* (London: Croom Helm, 1980); Carol Dyhouse, *Girls Growing Up in Late Victorian and Edwardian England* (London: Routledge and Kegan Paul, 1981); Deborah Gorham, *The Victorian Girl and the Feminine Ideal* (London: Croom Helm, 1982); and M. Jeanne Peterson, *Family, Love and Work in the Lives of Victorian Gentlewomen* (Bloomington and Indianapolis: Indiana University Press, 1989).

15 Parlby's eldest brother, Hugh Dennis, had entered the Royal Navy at age thirteen, as was customary at the time. In addition to Irene, the Marryat children living at home included her sisters Norah Isabel (who was next to Irene in age), Ruth, and Gladys. Two younger brothers, John Rudolph and Ulric Graham, were born at Limpsfield in the late 1880s, followed by Irene's youngest sister, Dorothy Sheila, who was born in 1890. A stepsister, Charlotte, the only child of Elizabeth Marryat's first marriage, died the year Irene was born. The Marryats' first son, born in Bombay in 1869, also died in childhood. The household also included the family's nanny and occasional governesses. Once Parlby was old enough to assume responsibility for teaching her younger sisters, the family was relieved of the expense of a governess. As was typical at the time, Irene's brothers went out to school. Dyhouse points out that this sex difference in educational opportunity was an important early lesson in Victorian femininity.

16 Parlby, "My Experiences."

17 Buffalo Lake is located just east of present-day Lacombe, Alberta. One of the early settlers in the district, Charles Westhead, took up a military homestead in 1892 and raised saddle horses and polo ponies for sale in England. According to the surveyor's report, he and his partner Rowe "had done a great deal of fencing and were actively engaged in ranching" as early as 1893. The Westhead home was "a large log house," estimated to have cost $2,500 to build. It was here that Parlby spent her first ten months in Canada. See *The Land of the Lakes* (Lamberton Historical Society, 1974), 48.

18 Aware of his daughter's discontent, Ernest Marryat readily agreed to allow Irene to go to Canada. See "Rambling Memories," Parlby's personal papers.

19 Parlby, "My Experiences."
20 Parlby, "Rambling Memories."
21 Ibid.
22 Walter was thirty-five years old when he and Irene married. He was the thirteenth youngest son of the Reverend John Hall Parlby and an Oxford graduate with a degree in classics. He arrived in the North-West in 1890 and initially ranched with his brother Edward before establishing his own homestead just north of Edward's on the shores of Parlby Lake, named for the brothers. Today the lake is a bird sanctuary on the outskirts of Alix.
23 Parlby returned to England to give birth to her son and only child Humphrey, who was born on 15 March 1899. During her first election campaign in 1921 Parlby came under severe attack by her Liberal opponent for this decision. He accused her of disloyalty, charging that she had chosen to have her child in England because she did not want him to be "called Canadian." See Parlby to McNaughton, 22 July 1921.
24 The election of 1921 was a landslide victory for the UFA, who unseated the governing Liberals. It was a hard-fought victory for Parlby, and it was marked by anti-British, anti-woman sentiments that left her feeling as though she had been through "rivers of mud and could never be clean again or trust anyone again." See Parlby to MacNaughton, 22 July 1921. She won her Lacombe seat by a comfortable margin in 1926 but narrowly in 1930. Ill health kept her away from the legislature throughout the latter part of that year and in the early months of 1931. Chronic illness was an important factor in her decision not to seek re-election in 1935.
25 On women in politics in the 1920s and 1930s see Sylvia Bashevkin, "Independence Versus Partisanship: Dilemas in the Political History of Women in English Canada," in *Rethinking Canada: The Promise of Women's History*, ed. Veronica Strong-Boag and Anita Clair Fellman, 2nd ed. (Toronto: Copp Clark Pitman, 1986), 246-75; Connie Carter and Eileen Daoust, "From Home to House: Women in the B.C. Legislature," in *Not Just Pin Money: Selected Essays on the History of Women's Work in British Columbia*, ed. Barbara K. Latham and Roberta J. Pazdro (Victoria: Camosun College, 1984), 389-405; Mary Kinnear, "Post-Suffrage Prairie Politics: Women Candidates in Winnipeg Municipal Elections, 1918-1938," *Prairie Forum* 16, 1 (Spring 1991): 41-58; Nanci Langford, "'All That Glitters'": The Political Apprenticeship of Alberta Women, 1916-1930," in *Standing on New Ground*, ed. Catherine A. Cavanaugh and Randi R. Warne (Edmonton: University of Alberta Press, 1993), 71-85; Patricia Roome, "Amelia Turner and Calgary Labour Women, 1919-1935," in *Beyond the Vote: Canadian Women and Politics*, ed. Linda Kealey and Joan Sangster (Toronto: University of Toronto Press, 1989), 89-117; Joan Sangster, *Dreams of Equality* (Toronto: McClelland and Stewart, 1989); and Georgina M. Taylor, "'The Women ... Shall Help to Lead the Way': Saskatchewan CCF-NDP Women Candidates in Provincial and Federal Elections, 1934-1965," in *"Building the Co-operative Commonwealth": Essays on the Democratic Socialist Tradition in Canada*, ed. J. William Drennan (Regina: Canadian Plains Research Centre, University of Regina, 1984), 141-60.
26 Irene Marryat Parlby, "Canada – The Hope of the World: An English Lady's Opinion of the Opportunities of the West," *Calgary Daily Herald*, June 1910.
27 Irene Marryat Parlby, "Awhile Ago – And Today!" Parlby's personal papers.
28 Parlby believed that the greater difference was between "men" and "women" and that each sex constituted a unified category with separate interests and responsibilities. For a further discussion of the political implications of the idea of a "unity of women," see Judith A. Allen's introduction to *Rose Scott: Vision and Revision in Feminism* (Oxford and Melbourne: Oxford University Press, 1994), especially 1-23.
29 This is not to overstate the inclusivity of Parlby's vision, which was bound by the class and racial conventions of her day. The point here is only that her view of exemplary womanhood had clearly shifted when compared to her earlier comments.
30 "Hon. Irene Parlby Visiting Scotland Tells of Women's Political Status," *Edmonton Journal*, 10 September 1928. It should also be noted that the question of women's political status was especially alive in Canada at the time. That year the Privy Council in London ruled that women were persons under the British North American Act and eligible for appointment to the Senate. Parlby was a co-appellant in the action, known as the "Persons Case,"

which marks the entry of Canadian women into the constitutional life of the nation. See Olive Stone, "Canadian women as Legal Persons," *Alberta Law Review* 17, 2 (1979): 357-82.

31 Ibid.

32 Irene Marryat Parlby, "The Great Adventure," Parlby's personal papers. See also Catherine A. Cavanaugh, "The Limitations of the Pioneering Partnership: The Alberta Campaign for Homestead Dower, 1905-25," *Canadian Historical Review*, 74, 2 (1993): 198-225.

33 Irene Marryat Parlby, "The Position of Women in Canada," notes from radio broadcast, Edmonton, CJCA, 1938, Parlby's personal papers.

34 Bush makes the point that appropriate colonial employment for British "ladies" was contested at the time, but for emigrationists it "remained an important end in itself." See Bush, "'The Right Sort of Woman,'" 390.

35 Parlby, "Canada – The Hope of the World."

36 Sheila immigrated to Alberta with her parents and younger brothers in 1905. After graduating from Olds Agricultural College she earned a degree in agriculture from the University of Alberta in 1923. She later worked in radio broadcasting and as a producer for the Canadian Broadcasting Corporation in Winnipeg before she and Reed retired to Victoria, British Columbia. Little is known of Jean Reed, who came to Canada with the Marryats. She is thought to have been active in the suffrage movement in Britain and was a founding member of the Women's Auxiliary of the United Farm Women of Alberta (1915). Parlby's sister Gladys came to Canada in 1899 to help with the infant Humphrey. Norah Marryat McDonnell settled in the Buffalo Lake District with her husband and children in 1901 and later moved to British Columbia. For one woman's account of farming on the Prairies, see Georgina Binnie-Clark, *Wheat and Woman*, Susan Jackel, introduction (Toronto: University of Toronto Press, 1979 [1914]).

37 Quoted in Carol Dyhouse, *Feminism and the Family in England, 1880-1939* (Oxford: Basil Blackwell, 1989), 16.

38 Irene Marryat Parlby, "The Milestones of My Life," *Canadian Magazine*, June 1928.

39 Irene Marryat Parlby, "I Shall Never Forget," notes for CJCA radio broadcast, Edmonton, February 1938, Parlby's personal papers.

40 Parlby to McNaughton, 12 June 1918.

41 Georgina Taylor, "A Personal Tragedy Shapes the Future," *Western Producer*, 10 January 1991, 10.

42 Parlby, "The Milestones of My Life."

43 The literature on the changing role of women in Victorian and Edwardian England is extensive, but see, in particular, J.F.C. Harrison, *Late Victorian Britain, 1875-1901* (London: Fontana, 1990), 157-83; Jill Liddington and Jill Norris, *One Hand Tied Behind Us* (London: Virago, 1978); David Rubinstein, *Before the Suffragettes: Women's Emancipation in the 1890s* (London: Harvester, 1986); Martha Vicinus, *Independent Women: Work and Community for Single Women, 1850-1020* (Chicago and London: University of Chicago Press, 1985); and Martha Vicinus, ed., *A Widening Sphere* (Bloomington: Indiana University Press, 1977).

44 The literature on the end of Empire is extensive, but for the idea of the Victorian age as an age of anxiety, see Walter E. Houghton, *The Victorian Frame of Mind, 1830-1870* (New Haven and London: Yale University Press, 1957). Harrison's *Late Victorian Britain* provides a good overall summary for the period. For a discussion of the sexual manifestations of the crisis of imperialism see Showalter, *Sexual Anarchy*.

45 Sandra M. Gilbert and Susan Gubar, *No Man's Land: The Place of the Woman Writer in the Twentieth Century,* vol. 2, *Sexchanges* (New Haven and London: Yale University Press, 1989), 36.

46 Karl Pearson, "Woman and Labour," *Fortnightly Review*, May 1894, quoted in Showalter, *Sexual Anarchy*, 7.

47 As UFWA president, Parlby was responsible for her own expenses. Under her leadership membership in the organization grew from 745 to just under 4,000 in 293 locals scattered across the province. At its peak in 1921, women represented about 13 percent of the total membership of the farmers' organization. See UFA "Annual Report" (1935): 37.

48 Parlby, "Awhile Ago – And Today."

49 Parlby's election in 1921 had fuelled speculation that she would be appointed minister of health, so being appointed minister without portfolio was a disappointment. While she was a member of the inner Cabinet, she did not have a department, budget, or salary of her own. A special order-in-council did provide her with compensation comparable to that available to other ministers, but it was made conditional on her attending Cabinet and other government meetings.

50 Parlby to McNaughton, 26 September 1918.

51 Parlby, "Awhile Ago – And Today."

52 Edmonton *Bulletin*, 10 February 1922.

53 Provincial Archives of Alberta, *Scrapbook Hansard*, 24 February 1923, 12-3. In her autobiography McClung also states that, despite party differences, as members of the legislature she and Parlby "united our efforts when questions relating to women were under discussion." See Nellie McClung, *The Stream Runs Fast* (Toronto: Thomas Allen, 1945), 175.

54 Jeffrey M. Taylor, "Dominant and Popular Ideologies in the Making of Rural Manitobans, 1890-1925" (PhD thesis, University of Manitoba, 1988), especially 310-37; Alvin Finkel, "Populism and Gender: The UFA and Social Credit Experiences," *Journal of Canadian Studies* 27, 4 (Winter 1992/3): 76-97.

55 Parlby, "The Great Adventure."

56 Ibid. For this interpretation of the nature of sex difference Parlby borrowed directly from Benjamin Kidd, *The Science of Power* (London: Methuen, 1918), echoing the pseudo-scientific opinion of the day. See Peter Gay, *The Cultivation of Hatred* (New York and London: Norton, 1993).

57 Parlby, "Canada – The Hope of the World."

58 Irene Marryat Parlby, "When East and West Meet," notes on an address to the Women's Canadian Club, Ottawa, 1930, Parlby's personal papers.

59 Gerald Friesen, *The Canadian Prairies: A History* (Toronto: University of Toronto Press, 1984), 304.

60 Parlby, "When East and West Meet."

61 Ibid.

62 See Timothy Christian, "The Mentally Ill and Human Rights in Alberta: A Study of the Alberta Sterilization Act," University of Alberta Faculty of Law, 1973.

63 On western Canadian Nativism, see Howard Palmer, "Strangers and Stereotypes: The Rise of Nativism, 1880-1920," in *The Prairie West*, ed. Douglas Francis and Howard Palmer, (Edmonton: Pica Pica, 1985), 309-33. For a discussion of the national debate, see Angus McLaren, *Our Own Master Race: Eugenics in Canada, 1885-1945* (Toronto: McClelland and Stewart, 1990).

64 UFA Annual Report, 1924.

65 Mariana Valverde, "'When the Mother of the Race Is Free': Race, Reproduction, and Sexuality in First-Wave Feminism," in *Gender Conflicts*, ed. Franca Iacovetta and Mariana Valverde (Toronto: University of Toronto Press, 1992), 20.

66 Margaret Strobel, *European Women and the Second British Empire* (Bloomington and Indianapolis: Indiana University Press, 1991), xi.

67 Whitford was a member of the Todd family of Buffalo Lake. She is described by Parlby's daughter-in-law Beatrice as "quietly dignified and unobtrusive ... a careful worker and a great comfort in her dependability." Her husband, Archie Whitford, the son of a Scottish father and Indian mother, was employed as a ranch hand by Ulrich Marryat. The Whitfords and their five children lived on the Marryat ranch. See *Pioneers and Progress* (Alix Clive Historical Club, 1974), 210.

68 Irene Marryat Parlby, notes from a campaign speech, c. 1940, Parlby's personal papers.

69 Wood's theory of "group government" was a contentious issue, and it divided the UFA from other agrarian political organizations. It aimed at breaking party dominance in Canadian politics by organizing representation on the basis of "occupational groups." For a more detailed discussion of Wood's ideas, see William Kirby Rolph, *Henry Wise Wood of Alberta* (Toronto: University of Toronto Press, 1950).

70 Irene Marryat Parlby, "On the Farm Front," notes for radio broadcast, CFCN, Calgary, March 1952, Parlby's personal papers.

71 Parlby's matrimonial property bill anticipated joint ownership in husband and wife. See Cavanaugh, "Women's Movement in Alberta."

72 J. Burgon Bickersteth, *The Land of Open Doors* (Toronto: University of Toronto Press, 1976 [1914]), described the ranch as "highly civilized ... quite different from anything I have as yet had the opportunity of seeing in the West ... not unlike ... the big stations in Australia," 233.

73 Parlby, "Forty Years Back," 1935, Parlby's personal papers.

74 Parlby, "The Great Adventure," *The Grain Growers Guide*, 1 April 1927, 47.

75 Parlby to McNaughton, 19 September 1916.

76 Ibid.

77 Irene Marryat Parlby, "Canada Must Choose Her Policy Among Nations," *Edmonton Journal*, 19 February 1934.

78 Ibid.

79 *Edmonton Journal*, 15 August 1930.

80 Edmanson to Parlby, March 1938, Parlby's personal papers.

81 Riley to Parlby, 19 February 1938, Parlby's personal papers.

82 A. Zella Spencer, "Mrs. Parlby's Appointment to League of Nations Assembly," *UFA*, September 1930.

83 Denise Riley, *"Am I That Name? Feminism and the Category of "Women" in History* (Minneapolis: University of Minnesota Press, 1988), 16.

84 Irene Marryat Parlby, "On the Farm Front," March 1952, Parlby's personal papers.

85 Irene Marryat Parlby, "What Business Have Women In Politics," Parlby's personal papers.

86 Margaret Strobel, "Gender and Race in the Nineteenth- and Twentieth-Century British Empire," in *Becoming Visible: Women in European History*, ed. Renate Bridenthal et al. (Boston: Houghton Mifflin, 1987), 377, summarizes the "myth of the destructive female" as the belief that "vulnerable European women provoked the sexual appetites of indigenous men, while as wives they replaced indigenous concubines (from whom male administrators had previously learned much about society and culture) and drew the attention of the men away from their official responsibilities."

87 For a further discussion of sex and gender in imperialism see, in particular, Ann Laura Stoler, "Carnal Knowledge and Imperial Power, Gender Race, and Morality in Colonial Asia," in *Gender at the Crossroads of Knowledge: Feminist Anthropology in the Postmodern Era*, ed. Micaela di Leonardo (Berkeley: University of California Press, 1991), 51-101; the essays in Nupur Chaudhuri and Margaret Strobel, eds., *Western Women and Imperialism: Complicity and Resistance* (Bloomington: Indiana University Press, 1992); and Jane Haggis, "Gendering Colonialism or Colonising Gender? Recent Women's Studies Approaches to White Women and the History of British Colonialism," *Women's Studies International Forum* 13, 1/2 (1990): 105-15.

88 Susan Armitage, "Through Women's Eyes: A New View of the West," in *The Women's West*, ed. Susan Armitage and Elizabeth Jameson (Norman: University of Oklahoma Press, 1987), 13.

89 For a further discussion of the "Employment or Marriage" debate within the female immigration societies, see Bush, "'The Right Sort of Woman,'" 388-94.

90 As Bush notes, this contradiction applied to all colonial economies. See ibid., 391.

91 Cran, *A Woman in Canada*, 282-3.

92 "Hon. Irene Parlby Visiting Scotland."

CHAPTER 5

Gender(ed) Tensions in the Work and Politics of Alberta Farm Women, 1905-29

SHEILA MCMANUS

The White, English-speaking women who settled Alberta's farms before 1929 came from the United States, England, and other parts of Canada. Some had previous farming experience, but many of them were confronting new and often very different living conditions from those they had left behind. These women brought with them conceptions of femininity, of what it meant to be a "woman," that were generally very like those of the places they had left behind. The varied responses of farm women to their work on North America's frontier farms has been the focus of much Canadian and American scholarship; this chapter examines the experiences of White, English-speaking women who settled in southern Alberta in the early twentieth century.[1]

For many of these women the experiences and challenges of indoor and outdoor farm work, reproductive and market-oriented, were a significant deviation from the gender constructions adhered to by "respectable" White, English-speaking women in more urban settings. Some women were able to accommodate this work to their construction of gender, while others continued to claim and preserve feminine domestic privilege.[2] These tensions underlying many farm women's understanding and use of gender would be played out in the political activism of the United Farm Women of Alberta (UFWA), particularly surrounding its demands for changes to married women's property law.

Utilizing women's diaries, the women's pages of farm newspapers, and the records of the UFWA, I examine the construction and meaning of gender in the lives of southern Alberta's White, English-speaking farm women, its impact on the division and valuing of farm work, and the role it played in their politics. By considering the gap between women's descriptions of their work in their diaries and memoirs, and the public representation of that work in the women's pages of the agricultural press, I will explore the difficulties women faced winning legal and political recognition for that work. In so doing, I use a gender analysis to bridge the gap between the histories of farm women's labour and their political activism.

Married, White, English-speaking farm women displayed a clear understanding of what a "woman" was supposed to be: preoccupied solely with the domestic concerns of her home and family; clean, neat, and modestly dressed; and an efficient household manager. Maintaining such high standards for womanhood might have seemed to be a daunting task in the overwhelmingly masculine environment of homesteading, but these women already had the advantage of being at the top of racial and ethnic hierarchies and so were in the best position to define, or attempt to redefine, what the gender of a "woman" was supposed to be. The boundaries of appropriate femininity were also collectively and strictly enforced by other White women in the area.

A key component of this femininity was a woman's ability to use whatever resources were at hand, scarce or ample, to create a more pleasant living environment for herself and her family. It mattered very much that "home" move beyond a merely functional use of space and become a comfortable and attractive place, even on the edges of recent White settlement. It would not have been easy to make a "soddie" aesthetically appealing, but many women tried hard to do just that. The White, English-speaking farm wife was usually the one person, even in a large family, who spent the majority of her time indoors, so the energy she devoted to making it "homelike" as well as comfortable and efficient had an immediate effect on her working environment. A desire to reproduce whatever sense of the home she had left behind also gave a woman a familiar base from which to face other challenges, and it could be, as historian Julie Roy Jeffrey has claimed, "an unconscious way of asserting female power and reassuring women of their sexual identity."[3] Contrary to any fears that the harsh conditions of homesteading might coarsen women, Jeffrey observes that "'Home,' crude and impermanent though it might be, received the kind of attention which would have pleased the proponents of domesticity."[4]

Kathleen Strange's family members, for example, started their lives in Alberta in 1920 with a tiny wooden shack as living space and two granaries for bedrooms. Strange decided to fix up the shack while waiting for their new two-storey lumber house to be built, "to make some changes and improvements that would render our living conditions there more practicable and pleasant." She used fabric to brighten the interior, added a tablecloth, a few pictures, "a vase or two of flowers," and "the place began to take on a new air. Of course, it was far from being the kind of home we had dreamed of, but at least it had now acquired some of our own personality and that gave it a homelike atmosphere."[5] Since it was Kathleen Strange's time, effort, and tastes that were involved, it was in fact her own personality that was being expressed and inscribed. The conflation of her self with her family and home was neither accidental nor uncommon.

Sarah Roberts also set about getting her household in order as soon as possible after the house was built on her family's homestead in 1906. Her husband built some shelves "so that I could have a place for dishes and other things which were scattered around wherever I could find a place for them. We lived in terrible confusion for five or six weeks, and until some of these things were done I couldn't bring order out of chaos, while the dust and dirt were simply terrible. I thought at times that I would just go crazy, but I've tried to be as patient as possible, for I knew that Papa and the boys were bringing things to pass as fast as they could."

Bringing order out of chaos meant, for her, an ongoing effort to keep the outside world of dirt and work clothes out of the house. She noted: "The hay on the ground floor was my worst trial, for it disintegrated into a fine powder, and I can never tell how I longed for a floor. One day in December I returned from the store with a broom, for which I had no earthly use. When Papa asked why I had bought it, I replied, 'For the moral effect. I am going to hang it on the wall and look at it often, and keep hoping that some day, I'll be able to sweep my floor with it.'"[6]

These quotes highlight Roberts's combination of womanly domesticity, cleanliness, and patience in her efforts to create and maintain a domestic space. During a subsequent winter, when her husband was finishing the house and making various improvements, she told him that she wanted a corner "in which I can express myself." She eventually got what she asked for, "as I usually did when it was at all possible."[7] Completely unquestioned was the assumption that a "cosy corner" within the home was the most, if not the only, appropriate place for a woman to express her personality. As she was in her fifties, Sarah spent almost all of her time indoors, but, within the homesteading ethos of the day, women were so strongly identified with hearth and home that, had she requested any other personal space (in the barn, for example), her request would likely have been viewed less favourably.

In a telling expression of her control over the domestic space, Sarah "decreed" that there would be an invisible line dividing their one main room, which measured approximately fourteen by eighteen feet, in half. The desired result of this partly humorous, partly serious, decree was to separate this one room into a "respectable" side and a "rough" side: "On the south side of the line would be our sitting room, drawing room, parlor, library and reception room, and on the north side would be the kitchen and dining room. I ruled that they must never cross the line into the south room while wearing their out-door garments, and moreover, that if they took them off they must leave them on the north side of the line." She noted that this "edict ... at first met with some opposition from Papa and the boys, who thought it violated their privileges," but they did comply. Their compliance meant that the one room could be imaginatively divided into a "respectable," "feminine" side and a "rough," "masculine" side, demarcated by the men's outdoor work clothes.[8]

When they visited another couple in the area on New Year's Day 1909, Roberts was impressed by the other woman's interior decorating. She wrote: "They had their house fixed up so much more cosily than it had been. Besides the improvements they had made in the house itself, Mrs. Preston had brought a number of decorations and accessories from Winnipeg, where she had gone for a visit; things that don't mean much to a man but which are dear to a woman's heart. These, with a canary and blooming plants, make it seem more homelike than any house I had been in since I came to Alberta."[9] As with the case of Kathleen Strange's conflation of herself and her home, here Roberts equates Mrs. Preston with the "they" who had "fixed up" their home. It was Mrs. Preston's effort, the small decorations and accessories, that signified homelike comfort. Within the gender system of the day men were expected to be content with mere functionalism but women were not.

Kathleen Strange, like Sarah Roberts, had to gain male compliance with her domestic changes: she had to "persuade" the men to hang their clothes on curtained pegs instead of bare nails. Although Roberts issued edicts and Strange had to persuade, in both situations the women had to get the men to adhere to certain unspecified domestic principles that were a "woman's" prerogative. In Roberts's case, her husband and sons thought they had a right to leave their outer garments wherever they wanted to but complied anyway and jokingly referred to the line as the "dead line." Roberts and Strange shared the conviction that it clearly took a woman's touch to make a house into a home.

Evelyn Slater McLeod's first house in Alberta reflected the extent of her family's fairly extensive material resources when they arrived in 1909, as it was a relatively spacious sixteen-by-forty-four-foot sod house with the added luxuries of a plank floor and a summer kitchen.[10] As soon as the Slater families' houses were up, the women "all learned firsthand how to use a whitewash brush." As time went on some "covered their walls with inexpensive cheesecloth and wallpaper," and "every family had a 'parlour' with a large rug, or all-over carpeting." McLeod recalled that her family's parlour was particularly well equipped, with "an ornate heater … a leather horsehair stuffed couch with raised head, as well as a fine pump organ. The 'frosting on the cake' was our large resplendent coal oil lamp with pink roses on its china base and globe. Potted plants always bloomed on the deep window-seats and were carried to the cellar at night during the winter months."[11]

Female power and a certain kind of heterosexual femininity were reinforced not only through time and effort devoted to the farm home but also via the individual and collective energy spent on maintaining appropriate standards of feminine appearance and behaviour. Many of the diarists wrote about relatives and neighbouring women, conveying a sense of what was perceived as "normal" for the times as well as revealing the characteristics that they admired or criticized in other women. McLeod, for example, wrote a detailed description of the aunt who raised her after her mother died. She "was quite good looking in a stern way – her gray-green eyes complementing her severe mouth. Her everyday gingham and Sunday challis were in the style of the period." Later in her life Evelyn recalled that "Aunt Ellen" had taken "good care" of her, braiding her hair "so tightly I had perpetually raised eyebrows" and not permitting her "to make mud-pies because I would soil my pinafore … She was a stickler for good manners and was determined that I should grow up to be a lady, an eventuality to which she referred often."[12] Whether McLeod ever achieved her aunt's standard of femininity is not revealed, but as she offered little more by way of description of her aunt it seems that Ellen's fashion sense, firmness, and determination to raise her niece "to be a lady" counted most in her favour.

The characteristics most often admired in other women were determination and courage, perseverance, and a refusal to let adverse conditions triumph or complain about those conditions – all of which were to be maintained within the bounds of appropriate and respectable femininity. In describing the trials and perseverance of the Houston family who moved into their area, for example, McLeod focused on Clara Houston's contributions. Mr. Houston was not very healthy but the sixty-mile trip from Stettler to their homestead had to be made, so he drove a "four-ox team" while his wife "Clara (with their 3-year old daughter Jean to care for) handled two half-wild cayuse ponies on the other wagon." The cattle were driven by their two eldest daughters, aged nine and eleven. Mr. Houston died two years later, and Clara "his indomitable widow ... was a familiar figure riding the plow in her field and driving four horses."[13] However much this "familiar figure" appeared to be abandoning a feminine ideal, that she did so to support her children and while wearing her widow's clothes was interpreted by her neighbours as remaining within acceptable gender boundaries. Clara Houston could have left the farm and moved to town instead of trying to keep it going on her own, but because she maintained her reproductive and familial position her active participation in production was recognized and valued by the community.

Apart from exhibiting as much stoicism as possible, women were, of course, still expected to be good cooks and housekeepers. Threshing season was often mentioned as bringing out a competitive streak among local women, as they each resolved to prepare the best and largest amounts of food for the large threshing crews. Sarah Roberts refused to be drawn into this sense of competition, and she wrote: "In Alberta, as in Illinois, each housewife vies with the others in demonstrating her ability as a cook, and I was almost in a panic. I finally decided that I would give them plenty of good food, but would not compete with the other women around in a line of work in which I did not excel."[14]

Characteristics such as uncomplaining perseverance and adapting to a challenging new environment were generally praised and occupied a central place in these farm women's construction of appropriate femininity. Not possessing these characteristics, or actively displaying their reverse, set a woman firmly outside what was acceptable. Native women were automatically excluded,[15] and belonging to a different ethnic group was often the first step towards marginalization. Sarah Roberts was particularly disparaging about a woman she only referred to as the "Dutch woman," "a big, raw-boned masculine looking woman whose general appearance would indicate that she had never had a bath. Her clothes looked as though they had never been washed and as though they had been thrown at her and fastened with a pin. Even her face and hands were as dirty as could be and her hair was the stringy, stiff kind that also plainly enough had never made the acquaintance of soap and water."[16]

This description provides a vivid contrast to the appearance of McLeod's Aunt Ellen. Instead of exhibiting cleanliness, fashionable clothes, and good manners, the "Dutch woman" was "masculine," dirty, and poorly dressed. She was known for being able to "stow away" large amounts of food, and Roberts heard from a neighbour that "the woman never cooked a meal or washed a dish."[17] She complained about having an abusive husband and mean neighbours, borrowed things and never returned them, and expected to get a large quantity of some food item every time she came by. Not only did she personally fail to display the appropriately feminine appearance and behaviour, she also failed to fulfil the womanly role of a good neighbour. One can only speculate as to whether this woman's female neighbours might have responded differently to her complaints of domestic abuse, her "borrowing," or her other habits if she had looked or acted more like "one of them."

As the contrasting descriptions of Aunt Ellen and the "Dutch woman" demonstrate, there were firm community standards for acceptable feminine appearance, even during the earliest and most difficult years of homesteading. A "masculine" appearance or wearing "masculine" apparel like trousers could either be merely noteworthy or it could provoke a harsh community response. In 1920 Kathleen Strange, having already caused a stir by arriving with a short haircut considered fashionable in England, "greatly shocked" her community when she wore breeches and her mother-in-law wore old army pants for horseback riding. A "deputation of ladies" called and insisted on speaking to her husband alone. They "told him they had called to protest against my wearing breeches. They said that no woman had ever appeared in such an immodest garb in that community before, and they wished to inform my husband that I must be stopped from ever appearing in such an outfit again. They did not mention Grandma, though I imagine they considered her appearance equally disgraceful."

Her husband "listened solemnly" and "promised that he would take me severely to task about it." All he did was tell her what the women had said; she was furious and went on wearing her breeches. She eventually "wore the resistance down. But it was by way of being a hard-won victory, for I had to endure a constant atmosphere of disapproval, at least in certain quarters, all of which made those early days of mine the harder to live through."[18]

What is key in this incident is not just that Strange's radical dress placed her very near the margin of female respectability but that the local women considered it their duty to confront this social deviant through her husband. Trousers were something men wore, and therefore it was immodest, disgraceful, and perhaps even dangerous for women to be seen in them. Apparently the presence of her mother-in-law did not signify the same sort of permission only a husband could grant. Grandma herself may have been exempted from the complaint because her pants were looser than Kathleen's breeches, or by virtue of her age, or because she was there without her husband and therefore lacked a keeper to whom the local women would have spoken.

This example demonstrates clearly that there were standards and expectations of femininity to which "real women" were supposed to adhere, along with a notion of gender that was not too far removed from what would have been considered acceptable for respectable, White, married, English-speaking women anywhere in Canada. A key difference, however, between the gender construction of these southern Alberta farm women and respectable married women in more urban settings was their participation in outdoor, market-oriented farm production and its potential impact on rural gender relations. Many of them regularly left the "feminine" space of the home to enter the "masculine" space of the fields to perform outdoor tasks that were the normal responsibility of men. In this way farm women deviated from traditional gender norms which generally precluded outdoor work and a market-oriented role; their construction of gender had to find some way to accommodate, or reject, this tension.

For the purposes of analysis, the kind of work most farm women did can be divided roughly between the unpaid, subsistence, and reproductive labour performed inside and the commodity, market-oriented, or income-generating labour performed outside.[19] Both kinds of labour were necessary for the survival of the farm. Women's work cannot be dismissed as mere subsistence labour, performed while the "real work" of the farm went on outside, because farm women's subsistence production freed other limited resources for market-oriented production.[20] Nor was their work confined solely to subsistence production; where a surplus and a market existed, for example, egg and butter sales often provided a vital cash income for the farm.

Most of the diarists faithfully recorded their own work, such as the chores associated with the despised washday, ironing, churning, all manner of food preparation, sewing, and numerous other tasks. The amount of inside work that had to be done and the amount of time a woman spent inside doing it generally varied according to the size of the family and the age and sex of her children. For example, Mary Crocker Wyndham had three young sons, and almost all of her work was concentrated inside. Just keeping her sons clothed meant that she spent a good deal of time sewing, as these entries from a two-week time period demonstrate:

> I finished blouse for A. [Alfred] today and got a play coat for R. [Ralph] nearly done – made it of Spencer's grey flannel coat ...

> ... I finished Ralph's coat.
> I sewed some today ...
> Sewed some today ...
> I sewed most of the day ...
> I sewed a little while this morning.[21]

The following New Year's Day she wrote that she had "celebrated by ironing most of the day," and added that her friend "Maryon says whatever you do on New Year's Day you'll do all the year – a nice prospect for me!"[22]

Most of the diarists would also note when they had received male assistance with their inside work, usually on washday,[23] and routinely shared tasks with female relatives or neighbours when they were available. Sharing her work with other women was one way for a farm woman to escape both the routine and the occasional isolation of housework; another way was to enter the "masculine" working spaces around the farm by participating in tasks such as milking and haying, or by conducting the farm's business affairs. While some women did not do any outside work, most did. Just as many diarists recorded their own daily work, so they also consistently noted when they had participated in outside work.

Emma Rowe, for example, was busy enough while she and her husband were farming near Vulcan, but her outside work increased dramatically when they moved to a ranch near MacLeod. Throughout the fall and winter when her husband was often away, she regularly wrote: "I did chores alone."[24] Although in July 1920 she vowed "no more milking for me," by August she wrote again "I did milking alone."[25] She continued to do the milking, as well as water and ride among the herd, and she helped her husband butcher from time to time. They may have shared the farm work on a more regular basis because they did not have children who might have assisted with the outside work or created more indoor work for Emma.

Ruth Bowlus, the youngest of the five Bowlus daughters, was routinely involved in the outdoor labour on her family's farm near Blackie, including some of the most demanding tasks. In the winter of 1919, for example, she helped her father unload two loads of baled hay, and during the 1920 harvest he recorded that Ruth drove a team of nine horses one day and stooked two acres of wheat the next.[26] She also accompanied her father on all of his business trips. In 1924, for example, he wrote, "Ruth & I in Calgary all day – on the Alix-Acme land deal. Pushed it thru today ... Ruth & I took in Picture show ... after our two days of strenuous work."[27] Even after her father's death in 1925 Ruth continued to spend most of her days working outside and helped her mother with all of the farm's business operations.

It is not surprising that there was a wide range of attitudes towards such forms of outside work. Ruth Bowlus clearly seems to have preferred working outdoors, while Eva Cumming recalled that she didn't really do any work outside: "I couldn't milk a cow and I wasn't sorry." She eventually had five children, however, and felt that her inside work "was enough at that time."[28] Mary Wyndham worked outside occasionally, when her help was needed, but did not like it or see it as her responsibility. In 1921, for example, she wrote that she "[l]eft all my morning work and went out when Spencer did. I raked while he mowed. I had all my morning work and the ironing to do this afternoon."[29]

Wyndham's last comment indicates that, although there were times when the outside tasks were pressing enough that her assistance was needed, she felt that her work also needed to be done and she resented the double duties. The dictates of the weather and urgency of the harvest regularly required that many women temporarily lay aside their own work to help outside; tasks like haying and harvesting "were both labor intensive and tightly time constrained" so having as many people as possible was critical. Some men would help with tasks like laundry which "required more sheer muscular strength than most of their own farm labor,"[30] but women still had to help outdoors far more often than men helped indoors. Even in the coldest winter months, when the outdoor tasks usually involved only the care of whatever livestock was on the property, few women found themselves with a full-time assistant. The allocation of various tasks was flexible, but the division of responsibility remained clear: women were responsible for the inside work, and men were responsible for the outside work.

In spite of the range of economic responsibilities assumed by women, then, the distinction between "inside" and "outside" work remained a crucial one in the division and valuing of labour on southern Alberta farms because of the differently gendered nature of the two spaces. This distinction was central to the valuing of work and its place in the construction of gender: the "masculine" outside work was most clearly oriented towards the market, and the constraints of time and weather meant that women had to put aside their own work and help outside far more frequently than men helped inside. Although most women likely would have agreed on the importance of outside work in terms of revenue for the farm, they also had a clear sense of how much work they did and the contribution they made to the farm's success or failure. They also knew how often they were involved in outdoor labour, but the gender division of labour was consistently maintained in the public forum. There was a clear relationship between many farm women's construction of gender and their experience, valuing, and representation of their work, and it was a construction that often belied the reality of most women's daily labour. Thus, in spite of the crucial "outside" labour performed by women, when the time came to talk about their daily lives in the public forum of the agrarian press it was the "inside" work that farm women celebrated. In doing so, they reinforced the theme of "separate but equal" by maintaining the centrality of inside work to the survival of the farm enterprise.

The extent to which women recognized both the volume and value of their own labour is evident from the women's pages of contemporary farm journals, but what was said in those pages was clearly framed by a sense of rigidly demarcated and gendered spheres of responsibility. The topic of labour savers, for example, appeared regularly, but focused on women's indoor labour. In March 1916 the *Grain Grower's Guide* sponsored a contest in which women were to send in descriptions and sketches of how they reorganized their work spaces to maximize efficiency. The winning articles stressed saving as much time and energy as possible by rearranging work spaces and equipment. One woman rearranged her pantry, adding shelves and storage cupboards for specific items, while another rearranged the whole kitchen around the one fixed cupboard.[31]

The *Farm and Ranch Review*'s women's page, "In The Country Home," published an article in 1917 called "Save Labor and Conserve Health," in which the author declared that "the women of the rural districts have always had an uphill fight, and probably always will," but urged them to make "more of a stand for their own good." She felt she needed to refute from the beginning any supposition that a woman who might not want to bear her burdens quietly was automatically being selfish. She stressed that she did not want "to plead the cause of selfishness" or imply "that men on the farm have indulged themselves and neglected the women," but only wanted "to impress on our women readers that they in their homes have a duty to perform to themselves, and their family through themselves." The author went on to point out that, while electricity was "looked upon as an absolute necessity" in the city, most farm women were still doing without. She concluded that once electricity was more widely available in farmhouses, a whole range of labour-saving devices would become available to the farm woman.[32]

In 1922 the *Guide* asked its women readers what they would do with $1,000 if it was given to them on the condition that it be spent to make their life on the farm happier. Almost all of the respondents said they would use the money to improve their working conditions in the house. Not surprisingly, 70 percent said they would purchase a water system, a cistern, or an indoor pump for the house, and the next most popular item was a power washer. Other smaller labour savers were also popular wishes, but only 4 percent said they would use part of the money to hire domestic help.[33] This may reflect the practical acceptance that hired domestic help was extremely hard to come by on the Prairies, but it also suggests that farm women accepted responsibility for the work, no matter how taxing. What they did not accept was that they should be worked to death as a result.[34]

Given the amount of discussion about labour savers inside the farm home, it is striking to note how rarely these pages discussed women's outside work, and how infrequently this major portion of many women's workloads was ever mentioned in a public forum. Even when it was raised, the examples used were from the shared space of the barnyard, the grey area of work that was neither a strictly "feminine" nor a strictly "masculine" responsibility. Many women might have entered the "masculine" space of the fields regularly, but in the women's pages the publicly appropriate division of labour and gender hierarchy was consistently maintained. In 1926, for example, the *Guide*'s women's page had started a question-and-answer box to serve as an ongoing forum for discussion of, and helpful strategies to cope with, problems encountered by the writers. In the first of these, "Mrs. R.B." of Saskatchewan asked if other readers thought that women should do outside work, referring only to milking cows, when they had more than enough to do inside. It was her opinion that "the state of culture in the farm home drops very rapidly when it is necessary for the woman to do outside work, but I would like to have the opinions of other farm women on this subject."[35]

The following month the *Guide* printed the responses: 50 agreed that women should help with the milking and other outside work if they are suited to it, 36 were against it, and 26 answered that it depended on the circumstances. One respondent, although she mentioned only having helped her husband to seed "two years ago" and the rest of her examples involved work around the barnyard, said that housewives need fresh air just as much as men and that it "is a great help to know how to take hold and do all these chores" if the "good man is sick." She noted, significantly, that she had "all the modern conveniences" that gave her "more time to help my husband outside" and concluded that she and her husband "work together. If I am sick he can clean the floor, or do any one of the many duties around the home. Our secret is co-operation."[36] Her response suggests that she and her husband had come to an equitable resolution for the inherently gendered tensions of farm work. Yet she chose to focus on and credit his ability to clean a floor, without mentioning whether she felt able and qualified to participate in the haying or threshing.

Examples of this kind of debate were uncommon, even though many women were doing considerably more work outside than milking the cows. Why, then, did these pages remain silent about farm women's outside labour? There are two possible answers, not necessarily mutually exclusive, both of which address the need to minimize the inherent tensions in farm women's gender constructions. Maintaining the conventional gender division of labour might have been necessary for White, English-speaking women to maintain their racial and ethnic privilege.[37] If, as Sarah Carter has shown, Native women were castigated for contravening domestic and sexual standards, then, presumably, White, English-speaking women had much to gain by adhering to community standards.[38] White women who were seen as working outside too often, or more often than was absolutely necessary, risked a loss of public respectability when "feminine" respectability (i.e., the sort to which only White, heterosexual, married women could gain access) was constructed around "non-productive" domesticity.

The other possible explanation for the discursive silence around women's outside labour lies in a consideration of farm women's political strategies. Upholding publicly appropriate gender norms and the notion of a woman's rightful "sphere" proved to be useful during organized farm women's legislative struggles, and it also kept the farm community from fracturing along gender lines. Farm women needed support from farm men to achieve their own goals, but they also needed to maintain a united front with the men as "farmers" against the external economic and political threats to their shared community.

Many of these women did deviate considerably from strict gender divisions of labour on their own farms, whether by choice or by necessity. As Nancy Grey Osterud has noted, however, they participated in larger, cooperative projects and represented their own labour in the women's pages "in accordance within the roles deemed appropriate to the community." A woman "might 'help' her husband with the haying on their own farm," for example, but would never have joined a haying or threshing crew that went to other farms. This highly gender-specific cooperative work and its representation characterize the "public gender division of labor."[39] On each individual farm it generally did not matter who actually did the work, as long as it got done; what mattered a great deal was who was seen to be doing it, and this throws into question the extent to which women would have been publicly recognized for their outside work.

This gap between the reality and the representation of women's work may be explained by considering the way most farm women constructed their own identities: they shared with their husbands a specific occupational disadvantage and shared with other women a gender-specific social disability. In neither case were their husbands portrayed as the direct cause of the difficulties in farm women's lives.[40] Most of the time most farm women did not see themselves as "women" first or as "farmers" first: only in certain circumstances would they try to claim one over the other. They were farm women, operating within a particular matrix of gender, political economy, and region, and they turned to the public purse and state policy to address the precariousness of their existence.

Many of Alberta's farm women entered the "masculine" world of politics through the UFWA. The wives and daughters of farmers were first officially admitted to the four-year-old United Farmers of Alberta (UFA) in 1913, and the women formed their own auxiliary in 1914. By the end of that year there were already twenty-three locals, with a membership of over 700, and the provincial executive for the Women's Auxiliary was formed in 1915. The UFWA became an autonomous organization in 1916, and membership climbed rapidly, reaching a peak in 1921 of 4,536 members in 309 locals.[41] The number of locals would continue to grow throughout the 1920s, although the total membership declined.

It was within and through this organization that many farm women articulated a complex notion of gender. Just as the UFWA's goals reflected farm women's individual and collective notions of womanhood, so its successes and failures had as much to do with dominant gender norms as with the prevailing political climate. For example, the organization was relatively successful in such areas as health and education, which were traditionally marked as "feminine" and safely fell within a woman's proper "sphere," but less successful when such aims as a married women's property act clashed with the dominant masculine legal and political culture. When the UFWA attempted to use a gender construction that recognized multiple forms of women's labour to make political and economic claims, it failed. Women's reproductive labour, and thus their efforts in areas like health care, were already visible in the public sphere and were rewarded; their productive or market-oriented labour, and so their claims for economic and legal equality, were not.

Such issues as health, education, young people's work, and reforming existing legislation (particularly the property rights of married women) dominated the UFWA's agenda through the late 1920s. These concerns had been taken up previously by other women's organizations in the province, but the farm women brought to them a distinctly rural perspective.

Health care and married women's property laws were of great interest to White, English-speaking farm women, as individuals and as a group. Struggling for provincially funded municipal hospitals and obstetrical training for nurses was a major concern because farm women were generally much further from medical care than were women in small towns and the growing urban centres.[42] Maternal and infant mortality rates were high during these years, a fact that did not escape the notice of neighbouring women. Emma Rowe, for example, noted local births and deaths in her diary, and from 10 December 1912 to 27 January 1915, a period of only twenty-six months, she recorded the births of five babies and the burials of three.[43] In the space of four days during an outbreak of "Infantile Paralysis," or polio, in 1928, Harriet Bowlus recorded the sudden deaths of three children in her area.[44]

In 1917 the UFWA Convention passed a resolution asking for the establishment of municipal hospitals. Largely as a result of pressure from the women's groups in the province, the provincial government created a Department of Health in 1918, and a resolution was passed at that year's convention asking that this new department, instead of local hospital boards, decide where new hospitals were to be located. This move was taken in an attempt to increase the chances that the more remote districts would be considered for new hospitals. In 1919 the UFWA helped other women's organizations convince the provincial government to start funding municipal hospitals.[45]

Kathleen Strange discussed the controversy that surrounded the building of a municipal hospital in Stettler in the early 1920s, and she noted that her "own home was divided on the subject." Her husband was against the hospital on the grounds that it would bring higher taxes, and he felt that most people "could be well enough looked after in their own homes." She countered that although babies "had been, and still were, successfully brought into the world on farmhouse kitchen tables, who knew how many had been lost, and how many mothers had suffered perhaps for years afterwards, because of it?"[46] She was pleased that the area did get its new hospital, particularly as her second child was born there.

As well as working for new and better hospitals, the UFWA struggled to get special obstetrical training for nurses. It realized that the remote rural areas were not at the top of the list for new hospitals but hoped that it could at least get trained nurses in the remote areas to help with childbirth. The question of midwives was raised at the 1919 convention, as it had been at previous conventions, and that year the UFWA passed a unanimous resolution "urgently" requesting "that registered nurses be permitted to qualify as midwives, wherever needed as such and that the Government undertake to supply both medical practitioners and service nurses prepared to act as midwives wherever needed in all those districts not supplied by independent workers."[47] There was a good deal of government opposition to this request, but UFWA president Irene Parlby was able to report in 1920 that "the Government finally passed legislation providing for the training of a certain number of these nurses at the expense of the Government."[48]

These limited improvements in health care proved to be easier to come by than any in the considerably more contentious area of married women's property rights. The relationship between land ownership and a woman's livelihood meant that farm women had an even greater stake than did urban women in the recognition of these rights, and the UFWA sought consistently to expand the terms of the debate. Throughout their struggle farm women were forced to confront existing gender relations and the inequality between women's and men's relationships to the land. It was in this area that they advanced most explicitly their vision for greater equality between farm men and farm women, by calling for property laws that would recognize farm women's labour and their right to own land and property. To do so, they had to negotiate the tensions behind their own understanding of what it meant to be a "woman" by articulating the value of labour that was still largely invisible.

In Alberta in the first three decades of the twentieth century, a married woman whose husband was still alive could not legally own property and had no legal claim to the product of her own labour. Except for independently wealthy single women, men were the only possible legal owners of farmland, machinery, and any profits. As early as 1915, therefore, the UFWA passed resolutions calling for a dower law that would guarantee a woman a share of her husband's property when he died, and it also called for legislation that would prevent a farmer from disposing of the property without his wife's consent.[49]

In 1917 the Alberta government did pass the Dower Act which granted a married woman a life estate in the homestead after the death of her husband. At the time the act was one of the most progressive in the country. As Catherine Cavanaugh and Margaret McCallum have shown, however, farm women soon became the most vocal critics of this act because it really "only went part way in recognizing the wife's interest in land she had helped to develop."[50] It did not create a property right that she could deal with in her own name, so she could not sell, mortgage, or even will the homestead to her children; it only specified a life interest in the home quarter. It excluded chattels and moveables, so a woman had no legal right to keep or use the furniture, the farm equipment, or even any seed after her husband died. Unless a woman's husband specifically willed the property to her, she was granted the right to keep an empty house and a piece of land that she could not even sell unassisted to feed herself. The "family home" was protected, but a woman was left without the means to support the family.[51]

The provision preventing husbands from disposing of the homestead without the wife's written consent might have been a more significant gain, but it was interpreted very narrowly in the courts. It was also soon realized that many women might be placed in a dangerous situation if they refused to sign away the homestead when their husbands wanted them to. Some changes were made to the act in 1919, but they reflected the narrow judicial interpretations of the act and served only to water down the original intent of the 1917 legislation.[52]

While some of the other women's organizations in the province continued to push for changes to the dower law, rural women soon expanded the terms of the debate by calling for the far more controversial principle of community property. At its 1920 convention the UFWA passed a resolution demanding that "all property of both or either shall be considered joint property unless it can be shown that it is not."[53] The resolution was referred to the UFWA's executive board, to be considered with the UFA's legal advisor, John Brownlee, in attendance. Brownlee, an urban lawyer who became attorney general in 1921 and premier in 1925, thought "it was unwise for women to insist on absolute equality with their husbands in regard to all property, as it would remove the protection" that he believed the existing Dower Law granted.[54] Nevertheless, the UFWA remained hopeful that, with the UFA's victory in the 1921 election, the new government would help them accomplish this goal.

In 1922 the UFWA passed a resolution calling for the abolition of homestead dower and the statutory recognition of the principle of community property. The concern for protecting the family home had become a claim to full and equal property rights, the idea being that what the husband and wife had acquired through joint effort should be recognized as being jointly owned.[55] While this resolution was endorsed by the UFWA and UFA conventions over the next four years, no progress was made on the issue at the provincial level until 1925. Once in the legislature, the UFA government "quickly put the reins on any radicalism" and, knowing they had to be seen to be able to govern for urban as well as rural voters, frequently ignored resolutions that came from the convention floor.[56]

In April 1925, however, Irene Parlby, having been elected as a UFA member in 1921, introduced Bill 54, An Act Establishing Community of

Property as Between Husband and Wife, into the legislative assembly. The bill was reprinted in full on the women's page of the *Western Producer* on 29 October 1925, where Violet McNaughton, Saskatchewan feminist and editor of the page, urged her readers to study it carefully. Bill 54 proposed that all property owned by the wife before marriage or acquired as a gift or as part of an inheritance after marriage was to remain her separate property, as was the husband's. All other property acquired by either husband or wife, or both, during the marriage, including any profits from the separate property of the husband and wife, was to be considered community property. The act did not go so far as to deny the husband's right to manage and control the community property, but he would not be allowed to "sell, convey, or encumber the community real estate" unless it was a joint action by him and his wife, and the wife was to be asked apart from her husband if her consent had been freely given. Upon divorce or the death of either spouse the property was to be equally divided.[57]

Other than the clause maintaining the husband's right to manage the community property during his lifetime and the fact that most of the provisions would still take effect only after the death of the husband, the bill Parlby brought before the legislative assembly was revolutionary. For the first time in Alberta an elected member of the government was insisting that a woman had her own property right to the community estate she and her husband had developed since being married, as well as a right to property she had acquired before her marriage or had inherited since. It was a key step towards closing the gap between the representation of farm women's labour as subsidiary and the recognition of it as central.

While feminists like Parlby and McNaughton were willing to challenge publicly the legal base of the family farm, the reaction of ordinary farm women was rather more muted. There was remarkably little discussion about Bill 54 on the women's pages of any of the major farm journals in the months following its publication. The two letters discussed below, however, indicate the way in which women's opinions seem to have divided: on this fundamental issue, the tensions within farm women's gender constructions began to show. Some women continued to support the separate-but-equal representation of their labour, and they expressed their identity as farmers first. On the same page of the *Western Producer* as the text of Bill 54 there was a letter from "Martha," who felt that the majority of farm women would hesitate to support the kinds of reforms Parlby was suggesting, because

> the keynote to our economic problems to day [sic] is co-operation, not coercion, which principle is being applied in most cases to home life also. It is not only the farm women who are suffering from insufficient remuneration for hard work – the men, too, have had to work hard for years, without sufficient returns from the farm to pay them a decent wage for work done, and I am sure most farm women are making willing sacrifices to help things along. Legislation along that line may be necessary in isolated cases. On the whole co-operation is, I believe, being put into practice in the home where most reforms begin. Let us do all we can to help co-operation … and our economic status will not need legislation to have equal rights in the home.[58]

Other women, who were clearly in the minority, put their identities as women first and called for greater rewards for women's labour. In June 1926 the *Western Producer* published a letter that expressed support for Parlby's bill and frustration at the apparent lack of interest among farm women. The author wrote to her "Sisters" that she was

> disappointed … that more women have not written to the page regarding Mrs. Parlby's work for women. Surely there are more women on the prairies that feel the injustice of the Canadian laws regarding what she should earn after years of hard work and broken health. What we call the Dower Act is poor compensation for the woman who has worked side by side with her partner in life and raised a large family. Surely she should have something to say regarding what she has helped to accumulate jointly. I understand the reason why these laws have not been changed is that women have not complained, but have just plodded along under the yoke. Now that Mrs. Parlby's work will make a better standard for the Canadian woman – let us co-operate along these lines to make a better and a higher standard for the next generation. I think the question deserves some discussion.[59]

Signed "A Progressive," this author's critique remained carefully within a familial and reproductive idiom.

As it was, the bill was referred to a committee headed by Parlby which included such women as Magistrate Emily Murphy, Henrietta Muir Edwards (then convenor of laws for the National Council of Women of Canada), and Gwendolyn Duff, a barrister from Edmonton. After two years of research into property laws around the world, the committee tabled its report in March 1928 and recommended that the bill not be adopted. The two major criticisms were that the bill constituted the husband as head of the community property and that "a wife's earnings, her wages, and her profits from her separate estate" would fall into the community estate and thus under the control of her husband. In effect, the committee believed the bill did not go far enough, even though it was a significant step forward.

These concerns on the part of the committee members, however, were not in step with those of most Alberta women who also opposed the bill; in their opinion, the bill went too far. The claim that their "property should be withheld entirely while they share in the husband's" was thought to be "an unfair position. There should be an equal sharing of both assets and liabilities." The committee did make other recommendations, like legislative recognition of "the economic value of a wife's contribution," but these were not acted upon.[60]

In 1926 the UFA government passed new legislation "aimed at eliminating some of the more objectionable defects in the existing Dower Act" but, in fact, did little but revert back to the intent of the 1917 act.[61] The one significant change was that the wife was given a life estate in her husband's personal property so that now she could keep the house and the furniture. The UFA government's failure to radically reform the legal and economic base of the "family farm" had various explanations, but what is clear is that the celebration of women's separate-but-equal sphere in the pages of the agrarian press was not transformed into a broader political debate of rural domestic relations.[62]

In 1927, the UFWA's president, Mrs. R.B. Gunn, said that the organized farm men and women were "the warp and woof of a fabric inextricably woven."[63] Constructions of gender and gender relations are fundamental to any social fabric; they affect women's personal spaces, their experiences and valuing of work, the ways their work is represented, and the way women enter and participate in political discourse. As Denise Riley has argued, gender definitions are always fundamentally unstable and are, therefore, always being contested and negotiated. Women never completely "inhabit" any gender role.[64] Perceptions of gender roles change depending on which sources, and which audiences, are being considered – from women's private diaries to their letters to the agrarian press to their calls for new legislation.

The White settlement phase of Alberta's agrarian frontier permitted women to transgress the conventional urban bourgeois feminine sphere, insofar as they could and did engage in a wider range of economic and political activities. Many of Alberta's White, English-speaking farm women were able to expand their notion of "womanhood" to accommodate the tensions created by their market-oriented labour and challenge the deeply embedded patriarchal system of land ownership.

Negotiating these tensions, however, meant that their understanding of what it meant to be a "woman" still had definite limits. It remained entrenched in a group of assumptions about "appropriate" femininity being rooted in the home and family, and transgressions were applauded or accepted only so long as these conventional symbols of femininity were maintained. Women who appeared too "masculine" were marginalized, or, if they belonged to a non-dominant group, excluded. Non-White or non-English speaking women, such as Sarah Roberts's "Dutch" neighbour, were left out of this gender scheme entirely, except as the "other" against which the appearance and behaviour of the dominant social group could be defined.

Furthermore, however much the sphere of women's work was expanded in daily life, when farm women discussed their work in the public forum of the agrarian press it was the significance of their reproductive "inside" work that was stressed, while their participation in the "outside" masculine sphere was downplayed or negated entirely. Explaining this gap between the reality and the representation of farm women's labour requires an examination of the ways in which many of these women constructed their identity. The dual nature of that identity meant that they generally saw themselves as farmers *and* as women, and were unwilling to implicate their husbands in any oppression they perceived as women while they still shared the category of "farmers." Instead, many farm women directed their political energy, and their calls for legal and economic redress, towards the state.

Advocating homesteading rights for unmarried women was quickly abandoned because few women were willing to pursue this basic but futile challenge to the established norm of male land ownership. Of the women who took part in the UFWA's discussions, meetings, and conventions, many were uncomfortable with any reforms that might portray their interests as being contrary to those of their husbands. There was a considerable amount of grassroots support for dower rights, but this support was much more difficult to generate when the more radical issue of community property was raised because it inferred that women had a right to claim full partnership in the "family" farm. Only such a fundamental challenge, which addressed directly the gendered inequalities of women's and men's relationships to the land, could force some women to pick sides as "farmers" or as "women." Most White, English-speaking farm women were aware of how often they contributed to market-oriented production, but they did not see that as sufficient reason to challenge the dominant gender hierarchy whereby only men legally profited from that production. Even in small farming communities the multiple definitions of "women's work" depended on who was in a position to create or shape those definitions and when.

In effect, representing their labour as separate but equal had a great deal of social utility in terms of structuring respectable femininity within the new economic context and maintaining women's position of racial and ethnic privilege, but it proved substantially less powerful as a radical political tool. The strands of connection between respectable White femininity, women's work on the edges of White settlement, and women's political activism, although rarely obvious, were in fact key to southern Alberta's "inextricably woven" social fabric.

Notes

1 Much of this early scholarship involved challenging the polarized images of farm women as being either "oppressed drudges" or "liberated" by the amount of work they had to do in the process of homesteading. Sara Brooks Sundberg has argued, for example, that female immigrants to western Canada in the late nineteenth century had a wide range of responses to their new homes and lives. Some saw the work of frontier farming as nothing but drudgery, while others saw it as welcome relief from the more restricted gender norms in the places they had left behind. Veronica Strong-Boag has further argued that Canadian farm women's awareness of the value of their labour would form the basis of their grassroots feminism in the early years of the twentieth century. See Sara Brooks Sundberg, "Farm Women on the Canadian Prairie Frontier: The Helpmate Image," in *Rethinking Canada: The Promise of Women's History*, ed. Veronica Strong-Boag and Anita Fellman (Toronto: Copp Clark Pitman, 1986); Veronica Strong-Boag, "Pulling in Double Harness or Hauling a Double Load: Women, Work and Feminism on the Canadian Prairie," *Journal of Canadian Studies* 21, 3 (Fall 1986): 32-52. Another early Canadian example is Susan Jackel, ed., *A Flannel Shirt and Liberty: English Emigrant Gentlewomen in the Canadian West, 1880-1914* (Vancouver: UBC Press, 1982). The American historiography includes numerous volumes on western women, including Sandra Myers, *Westering Women and the Frontier Experience, 1800-1915* (Albuquerque: University of New Mexico Press, 1982); Susan Armitage and Elizabeth Jameson, eds., *The Women's West* (Norman: University of Oklahoma Press, 1987); and Lillian Schlissel, Vicki Ruiz, and Janice Monk, eds., *Western Women: Their Land, Their Lives* (Albuquerque: University of New Mexico Press, 1988).

2 Gender does not merely reside in the opposition of "feminine" and "masculine" but also in the multiple possibilities of "femininities," of ways of being a "woman." A powerful challenge to the immutability of the category "woman" is set out in Denise Riley's *"Am I That Name?": Feminism and the Category of "Women" in History* (Minneapolis: University of Minnesota Press, 1988).

3 Julie Roy Jeffrey, *Frontier Women: The Trans-Mississippi West, 1840-1880* (New York: Hill and Wang, 1979), 38.

4 Ibid., 73.

5 Kathleen Strange, *With the West in Her Eyes: The Story of a Modern Pioneer* (New York: Dodge, 1937), 57-8.

6 Sarah Roberts, *Of Us and the Oxen* (Saskatoon: Modern, 1968), 52-3.

7 Ibid., 168-9.

8 Ibid., 169. Although in more urban settings the kitchen and dining room were often the most "feminine" spaces in the house, in small houses on the frontier of White settlement these "rooms" often appear to have been used by farm women and their families as transitional spaces between the dust and dirt of the outside and the rest of the living area.

9 Ibid., 153.

10 Evelyn Slater McLeod, "Our Sod House," Provincial Archives of Alberta (PAA) 78.12SE. The Slater families had come to southern Alberta as a group of extended kin, and the pooled resources ensured each family a better start than was the case with many new homesteaders.
11 McLeod, "Restless Pioneers" PAA 77.39SE.
12 Ibid.
13 Ibid.
14 Roberts, *Of Us and the Oxen*, 222.
15 See, for example, Sarah Carter, "Categories and Terrains of Exclusion: Constructing the 'Indian Woman' in the Early Settlement Era in Western Canada," this volume.
16 Roberts, *Of Us and the Oxen*, 163. There is no evidence that the woman was actually Dutch. As Roberts could never remember or pronounce her name, the woman could have come from any number of central or northern European countries.
17 Ibid., 165.
18 Strange, *With the West in Her Eyes*, 39-41.
19 I am using the words "inside/outside" in a strictly physical sense and not to suggest a rigid "separate spheres" dichotomy. As Nancy Grey Osterud has suggested, the terms represent two differently gendered but highly permeable work spaces: women were responsible for the "feminine" indoor work, men were responsible for the "masculine" outdoor work, and the barnyard was an in-between area of activities where women's and men's responsibilities generally overlapped. See Osterud, "Gender and the Transition to Capitalism in Rural America," *Agricultural History*, 67, 2 (Spring 1993): 19.
20 Marjorie Griffin Cohen, *Women's Work, Markets, and Economic Development in Nineteenth-Century Ontario* (Toronto: University of Toronto Press, 1988), 41.
21 Mary Crocker Wyndham, 1, 2, 9, 13-5 May 1913. Glenbow Archives, microfilm AB.
22 Ibid., 1 January 1914.
23 See, for example, Wyndham, 26 January and 22 July 1914.
24 Emma Rowe, March 1919, November and December 1919, Glenbow Archives M7076, box 1, file 2.
25 Ibid., 10 July and 29 August 1920. Cohen argues in *Women's Work* that in nineteenth-century Ontario, dairying was seen as a woman's responsibility because of its association with the home, but in these examples from early twentieth-century Alberta it was more often seen as one of the tasks belonging to the shared space of the barnyard.
26 Bowlus, 20 January 1919 and 20-1 August 1920. Glenbow Archives M5789, box 1, file 1.
27 Ibid., 30 May 1924.
28 Eva Cumming, PAA Eliane Silverman fonds 81.279, no. 54.
29 Wyndham, 26 August 1921.
30 Nancy Grey Osterud, *Bonds of Community: The Lives of Farm Women in Nineteenth-Century New York* (Ithaca and London: Cornell University Press, 1991), 186.
31 *Grain Grower's Guide* (*GGG*), Winnipeg, Manitoba, 29 March 1916.
32 *Farm and Ranch Review* (*FRR*), Calgary, Alberta, 20 December 1917.
33 *GGG*, 11 October 1922.
34 In Mary Kinnear's article on Manitoba farm women, "'Do you want your daughter to marry a farmer?': Women's Work on the Farm, 1922," most of the women who responded did want their daughters to marry farmers, but their main complaint was "overwork." See Donald Akenson, ed., *Canadian Papers in Rural History*, vol. 6 (Gananoque: Langdale, 1988).
35 *GGG*, 3 March 1926.
36 Ibid., 1 April 1926. While the sources of the various letters were not given, it is reasonable to assume that at least some of them came from Alberta, and the nature of the discussion suggests that provincial divisions may not have made a great deal of difference.
37 See Frances Swyripa's study of Ukrainian-Canadian women, *Wedded to the Cause: Ukrainian-Canadian Women and Ethnic Identity, 1891-1991* (Toronto: University of Toronto Press, 1992), for a discussion of the experiences of a large number of "White" but not English-speaking women.
38 Carter, "Categories and Terrains of Exclusion."
39 Osterud, *Bonds of Community*, 217-8.
40 As Heidi Hartmann has pointed out, the debate over "the significance of patriarchy in

women's lives" must revolve "around whether or not women *perceive* patriarchy as oppressive." Most farm women obviously did not perceive any such oppression in their lives, given the number of times they argued that they would have all the labour-savers they needed if the government would just give farmers a fair deal. See Heidi I. Hartmann, "The Family as the Locus of Gender, Class and Political Struggle: The Example of Housework," *Signs* 6, 3 (1981): 387. Emphasis in original.

41 Eva Carter, *The History of Organized Farm Women of Alberta* (Edmonton: Douglas, 1954), 23-4.

42 See Nanci Langford's discussion of the state of maternal medical care in "Home Was Never Like This: The Lives of First Generation Homestead Women," paper presented to the Canadian Historical Association, June 1994.

43 Rowe, 10 December 1912 to 27 January 1915.

44 Bowlus, 29 January to 1 February 1928.

45 Howard Palmer, with Tamara Palmer, *Alberta: A New History (*Edmonton: Hurtig, 1990), 182.

46 Strange, *With the West in Her Eyes*, 267.

47 UFA Annual Report, 1919, 95.

48 Ibid., 82.

49 UFA Annual Report, 1914, 39.

50 Catherine Cavanaugh, "The Women's Movement in Alberta as Seen through the Campaign for Dower Rights" (MA thesis, University of Alberta, 1986), 53. See also Cavanaugh, "The Limitations of the Pioneering Partnership: The Alberta Campaign for Homestead Dower, 1909-1925," *Canadian Historical Review* 74, 2 (1993): 198-225; and Margaret McCallum, "Prairie Women and the Struggle for a Dower Law, 1905-1920," *Prairie Forum* 18, 1 (Spring 1993): 19-34.

51 Cavanaugh, "The Women's Movement in Alberta," 53.

52 Ibid., 59.

53 Minutes, UFWA Convention, in UFA Annual Report, 1919, 124.

54 Minutes, UFWA Executive Board Meeting, 24 January 1920.

55 UFA Annual Report, 1921, 39.

56 Palmer, *Alberta*, 217. I am indebted to Jim Hansen for this observation.

57 *Western Producer*, Saskatoon, Saskatchewan, 29 October 1925.

58 Ibid.

59 Ibid., 3 June 1926.

60 *GGG*, 2 April 1928.

61 Cavanaugh, "Women's Movement in Alberta," 66.

62 The more radical nature of Alberta's political climate only a few years earlier was being tempered by the mid-1920s, and the provincial government remained dominated by conservatives. As it was, federal legislation was finally changed in 1930 to allow women to take up homesteads, but there was little land left, and farming was rapidly becoming an unprofitable venture. See Palmer, *Alberta*, 218-9. I am indebted to Jim Hansen for this observation.

63 *GGG*, 1 February 1927.

64 Riley, *"Am I That Name?"*

CHAPTER 6

Childbirth on the Canadian Prairies, 1880-1930

NANCI LANGFORD

The provinces of Saskatchewan and Alberta were the last Canadian region to be settled by migrants from other countries and other regions of Canada. The largest wave of settlement began at the turn of the twentieth century and peaked in 1911, increasing the population of female inhabitants tenfold in a decade. While this region can be characterized as a twentieth-century frontier, families who settled there found few or no twentieth-century amenities and services available to them. Those most acutely missed were medical and health practitioners to assist with medical emergencies and with childbirth.

Geographical isolation and the high cost of doctors' care were major issues for homestead families. Other factors served to make childbirth, in particular, a serious risk for homestead women and babies for decades. These included the living conditions and work roles of expectant women; professional protectionism and prejudices about midwives; and the fact that federal and provincial governments did not address a social problem of epidemic proportions.

My research into the lives of seventy-eight homestead women on the Canadian Prairies reveals a rich store of anecdotes about women's childbirth experiences during the settlement years. These stories hint at a larger picture – the politics and social organization of childbirth on the Prairies through the period 1880 to 1930. This chapter blends homestead women's childbirth stories with an analysis of public and professional responses to women's maternity care needs, revealing both the complexities and the tragedies of this time and place in Canadian history.

The women in this study are those of the "first generation": women who came to Saskatchewan or Alberta as adults to homestead and who, in most cases, were the first to settle on their farm.[1] Most of the women included in the study were English-speaking and came from the British Isles, the United States, or other parts of Canada. About 10 percent of the immigrants came directly from eastern and central Europe and from Russia and Scandinavia. I used as sources only the material women had spoken or written themselves, their diaries, letters, oral histories, and memoirs, and so these accounts reflect their perspectives on their childbirth experiences. This research focuses on childbirth in rural areas of both provinces, not in the cities and towns, although rural women sometimes used the services available to them in urban centres.

In learning about these women's experiences, I came to the conclusion that childbirth stood out as an experience that captured the essence of all that was bad and good about homestead life, that in many ways it was a microcosm of what homesteading meant for women of this generation. Conditions and circumstances converged to make an expectant homestead woman vulnerable and powerless: the isolation, the poor trails and slow means of transportation, the uncomfortably cold (or hot) shack, the unpredictable weather, the lack of medical facilities and personnel, the lack of friends and relatives, the lack of compassion and understanding from her partner, her lack of knowledge about childbirth, her own weakened condition from overwork and an inadequate diet, and her inability to abandon even temporarily her responsibilities on the homestead. At the same time, the ways in which Prairie women approached the challenge of childbirth, sometimes many times over, demonstrated remarkable resourcefulness and fortitude. Homestead families used three strategies to ensure the safe births of their children: managing the birth on their own without any outside help; sending for some assistance – whatever was available and affordable; or transporting the mother, either in labour or well in advance of it, to a place where help could be obtained. Whatever choice was made, childbirth was a family affair, and every available adult, including hired men, had a role in the delivery of each child.

Childbirth was also a time of sisterhood during the Prairie settlement years. Homestead women became midwives for each other out of necessity, despite their fears about their lack of knowledge and training in childbirth and about the tremendous responsibility this role entailed. This situation underscores the position of women in settlement areas. Women were integral to the success of expansionist dreams of the nation and essential to the survival of their own families. Yet these women's lives were at risk each time they became pregnant. They were also burdened with the worry of their neighbours' well-being and their own helplessness to assist them when called to attend their childbirths. In settlement policy, and, in particular, in the system used to carve the Prairies up into homesteads, little thought had been given to the needs of women and children. Limited recognition by governments of the conditions in which homestead families lived resulted in, for many years, few resources and no services being available to women who were in desperate need of them to ensure the safest possible births of their children.

In letters, diaries, and memoirs, Prairie homestead women described their birth experiences and their preparations, both psychological and practical, for bringing children safely into the world. Pregnancies, however, are less frequently mentioned. This was a generation that maintained a veil of privacy around pregnancy but that acknowledged birth as the social event that it, of necessity, had become. Gertrude Chase did not even tell her own mother about her pregnancies in her letters home, and she mentioned the children only after they were born.[2] There was a difference between educated women and uneducated women with regard to attitudes towards pregnancy and childbirth accounts. In their writing educated women are more descriptive about their pregnancies and also about how the birth progressed. In a display of anticipation and excitement rarely found in these women's accounts, Barbara Slater revealed the news of her pregnancy and her physical discomforts in a letter to a friend in 1912: "You ask how I am!!!!!! Guess!!!!! As busy as usual and more so preparing a layette for a little stranger due to arrive at the end of the month. The first three or four months I was too horribly sick to care about anything and didn't do as much sewing as I would have wished ... I had the *awfullest(!!)* struggle to prepare Xmas dinner. However that is all over and since March I have been like a fighting bird, and on the whole so well."[3]

The major barriers women had to overcome in their preparations for childbirth on the Prairies during these years were the lack of trained medical practitioners (whether nurses, doctors, or midwives); the long distances to be travelled to obtain whatever help might be available; the lack of facilities at home (e.g., heat, water, and privacy for birthing a baby safely and comfortably); and the lack of alternative birthing places, such as maternity homes or hospitals. In addition, with the exception of the homesteaders who were trained nurses or midwives, most women faced the limitations imposed by their own ignorance, particularly of the birth process, but also of appropriate prenatal and postnatal care. These women were cut off from the usual support persons who surrounded women through pregnancy and childbirth. They had no regular access to the care and knowledge of mothers, sisters, and aunts – or even of friends and neighbours – except through letters. At best, these experienced women could give advice and voice concern about the kind of help the woman might need and should have available to her when giving birth only in their letters.

Because of the conditions in which they bore and delivered their babies, and also because of the status of medical knowledge and practice with regard to childbirth, Prairie women faced the possibility that either they or their babies might not survive. In her 1905 diary Sophie Puckette told the story of her neighbour's preparation for childbirth: "Then she took me upstairs and showed me all her wedding outfit she had laid carefully away for them to put on her should she die. She imagines so strongly that her life will be given for the little life she is expecting in Jan., that she has all her things put in her trunk in order, and each is marked so Mr. Bond will know what to do with them all. It made me want to cry to see the things all ready for her to die, and to hear her talk of them."[4]

Women's fears were realistic, particularly because, if the birth or post-partum period involved any complications, then the chances of both mother and baby surviving were slim. Judith Leavitt also found a profound and realistic fear of death among American women at the turn of the twentieth century.[5] While the possibility of death in childbirth confronted every pregnant woman during this period, the homestead woman was at particular risk because of her isolation and, thus, her inability to call on experienced childbirth attendants. Women had few career choices outside of marriage, particularly in settlement areas, and most married women had little access to, or knowledge of, birth control. As these accounts reveal, even homestead women who remained childless worried about their chances of surviving childbirth should they become pregnant. The feelings of Monica Hopkins are understandable, as, in 1901, she assessed the situations her friends and neighbours found themselves in at childbirth: "I had heard so many appalling stories of abnormal births since I came out here that I have made up my mind to spend the nine months in a hospital to be on the safe side! Mrs. B. has just had her second babe, under the most unpleasant circumstances to my mind, though they seem fairly ordinary out here."[6]

Perhaps no other aspect of life on the Prairies endangered women as much as did the birthing of their children. It is not surprising that the maternal mortality rate was high.[7] "Quite a few, quite a few died. And even then with the doctors ... So many died so quick. And they didn't know what it was," Magdalena Zeidler remembered.[8] Harriett Neville, who assisted at many of her neighbours' births from 1895 to 1914, wrote in her memoirs that "out of one family who were neighbours, two of the women died in childbirth."[9] Peggy Holmes wrote: "There were so many bereavements in the district. Two widowers were left with seven children each. That made fourteen more motherless children to be cared for. Most of the deaths were caused by neglect at childbirth and still the government would not allow midwives to be licensed in Canada. Why not I wonder?"[10]

Holmes's question pinpoints the major problem for women on the Prairies. While professionals and politicians discussed the problems of maternal and infant mortality in the West at great length, and while they debated issues of professional jurisdiction and qualifications, women continued for many years to birth their children without benefit of any trained attendants.[11] Prairie farm women were also forced into the uneasy role of untrained midwife because there was simply no one else to call upon. Marion Cran, a visiting author from England touring the Canadian West to promote it to English women immigrants, raised the issue publicly in Winnipeg in 1908. She later wrote in her book, *A Woman in Canada*, "At last I found what I felt all along must exist; a hardship to be faced which make women justly shrink from the country. First from one prairie wife, and then from another I heard a cry about the hardships of birth on the homesteads ... I heard many stories of courage, stories of disaster."[12] Cran felt the situation was serious enough to deter women from migrating to Western Canada. Many women, however, were unaware of the conditions on the Prairies until they arrived there, their commitment to establishing a new life already made.

Some women felt they had to measure up to the standards of bravery and resourcefulness they saw in other homestead women around them. Kathleen Strange wrote in 1919: "When I observed with what serene confidence and lack of excitement the country mothers faced it, many of them giving birth to their babies without either a doctor or a nurse's care, I realized that whatever my personal fears and qualms might be, I must try to face it in the same courageous and confident fashion if I was ever to hold my end up with them."[13]

And Margaret Thompson, too, despite her knowledge (as a trained nurse) of the complications that could arise in childbirth, wrote that she thought, as she became pregnant in 1921, "if other homesteaders' wives could take it, why not I?"[14] She thought her nurse's training would help her through even if the doctor, who was fifty miles away, could not make it.

When the anxious waiting was over and the time to give birth finally came, it was not uncommon for women to be alone, without anyone to assist them or to comfort them. This occurred because husbands were away or because they did not return with a neighbour, midwives, or doctors in time for the birth. As Mary Edey recalled, "The first child I had I think I was all alone when he was born. My husband went for a neighbour woman and the neighbours were so far away I think I had him before they got back."[15]

The long distance from medical care was a problem for most rural families. Three times Margaret Shaw delivered a child before the doctor who had been sent for arrived. Two of those births took place in town, where she had moved temporarily to be close to medical aid only to find on one occasion that the doctor was out of town when her time came.[16] In most cases town conditions and services on the Prairies for many of the settlement years were not significantly better for expectant women than was what was available to them on their own farms. The need to rely on others to fetch doctors, midwives, or nurses, and the distances these messengers had to cover, often put women at risk. Mary Cummins remembered two of her birthing experiences, both in the mid 1890s: "When Tom was to be born Colin sent a man off to Broadview for the doctor but he fell foul of the drink. He and the doctor slept on the prairie arriving at the house when Tom was already 12 hours old ... when Marjorie was born in March 1889, I broke down completely and nearly died before the doctor could get to me."[17]

Alice Self began her first labour on Christmas Eve, 1912. Her husband and the hired man took turns driving to town to fetch the doctor and to return him, four trips of twenty-eight miles each.[18] Even when distances could be overcome, and appropriate maternity care obtained, the course a birth might take was unpredictable. It was the combination of this unpredictability, a natural feature of childbirth, and the isolation of farms and ranches that increased the risks for expectant homestead women. Monica Hopkins told the story of her neighbour Joan, who became very ill during her delivery in 1912: "The nurse got very alarmed and Mr. C., went galloping to his nearest neighbour, John B., in the middle of the night to get him to go for the doctor, twenty miles across the reserve. John made simply wonderful time for the doctor was out before midday. It's dangerous having a baby so far away from a doctor. Of course, in a normal case the nurse was capable of doing everything, but who is going to know if it is going to be a normal birth. Joan had been wonderfully well all of the time."[19]

Even when doctors were available, many homesteaders could not afford them. As Eliza May recalled: "People didn't have money to spend on doctors. It cost $25 and mileage at the rate of $1.00 per mile to have a doctor tend a maternity case."[20] Women relied on the help of a neighbour woman, a midwife, their husband, or, occasionally, a trained nurse. Young women were often hired to help out around the house for a few weeks after the baby arrived, but even this was a luxury for some. As Maria Potter recalled, "We didn't have doctors, nurses or hired girls in those days but my husband was very handy around the house and could even bake bread, so we managed fine, with an occasional neighbour dropping in once in a while to help out. The drawback was that we were so far apart."[21] Sometimes the lack of professional care had serious consequences. As Catharine Neil wrote in 1906:

> Someone told me that the girl's mother was very ill and not expected to recover. I went to see her and offer my help. Mrs. Kirk was there nursing her and told me it was a case of blood poisoning through neglect at childbirth. The woman was German and had quite a number of little ones, and as doctors were far away and the cost of bringing them too much for these poor people, they had a neighbour come in whenever a baby was expected.[22]

Most women during this period had their babies at home; homesteaders were not unusual in that respect. However, most homestead mothers were disadvantaged because they were without the assistance of a trained attendant; instead, many relied on experienced midwives, while others called on inexperienced neighbours. These women had no training in childbirth. In turn, these mothers were also called upon to attend other women in childbirth, and for some it was a responsibility they did not take lightly. Unfortunately, it was also one for which they felt inadequately prepared. Clara Middleton's story points out that, regardless of their preparedness, homestead women were expected to respond when other women needed them. "You're a woman and you're needed" – that was what she believed the woman's husband was thinking when she tried to decline to help:

> His wife was in labour and would I come? I protested that I wouldn't be any good, that I knew nothing, and urged him to go at once for Mrs. Lane. No, his wife wanted me ... In a rebellious mood I dressed, and while still sure that I must refuse got into the wagon. My own child had been born with a doctor and a nurse in attendance. I had been a passive figure in their hands. What I knew or didn't know was of no consequence. Now it was of terrible consequence. So I arrived at the house distinctly "in a state" ... I waited until the doctor [who arrived after the birth] said the mother would be all right, and then went home to stumble into bed and gave my ragged nerves a rest by a

fit of wild crying ... I went there every day for two weeks, and the Barnes family, quite foolishly, regarded me as a sort of benefactor, when in reality I was only an ignorant woman standing around helpless in the face of a crisis.[23]

Harriett Neville described the situation in which many homestead women found themselves: "I tried recently to count the number of births at which I was the only assistant. I was never thought very strong but for years I never went to my bed without leaving my clothes ready to slip on at a moment's notice and a candle ready for my husband to light and go to the door when a call came."[24] Kaja Froyen referred to the "midwife from Denmark," Mrs. Sorenson, who travelled from her farm nine miles away to attend several of Froyen's births.[25]

Some of the homesteaders were trained nurses. In 1921, Margaret Thompson, a trained nurse and homesteader, found herself feeling apprehensive about being a midwife for her neighbours:

He [a neighbour] was visibly excited and said "I'm Tony. – Misses you come quick-a, my signora very sick-a, bambina stuck and won't come out-a!" I did some rapid thinking. How was I to cope with such an unknown predicament and nobody to help me but Mother Nature? No pre-natal care, no district nurse, and the only doctor 50 miles away! His horse and buggy could never make it over bumpy roads full of potholes, even if the only telephone in the district could be reached ... I had heard that homesteaders' wives learn to be resourceful and were quick to learn the procedure of normal childbirth – "nolens volens" ... I was conducted into the small bedroom where the patient lay in agony. The clean bed was surrounded by several frustrated women, who were counting their rosary beads while praying loudly and fervently. I asked them to leave the room and fill every available pot and kettle with water to bring to a boil on the cookstove in the kitchen ... I recognized a breech presentation; the delivery would indeed be a complicated and difficult one. It finally was successful. A perfect bambino made his entrance into the world, rather limp just now, but no doubt a future good Albertan ... A feeling of a job well done came over me. Like most of us, I marvelled at the ever new miracle of birth.[26]

Lena Kernen Bacon used her nursing training to educate and serve women in her community. She held social gatherings for women at her home, where the birth and care of a baby were discussed. And she went to whatever births she was asked to attend. She wrote in her memoirs: "In my three and one half years on the prairie I cared for thirteen obstetrical cases without the aid of a doctor, as we were thirty miles from Davidson and that was too far to go by horse and buggy. One baby born near Girvin, died in spite of a doctor in attendance. Here I was, nurse and undertaker, and even lined a homemade casket with white silk and artificial flowers. The mother asked me to hold a bedside service."[27]

Women responded to each others' needs by providing essential medical and social services where none had been organized. Midwives, including those who were nurses, provided an invaluable and usually free service to whomever asked for it, regardless of economic circumstance or ethnic background. As R.E. Sparks wrote about the welcome arrival of her Scottish sister-in-law, who was a trained nurse, "After that no little new Canadian ever arrived in Township 23 or surrounding townships, be he English, Irish, Scotch, Danish or German but was thoroughly scrubbed by her."[28] A few nurses and midwives did receive some pay for their work, but the fees were small and rarely solicited. Lena Kernen Bacon wrote about charging three dollars for her maternity nursing care, in her case a necessary request because she was a widow with a young daughter. Those who could not pay cash paid in kind with gifts of chickens, butter, eggs, or other staples. At the time, however, Bacon could have been prosecuted, for only doctors were legally entitled to charge for maternity cases, according to an 1885 ordinance of the North-West Territories still in effect after Saskatchewan and Alberta were created in 1905. Underlying this slow development of needed services to settlement families was a frontier ethic that valued property and profit more highly than people. Campaigns for medical care initiated by western women, as outlined by Beverly Boutilier, directly attacked this ethic and revealed its high human cost.

Sometimes motivated by cultural norms, but more often out of necessity, many families managed childbirth without any outside help. Husbands and fathers found themselves in the unfamiliar role of midwife. Mary Lawrence lived in the far north of Alberta, in Fort Vermilion, where no medical services of any kind were available. Her father-in-law had spent some time in Edmonton, studying obstetrics with various doctors in order to return to the North to be, as Lawrence described it, "a sort of amateur interne during my first child-birth" in 1899. Still, "all the remedies father had learned, all the medicines he had brought with him for this emergency were useless," as Lawrence wrote later, for she almost died from a postpartum haemorrhage.[29] Before he left the North again, her father-in-law gave the Native midwife who had assisted him with the Lawrences' first birth careful instructions on how to proceed with future births.

This account is unusual in that the cultural norm for childbirth was that it was a woman's event, to be managed by women for women. According to Judith Leavitt there was a female culture around the birthing bed, and for women from some European countries, the presence of a man, other than the husband, was forbidden.[30] Irene Parlby, president of the United Farm Women of Alberta, wrote to Violet McNaughton in Saskatchewan in 1916: "One thing we are up against are the men and their wives who refuse to have any medical or nursing aid at childbirth. I know of *many* instances where the wife has never had anyone but her husband and they don't seem to want anyone else, many of them."[31] In most cases, even when male doctors were in attendance, a nurse, midwife, or woman neighbour was present and was involved in the care of mother and baby. In some families, necessity demanded innovation, and many husbands (and sometimes other men) who were not doctors were actively involved in childbirth. As one woman described her family's approach to childbirth: "I stay right here and when my time comes, I call Bill in from the field and he delivers them."[32] Due to bad weather, Harriett Neville's husband also was her only attendant at the birth of their son.

Mary Lawrence's subsequent births were also unusual because the midwife was a Native woman. In the culture in which Lawrence had lived in the North this was not unusual; but for the settlers included in this study, it was atypical. Only one other birth story mentioned a Native woman as a birth attendant. The accounts of Lawrence's five subsequent childbirths demonstrate that Native expertise in childbirth was far more useful than was the knowledge brought by her father-in-law from the Edmonton doctors. By following the Native custom of kneeling to give birth, Lawrence found that her third childbirth, again under the direction of the Native midwife, Nokum Julie, was "the easiest of any childbirth so far." She wrote in her memoirs: "And I was so convinced of the logic of this natural method over that to which white women are enforced that I abided by it henceforth."[33]

Mary Lawrence was a trained nurse, which proved to be an asset because she knew about the prenatal and postnatal care she and her babies needed in order to survive the six pregnancies she had in her nine years in the North. Even then, the conditions in which she gave birth to her largest and strongest baby, a ten-pound boy, conspired against her, and she lost him to croup within thirty-six hours. Infant mortality rates on the Prairies were high, and, as Canadian statistics show, most infant deaths occurred within the first week of life.[34] It is not an exaggeration to say that almost every family lost at least one infant at birth or shortly after birth. Sometimes it was the circumstances of the birth that caused the death, and occasionally it was the conditions into which the baby was born. Margaret Shaw wrote of her first birth in 1902, in a rented room in town, "it was a chilly April morning and the room was far too cold for a new born baby ... She was blue with cold."[35] Evelyn Springett wrote: "I shall never forget those awful hours before the doctor arrived. The heat was terrific and I was devoured by flies."[36] Elone Stobaugh and her family shared their cabin with another family in 1930, so privacy for childbirth had to be found elsewhere. She delivered her child with the help of her friend while waiting for the doctor to arrive.

> A baby being born at the mill was quite an event. We were living in a small house with another family so what were we to do? There was a small shack used as an office. It was decided that we would clear it out and use it. There was a built in bunk and a stove. That would do. Mail came in once a week. Someone would go to town to bring it back. That was an important day. That morning I knew was *the day*. I was already in labour but I had to have breakfast and read the letter from my mother so I put off going to the shack until I knew I could wait no longer. I walked about fifty yards to the little house I was to be in. A very short time later she was born. We were waiting for the only doctor in the area to come. She was paid by the government. A young English woman who had come out to take care of people in a 100 mile area. She too got thrown in a snowdrift and so didn't make it until too late for any help.[37]

The quality of professional care, when available, also proved, in some instances, to put women and infants at risk. Margaret Shaw and Mary Unger described their experiences:

> When the doctor arrived the baby had beat him to it. Remember he had just come out of a *livery stable*. He wore a big coon skin coat which he threw over a chair just four feet from my bed. He may have washed his hands, I'm not sure, but I know he didn't use any disinfectant.[38]
>
> There were no hospitals, no nurse, and just an old, old doctor. And he was going deaf ... Well that old doctor he waited on the couch and he helped me. He laid down and he slept and when it got too hard he helped me a little, then he went away.[39]

Some doctors who were recent graduates had little or no practical experience, especially with childbirth, and certainly not with home births, which ensured that no facilities were available to them. Many of the local doctors spent most of their time farming, and there was a high turnover of doctors on the Prairies for many years during this period. It was difficult to make a living as a doctor on the Prairies during settlement years, as homesteaders had little money to pay for professional services. Lillian Turner described the birth of her third child, the first birth for which she had a doctor's assistance: "I have been very far down in the valley this time and I pray the dear Lord I may never have to go again. I feel so glad I have been spared to the children … We had the Dr. here three times and the last time he waited from midnight until noon the next day before he gave me chloroform. He is the same fellow who was on the threshing outfit with John. So you will know not very experienced. But he seems to have had good training."[40]

Doctors in other parts of the country, particularly in urban centres, criticized women who attended at childbirths, whether as trained nurses or as midwives. In contrast, some Prairie doctors recognized the shortage of help available to farm women and provided informal on-the-job training to women who continued to practise as midwives for their neighbours. While they expressed some concerns about these attendants' abilities to handle more complicated deliveries, they understood that even someone with a little training and experience was better than a neighbour woman with none. Mary Dawes explained how she became a midwife in 1923:

> I was helping the doctor one time and he come down and said, the lady upstairs said she's feeling sick and going to have the baby but my nurse is sick. Well I said, I ain't a nurse … but if I can help you, I'll come up and help. So I washed and put on a clean apron and went upstairs and helped him with this baby when it was born … I didn't know that to slap their bottoms to make them cry you see and he slapped the baby's bottom to make it cry and I punched him in the back. I laughed so much afterwards and I hugged him afterwards. I said forgive me I didn't know … well I brought twenty-six babies into the world now on the farms, all on my own with no doctor … it's give me such a gorgeous feeling … I really enjoyed it because I wanted to be a nurse … We didn't charge no money. I never charged a lady a nickel … It all worked beautiful. Of course lots of times we never had the things we wanted to put on the children and do the things we wanted to but as long as I had lots of hot water and lots of clean clothes I managed pretty nice. Well Dr. Olibisky … I was with him three or four times and he said "I don't know," he said, "whatever you'll do if you had to go somewhere where there was something bad," and I said that's the only thing that I didn't want to go for because I said if anything went wrong I didn't want them to blame me because I wasn't a nurse and I had no papers. But you're always there ready to help somebody if you can … And they say you can't do those things if you're not a nurse but the doctor just told me what he did when that baby was born, showed me how to cut the cord and wait for the afterbirth and told me if it was all perfect that was everything. Well everything went fine.[41]

The issue of midwifery in settlement areas became a subject of intense debate among women's groups and health care providers. Suzann Buckley identified a thirty-year period, from 1890 to 1920, in Canada, during which there were considerable efforts made by women's organizations, led by the National Council of Women of Canada and by women reformers, to address the infant mortality and maternal mortality rates in Canada.[42] The trained midwife was seen as an immediate solution to this pressing problem. The maternal mortality and infant mortality rates of the Prairie provinces were higher than in most other provinces until about 1924. Alberta had the highest rates in the country in 1921.[43] Statistics gathered in 1914 in Saskatchewan showed that almost one-half of 1,637 infant deaths under the age of five were attributable to problems related to the mother's pregnancy or to the delivery of the baby.[44] The report on maternal mortality rates prepared by the federal government in 1925 showed that, for adult women, maternity was the second leading cause of death, after tuberculosis.[45] Maternal morbidity as a result of pregnancy and childbirth was also a significant and hidden problem.[46]

Farm women and nurses involved in the Victorian Order of Nurses responded to this crisis, with limited success. In 1916 Violet McNaughton, president of the Women's Section of the Saskatchewan Grain Growers, presented a brief on behalf of Prairie farm women to a subcommittee of the Canadian National Association of Trained Nurses (CNATN) outlining the needs of Prairie women with respect to maternity care and some of the difficulties the Prairie environment and lifestyle posed. She proposed a scheme that incorporated the partnership of "strong women who are trained midwives and can also take charge of the household" and district nurses, paid for by provincial and federal governments.[47] She had some confidence, gained through her work with the Colonial Nursing Association of Britain, that trained midwives would be readily available.[48] The executive minutes of the CNATN acknowledged McNaughton's valuable input and the strong impression she made on those present at the subcommittee meeting.[49]

McNaughton was a practical woman offering a practical solution to a serious social problem. She had done her research: Saskatchewan was one of the few Canadian provinces to gather statistics on infant and maternal mortality before 1916.[50] She had the support of the Victorian Order of Nurses, which had participated in putting the scheme together. She also had the full support and keen interest of her counterpart, Irene Parlby, president of the United Farm Women of Alberta, as correspondence between the two women in early 1916 shows. In a letter to McNaughton written in February 1916, Parlby says:

> There seems to be nothing to go upon and yet one knows of what one hears, that there are any amount of women in the rural districts who go without any

> aid but their husbands during their confinements, or perhaps that of a neighbour who will come in. I remember reading or hearing years ago that at some medical board or convention in the West, I think in Alberta, it was said that the province would never be able to provide sufficient population from within as the conditions of climate and everything were so against the women at the time of childbirth ... What is the Government's objection I wonder to properly trained and qualified midwives?[51]

The response of Canadian doctors and nurses to McNaughton's proposal, as it was to the previous two put forward by Lady Aberdeen in 1897 and Marion Cran in 1908, was strong opposition. They were motivated to protect their professional turfs and incomes, and objected to midwives based on a variety of prejudices, including their belief that midwives lacked adequate training, were unclean, and were willing to perform domestic chores. The CNATN aligned with the doctors to insist on doctors' rights to the delivery fee and the right of nurses to be trained assistants at births. Neither doctor nor nurse would do housework. The CNATN executive felt pressed to respond immediately to the doctors on the issue, and they decided that their recommendation and, indeed, their lobbying strategies would be directed at requests to governments to provide small hospitals throughout the western provinces where trained nurses could work in conjunction with doctors. They could not see nurses making home visits into remote areas, and they agreed to supply nurses if suitable facilities were provided.[52] The position of the nurses in the CNATN made some professional medical people uneasy. Charlotte Hannington, who was chief superintendent of the Victorian Order of Nurses (VON), supported the introduction of midwives as a temporary measure, as did Dr. Thomas Gibson, also of the VON. They both felt the mothers of the West deserved some help, even if it wasn't highly trained help, and that the scheme presented by the CNATN was not an adequate solution.[53] As honourable secretaries of the board of governors, Thomas Gibson and Charles Morse included in their 1916 report to the board a reminder that the original reason for the existence of the VON was to serve the nursing needs of the West and the sparsely settled parts of Canada. They suggested that it was "quite probable that the obstetric needs of the West cannot be satisfied by small hospitals and regular district nurses, at least for many years to come,"[54] citing the scarcity of trained nurses, the heavy demands put upon a nurse to serve all citizens in a district, and the difficulties that, due to their family responsibilities at home, mothers would experience in utilizing the services of a hospital. Hannington never gave up her campaign to improve the maternity care for mothers in rural areas. In her report to the board of governors of the VON in 1919, she stated:

> I cannot close this report without calling the attention of all present, and I wish it could be all the citizens of Canada, to the neglect of proper provision for the care of child-bearing women in the rural districts of Canada ... The condition cannot be met by a graduate nurse for two reasons: first, her graduate training is not sufficient to enable her with confidence to take care of normal cases without a doctor or to recognize abnormal conditions in time to get medical help ... second, when the nurse is willing to go and do her best she has no legal protection ... Though red tape has crept into the medical and nursing profession regarding this matter, their rules were originally intended as an earnest effort to protect the mother from ignorant and untrained service. But so far the State refuses to accept its full responsibility in the matter. The full protection of all bodies engaged in Public Health work and all their resources should be thrown about the women of this country who are bringing to the nation the gift of life.[55]

The position of some of the VON members was based on experience. As Beverly Boutilier explains in Chapter 8, the VON had set up small cottage hospitals in the western territories by 1904, originally with the idea that they would provide mostly maternity care. But once the start-up grants from the VON had been expended, most of the communities were unable to sustain the hospitals, and maternity cases occupied fewer than 10 percent of the beds.[56] Few women were able to take advantage of the care the VON had set out to provide because women were generally reluctant to use hospitals, the fees were prohibitive, and hospitals were difficult to reach from remote areas. Historically, this was just the beginning of the period in which women would start to choose to give birth in institutional settings, with trained personnel, rather than at home, preferably with a doctor in attendance. The particular situation of a homestead woman, whose work was essential to the maintenance of the farm, dictated that she not leave the farm to have her babies, especially after the first child had arrived. The failure of the cottage hospital program led the VON to support the British midwife plan in 1916.

Government response was slow and inadequate. In 1910, Saskatchewan introduced a maternity package and maternity grant system for poor mothers. The maternity package contained a few basic supplies needed for a newborn infant. The maternity grant was designed to help mothers in remote areas and in financial need pay for doctors' services. Eligibility for the grant had to be determined by a municipal secretary, a justice of the peace, or the local member of the legislature. Between 1921 and 1923, applications for the grant tripled, as a small depression hit the farming community during those years.[57]

In Saskatchewan the municipal-doctor scheme was implemented in 1916, and it placed doctors in small rural centres that were designed to serve a wide rural area. Although these doctors' basic salaries were paid from public funds, a fee for maternity cases was allowed. Half of the doctors working under the scheme worked on a part-time basis, and the program did not grow significantly until the depression years of 1931-6.

Alberta introduced a municipal hospital system in 1917. By 1935 twenty-two rural municipal hospitals had been built or purchased, some of them from the VON. The areas they served represented approximately one-third of the rural population. This system had its origins in Saskatchewan, where "Union Hospitals" were established under a similar scheme. By 1920 the Red Cross had also established eighteen community hospitals in Saskatchewan; these were designed to serve maternity cases, minor surgery, and accident cases, although by 1924 only seven of them remained open. The Union Hospital plan also did not prove to be the answer to women's maternity needs. The minister of health reported in 1924 that hospitals handled only 26 percent of the province's maternity cases.[58] It is clear that hospitals were not the answer to the maternity care needs of rural women.

The informal nursing services that homesteading women provided to each other in Alberta were partially replaced in 1918 by public health nurses who were employed by the Alberta government and placed in towns where women could visit them for prenatal and postnatal care. However, public health nurses were not legally permitted to attend childbirths. Only specially trained district nurses were allowed to deliver babies, and the Alberta Nursing Act was changed in 1919 to accommodate the role of the district nurse. The first three district nurses were hired in 1919, two for remote northern areas, where no medical care of any kind was available. At its peak level, the district nursing service would provide full maternity care in fifteen districts in Alberta. The idea of having a district nurse, with training in obstetrics, attend maternity cases in remote areas, stemmed from farm women who, both individually and collectively, lobbied the provincial government. Tony Cashman, in his history of nursing in Alberta, claims that some doctors were opposed to district nurses delivering babies. "The idea was new in Canada ... on the frontier in Alberta it was supported by the unwritten law that there is a duty for one woman to help another."[59] However, some doctors recognized that the needs of rural mothers were urgent, and they ensured that nurses were appropriately trained and given legal status as midwives.

In 1930 the Alberta government took some responsibility for placing doctors in four remote northern areas. They recruited four doctors from England, all of them women, and the local people provided them with cabins centrally located in the district they were to serve as well as a horse to ride to all corners of their district.[60] In eleven other Alberta pioneer districts the Alberta government subsidized private physicians for their services. Anecdotal histories of the doctors' experiences reveal that a significant number of mothers' and babies' lives were saved by having practitioners trained in obstetrics to call upon during childbirth.

Some Prairie women, mostly in the later settlement years, travelled to hospitals or to private maternity homes in towns or cities to birth their children. The travel was often rough and uncomfortable, with women exposed to the elements, as this account by Elone Stobaugh, who lived in one of the northern areas served by a British doctor, shows:

> We sent word to the doctor nine miles away. She came and found I needed to go to a hospital. She gave me some morphine to slow things so I could get to some professional care she couldn't give. We had no car but a neighbour had an open grain truck in which an army cot was placed and we started eighty miles to the town of Peace River. The sky was clear and the sun was bright. I got a severe sunburn. We reached the hospital without much problem though the canvas on the cot was rotten and split down the middle.[61]

Kathleen Strange, a war bride who began homesteading in 1918, travelled to a hospital in Edmonton for her first child's birth and to a hospital in Calgary for her second's; both hospitals were a considerable distance from her farm. Her third child was born in Stettler, twenty miles from her farm, where a new doctor and hospital were established. She told a horrendous tale of the four hours it took to cover the twenty miles – in a car without a roof, in a severe rainstorm, and in the advanced stages of labour – all the while trying to delay the birth until she arrived at the hospital.[62] Esme Tuck included in her memoirs some notes from a hospital nurse, who wrote about a woman who travelled eighty miles in forty below zero weather in January to have her baby in the hospital. The baby did not survive.[63] Eliza Wilson lost her first child in hospital when the baby was four days old. For the birth of her second child in 1902, she travelled in a cold rainstorm on an open wagon, arriving sixteen hours later, chilled and numb, at the home of a friend. She rested for a few days before travelling alone by train to admit herself to the town hospital. She wrote that she was "very weary" when labour finally began.[64] Travel to hospitals was a hardship for many women, and it made life more difficult for families with children who were left behind to cope on their own. Hospitals proved to be a mixed blessing, as the quality of care there was not significantly better than what could be obtained at home, and the long journey in rough conditions to get there put many mothers and babies at risk.

As an alternative to last-minute travel, some women, like Margaret Shaw, moved into town to rented rooms or the home of a friend to await the births. Barbara Slater moved to town for the winter to birth her second child after a bad experience with the birth of her first child on the homestead. There she had the assistance of a new doctor, whom she declared "decidedly clever" and a "qualified nurse."[65] In some cases, women travelled to a nurse's or midwife's home to give birth. As one midwife wrote, this put labouring mothers at considerable risk:

> I was midwife during the poor years and brought many babies into this world. Sometimes the men had to come many miles by team and sleigh through deep snowdrifts to get me to help the women. Others would bring their wives to my home to have their babies. I remember one woman coming very early one very cold winter morning, they had tried to get to Empress, Alberta but the roads were so bad they couldn't get through. Turned around and headed for our farm … That woman was so cold … I remember it took me all day to get that woman warm, her baby girl being born soon after they got in our house. Even that poor baby was cold when it was born.[66]

Even hospital births were not free of risk for mother and baby. Hospitals were ill equipped to deal with some neo-natal needs, and personnel denied mothers' expertise and participation in the care of their own babies. Beatrice Whitehair described her tragic hospital experience in Calgary:

> The new General was open by the time my twins were born … But I lost the boy. He was twelve days old but he was dying. I never brought him home … Oh he just went bad and yet when he was born the doctor says "Well your boy is fine but I'll not give you much for your girl." And I've still got her … Well I put it down to that they didn't bring him often enough to have nurse. And I told the doctor so. I said "You know Dr. Crawford that baby isn't getting any nourishment. I have to squeeze it into his mouth, he hasn't got the power to, he's getting weaker and weaker." Well he said, "I'll tell them to bring him to you all the time." But they didn't … You see at the time there was nothing to help the babies in the hospital. It should have been put in the incubator and got some more strength because they were over five pounds each. So they were good sized babies.[67]

Some women also chose to travel to their parents' or other relatives' homes in other provinces or countries to deliver their babies. Socio-economic status determined who could choose this option, just as it determined the decision to call a doctor to the homestead. Evelyn Springett, after a bad experience with her first child's birth on the ranch, travelled to Winnipeg to stay at her brother's home for the birth of her second child.[68] Lillian Turner sent a private note to her mother, separate from her newsy family letter, telling her not to worry about her daughter's first pregnancy. She mentioned that the doctor who was presently in the district was leaving, so she decided to return by train to her mother's home in Ontario to birth her child there.[69]

Among the more unusual birth stories I found in women's accounts is a story told by Ellen Lowes about a neighbour woman's experience. As Lowes indicated, it was a story that was widely shared as an example of the situations and conditions in which women experienced childbirth:

> Shortly after the train service to Yorkton became regular, an event almost unbelievable occurred in the train. The usual Saturday night train leaving Portage La Prairie for Yorkton had as a passenger a lady travelling from England. She was expecting very shortly to become a mother, but was suddenly taken ill on the train. The baby was born in the women's lavatory, but disappeared through the toilet. The conductor stopped the train, and went back and picked up the young man. Many people consider this an impossible yarn, but I watched this baby grow to young manhood.[70]

Ignorance about pregnancy and childbirth was a problem for some mothers. The inaccessibility of medical personnel and the lack of reading materials on these subjects made self-education impossible. Some women indicated a cultural taboo about discussing such topics, even with one's own mother, so intergenerational knowledge and experience was not available to them. One woman claimed that her parents had deliberately kept her in the dark about how babies were conceived. She knew her husband knew, but she would not discuss it with him. It was only after her two children were older that she found out from other women how they had been created. The number of trained nurses who were also homesteaders alleviated the problem about lack of knowledge to some extent, as the examples of Mary Lawrence and Lena Kernen Bacon demonstrate. They both provided informal pregnancy and sex education to women they knew. However, many women reflected with regret on their lack of knowledge of childbirth as they faced it for the first time. "As for prenatal care, there was no such thing for pioneer homesteaders," wrote Margaret Thompson, a trained nurse who homesteaded in the Fort Assiniboine area.[71] The first time many practitioners saw their maternity patients was at the birth.

Several women, including Mary Lawrence, also mentioned that they had no knowledge of how to prevent pregnancies but that if they had it they would use it. Without this knowledge many women had large families in a short space of time and spent the better part of their reproductive years either carrying or nursing infants.[72] When the enormous workloads homestead women were responsible for are considered, as well as the conditions in which they lived and worked, the additional burden of continuous pregnancies – sometimes for up to twenty years – may be seen as an onerous one indeed. Women could not easily set aside their work to rest. Some farm women cut back on some of their heavier farm chores, but for the most part, both farm and ranch women carried on as usual. Many women faced heavy physical and emotional demands throughout their pregnancies. Eliza May found herself a midwife and housekeeper for her neighbour while very close to delivering her own child: "We took care of each other in case of illness in those days. I never had any training, but was never afraid and was guided to do what was needed. Once a call came for me to go to a neighbour. This was six weeks before my own daughter was born, in November and very cold. It was a two and a half mile drive with an old team and a jumper. When I got there I found it was a false alarm. Next morning I had to come back home and get my little son and bring him to the house. A week later her baby was born."[73]

Peggy Holmes wrote that she continued working as a hired cook for harvest crews, a physically exhausting job, through six months of pregnancy. And Mary Cummins described an incident on her farm in which she found herself, at nine months pregnant, sprawled across the top of an eighty-foot well, assisting the hired man to hoist himself out after rescuing a foal who had fallen down it.

There was also little opportunity for postpartum healing and rest when, as Mary Lawrence put it, "men must eat," and many women delayed their recoveries by returning to their regular work routines too quickly after birth. Farms and ranches were dependent on women's work. After her fifth child was born, Mary Cummins had a difficult time recuperating, particularly after four pregnancies close together and a growing workload, and she "withered away" to a weight of fifty-eight pounds (from her usual ninety). She was sent "home" to England to rest and recuperate.[74] Hilda Rose's birth brought her so near death that she barely hung on to life for five weeks, and it took her another six months to learn to walk alone.[75] Postpartum complications were responsible for most of the childbirth deaths. While this was true for women across Canada during this period, it was perhaps especially the case for Prairie women who were without the care they required.[76] Sarah Roberts wrote of her doctor husband's visit to a woman twenty miles away – a woman "who had not had the services of a physician during confinement. He found her in a raving delirium. He advised her husband to take her at once to the hospital in Castor. This was done, but she died a few days later, just for the lack of proper care when her child was born."[77] If women did recover from childbirth, for many their former state of health never returned. Peggy Holmes wrote about a homestead woman she met who had borne many children and worked hard and continuously for many years: "It was difficult to imagine how she looked when she was young, as she was in such poor condition physically and mentally ... How she must have suffered! Here was a happy bride, full of hope but now a human wreck."[78]

Women did not passively accept the lack of medical services and facilities at this crucial time in their lives. Some organized committees or raised funds to establish hospitals or maternity homes. Alice Rendell, after a difficult time with a birth several months after her arrival on the homestead in 1903, immediately began a fund-raising campaign for a little hospital for the Barr settlement. She appealed to her friends and relations in England, and she wrote in a subsequent letter: "Some of you are just working hard for the benefit of the hospital here in response to my appeal ... A little lumber shack is to be put up almost immediately so great is the need for it ... You would not wonder at my taking this so much to heart could you have but witnessed what I have or been through what I myself have suffered. You cannot realize how awful it is."[79]

Women in many communities on the Prairies took the initiative to raise funds for private or community-sponsored hospitals. In this way, women's nursing responsibilities in the home were extended into the community (the expectation that doctors and nurses could provide better care than untrained women had been their cultural experience in their "home" communities). Later, shared concerns about the safety of mothers and babies would move individual farm women and farm women's organizations in both provinces to put demands for health care services at the top of their lobbying agendas, as they became engaged in the midwifery debate at both provincial and national levels.

The stories of homestead women's birth experiences are diverse and reflect differences of ethnic background, socio-economic class, and education. Common to all was the resourcefulness of couples in attempting to achieve as safe a birth situation as they possibly could within the restrictions imposed by their families' limited resources, the lack of trained personnel available to them, and their families' geographical locations. As these accounts show, this was not an easy undertaking: it was often filled with fear and apprehension, and it brought hardship and sometimes tragedy.

On the Prairies during the settlement years, efforts to ensure safe childbirths were complicated by the isolation and conditions of homestead life as well as the lack of social and government structures that could respond to settlers' needs. Efforts by the medical profession and federal and provincial governments to address the maternity and child health needs of Prairie homesteaders were hampered by a number of factors. One was the limited knowledge of decision makers about the conditions in which homesteaders lived, including their financial resources, the distances they lived from service centres, the methods by which they had to travel, and the workloads of expectant women. Canadian doctors and nurses did not give the suggestions of farm women from Saskatchewan and Alberta, who were most familiar with families' needs and circumstances, adequate consideration in the development of services to respond to homesteaders' needs. This short-sightedness was coupled with the prejudices of medical practitioners, both doctors and nurses, concerning the effectiveness of midwives. Such views were not based on research of any kind and did not discriminate between trained and untrained midwives. Some of these concerns thinly masked a xenophobia directed at anyone not of British origins and of a certain class, thus the condemnations of the practice of midwifery were also an attempt to "civilize" the Prairies – to make them conform to a White, Anglo-Canadian middle-class norm.

There was also a lack of recognition that safe childbirth was a social problem, not just a medical one, and that it required the consideration of families' needs (e.g., for help with household work) as well as an understanding of the efficacy of proposed solutions and their consequences should they not be effective. Several anecdotes reported in the maternal mortality research conducted by the federal government pointed to the collapse of families and of farm operations when the mother died.[80]

Other historical developments affected the response to the maternity care needs of homestead families. One was the professional territoriality of the doctors and nurses, both of whom were trying to establish themselves more firmly in their professions. For doctors, delivering a baby was often their first point of contact with a family; as for nurses, they were trying to improve their professional position within the medical hierarchy by doing only medical care and by strengthening their relationships with doctors. Another was the historical changes that were taking place in the delivery of health care generally, which was moving away from the home and into institutions. Hospitals were perceived as the answer to every health issue when, in fact, for people on farms and ranches, a hospital located many miles away was useless in many medical emergencies. Because of their distance from medical centres, women were often unable to receive appropriate prenatal and postnatal care, and many had no opportunities to take a break from their heavy workloads. These circumstances often complicated the birth situations that medical practitioners were called to attend, whether in the home or in the hospital. At the same time, childbirth was becoming increasingly medicalized, even in the home, because women wanted every defence they could get against death or debility.

The situations specific to Saskatchewan and Alberta, established as new provinces in 1905, were the difficulties they faced in setting up needed services quickly. The funds and the trained personnel had to be found and the structures for service delivery had to be developed. The new provinces sometimes looked to England for doctors and nurses, and they

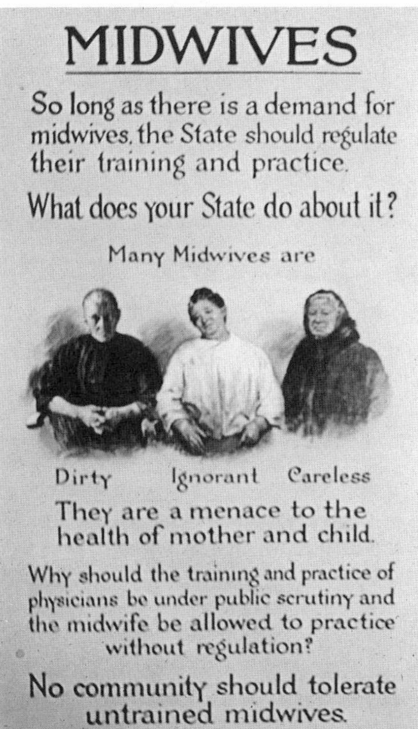

Anti-midwife poster distributed by the Department of Public Health, 1924

attempted to adopt programs and delivery mechanisms identical to those developed in provinces whose geographies and populations differed significantly from their own.

For many years, while the medical profession, women's organizations, and governments sorted out which solutions were best suited to providing safe maternity care to Prairie women, many homestead families were left to cope on their own. The numbers of women affected by the situation increased dramatically during this period, the population of women in Saskatchewan and Alberta multiplying ten times over in the decade between 1901 and 1911. Homesteading was indeed a different experience for women than it was for men. Women literally risked their lives to establish their families and a future for their children in the Canadian West. In a contradictory social context, in which women were indispensable to successful settlement yet treated as dispensable by negligent and irresponsible governments, homestead women responded to each other's needs – sometimes with hesitation and fear, but they always responded. They provided each other with the practical and emotional support that childbirth demanded, and they often did this in defiance of legislation or medical practitioners' attempts to control childbirth. They assisted each other at childbirth because they were the only ones available to do so. As one woman characterized it, childbirth was a time of sisterhood for many women of this generation on the Prairies, a sisterhood based on a bond central to their lives as homestead women: they were women, and they were needed.

Acknowledgments

This chapter is reprinted courtesy of the *Journal of Historical Sociology* 8, 3 (1995): 278-302. I am grateful to Susan Smith, Diana Chown, and Catherine Cavanaugh for their helpful comments on this chapter.

Notes

1 I categorize these women as the "first generation" of mass European agricultural settlement on the Prairies, recognizing that Aboriginal peoples had made the Canadian Prairies their home for thousands of years before the Europeans arrived and that other White women had served in missions before the migration of settlers to the West.
2 G. Chase, Letter to her mother, 1920. Provincial Archives of Alberta, Accession no. 73.569SE.
3 B. Slater, Letter to a friend, 1912. Provincial Archives of Alberta, Accession no. 78.79.
4 S. Puckette, Diary, 1903-5. Glenbow Archives, Accession no. M843.
5 J. Leavitt, *Brought to Bed: Childbearing in America, 1750-1950* (New York: Oxford University Press 1986).
6 M. Hopkins, *Letters from a Lady Rancher* (Halifax: Goodread Biographies, 1981).
7 Statistics on maternal mortality in Canada were not collected until 1921, although some

provinces collected their own statistics before that date. Maternal mortality was not studied in Canada until 1925. In the period studied, 1 July 1925 to 1 July 1926, there were 1,532 maternal deaths, and the 1928 report, *Maternal Mortality in Canada* (H. MacMurchy), claimed that "most of these deaths can be prevented." Of the 1,532 women who died, 1,302 had no prenatal care at all. Septicemia was the major cause of death, closely followed by hemorrhage, although this order was reversed in Alberta. The third major cause was toxemia. In Alberta, there were 111 maternal deaths in both 1921 and 1922, and 84 of these occurred in rural areas. In 1929 there were 123 maternal deaths in Alberta, 78 of them occurring in rural areas. In Saskatchewan, there were 127 maternal deaths in 1922, 74 of them occurring in rural areas. Until 1933 maternity followed only tuberculosis as the leading cause of death for adult women in Canada.

8 M. Zeidler, Oral history, Provincial Archives of Alberta, Accession no. 81.279/16.

9 H. Neville, Memoirs, "Pioneering in the Northwest Territories, 1882-1905," Saskatchewan Archives Board, Accession no. R-E2883, 44.

10 P. Holmes, and J. Roberts, *It Could Have Been Worse* (Toronto: Collins, 1980), 164.

11 For a full discussion of this professional debate conducted at the national level, see S. Buckley, "Ladies or Midwives? Efforts to Reduce Infant and Maternal Mortality," in *A Not Unreasonable Claim*, ed. L. Kealey (Toronto: Women's Educational Press, 1979), 131-49.

12 M. Cran, *A Woman in Canada* (Toronto: Musson, 1910).

13 K. Strange, *With the West in Her Eyes: The Story of a Modern Pioneer* (New York: Dodge, 1937), 164.

14 M. Thompson, Memoirs, Provincial Archives of Alberta, Accession no. 84.156SE.

15 M. Edey, Oral history, Provincial Archives of Alberta, Accession no. 81.279.

16 M. Shaw, Autobiography, 1964, Glenbow Archives, Accession no. M4168.

17 M. Cummins, Memoirs, "How About It? The Story of a Woman's Life," Saskatchewan Archives Board, Accession no. R-E2552.

18 A. Self, Oral history, 1973, Saskatchewan Archives Board.

19 Hopkins, *Letters from a Lady Rancher*, 50.

20 E. May, Memoirs, "Reminiscences of an Old-timer," 1929, Glenbow Archives, Accession no. M1002.

21 M. Potter, Memoirs, 1948, Saskatchewan Archives Board, 12.

22 C. Neil, Memoirs, "One Big Family," Glenbow Archives, Accession no. M888, M4116.

23 C. Middleton, *Green Fields Afar: Memoirs of Alberta Days* (Toronto: Ryerson, 1947), 48-50.

24 H. Neville, Memoirs, "Pioneering in the Northwest Territories, 1882-1905," Saskatchewan Archives Board, Accession no. R-E2883, 44.

25 K. Froyen, Memoirs, 1934, Provincial Archives of Alberta, Accession no. 74.172.

26 M. Thompson, Memoirs, Provincial Archives of Alberta, Accession no. 84.156SE.

27 Lena Kernen Bacon, Memoirs, "Fours Years in Saskatchewan from June 1904 to July 1908," Saskatchewan Archives, Accession no. R-E30, 7.

28 R.E. Sparks, Memoirs, "A Pioneer Mother," Provincial Archives of Alberta, Accession no. 74.444.

29 M. Lawrence, Memoirs, "Keewaiten," Glenbow Archives, Accession no. M3841, 86.

30 Leavitt, *Brought to Bed*.

31 Parlby to McNaughton, 14 March 1916, Violet McNaughton Papers, Saskatchewan Archives Board, Accession no. A1.

32 Homes and Roberts, *It Could Have Been Worse*, 119.

33 M. Lawrence, Memoirs "Keewaiten," Glenbow Archives, Accession no. M3841, 163.

34 Infant deaths from premature births, injuries at birth, congenital debility, and congenital malformation constitute 44.6 percent of all infants who died under the age of one in Alberta in 1921. This number actually increased in the second part of the decade. The stillbirth rate also increased throughout the 1920s. In Saskatchewan in 1914, 31 percent of infant deaths in the first year were neonatal deaths, and the rate of still births dramatically increased from 1914 to 1916 (from 182 to 285, respectively). Prenatal care of mothers, as well as better obstetric care at birth, was cited as a major preventive measure for dealing with the high incidence of infant mortality.

35 M. Shaw, Autobiography, 1964, Glenbow Archives, Accession no. M4168.

36 E. Springett, *For My Children's Children* (Montreal: Unity, 1937), 97.
37 E. Stobaugh, Memoirs, Provincial Archives of Alberta, Accession no. 88.638.
38 M. Shaw, Autobiography, 1964, Glenbow Archives, Accession no. M4168.
39 M. Unger, Oral history, Provincial Archives of Alberta, Accession no. 81.279/67.
40 L. Turner, Letters, Glenbow Archives, Accession no. M8244.
41 M. Dawes, Oral history, Provincial Archives of Alberta, Accession no. 81.279/111.
42 Buckley, "Ladies or Midwives?" Also see Boutilier, this volume, 174-99.
43 H. McMurchy, *Maternal Mortality in Canada* (Ottawa: Department of Health, 1928).
44 J.A. Rose, *Infantile Mortality in Saskatchewan* (Regina: Department of Public Health, 1915).
45 McMurchy, *Maternal Mortality.*
46 Ibid.
47 V. McNaughton, "Some of the Difficulties in Connection with Maternity Nursing on the Prairie," a brief to the Canadian Nursing Association "Canada" Subcommittee, 1916. Saskatchewan Archives Board, Violet McNaughton Papers, Accession no. A1.
48 Report on the Friday, 3 November 1916 meeting of the Colonial Nursing Association, London, England, reprinted from the *Imperial Colonist* (London), December 1916.
49 Proceedings of the Fifth Annual Convention of the Canadian National Association of Trained Nurses, Ottawa, 1916
50 Rose, "Infantile Mortality."
51 Parlby to McNaughton, 19 February 1916. Saskatchewan Archives Board, Violet McNaughton Papers, Accession no. A1.
52 Proceedings of the Fifth Annual Convention of the Canadian National Association of Trained Nurses, Ottawa, 1916.
53 The Victorian Order of Nurses for Canada, *Report of the Board of Governors*, 1916.
54 T. Gibson and C. Morse, honourable secretaries, Victorian Order of Nurses for Canada, *Report of the Board of Governors, 1916*, 15.
55 C. Hannington, Chief Superintendent's Report, Victorian Order of Nurses for Canada, *Report of the Board of Governors, 1919*, 27.
56 Report of the Board of Governors, Victorian Order of Nurses for Canada, 1906, indicated that at the Indian Head hospital, only 11 of 206 cases were obstetric cases; in Regina hospital, 10 of 416 cases were obstetric cases; and in Yorkton hospital, only 9 of 252 cases were obstetric cases (see p. 13).
57 Sessional Papers, Saskatchewan Legislature, 1924.
58 Ibid.
59 T. Cashman, *Heritage of Service: The History of Nursing in Alberta* (Edmonton: Alberta Association of Registered Nurses, 1966), 196.
60 For a remarkable account of one doctor's experiences, see Mary Percy Jackson's *The Homemade Brass Plate* (Sardis, BC: Cedar-Cott Enterprises, 1988).
61 E. Stobaugh, Memoirs, Provincial Archives of Alberta, Accession no. 88.638.
62 Strange, *With the West in Her Eyes.*
63 E. Tuck, Memoirs, Glenbow Archives, Accession no. M1254.
64 E. Wilson, Diary, 1902, Glenbow Archives, Accession no. M1320.
65 B. Slater, Letters, Provincial Archives of Alberta, Accession no. 78.79B.
66 H. Campbell, Memoirs, Saskatchewan Archives.
67 B. Whitehair, Oral history, Provincial Archives of Alberta, Accession no. 81.279/72.
68 Springett, *For My Children's Children.*
69 L. Turner, Letters, Glenbow Archives, Accession no. M8244.
70 E. Lowes, Memoirs, "The Diary of Ellen McFadden Lowes," Saskatchewan Archives Board, Accession no. SHS 148, SHS 235.
71 M. Thompson, Memoirs, Provincial Archives of Alberta, Accession no. 84.156SE.
72 Judith Leavitt's research also demonstrated the long periods, often twenty years or more, during which women were either pregnant or nursing a child. Birth control was unevenly used among women on the Prairies, some of whom managed to restrict their families, by some means, to two or three children, while other women found themselves continually pregnant, having as many as fourteen children. Religion, accessibility to birth control infor-

mation, and education were the determinants of women's birth control use.

73 E. May, Memoirs "Reminiscences of an Old Timer," 1929, Glenbow Archives, Accession no. M1002.

74 M. Cummins, Memoirs, "How About It? The Story of a Woman's Life," Saskatchewan Archives, Accession no. R-E2552.

75 H. Rose, *The Stump Farm* (Boston: Little Brown, 1928).

76 McMurchy, *Maternal Mortality.*

77 S. Roberts, *Of Us and Oxen* (Saskatoon: Modern, 1968), 248.

78 Holmes and Roberts, *It Could Have Been Worse*, 119.

79 A. Rendell, Letters, Saskatchewan Archives, Accession no. SF175.4.

80 McMurchy, *Maternal Mortality.*

CHAPTER 7

Nursing Nation Builders

The "Council Idea," Western Women, and the Founding of the Victorian Order of Nurses for Canada, 1896–1900

BEVERLY BOUTILIER

By 1900, when its first chief superintendent of nurses submitted her third annual report, the self-sacrificing and adaptable Victorian Order nurse had emerged as the sole heroine of the nation-building discourse that framed the early work of the Victorian Order of Nurses (VON) for Canada. Too much could not be said, Charlotte Macleod wrote, of those "who, in the midst of heavy work, deprived of many of the comforts of life and at long distances from their homes and friends, still work on cheerfully in spite of the many difficulties and inconveniences inseparable from life in such remote districts."[1] Macleod's comment was meant to highlight the special vocation of the trained district nurses who now staffed Victorian Order cottage hospitals in western Canada, northern Ontario, and parts of rural Quebec and Nova Scotia. But, removed from their immediate context, the images of sacrifice, hardship, and duty that she evoked could also describe that other stock character of female nation building in late Victorian Canada, the pioneer Prairie mother, whose life and children the VON was originally founded to preserve.[2]

The twin images of the homesteading Western woman and the trained district nurse dominated the year-long debate that occasioned the founding of the VON by the National Council of Women of Canada (NCWC) in 1897. The immediate object of the "Victorian Order of Home Helpers," as the scheme was originally known, was to provide rural parturient women in the Canadian North-West with skilled maternity aid, but not necessarily with the services of hospital-trained nurses, who were neither equipped nor permitted to practise "midwifery" in Canada. Through the creation of this specially trained corps of "pioneer helpers," the NCWC would enable western women to fulfil their God-given duties as mothers, as homemakers, and, ultimately, as nation builders. The chorus of sustained and sometimes virulent opposition that plagued the scheme, even after its reformation as the VON, was an unexpected obstacle that eventually silenced the NCWC's discourse of patriotic motherhood and forced its leaders to reconsider the extent of their collective authority as members of a self-styled union of the "representative" women of Canada.

In the past, historians of the middle-class women's movement in Canada have generally represented the NCWC as an institution motivated by class interest and by "feminine," rather than feminist, politics. Using a narrow, legalistic definition of "politics," which conflated advocacy of women's suffrage reform with feminist consciousness, they dismissed the majority of NCWC leaders in this period as "maternal feminists" whose conservatism retarded the development of a viable women's rights movement in Canada.[3] Similarly, the clique of central Canadian women who inaugurated and led the NCWC after 1893 has been censured for alienating western women activists, many of whom self-consciously rejected membership in the council after the turn of the century.[4] But the well-justified sense of regional alienation that characterized western women's relations with the NCWC in subsequent decades was not a factor in the 1890s, when organized middle-class women in towns and cities across western Canada embraced "the Council idea" with an enthusiasm bordering on zeal, using its promise of power and prestige to claim a new and expanded public role for themselves as civic leaders.

As originally conceived by its American progenitors in 1888, the object of the NCWC movement was to create a federation of local and national women's societies whose representatives would work together to effect cooperative solutions to women's shared concerns – as such, it was an umbrella group that aspired to unite ideas rather than individuals. The most salient feature of the NCWC movement in Canada after 1893 was its leaders' determination to shape their new institution as a union of faithful women working to serve the divine in an organized way. United by their gender rather than by their faith, for the first time Protestant, Roman Catholic, and Jewish women would apply their combined energies to the common causes of womanhood: the protection and uplift of the Canadian home and family. Early NCWC leaders used this non-sectarian ideal of female unity, and the heightened sense of gender consciousness that resulted from it, to forge a new corporate political culture predicated on a complementary construction of gender relations on the one hand, and a domestic, religious, and voluntary construction of "woman's work" on the other.[5] By 1896, when western NCWC leaders first highlighted the medical needs of women and children in the Canadian North-West, NCWC leaders firmly believed that, as a result of their unprecedented "confederation," Canada's organized middle-class women now possessed the power to define as well as defend the national interests of "woman's sphere."

The VON was the first major expression – and test – of the expanded notion of female authority that underwrote the NCWC's new inter-faith political culture in the 1890s. This chapter examines both the role and the image of western women in the national and local institution-building campaigns that finally brought the VON to western Canada between 1896 and 1900. It begins with an examination of the meaning of the NCWC idea for organized women in western Canada and briefly outlines the intellectual foundations of the Council's early political culture. This is followed with a discussion of the NCWC's discourse on female nation building; this shows how various regional constituencies within the NCWC used the image of the western pioneer mother to empower themselves as nation builders. I conclude with an assessment of the impact of the NCWC's gendered institution-building strategies on the original Home Helper scheme as well as an assessment of how the power struggle over the purpose and personnel of the VON shaped its early work in the pioneer districts of western Canada before 1900.

The Council Idea

By 1896, the NCWC was a national institution by membership as well as by name. At least one local Council of Women was established in each province or territory (except Prince Edward Island), and there was a total local affiliation of more than 300 women's societies nation-wide. The NCWC's leaders had good reason to believe that this new federation of middle-class women's organizations had overcome its initial growing pains and could now look forward to a more ambitious program of work. As one might expect, given the demographic landscape of late Victorian Canada, more than two-thirds of the NCWC's locally affiliated societies at mid-decade were concentrated in urban centres east of Manitoba. It is remarkable, therefore, that almost half of the twenty local councils of women established by 1896 were situated in western Canada.[6]

The tremendous popularity of "the Council idea" among Canadian women in the early 1890s, and its rapid adoption by western women in particular, is largely attributable to the unflagging effort and personal appeal of the NCWC's first president and mentor, Lady Isabel Aberdeen, whose term of office coincided with her husband's tenure as governor general of Canada between 1893 and 1898.[7] A part-time resident of British Columbia since purchasing a farm near Vernon in 1891, Lady Aberdeen felt a special obligation to involve western women in an organization that was otherwise dominated by the concerns and personnel of the central Canadian women's movement. Her official duties as vice-regal consort took her across the country by train several times, thus affording her the opportunity to introduce western women to the Council idea first hand. By the time delegates convened at Montreal for the NCWC's third annual meeting in 1896, organized women in Victoria, Vancouver, Vernon, East Kootenay, Calgary, Regina, Winnipeg, and Brandon, as well as in the remote northern Ontario towns of Port Arthur and Rat Portage, had united to form local councils of women as a result of Lady Aberdeen's direct intervention.[8]

For local council activists in the West, especially those living in such recently settled towns as Regina in Assiniboia and Vernon in British Columbia, the introduction of the Council idea to their communities in the mid-1890s had immediate and tangible results. Quite apart from the social cachet that attached to the NCWC during Lady Aberdeen's presidency, the formation of local councils of women in these towns brought into association female community leaders who, because of sectarian divisions, had not previously engaged in associated work with one another, despite belonging to similar kinds of organizations and sharing the same basic class affiliation. As in the East, Council leaders in the West focused their attention primarily on local and sometimes regional concerns. In 1895, for example, Council enthusiasts in Regina and Vernon used their new-found unity to initiate fund-raising campaigns for community hospitals, while in January 1896, members of the Regina executive committee organized a branch of the Aberdeen Association to collect and distribute "good" reading materials to isolated homesteaders in the surrounding territories.[9] The significance of western women's ready adoption of the Council idea extended beyond the confines of their own towns, however. For local and national Council leaders in the East, the successful propagation of the Council movement in the pioneer districts of western Canada and northern Ontario symbolized the unprecedented power of their new institution to unite, and speak for, the "women of Canada."

Lady Aberdeen and the NCWC's other national leaders viewed the rapid proliferation of the Council idea among organized Canadian women as a sign of their willingness to cooperate with one another to achieve a mutually agreeable program of reform. But more than this, by demonstrating their enthusiasm for a new kind of associated work, NCWC leaders believed that Canada's organized middle-class women had also signalled their collective determination to overcome the religious divisions that had prevented them from fully realizing the "divine power" of their gender and class. Although the NCWC itself was an officially non-partisan and non-sectarian organization, evangelical sentiment underwrote much of the organized activism of its overwhelmingly Protestant membership. In order to temper the overt sectarianism of this group, Lady Aberdeen elaborated a non-sectarian but still religious ideal of female unity that emphasized Council members' shared experience of womanhood rather than adherence to one faith. By uncoupling womanhood from an expressly evangelical Protestant construction of female religiosity – but not from the female religious mission to edify and uplift – Lady Aberdeen self-consciously fostered the development of a new corporate political culture whose defining characteristic was its unification of Protestant, Roman Catholic, and Jewish women's societies in one national institution. Voluntary sector activists who had previously organized as members of one church, sect, or creed would now combine first and foremost as women. More than anything else in the 1890s, this spiritual innovation supported the NCWC's sustained but otherwise dubious assertion that, as a religious and regional sampler of organized middle-class womanhood, it represented the interests not only of its own members but of Canadian women generally.[10]

Local and national Council leaders shared more than a common sense of religious purpose. For the most part, they also ascribed to a complementary view of gender relations, arguing that women and men had separate but equally important "spheres" of private and public responsibility. This essentially conservative social creed had more radical implications than the church and charity women, whose societies dominated local council rosters in all regions of the country, were perhaps prepared to acknowledge. Just as the NCWC's professed non-sectarianism did not necessitate a disavowal of religion, the non-partisan complexion of its membership did not impose an apolitical attitude on the institution as a whole. Rather, conflating the "representative" character of their new institution with an expansion of female power in the public sector, its national leaders claimed moral jurisdiction over "woman's sphere" – a traditional construct whose meaning Council leaders renovated to assert their specialized knowledge as "home women" and to justify their corporate intervention in public policy making on behalf of Canadian women and children, wherever they were found. Defined in this way, "woman's sphere" encompassed not only the home, but also such non-traditional work places as factories and shops, where the archetypal mothers-of-the-next-generation were now routinely employed. Although circumspect and non-confrontational, in practice this innovation of thought constituted a real attempt by a core group of seemingly "conservative" activists within the NCWC leadership to renegotiate the existing balance of power between the sexes by forging a public leadership role for its members.

For NCWC leaders, "woman's sphere" was synonymous with the welfare of the nation. By conflating homemaking with nation building and motherhood with statecraft, they created a new political creed that both challenged and conceded the practical division of male and female labour prescribed by the middle-class ideology of separate spheres. Lady Aberdeen was especially anxious to assure prospective confederates that the NCWC would work to fulfil "women's duties" rather than to agitate for "women's rights," a distinction that reflected her distaste for the individualist rhetoric and "aggressive" tactics that she associated with the American women's movement.[11] Although voting was women's Christian duty in Lady Aberdeen's estimation, she temporarily set aside this highly controversial view to convince her more dubious Canadian followers that the object of the NCWC was not to reform public institutions but, through collective action at both the local and national levels, to enhance women's access to the men who governed them. In this way, the NCWC would function as the helpmate of the state, exercising the power of influence rather than direct political power, which, in the estimation of most Council leaders, remained the legitimate purview of men.[12]

Most of the women who took a leading part in the NCWC in the early 1890s represented this enlargement of their public work as a source of personal empowerment.[13] In turn, they declared that it was now their sacred and patriotic obligation to help other "less fortunate" women and girls realize their full potential as the maternal builders of Canada. Ontario women took the lead in 1894, using the NCWC to convince the provincial legislature that female inspectors and police matrons were needed in the region's factories, workshops, and jails. Other regional lobbies, including British Columbia women who wanted opium shipments to the West Coast curtailed, asked the NCWC to memorialize the federal government on their behalf. Both of these initiatives were justified as "preventive" measures that would enhance the power of individual women to safeguard their own morality and that of the nation at large.[14] The apparent willingness of local, provincial, and federal legislators to facilitate or adopt many of the reforms proposed by the NCWC during its first three years of work only affirmed its members' confidence in their ability to reshape the nation in their own image. More importantly, their authority to do so was officially recognized.

Nation Building

It was in this heady climate of success that, in 1896, delegates to the third annual meeting of the NCWC turned their attention to the needs of women and children in the Canadian North-West.[15] Local and national Council leaders expressed empathy for the hardships faced by rural pioneer women in the West. For Council leaders living in the longer settled regions of the country, the current generation of pioneer women mirrored their own aspirations as nation builders. Edith Archibald of the Halifax Local Council of Women, for example, asserted that, as the beneficiaries of a hard-won legacy of progress and prosperity secured for them by their own pioneer "foremothers," NCWC leaders had also inherited an obligation to further the welfare of pioneer women in their own day. In Archibald's estimation, the NCWC was first and foremost an agent of female nation building. Through its members' associated work to enhance and safeguard "woman's sphere" of influence, the NCWC would help a new generation of women pioneers realize their assigned task as the architects of the nation's homes and families. In this way, members of the Council would themselves become nation builders. "Like them," Archibald declared, "we are builders."[16]

At the 1896 meeting, two separate resolutions, one originating from the Vancouver Local Council of Women and the other from the Women's Protective Immigration Society (WPIS) of Montreal, highlighted the region's acute need for increased medical and nursing aid. On the surface these two initiatives seemed to ask for much the same thing, but on closer inspection their immediate objectives were quite different. Whereas the Vancouver proposal sought to alleviate the suffering of women and children already resident in the Canadian North-West, expanding medical services was only one of several improvements suggested by the WPIS in order to make the region's urban households and rural bachelor homes more attractive to Britain's "excess" pool of emigrant women. In practice this difference of approach augured future debates between western Council leaders and their counterparts in central Canada not just over the social and political needs of their region, but also over who possessed the authority to speak on its behalf. While reflecting regional sensibilities, each resolution also epitomized the NCWC's corporate belief that, as homemakers, as mothers, and, most especially, as nation builders, women would play a crucial role in claiming the western territories for Canada.

At a special evening conference on female immigration convened by the WPIS on the third day of proceedings, its leaders argued that organized middle-class women should use the local council structure to establish a national network of female-administered immigration "homes" to supervise the distribution of British immigrant women in Canada.[17] Originally organized in 1881 to provide Montreal's elite households with female domestic servants from Great Britain, in the 1890s membership in the Montreal Local Council of Women urged the WPIS to view the question of female immigration more broadly. Its leaders now argued that women immigration activists should themselves become nation builders by working to provide the Canadian North-West with "worthy women," whose good character, physical hardiness, and collective fecundity would build up the region's homes and families. The contribution of such women to the region would be inestimable, they argued, for only the diffuse moral influence of women could counterbalance the single-minded preoccupation of pioneer men with material progress. "It would be impossible to speak too strongly about the need of a wife and mother for the settler's home," Caroline Cox of the WPIS stated. "As a sympathetic companion, an economical manager, an actual helpmeet in the farm work, as a mother of future citizens, and as a standard bearer of civilization, she will always be invaluable."[18]

In order to secure British emigrant women who were "suitable, healthy and the right kind for settlers' wives," the WPIS counselled delegates that conditions of settlement in the Canadian North-West would first have to be improved. At its sectional conference the WPIS proposed three resolutions, each of which required the federal government to acknowledge women's contribution to nation building in some way. While the first two requested an expanded role for organized middle-class women in the management of female immigration at home and abroad, the third resolution urged the federal government to review land distribution policies in the North-West in order to make farm life on the Prairies more amenable to women settlers. The WPIS viewed the government's existing system of alternating railway land reserves with homestead sections as the chief impediment to female settlement in the region because it isolated homesteading women from one another, inhibited the development of rural Prairie communities, and deprived settlers who were raising "the future citizens of the Dominion" of needed educational, medical, and cultural services. By remedying its land allocation policies, and by recognizing the authority of female immigration activists to receive, shelter, and distribute immigrant women, the WPIS believed that the federal government could dramatically increase the rate of female settlement in the North-West.[19]

Although WPIS leaders interpreted the meeting's unanimous endorsement of its national immigration scheme as a mandate to assume responsibility for the welfare of women in the Canadian North-West, several western Canadian delegates expressed impatience with its characterization of the North-West as a region in need of "civilization." Mrs. Beneke of the Regina Local Council of Women, for example, stood to defend the educational system of Assiniboia and to boost the comparative attributes of her territory and town. Similarly, another western delegate, Mrs. Grant McEwen of Brandon, criticized the meeting's parallel suggestion that British "pauper children" be resettled in the Canadian North-West, arguing that her region should not be used as an indiscriminate receptacle for the unwanted and morally suspect children of the Empire.[20] The implied metropolitanism of the WPIS rankled Beneke and McEwen, each of whom viewed her adopted region as a new society founded on the self-reliance and fortitude of its citizens, both male and female, rather than as a laboratory for social imperialist experimentation.

The remarks of McEwen, the only western woman invited by the WPIS to speak at its meeting, brought the different perspective of the meeting's small delegation of western women sharply into focus. McEwen had joined the westward migration of Ontarians in the 1880s, leaving behind a comfortable life in Toronto to build a home for her daughters in rural Manitoba. Her success as a farmer – she was a perennial butter-making champion, for example – had made her a respected leader of women in nearby Brandon, where she helped to found both the town's hospital and its local Council of Women. McEwen agreed with the WPIS that female companionship, medical and nursing services, and cottage hospitals were desperately needed by rural women and children in Manitoba and the North-West, some of whom were "forty-five, fifty or sixty miles from the doctor." Although McEwen's presence on the platform implied support for each of the three resolutions proposed by the WPIS, she limited her remarks to the third (i.e., the regional) plank of its program. This omission suggests that, for McEwen, improving rural women's access to medical aid and female companionship took precedence over implementing an ultimately self-aggrandizing scheme that might or might not attract more women to the region; rather, McEwen used the WPIS meeting, and her unexpected authority as a regional spokeswoman, to solicit support for an alternative measure – one whose only object was to provide western women and children with increased medical and nursing aid – that the Vancouver and Brandon local councils of women would present to the NCWC meeting on the following day.[21]

This western initiative had been more than a year in the making. During a trip to British Columbia in November 1894, Lady Aberdeen had helped launch local councils of women in Victoria and Vancouver. While in Vancouver, two local council supporters, Mrs. James Macaulay and Mrs. Duncan Gavin, drew Lady Aberdeen's attention to the plight of sick women and children in the remote settlements of British Columbia and the Canadian North-West. They urged her to use the influence of her vice-regal office to remedy this situation, either by organizing a corps of district nurses for the region or, as women in Kaslo later suggested, by helping to establish a regional network of local cottage hospitals. On the one hand, despite her elevated social position, Lady Aberdeen alone was powerless to implement a scheme of such immense proportions; on the other hand, as the leader of a self-styled union of the "representative" women of Canada, whose members claimed moral jurisdiction over "woman's sphere," it was her self-appointed duty to safeguard the lives of all Canadian women. She therefore advised Macaulay and Gavin to write to her as the president of the NCWC and to make the health of women and children in the Canadian North-West a priority of Vancouver's new women's council.[22]

When the Vancouver Local Council of Women finally submitted a formal resolution to the NCWC in 1896, the scope of its proposal was much less ambitious than was the district nursing scheme its representatives had suggested to Lady Aberdeen in 1894. The resolution itself asked the governments of Canada to alleviate "the sufferings endured by women and children in the North-West Territories and other outlying districts of Canada from want of medical aid; either by offering inducements to medical men and women and efficiently trained nurses to settle in those districts, or in any other way which they may see fit."[23] This was not a general call for improved health care facilities in the North-West. For most western delegates, the resolution had a very specific meaning, which was implied by the words "sufferings" and "endured." When applied to women and children, these otherwise generic references to sickness and ill health would be understood by contemporaries as oblique but readily discernible allusions to the pain and anxiety that so many late Victorian women associated with the ordeal of childbirth, whether or not they had the benefit of "professional" maternity care.[24] The remedy sought by the Vancouver Local Council of Women – immediate government intervention on behalf of "woman's sphere" as directed by the NCWC – suggests the sense of crisis that underlay this initiative. The prospect of a whole generation of British and Canadian mothers, so many of whom had already sacrificed domestic comfort and the other trappings of "civilization" to accompany their husbands to the western "frontier," facing the perils of childbirth without adequate medical or nursing aid was a matter of the gravest national concern. It was also, therefore, a matter for immediate government action.

The discussion that followed the introduction of the Vancouver resolution supports this reading of the text. To underscore the urgency of their region's need for immediate medical and nursing relief, western delegates recounted a series of compelling stories about the often tragic circumstances of rural childbearing women. Mrs. Davidson of Brandon, whose local council seconded the Vancouver initiative, used class language to heighten the impression of suffering among western pioneer women. Many of them, she declared, were "ladies in reduced circumstances," unaccustomed to the kind of rough life they had found on the prairie. Davidson described the experience of childbirth in the region as one of unmitigated misery, as rural childbearing women were left alone to suffer, and sometimes to die, with their babies, while their husbands travelled great distances in search of a doctor. When the doctor finally arrived, "he" often found "his patients lying in such misery and discomfort that it is almost impossible for him to do anything – a mother and child lying in a little shanty, with a large stove kept red hot day and night to give heat to other rooms – he finds that woman lying there with no one to assist her." "Those who live in the centres of civilization," Davidson charged, "can never understand what these poor settlers have to undergo. The pioneers are always the martyrs."[25]

In common with the resolution that sparked it, this lament for professional medical, nursing, and domestic help during and after childbirth reveals more about the standard of obstetrical care expected by NCWC leaders in the 1890s than it does about the actual incidence of maternal mortality in the Canadian North-West. But perhaps more important, as Nanci Langford shows, it also suggests that fear of death in childbirth was an integral part of the experience of motherhood. Historians of women and childbirth have demonstrated that even women with recourse to what Judith Walzer Leavitt has called "privileged" maternity care – that is, a physician-managed birth with extended postpartum nursing and domestic support – regarded pregnancy and childbirth as something of a mixed blessing. In Canada, only a small percentage of women of childbearing age actually died of childbirth complications in this period; but, as Wendy Mitchinson has argued, enough women from all strata of society did succumb to convince prospective mothers "that childbirth could be dangerous if not fatal."[26] Various groups of organized middle-class women, some of them active members of the NCWC movement after 1893, had already acted on these fears, either by founding "nursing homes" or by building more substantial maternity hospitals in urban centres across the country. Through institution-building projects of this sort, elite urban women worked to provide their "less fortunate sisters" with the kind of medicalized childbirth and trained nursing care that most women of their class now considered basic to their own survival. By asking Canadian legislators to facilitate the settlement of health professionals in the Canadian North-West, leaders of the Vancouver and Brandon Local Councils of Women hoped that the NCWC would be the means of securing an approximate degree of protection for that region's rural mothers.[27]

Not all western NCWC leaders regarded this comparatively modest but still innovative request for government action on behalf of "woman's sphere" as an exclusive plea for improved rural maternity care. Local council leaders from Regina in Assiniboia and West Algoma in northern Ontario used the resolution to acquaint delegates with the various public health crises confronting urban communities in Canada's pioneer districts. Mrs. Beneke of Regina, who had been authorized by her local council to solicit donations from Council delegates and supporters in Montreal, informed delegates that her local council had initiated a fundraising campaign to build and endow a municipal cottage hospital which, in addition to rural maternity cases, would be used to combat the periodic outbreaks of typhoid fever that afflicted her town.[28] The object of this initiative was not simply to quarantine those individuals suffering from contagious disease, however. In common with the Vancouver resolution, Beneke believed that the real benefit to be derived from a hospital in Regina was the extension of professional medical and nursing attendance to individuals who would otherwise go without such care.[29]

Although most delegates seemed to concur that providing professional maternity care, rather than containing contagious disease, was the principal object of the Vancouver resolution, several women representing local councils in central Canada questioned the course of action it specified. Mrs. Grant Macdonald of Toronto argued that government action in this matter was inappropriate. "One's heart is so touched by the stories of suffering and misery that one does not like to say a word, but it seems to me that if they wanted missionaries in the North-West, we would certainly not expect the Government to send them. The question is: shall we ask them to send one particular profession to the exclusion of others?" Elizabeth Tilley of the London Local Council of Women suggested an alternative course of action. Because she believed the women of "the far west territories" looked to the NCWC "for aid and advice," she declared that "all these resolutions dealing with the North-West Territories should be regarded as special appeals to the National Council, and we should try to aid them in what they want." Caroline Cox of the WPIS, on the other hand, reminded delegates that they had already given her society a national mandate to oversee female immigration in Canada, a charge that included improving conditions of settlement for women in the Canadian North-West. She therefore urged delegates not to squander the limited nation-building resources of the NCWC on a second, purely regional, health care initiative.[30]

The final wording of the Vancouver resolution suggests that most NCWC leaders shared Elizabeth Tilley's view of the NCWC as a protector of pioneer women in the west. Enhancing the power of the nation's mothers was consistently invoked as part of the corporate mandate of the NCWC during the early 1890s. As a problem that most intimately affected women and children, members of the Council's national executive committee believed that its resolution could be effected wholly within the confines of the female-dominated voluntary sector. This decision reflected their perception of the NCWC as a female parliament working to protect the interests of their sex. Accordingly, this small clique of elite central Canadian women used its influence over the conference agenda and over the Ottawa Local Council of Women, whose meetings were usually chaired by Lady Aberdeen, to engineer an amended resolution that obliged the NCWC itself to devise a "practical" scheme to help rural parturient women in the Canadian North-West.

To realize this ambition, two crucial amendments were put before the meeting. The first removed all references to medical men and trained nurses. The direct involvement of these health care professionals in any scheme devised by the National Council would only undermine its members' self-declared authority to define and resolve the problems of "woman's sphere." The second amendment, which effectively corroded the authority of western Council leaders to implement a solution specific to their own regional problems, demanded that any scheme proposed by a local council first be approved by the national executive committee – at least one of whose members had already conceived a plan to train a corps of pioneer helpers in nursing and housewifery through the new Household Science Department at the Ontario Agricultural College.[31] By centralizing authority in the hands of the Council's national executive committee, the amended resolution would ensure that, rather than simply functioning as a point of access to male legislators, leaders of the NCWC would themselves be the means of bringing skilled nursing care – but not necessarily trained nurses – to Canada's heroic female nation builders in the West.[32]

Institution Building

The original sponsor of the VON was the executive committee of the NCWC. Under the direction of Lady Aberdeen, between January and February of 1897 NCWC members devised a national scheme to blanket the Canadian North-West with trained nursing practitioners. In its first incarnation, the NCWC's memorial to Queen Victoria's diamond jubilee was a regional initiative known as the Victorian Order of Home Helpers (VOHH). Ideally, its members would be older, "practical" women from the West, trained for one year by the Victorian Order in midwifery, simple nursing, and housewifery. Once returned to their communities in western Canada, these home helpers would minister to their neighbours, going from house to house "spreading all kinds of mercy and kindnesses" in exchange for a nominal salary paid by local subscription to the Order. Physicians would oversee the training and examination of home helpers, but, in practice, members of the Order would work without direct medical supervision.[33] Although home helpers would be equipped to handle a variety of medical emergencies, as their prescribed training suggests, their primary function was to assist parturient Prairie women during and after childbirth. As originally envisaged by NCWC leaders, then, this corps of specially trained "pioneer helpers" would provide western mothers not only with the skilled help that elite women now associated with successful childbirthing, but also with the necessary means to fulfil their heroic destiny as the domestic and maternal builders of Canada.

The institution-building strategies adopted by Lady Aberdeen, who was the principal author and supporter of the VOHH, even within the NCWC executive committee, reflected the complementary view of gender relations that informed the Council's political culture during the 1890s. She hoped to endow the Victorian Order with an initial income of $1 million, and recruited a carefully crafted committee of elite businessmen, civil servants, politicians, and clergymen to oversee the collection of the fund, and, more important, to help the Victorian Order's select group of female managers tap the more extensive financial and political resources available to men. Although Lady Aberdeen represented the VOHH as a "national" undertaking, her choice of male allies highlighted the regional impetus of the scheme. In addition to Prime Minister Wilfrid Laurier, who served as a trustee of the Victorian Order fund, Lady Aberdeen secured the support of Clifford Sifton, the federal minister of the interior, as well as several western MPs. Echoing the hopes of WPIS activists, in letters to Laurier and Sifton – each of whom represented a western constituency and was married to a member of the NCWC executive committee – Lady Aberdeen promoted the VOHH as an aid to female immigration in the North-West. For their part, in early February Laurier and Sifton publicly endorsed the Home Helper scheme as Canada's national memorial to Queen Victoria's diamond jubilee.[34]

Lady Aberdeen's most significant male ally was Professor James Robertson of Ottawa. As the Dominion agricultural commissioner, he was anxious to increase agricultural production in Manitoba and the Canadian North-West. Robertson's professional preoccupation with regional development no doubt played a part in his acceptance of the honorary secretariat of the Victorian Order provisional committee in March. His enthusiasm was likely enhanced, however, by his wife's support of the NCWC and by her friendship with Lady Aberdeen.[35] In common with the Victorian Order's other early supporters, both male and female, Robertson regarded the scheme as a vehicle for implementing his own particular reform agenda. But in contrast to most local Victorian Order boosters in central and eastern Canada, who regarded it as an urban rather than a rural public health measure, Robertson's aspirations for the Order directly complemented those of Lady Aberdeen. Like her, he regarded the Victorian Order primarily as a self-help initiative for western homesteaders. In addition to providing rural dwellers with skilled maternity care, Robertson also believed that the Victorian Order could be used to establish an extensive network of locally administered cottage hospitals throughout rural Manitoba and the North-West.[36]

Lady Aberdeen's gendered institution-building strategies did not realize the benefits she had originally envisaged. She successfully recruited a sympathetic panel of medical specialists to examine and oversee the training of home helpers, but most leading medical journals and medical societies viewed the Victorian Order as a menace to public health and as a threat to the already meagre livelihoods of country doctors and urban private duty nurses.[37] By mid-March, additional pressure from within the Victorian Order's elite group of lay and medical supporters, and from within the NCWC itself, forced Lady Aberdeen to accept a number of changes to the scheme. Local council leaders in Ottawa, Montreal, and Halifax, for example, demanded that the mandate of the Victorian Order be expanded to include urban as well as rural "districts" of the country. Several influential female correspondents, including the president of the Montreal Local Council of Women and the lady superintendent of nurses at Montreal General Hospital, also urged Lady Aberdeen to reconsider the name of the Order and the professional qualifications of its workers.[38] The Order's medical advisors did not immediately contest the length of training specified by Lady Aberdeen for home helpers, which reflected her assimilation of British rather than North American standards of nurse training. They were nevertheless adamant that members of the Order be subject to direct medical supervision and that their ministrations be limited to the care rather than the cure of patients – a stipulation that precluded the practice of "midwifery" by Victorian Order "nurses," whatever their qualifications or length of training.[39]

The first official circular describing the newly reconstituted "Victorian Order of Nurses for Canada" gave expression to these competing reform and professional agendas. Although not an unequivocal statement of intent, the wording of the circular suggests that a major renovation of the Victorian Order's original purpose and personnel had been effected. The stated object of the VON was now to place "the aid of trained skilful nurses within the reach of all classes of the population." As a graduate of a medically supervised hospital training program, the fully trained Victorian Order nurse would aspire "not to supplant but to supplement" the work of physicians. By nursing the sick poor in their own homes, the district nurses of the VON would also be the means of introducing middle-class standards of hygiene and health care to the poor homes and neighbourhoods of urban Canada. Thus, rather than creating an institution with a unique health care mandate that employed a distinct and specially trained corps of female workers, the revised Victorian Order scheme was now envisaged, by some of its supporters at least, as an adjunct to the existing system of urban poor relief – a system organized and staffed by the kind of lay hospital builders and medical specialists recruited by Lady Aberdeen to bring the Victorian Order to fruition. But, even within this document, the original formulation of the Victorian Order as a band of women "helpers" specially trained to safeguard the lives of Canada's heroic pioneer mothers persisted.[40]

The personal authority of Lady Aberdeen, combined with James Robertson's determination to extend health care services to western agricultural districts, ensured that the regional orientation of the Home Helper scheme was not entirely abandoned by national supporters of the VON. Although publicly Lady Aberdeen agreed that urban districts were a necessary component of the VON scheme, privately she maintained that the kind of emergency conditions that made a national health care organization like the VON necessary in the rural districts of western Canada simply did not prevail in eastern cities. Both Lady Aberdeen and Robertson continued to insist that the urgent need of the North-West for health care workers justified the sending of "specially trained nurses" to the region. In a letter soliciting support for the VON, for example,

Lady Aberdeen assured MPs that the training of Victorian Order nurses would be "absolutely adequate" for their prescribed work.[41] Similarly, in an address to the Ottawa Local Council of Women in March, Robertson declared that "the best trained nurse in all of Canada is none too good for the outlying districts; but until all the women who take this work up can be thoroughly trained, it would certainly be better to have some nurses, even if trained only for particular cases and emergencies and trained well for them, than to let the people go without altogether." In his estimation, the spectre of a whole generation of women in the North-West left to face the "unspoken fear of approaching the gate that swings both ways – into new life or into death – without competent skilled help" justified the creation and deployment of a corps of nurses specially trained in midwifery and housewifery – skills that hospital trained nurses did not routinely acquire or practice. Once again, although the reference to maternal death is implied rather than stated, the meaning of Robertson's graphic metaphor is unmistakable. "Nothing that can be done to lift that dull dread out of the lives of pioneers should be left undone," he contended, "when a National and Empire Jubilation is in prospect."[42]

Lady Aberdeen endured a summer of controversy precipitated by the Ontario Medical Association's condemnation of the VON as a positive threat to the commonweal. Then, in the autumn of 1897, she gave way to the opinion of her medical supporters and abandoned her original vision of the Victorian Order as a corps of autonomous and specially trained female maternity attendants. All references to Victorian Order nurses either training in or practising midwifery were therefore omitted from the provisional constitution drafted by the Order's key supporters in mid-November. The addition of a clause declaring Victorian Order nurses subject to the authority of individual physicians in the sick room further signalled the integration of the VON into the nation's increasingly medicalized system of health care delivery.[43]

Prevented by medical opposition to nurse-midwifery from directly aiding western pioneer mothers, Lady Aberdeen mobilized her remaining allies to constitute the VON as a self-governing order, or hierarchy, of nurses. This provision reflected her new vision of the VON as an elite corps of professional women, set apart from other graduate nurses by a training that not only met but exceeded Canadian standards and by a powerful vocation to serve "humanity." Some local VON supporters strenuously resisted this centralization of authority as an infringement of local and medical prerogative, for, in making the VON's district nurses subject to one central authority, Lady Aberdeen also increased the power of its national board of governors. To some extent, the immediate beneficiary of this decision was the VON's small clique of nursing leaders, for whom autonomy from lay, if not medical, control was basic to their professional identity. But the outcome of this power struggle over local versus national control of Victorian Order nurses had an equally significant impact on the future work of the Order in western Canada. By creating two levels of government within the VON, and by investing its central board with the authority to recruit and deploy its workers, Lady Aberdeen and her national supporters ensured that both the power and the personnel needed to provide the Canadian North-West with skilled nursing aid would remain in their hands.[44]

According to the royal charter granted to the VON by the British Privy Council in May 1898, its central board of management was constituted expressly to provide Canada's "outlying districts" with fully trained nurses and cottage hospitals. During and after Lady Aberdeen's presidency of the VON, which ended in 1899, the central board adopted the Canadian North-West as its special field of work. Two factors inhibited the expansion of its work in this region, however. First, it was not able to recruit and retain a sufficient number of women to meet the demand for nurses from urban local associations in the East or from aspiring district committees in the West, largely because graduate nurses continued to regard the VON as a source of competition rather than as an alternative form of remunerative employment. Second, the central board was perennially short of funds. Most rural communities in western Canada could not guarantee the salary of a Victorian Order nurse without some kind of financial assistance from the central board. But, because the small amount of money raised by the VON during the jubilee year was collected and controlled by local associations, the central board lacked a regular income with which to provide such aid. Special grants were made by the governments of Ontario and Nova Scotia to assist the development of Victorian Order cottage hospitals in the remote districts of these provinces, but in rural Manitoba, British Columbia, and the Canadian North-West no such aid was available before 1900. Despite these financial constraints, however, during its first two years of work the VON helped to establish one cottage hospital in each of these western jurisdictions.

Before 1900, the VON was most successful in western Canada when the nation-building impulse of its central board complemented local efforts to found community hospitals in the region's pioneer districts. It had considerably less success founding or sustaining branches in large western cities, despite the presence of well-established local councils of women in most of these centres. In Vancouver, where local council leaders founded but quickly disbanded a branch of the VON in 1899, local enthusiasm for the VON was temporarily dampened by a disagreement with the central board over who controlled the work of Victorian Order nurses, the chief lady superintendent or the local board's "lady managers." There were several hopeful signs that Council leaders in Victoria and Winnipeg might found branches but, before 1900 at least, neither group attempted to do so. After securing the permission of local subscribers, the VON's female supporters in Victoria decided to use their money to establish a rival district nursing association known as the Home Nursing Society. Winnipeg local council leaders, on the other hand, were too preoccupied in the late 1890s with their own efforts to establish a government-sanctioned female immigration hostel to provide the kind of community leadership needed to found a viable branch of the VON. The claims of a pre-existing urban district nursing society in Winnipeg may also account for their initial lack of support.[45] Until the Vancouver local association was reactivated in 1901, then, the VON's work in western Canada was restricted to underwriting and staffing cottage hospitals at Vernon, BC, Regina, Saskatchewan, and Shoal Lake, Manitoba.

The VON's association with each of these cottage hospitals was initiated by women community leaders. In Shoal Lake, the promise of financial help from the VON encouraged local women activists to initiate a local hospital building program in 1898.[46] In Vernon the Local Council of Women had been actively working to finance and build a community cottage hospital since 1896. Although it had transferred control of both its hospital project and its $2,000 fund to the town council in June 1897, after receiving a visit from Lady Aberdeen and Charlotte Macleod in July 1898 local council leaders agreed to donate $100 annually towards the salary of the Victorian Order nurse sent by the central board to staff Vernon's new cottage hospital. From 1899 onward, the Vernon women's council functioned as a de facto ladies' aid for the hospital, using virtually all of its energy to raise its promised donation, usually by hosting a berry and ice cream festival each summer. By 1900, with belated assistance from the provincial government, the Vernon cottage hospital had begun to renovate its building to accommodate private as well as public patients and had expanded its staff of Victorian Order nurses to three, two for the hospital and one for district nursing in the surrounding countryside.[47] In Regina, leaders of the local Council of Women were likewise preoccupied with the extension of hospital services to their town. Their initial object, in 1895, was to establish a temporary winter hospital in rented rooms in order to provide medical and nursing relief to the town's sick poor on a seasonal basis. Within a few months, however, they had determined to build a seven-bed cottage hospital on land donated by the Northwest Land Company. When it was paid for, the hospital building and property would be deeded from the local Council of Women to the town and subsequently maintained by annual subscriptions, entertainments, and government grants.[48]

The refusal of the Regina town council to lend financial support to the local council's hospital project in 1896, and an apparent misunderstanding over the rental of rooms for its temporary hospital, briefly soured feeling towards the hospital in some quarters of the town. A satirical article published in the *Standard* in mid-December 1896, which, in contrast to notices about previous meetings of the local women's council, was prominently placed on the front page, suggests that Regina Council leaders encountered many of the same difficulties faced by Lady Aberdeen during her year-long effort to establish the VON. After ridiculing the Council's practice of solemnizing its proceedings with silent prayer, and implying that its members could not distinguish between their affected interest in political affairs and their real interest in the matrimonial status of the *Standard*'s bachelor reporter, the newspaper reported the following exchange regarding their plan to open a cottage hospital:

> Mrs. Mixer then moved that "in the opinion of this council it is deemed advisable to open a hospital for maternity cases; that the house of Thomas Young be taken for that purpose." At this juncture Mrs. Giddy, who had agreed to second the motion, announced that she had changed her mind, and for a time it seemed as tho' the motion would drop for want of support. Some differences of opinion were freely expressed, one member declaring the view to be too *essential* for convalescent patients. Another said a person told her that Mrs. Somebody said Miss A. had told Miss B. it was too far from town. Miss Smiler stood up and asked that the Town Council be petitioned to move the town up a little bit; whereupon Mrs. Twaddle remarked that "while that man McInnis was on the Council Board he would certainly oppose doing anything like that." Miss Boxer said "he's too careful and economic anyway!" Mrs. Good put in another chunk of coal, remarking "it doesn't cost us anything!"[49]

It does not take too great a leap of imagination to divine, as the masthead confirms, that "that man McInnis" was the editor of the *Standard* as well as a member of the town council whose members had thus far refused to support the local council's hospital scheme with a grant of money. The implication of the passage is clear: women had neither the experience nor the expertise to interfere in the work of local, let alone national, government, however good their intentions might be. In other words, even an elite group of organized women like the Regina Local

Council of Women and, by extension, like the NCWC as a whole, could still overestimate and overstep the bounds of "woman's sphere."

By helping to offset its funding deficit, the affiliation of the Regina cottage hospital with the VON in 1898 may have helped local council leaders circumvent the simmering opposition to female civic leadership that continued to hinder their work.[50] The appointment of an eight-man board of directors, to whom Regina NCWC leaders voluntarily relinquished responsibility for management of the hospital, probably deflected any remaining hostility from their scheme. But it was very likely a shared willingness to acknowledge the professional authority of Victorian Order nurses that enabled residents of Regina to mend their differences and support the work of the town's new tenement hospital. Whereas the ability of NCWC women to define the health needs of the town and to select adequate quarters for even a temporary hospital had been publicly questioned and ridiculed, that of Charlotte Macleod was not. During a visit to Regina, the Victorian Order's chief lady superintendent of nurses chose a suitable house that, after securing the advise of local physicians, Council leaders equipped with the necessary hospital furnishings and supplies. Within three years their ambition to erect a specially constructed hospital building was finally realized, and the Victoria Cottage Hospital of Regina opened in September 1901 with an enlarged staff of three Victorian Order nurses.[51] Ironically, the shift in the Victorian Order's nation-building rhetoric away from helping western pioneer mothers by providing the region with trained district nurses may have increased its appeal to male and female institution builders in the West. In its final incarnation as an order of skilled professional women, the VON now promised to provide the very thing that the Vancouver Local Council of Women had originally requested in 1896, and that local hospital builders in the pioneer towns of western Canada had consistently worked to acquire: the services of trained hospital nurses.

In the end, the chief virtue of the newly founded VON for Canada was its malleability. Through its various constituent parts, it functioned simultaneously as an urban district nursing association in eastern Canada and, after 1901, in a handful of western cities; a purveyor of trained nurses and (especially after the Lady Minto Cottage Hospital Fund raised nearly $30,000 for the central board between 1900 and 1901) of funds to community cottage hospitals in Canada's "outlying districts"; a rural district nursing service; and, in its own specific way, an agent of nurse professionalization. By 1900, VON supporters at the local and national levels now acknowledged the necessity of uniform professional qualifications for the Order's nursing personnel. But the several and often conflicting opinions about the ultimate purpose of the VON that threatened to derail Lady Aberdeen and the NCWC from their institution-building course during the jubilee year were never entirely resolved.[52]

The founding of the VON for Canada between 1896 and 1900 suggests that the ideal of female unity that underwrote the development of the Council idea in Canada did not necessarily translate into female power in the public sector, as its early leaders had initially supposed. Nor, as the experience of women institution builders in western Canada suggests, did it result in an equal distribution of authority within the NCWC itself. Western Council leaders were instrumental in bringing the health care needs of pioneer women and children in the Canadian North-West to the NCWC's attention in 1896. But this regional concern was quickly appropriated for "national" purposes by Council leaders in central Canada who were anxious to demonstrate the utility of the Council idea and its power to safeguard "woman's sphere." In practice, during the year-long campaign that finally resulted in the promulgation of a modified version of the VON, the image of the western woman as a nation builder became more important than the more modest aspiration of local Council leaders in the West to provide their region with skilled nursing care. The easy substitution of the well-qualified Victorian Order nurse for the western pioneer mother as the heroine of the VON's nation-building enterprise was not without ramifications for the political culture created by NCWC leaders in the 1890s. Nevertheless, it was this shift of emphasis, combined with its new mandate to provide trained nurses rather than simply skilled nursing care, that finally made the VON a useful tool for institution builders and community builders in the West.

Acknowledgment

I wish to acknowledge the financial support of doctoral and postdoctoral fellowships from the Social Sciences and Humanities Research Council of Canada, which made the preparation of this chapter possible.

Notes

1 Charlotte Macleod, "Report of the Chief Lady Superintendent of Nurses," in VON, *Report of the Board of Governors,* 1900, 27.

2 Although initially inspired by the example of Queen Victoria's Jubilee Institute for Nurses (QVJIN), which was founded with funds collected by the women of Great Britain to commemorate the Queen's golden jubilee in 1887, the VON for Canada was a separate and entirely Canadian organization. Other than seeking permission for its nurses to wear a badge of similar design to that won by Jubilee Institute nurses, and to be known as Queen's Nurses, there was no formal association between the VON for Canada and the QVJIN, now known

as the Queen's Nursing Institute. For more on the institutional and intellectual roots of the VON, see Beverly Boutilier, "Helpers or Heroines? The National Council of Women, Nursing, and 'Woman's Work' in Late Victorian Canada," in *Caring and Curing: Historical Perspectives on Women and Healing in Canada,* ed. Dianne Dodd and Deborah Gorham (Ottawa: University of Ottawa Press, 1994), 33-4.

3 On the NCWC, see Veronica Strong-Boag, *The Parliament of Women: The National Council of Women of Canada, 1893-1929* (Ottawa: National Museums of Canada, 1976); Carol Lee Bacchi, *Liberation Deferred? The Ideas of the Women's Suffrage Movement in English Canada, 1883-1918* (Toronto: University of Toronto Press, 1983); Wayne Roberts, "'Rocking the Cradle for the World": The New Woman and Maternal Feminism, Toronto, 1877-1914," in *A Not Unreasonable Claim: Women and Reform in Canada, 1880s-1920s,* ed. Linda Kealey (Toronto: Women's Press, 1979), 15-46. Veronica Strong-Boag has since re-assessed her own interpretation of the turn-of-the-century women's movement. See "Pulling in Double Harness or Hauling a Double Load: Women, Work, and Feminism on the Canadian Prairie," *Journal of Canadian Studies* 21, 3 (1986): 32-3. For a new assessment of the NCWC, prepared for its centenary, see N.E.S. Griffiths, *The Splendid Vision: Centennial History of the National Council of Women of Canada, 1893-1993* (Ottawa: Carleton University Press, 1993).

4 For example, Carol Lee Bacchi, "Divided Allegiances: The Response of Farm and Labour Women to Suffrage," in *A Not Unreasonable Claim: Women and Reform in Canada, 1880s-1920s,* ed. Linda Kealey (Toronto: Women's Press, 1979), 89-108.

5 Much of the new feminist literature on women's "politics" is American and British in origin. For an overview of the problem of redefining feminism as an expression of political consciousness, see Karen Offen, "Defining Feminism: A Comparative Historical Approach," *Signs* 14, 1 (1988): 119-57; Elizabeth Fox Genovese, "Individualism and Women's History," in *Feminism without Illusions: A Critique of Individualism* (Chapel Hill: University of North Carolina Press, 1991), 113-38; Jane Rendall, "Introduction," in *Equal or Different: Women's Politics 1800-1914,* ed. Jane Rendall (Oxford: Blackwell, 1987). On the concept of women's political culture as derivative of women's culture methodology, see Beverly Boutilier, "Gender, Organized Women, and the Politics of Institution Building: Founding the Victorian Order of Nurses for Canada, 1893-1900" (PhD thesis, Carleton University, 1994), chap. 1.

6 In 1896, 91 societies, or 30 percent of the NCWC's 306 local affiliates, belonged to one of eight local councils of women located in western Canada; 50 societies, or 16 percent, belonged to one of three Maritime local councils; and 165 societies, or 54 percent of the total, belonged to one of nine central Canadian local councils. See "List of Local Councils," in National Council of Women of Canada (hereafter NCWC), *Women Workers of Canada,* 1896, 3-23.

7 For a persuasive analysis of the intellectual foundations of Lady Aberdeen's social activism in Canada, see Joanna Dean, "Lady Aberdeen's Vision for Canadian Women: A Study of Evangelism, Liberalism and the Woman Question" (MA essay, Carleton University, 1989).

8 Edmonton women also established a local Council of Women in October 1894 after a visit from Lady Aberdeen, but it disbanded for "local reasons" after one year of work. See "Secretary's Report," in NCWC, *Women Workers of Canada,* 1896, 34. An Edmonton local was re-established in 1908. See Griffiths, *The Splendid Vision*, 89.

9 Greater Vernon Museum and Archives (hereafter GVMA), Vernon Local Council of Women Papers, Minute Book, 4 December 1896, 8 February 1897, 6 June 1897; Saskatchewan Archives Board (hereafter SAB), coil. R-136, Regina Local Council of Women Papers, file 23a, Minute Book, 22 November 1895, 13 December 1895, 14 January 1896.

10 The national branches of Canada's two largest inter-denominational women's societies, the Woman's Christian Temperance Union and the Young Women's Christian Association, refused to affiliate with the NCWC in the 1890s because of its failure to institute some form of audible Christian prayer at its annual meetings. The NCWC did retain the support of many local branches of these organizations, however. See Boutilier, "Gender, Organized Women, and the Politics of Institution Building," chap. 2.

11 Lady Aberdeen, "Public Meeting," in NCWC, *Women Workers of Canada,* 1894, 176-9. On Lady Aberdeen's view of the American women's movement, see Dean, "Lady Aberdeen's Vision," 99-100.

12 The Countess of Aberdeen, "Woman as an Actual Force in Politics," in *The World's Congress*

of Representative Women, ed. May Wright Sewall (Chicago: Rand, McNally, 1894), 424-30. See also Boutilier, "Gender, Organized Women, and the Politics of Institution Building," chap. 3.

13 For example, see Mrs. Schultz (Winnipeg), "The Women Workers of Manitoba," in NCWC, *Women Workers of Canada,* 1894, 212-7.

14 "Resolution on Appointment of Women Inspectors for Factories and Workshops where Women are Employed" and "Resolution on Appointment of Police Matrons," in NCWC, *Women Workers of Canada,* 1894, 110-4; "Duty on Opium," in ibid., 1895, 213.

15 Acquired from the Hudson's Bay Company by the federal government in 1870, the North-West Territories encompassed a vast region that included present-day Alberta, Saskatchewan, northern Manitoba, northern Ontario, northern Quebec, and the Canadian North. NCWC leaders generally used the term as a synonym for the Canadian Prairies, however.

16 Mrs. Archibald (Halifax), "The Importance of the National Council in Fostering and Developing the Patriotism of Canadian Women," in NCWC, *Women Workers of Canada,* 1896, 73-7.

17 On the WPIS, see Barbara Roberts, "Sex, Politics, and Religion: Controversies in Female Immigration Work in Montreal, 1881-1919," *Atlantis* 6, 1 (Fall 1980): 25-38; Barbara Roberts, "A Work of Empire: Canadian Reformers and the British Female Immigration," in *A Not Unreasonable Claim: Women and Reform in Canada 1880s-1920s,* ed. Linda Kealey (Toronto: Women's Press, 1979), 148-86.

18 Mrs. John Cox (Montreal), "The Immigration of Women," in NCWC, *Women Workers of Canada,* 1896, 197; "Sectional Conference Meeting on Women's Immigration," in ibid., 502, 519-20, 522, 523. See also Elizabeth Jameson, "Women as Workers, Women as Civilizers: True Womanhood in the American West," in *The Women's West,* ed. Susan Armitage and Elizabeth Jameson (Norman: University of Oklahoma Press, 1987), 145-64; James Hammerton, *Emigrant Gentlewomen: Genteel Poverty and Female Emigration, 1830-1914* (London: Croom Helm, 1979), 163.

19 "Sectional Conference Meeting on Women's Immigration," in NCWC, *Women Workers of Canada,* 1896, 500-39, esp. 520-39.

20 Ibid., 534-5, 537-58.

21 Ibid., 535-7.

22 John Murray Gibbon, *The Victorian Order of Nurses for Canada: 50th Anniversary, 1897-1947* (Montreal: Southam, 1947), 1, 4. Gibbon wrongly states that the Vancouver Local Council of Women was founded in 1896.

23 "Need of Medical Aid in the North-West Territories," in NCWC, *Women Workers of Canada,* 1896, 439-45, esp. 439.

24 Pat Jalland, *Women, Marriage and Politics, 1860-1914* (Oxford: Oxford University Press, 1986), chaps. 5 and 6. See also Langford, this volume, 147-73.

25 "Need of Medical Aid," 1896, 440-1.

26 Judith Walzer Leavitt, *Brought to Bed: Childbearing in America, 1750-1950* (New York: Oxford University Press, 1986), 74-5; Wendy Mitchinson, *The Nature of Their Bodies: Women and Their Doctors in Victorian Canada* (Toronto: University of Toronto Press, 1991), 224-8, esp. 228. See also Edward Shorter, *A History of Women's Bodies* (New York: Basic, 1982), 69.

27 For example, see the 1894 prospectus of the Ottawa Maternity Hospital, reprinted in Beth Light and Joy Parr, *Canadian Women on the Move, 1867-1920* (Toronto: New Hogtown, 1983), 136-8. In the case of the Winnipeg Maternity Hospital, its female founders also intended that local farm women should avail themselves of its services. See Mrs. George Bryce, *Historical Sketch of the Charitable Institutions of Winnipeg* (Winnipeg: Historical and Scientific Society of Manitoba, *Transaction* No. 54, 1899).

28 5AB, coil. R-136, Regina Local Council of Women Papers, file 23a, Minute Book, 1 May 1896. See also a speech given by Beneke, who travelled to England from Montreal, before a Presbyterian congregation in London about the work of the Aberdeen Association in the Canadian North-West and the efforts of her local council to raise funds for a cottage hospital in Regina. National Archives of Canada (hereafter NAC), MG 27, I BS, Aberdeen Papers, vol. 5, file "NCWC," "Paper read at St. James, Hatcham London on January 23rd. 1897 afterwards at Manchester and lastly at Liverpool," n.d.

29 "Need of Medical Aid," 1896, 443-4.

30 Ibid., 439-40, 441-2.

31 Ibid., 444-5.

32 On the distinction made by early NCWC leaders between nursing as "woman's work" and the work of hospital-trained nurses, see Beverly Boutilier, "Helpers or Heroines? The National Council of Women, Nursing, and 'Woman's Work' in Late Victorian Canada," in *Caring and Curing: Historical Perspectives on Women and Health in Canada,* ed. Dianne Dodd and Deborah Gorham (Ottawa: University of Ottawa Press, 1994), 17-47.

33 For a more detailed discussion of the VOHH scheme, see Boutilier, "Gender, Organized Women, and the Politics of Institution Building," chap. 3.

34 NAC, MG 26, G, Sir Wilfrid Laurier Papers, Mfm reel C-746, frames 11306-14, Lady Aberdeen to Wilfrid Laurier, 22 January 1897; NAC, MG 27, II DS, Clifford Sifton Papers, Mfm reel C-454, vol. 10, file: Lady Aberdeen, Aberdeen to Sifton, 19 January 1897. For an account of the inaugural meeting of the VOHH, at which both Laurier and Sifton spoke in favour of the scheme, see the *Citizen* (Ottawa), 11 February 1897.

35 Robertson was also a great admirer of Lady Aberdeen, who shared his commitment to evangelical Presbyterianism. The Robertsons named their first daughter, Ishbel, for Lady Aberdeen. See NAC, MG 30, Dli, Ishbel Robertson Currier Papers, typescript, "James Wilson Robertson," by Ishbel Robertson Currier; Henry Morgan, ed., *Canadian Men and Women of the Time: A Hand-book of Canadian Biography* (Toronto: William Briggs, 1898).

36 NAC, MG 27, I BS, Aberdeen Papers, Journal of Lady Aberdeen, pamphlet insert, *Report of an Address by Professor James Robertson at the Annual Meeting of the Local Council of Women of Ottawa, on 10th March, 1897* (Ottawa: Paynter and Abbott, 1897).

37 Among the medical journals to condemn the VOHH and the VON were the *Canada Lancet,* the *Maritime Medical News,* the *Canadian Practitioner,* and the *Canadian Journal of Medicine and Surgery.* Only the *Montreal Medical Journal,* whose editors were members of the Victorian Order's ad hoc medical advisory council, publicly asserted the need for a district nursing organization like the Victorian Order. It did, however, criticize the creation of a two-tier standard of home nursing according to a patient's ability to pay. See *Montreal Medical Journal* 25, 10 (April 1897): 837-8.

38 NAC, MG 28, 1171, VON Papers, vol. 5, file 30, Julia Drummond to Lady Aberdeen, 8 February 1897; ibid., Nora Livingston to Lady Aberdeen, 20 February 1897.

39 Ibid., J.C. Cameron to Lady Aberdeen, 3 February 1897.

40 NAC, MG 28, 1171, VON Papers, vol. 1, file 2, pamphlet, *The Canadian Fund for the Commemoration* of the Queen's Diamond Jubilee, n.d.

41 NAC, MG 27, I E17, Sir James Gowan Papers, Mfm reel M-1897, Al General Correspondence, typescript letter, Lady Aberdeen to Senator Gowan, 13 March 1897.

42 NAC, MG 27, I BS, Aberdeen Papers, Journal of Lady Aberdeen, pamphlet, *Report of an Address by Professor Robertson,* 9-10. See a report of the same speech in the *Standard* (Regina), 25 March 1897.

43 Geoffrey Bilson, "Public Health and the Medical Profession in Nineteenth-Century Canada," in *Disease, Medicine, and Empire: Perspectives on Western Medicine and the Experience of European Expansion,* ed. Roy Macleod and Milton Lewis (London: Routledge, 1988), 156-75.

44 *Canadian Journal of Medicine and Surgery* 1, 6 (June 1897), 269-71; NAC, MG 28, 1171, VON Papers, vol. 1, file 15, *Provisional Constitution of the Victorian Order of Nurses in Canada founded in Commemoration of the Queen's Diamond Jubilee,* 1897. See also *Royal Charter and By-Laws of the Victorian Order of Nurses for Canada*; *Resolutions Passed at a Meeting of the Board of Governors on 4th January, 1900* (Ottawa: Mortimer, 1901).

45 VON, *Report of Board of Governors,* 1901, 11; NCWC, *Women of Canada: Their Life and Work* (Ottawa: Department of Agriculture, 1900), 364-5. On the immigration work of the Winnipeg Local Council of Women, see Marilyn Barber, "The Servant Problem in Manitoba, 1896-1930," in *First Days, Fighting Days: Women in Manitoba History,* ed. Mary Kinnear (Regina: Canadian Plains Research Centre, University of Regina, 1987), 100-19.

46 Lady Aberdeen, *What Is the Use of the Victorian Order of Nurses for Canada* (Ottawa: Mortimer, 1900); NAC, MG 28, 1171, VON Papers, vol. 5, file 20, Shoal Lake Cottage Hospital.

47 GVMA, Vernon Local Council of Women Papers, Minute Book, 4 December 1896, 8 February 1897, 30 July 1898, 8 December 1898; VON, *Report of the Board of Governors,* 1900, 27, 32.

48 E. Perry, rec. secy, Regina Local Council of Women, to Editor, the *Standard* (Regina), 12

December 1896; M.H. Herchmer, pres., Regina Local Council of Women, to Editor, ibid., 13 February 1896.

49 "The Women's Council: A Report of a Recent Meeting of that Energetic Body," the *Standard* (Regina), 17 December 1896. See also "The Cottage Hospital," ibid., 30 July 1896.

50 The Regina Local Council of Women first expressed interest in the VON in April 1897; see SAB, coll. R-136, Regina Local Council of Women Papers, file 23a, Minute Book, 29 April 1897. On the creation of the male board of directors, see SAB, coll. R-136, Regina Local Council of Women Papers, file 11, Letter Book, Corresponding Secretary to Lady Aberdeen, 8 October 1898.

51 SAB, Coll. R-136, Regina Local Council of Women Papers, file 11, Letter Book, Corresponding Secretary to Lady Aberdeen, 8 October 1898; VON, *Report of the Board of Governors,* 1901, 52.

52 For a prospectus of the cottage hospital fund-raising scheme inaugurated by Lady Mary Minto, who was the VON's honorary president between 1898 and 1904, see VON, *Report of the Board of Governors,* 1900.

CHAPTER 8

Scattered but Not Lost

Mennonite Domestic Servants in Winnipeg, 1920s–50s

FRIEDA ESAU KLIPPENSTEIN

The "story" of a people is a touchstone of cultural identity. Story is expressed in icons, rituals, music, and dance as well as in literary, architectural, and culinary traditions passed down through generations. It is contained in oral and written accounts, some of which achieve the status of "official" versions of a story. In literate societies these official histories are typically preserved in a documentary canon that is systematically assembled over time and that gains authoritative power, correcting and shaping the collective memory. In it a chorus of individual voices is reduced to some consensus. The writers of the official histories are usually dominant in their societies, and it is no coincidence that the events and heroes selected for prominence are often in their image.

This pattern is also evident in the history of the Mennonite peoples, descendants of the radical, Anabaptist wing of the sixteenth-century Reformation in Europe. Mennonite history has traditionally been a lineup of "great men": those religious and political leaders, farmers, businessmen, preachers, teachers, and missionaries credited with a long catalogue of sectarian divisions and migrations. In the last few decades, however, historians have asked new questions about the lives of women in the group – about their domestic and public spheres, their roles and contributions, attitudes and world views. As an ethnohistorian and a Mennonite woman myself, I have a particular interest in recovering the lost voices of women of this community. Sometimes these voices speak in unison with the official histories, and sometimes they speak in significant and revealing counterpoint.

This chapter is based primarily on interviews conducted with some thirty-four Mennonite women in the spring of 1987 concerning their immigration experiences and early years in Canada. Most of the women were born in what was then Imperial Russia in towns and villages within the Mennonite colonies, the oldest of which were located in Ukraine, and the newest in Crimea, Middle Volga, Caucasus, and Siberia.[1] Their families had migrated to Russia from Prussia and other parts of Europe in the late 1700s in order to retain group identity and religious freedoms. After generations of relative peace and seclusion, life in Russia changed completely. The women talked about the Russian Revolution (1917) and ensuing civil war (1918-21), about immigrating to Canada between 1923 and 1929, and about their experience of starting over in a new land. Their stories shed new light on a complex process of adaptation, accommodation, and resistance in a period of community transition following resettlement in Canada.

The 20,000 Mennonites who came to Canada in the 1920s arrived virtually empty-handed. Because of their extensive land holdings and their bourgeois lifestyles in Russia, they were severely targeted in the communist takeover.[2] Thousands of lives were cruelly lost. Vast properties were lost. Also lost were the freedoms that had originally lured the Mennonites to the steppes of Russia – freedom to worship, to teach their children, and to refrain from military service. Although they immigrated to Canada in groups, the newcomers were actually disassociated, broken remnants of once tight-knit communities. They were orphans, widows, and fragments of families, traumatized by their personal and collective experiences of gruesome murders, plunder, rape, and famine, during which their most fundamental faith in God and their most basic value of non-resistance were severely tested.

The Mennonites who arrived in Canada in the 1920s were ill equipped for the challenges of re-establishing livelihoods, making it through the lean years of the 1930s, and paying off the substantial travel debts they owed to the Canadian Pacific Railway.[3] For many of the women, a central part of this experience was leaving their families in the countryside and going to work as live-in maids in middle- and upper-class homes in the cities. Across western Canada, in Winnipeg, Saskatoon, Calgary, and Vancouver, as well as in some smaller centres, *Maedchenheime* (hostels, or girls' homes, for working women) arose in response to the needs of the women and their families who were concerned about them.

All of the women interviewed had some connection to the Mennonite Girls' Homes in Winnipeg.[4] One woman remarked, "We never thought this Maedchenheim would make a big story." Indeed, so far it has not. Most of the standard Mennonite history texts mention the women's maid experience in passing, if at all.[5] Yet it is an important chapter in the story of the immigrant experience in Canada. Some writers have recently suggested that it contributed to the group's urbanization and their adjustment to Canadian life.[6] While researching this topic the question posed repeatedly by colleagues and observers was, how did the pattern of urban domestic service become so well established? The Mennonites reputedly had a long tradition of protectiveness over their children and seclusion from "the outside world." Moreover, while in Russia domestic service was associated with the lower classes, in Canada it was tainted by a reputation far less respectable, being associated with prostitution, abortion, and other vices.[7] It seems a sharp contradiction, then, that the Mennonite newcomers would so freely allow their daughters to be scattered in the cities to live under the roofs of strangers.

The women interviewed here explained their entry into domestic service by referring to their hardships in Russia, their families' great financial need, their parents' attitudes, and their own resources and goals. Overall, their entry into domestic service was shaped by two factors: one from within the Canadian society and the other from within the immigrant group itself. The first is that during those decades Canada systematically channelled immigrant women into domestic service. The second, which is the focus of this chapter, is that some segments of the Mennonite community worked to conceptualize the situation of the young women in such a way that the group could accept and support it. Specifically, by applying the imagery and language of their religious tradition to the work of domestic service, leaders presented domestic work as a "mission," thus making it acceptable to the women, their families, and Mennonite communities. This was similar to what Mennonite women in non-traditional roles did in the Old World, where leadership, world travel, education, and other adventures could comfortably be condoned only for women who were performing, or preparing for, "church work." For immigrant Mennonite women, then, familiar religious traditions were evoked to mediate their new experience in Canada. The use of religious imagery and rhetoric helped these women to cope, and their communities to allow, justify, and even facilitate the break with propriety and tradition. Through this unique adaptation, the community could benefit from their daughters' labour, while the women themselves could remain safely in the centre, rather than on the fringe, of their own communities.

This is in contrast, for example, to the experience of Finnish women in Canada. According to Varpu Lindstrom-Best, the Finnish women who took on the role of domestic servants during the same time period became "defiant sisters," increasingly articulate, independent-minded, stubborn, and strong.[8] They became bold in their espousal of socialism, developing a strong collective class consciousness, fighting for legal rights for domestic workers, and rebelling against the conservatism of the Lutheran Church in Canada. Similarly, Christine Stansell maintains that, for the Irish women who comprised 74 percent of the domestic servants in New York in 1855, the effect of the experience was to unite the women in their disdain for the cultural, class, and gender discrimination they experienced in the parlours of their employers. She argues that, far from "timid and downtrodden souls, too miserable and oppressed to take much of a part in making history," these women "played a part in the thoroughgoing changes in work, family and politics in nineteenth-century New York."[9] In both cases it would appear that the experience in domestic service contributed to the empowerment of the women while it separated them from their previous traditions and communities.

Like the studies by Lindstrom-Best and Stansell, most of the literature on female domestic workers in North America focuses on the large groups of orphaned and single immigrant women who were separated from their Old World communities and entered North American life in a socially directed manner. The example of the Mennonites shows that, in large-group immigration as well, women were siphoned away from their communities into a special category of labour through a process that Roxana Ng has termed the "commodification" of immigrant women.[10] This occurred even though the Mennonites formally entered Canada as "agriculturalists" rather than as "domestics" or "labourers," the two other common categories. Indeed, taking up farming was a condition of the immigration agreement negotiated on their behalf by federal immigration officials and the Canadian Mennonite Board of Colonization. But unlike the Ukrainian women in Frances Swyripa's chapter in this book, the experience of immigrant Mennonite women differed significantly from that of the men in their communities. Mennonite women laboured as exiles from their community in a very low-status occupation. Many of them never moved directly onto farms, but remained in the urban centres where they disembarked to take up work in other peoples' homes.

These events must be understood in the context of the late nineteenth and early twentieth centuries, when female domestic service constituted an overwhelming percentage of Canada's female workforce and was considered appropriate employment for each new wave of immigrants. The female newcomers' experience fell into a typical "story pattern," involving entry into live-in domestic service immediately after their arrival, continuation in this work through the 1920s and 1930s, and a transfer either to domestic day-work or assembly-line labour in factories during the Second World War. Although this pattern describes the experience of countless immigrant women, their varied cultural responses made their stories unique. In the case of the Mennonite women, leaving home to work for wages in the city violated a primary rule of Mennonite family order. The traditional "Mennonite way" was for extended families to work together on family farms or businesses under the highly visible leadership of a patriarch. Women were an integral part of the effort, working in important though clearly supportive roles. In Canada the young women found themselves in an uncomfortable, if not bewildering, role reversal, where, instead of being supported by their fathers, their fathers – and, indeed, their entire families – depended on them for financial provision.

In their interviews the women spoke about their experiences in domestic service, about the people who worked to establish and shape institutions (girls' homes) to aid them, the support these institutions gained from the Mennonite communities, and the various functions the homes served. An important part of their story continues into the 1950s when, without warning or consultation, the girls' homes across western Canada were closed as male church leaders began to question the homes' functions and implications. Essentially the same forces that worked to rationalize and to allow the young women's separation from their communities – namely, religious symbolism, patriarchal structures, ethnic and class values – eventually called them back, as the community struggled to achieve cultural continuity in the midst of change.

The Channel into Domestic Service

In the 1920s newly arrived Mennonites entered a society that systematically channelled immigrant women into domestic service. From the 1880s to the 1930s there was an "acute" and much publicized "servant problem" – the "regrettable," even "tragic," shortage of women to work as domestics in Canadian homes. Enormous effort was exerted by private agencies and by the Canadian Immigration Department through the Canadian Council of Immigration of Women for Household Service to carry out elaborate schemes whereby large groups of women were recruited specifically for domestic work. The targets of recruitment for domestic work were young single women, war widows, and orphans (preferably English speakers of "desirable character"). Throughout the nineteenth century, efforts to obtain domestics focused first on the British Isles, where statistics showed "a great surplus of women," then on continental Europe. Advance ship passages were offered to women, while bonuses and commissions were given to shipping companies for bringing maids and to their chaperons for accompanying, protecting, and registering them at special hostels. These hostels, some supported by federal and provincial grants, others by private sector agencies such as the YWCA, and church, ethnic, and women's organizations, were set up across Canada to receive and place immigrant girls and women in domestic jobs. From 1870 to 1930, over 250,000 women came to Canada, stating their intended occupation as domestic service.[11]

In the early 1900s, having domestic help was a class indicator for the middle and upper echelons of Canadian society. Finding cheap, reliable help in the form of domestic servants was considered urgent for both symbolic and practical reasons. Certainly, in the days before sophisticated household technology, it was virtually impossible for women to achieve the dual expectations of domestic orderliness and leisure without hiring help. The Mennonite domestics lived in homes throughout Winnipeg, from the North End to River Heights. The "ladies" of the homes were often women who spent much of their time in club, charity, and church

Mennonite domestic servants

work; in family life; and on social events such as bridge afternoons, dinner parties, and arts events. To achieve this lifestyle, they needed to free themselves of a tremendous amount of housework. Besides often being in complete charge of the children in these homes, servants were expected to scrub floors; cook and serve meals; wash and dry dishes; polish silver; dust and oil woodwork; sweep carpets; clean and hand polish hardwood floors; and wash, dry, iron, and sometimes mend the entire family's laundry. This work was commonly done on a live-in basis, as domestics were expected to be on duty at almost any hour from six to six-and-a-half long days a week.

Acquiring domestic servants was considered so important that people scrambled to engage anyone willing to do the work. Young immigrant women were the most common targets of recruitment. In Winnipeg, a major terminus for large groups of newcomers, immigrant women were often approached by potential employers on the train platforms or in the Immigration Hall.[12] In this way many Mennonite girls, some as young as thirteen or fourteen, were separated from their families or fellow travellers shortly after arrival.[13] Their powerlessness to reconnect with family or friends on their own and, indeed, the worry of whether they would again be "findable" in the maze of the foreign city, weighed heavily. Bewildered, they found themselves in the homes of complete strangers, with whom they could not converse and who had enormous expectations of them. They were sought and hired even though they could not understand directions, read recipes, or make their questions understood. They knew little of the manners deemed "proper" or of the particular customs and cooking styles appropriate to the Jewish, English, Scottish, Icelandic, and other families for whom they worked. In general, willingness to do the work was the main criterion for being hired. At the same time that domestic work was widely available, it was reputedly the only work to be found for immigrant women.

The channel into domestic service was made even wider by the severe economic depression beginning shortly after the Mennonites arrived. The onset of drought in the late 1920s brought a series of crop failures. Many of the Mennonites lived in debilitating poverty during their first years in Canada. Most, in accordance with the understanding they had with the Canadian Pacific Railway, tried to establish farms, some joining relatives, some buying farms from "Canadian" Mennonites who were immigrating to South America and Mexico at the time. However, because most of the viable free homestead allotments near the railways were taken by the 1920s, the majority of the Mennonite immigrants purchased lands under a variety of agreements with the help of land agents. In Manitoba these were lands near Holmfield, Whitewater, Morris, Osborne, Arnaud, and Pigeon Lake. They also included lands near such centres as Altona, Niverville, Winkler, and Steinbach on the Mennonite "reserves" – two substantial blocks of land south of Winnipeg originally set aside for the first large wave of Mennonite immigration in the 1870s.[14] Among the newcomers, cash was very scarce. Though usually needed on the family farm, some young men found employment as casual workers on threshing crews and in construction, lumber, and mining camps. But because of the so-called "servant problem," it seemed that unmarried women – widows, daughters, and orphan girls – often had the best chance to earn wages.

The interviewees insisted that parents did not want to leave their daughters in the city, but they could not find a viable alternative. For many it is a bitter memory. One woman recalled how, in 1925, when she was thirteen and had been in Canada for less than a month, her father took her to Winnipeg to find her a place to work and live. She cried while walking up and down the city streets until she was finally hired for three dollars a month and a bed in her employers' living room.[15] While this kind of arrangement was not uncommon for very young girls, those in their mid-teens could expect a half day off a week, room and board, and a monthly wage starting at ten to fifteen dollars. Their income went almost entirely to their families.

In addition to individual family needs, there was also community pressure channelling Mennonite women into domestic service. The groups' collective debt to the Canadian Pacific Railway was still near an enormous three-quarters of a million dollars in the late 1930s.[16] Some of the newcomers considered the debt overwhelming and the attempts to repay it futile. But to community leaders, paying the travel debt became a crusade to defend the respectability and trustworthiness of the group. The Canadian Mennonite Board of Colonization, which had negotiated the immigration to Canada, had achieved contracts with the Canadian Pacific Railway partially on the basis of the Mennonites' acclaimed honesty with regard to repaying debts. Board representatives lobbied churches and private homes emphasizing the need to complete this obligation, and they even appointed a full-time collector to facilitate the process. Through domestic work the young women were the most active in paying off their own travel debt, then often single-handedly paying off the debt of their parents and siblings. For some this took only three to five years, while others spent ten or fifteen years at it.[17]

Family and community willingness to release the young women into domestic service also reflected attitudes and expectations formed in the process of the group's immigration. The violence of revolution, civil war, and famine that spread throughout south Russia (1917 to 1921) left the Mennonite settlements in ruins. These events prepared the immigrants to work without complaint to establish themselves in Canada. In some cases, news of Canadian life had travelled back to Russia; as Agatha Isaak explained, she expected to be a "servant girl" in Canada because she had already heard that her family would initially need to be separated and to do any work available until they were established. As well, many of the girls had experienced "working out" during the difficult times in Russia. Elizabeth Friesen described how, at the age of eight, when her family members were refugees in war-torn Russia, she worked as a field hand clearing thistles and as a babysitter for seven pounds of flour a week. Nevertheless, becoming a servant in Canada was a hard pill to swallow. Most of the women were old enough to remember the years of prosperity in Russia, when they themselves had servants.

The stratified Mennonite society was crushed flat in the Russian Revolution, and in Canada those who had been moguls of land and industry stood empty-handed alongside those who had been the village paupers. Indeed, the descent of the group from wealth and privilege in Russia to that of the poor and often disdained immigrants in the New World was tremendously deflating. Sometimes it was explained in terms of biblical judgment or justice. For instance, Betty Olfert recalled being told by her mother that she should not be shocked that, as a maid, she would have to eat alone in the kitchen. Her mother told her that this was how they had treated their own maids in Russia, so perhaps they were "getting back" some of their own treatment.

Hardships endured in the Old World reduced immigrants' expectations. But, despite their struggles, several of the women mentioned how free their families felt in Canada. Mary Suderman, after describing efforts of her widowed mother and four siblings to make a living selling eggs and garden vegetables in Winnipeg, revealed the immense gratitude they had for the bare essentials of life: "We had a good life. Nobody bothered us. We could do as we pleased. We had food. We had shelter. So what more do you want?" Others mentioned that their parents "never looked back" and that they themselves were "just grateful to have jobs" and the "opportunity to work." In concert with the forces in Canadian society, then, these attitudes of desperation, inferiority, contrition, and gratitude all contributed towards the channelling of the Mennonite women into domestic service.

Mennonite Girls' Homes as Refuge

For Mennonite immigrant women one of the strongest channels into domestic service – the girls' homes – arose from within the Mennonite community. This is somewhat ironic, as the homes were originally intended to be a refuge protecting, and even rescuing, the women from the perils of their work. But so effective were the girls' homes in meeting the needs and allaying the fears of the girls and their families that they came to serve as an important conduit into domestic service.

Although in Russia the Mennonites were not strictly rural people, many of them had a suspicion, or "fear," of the city. This fear ranged from timidity due to unfamiliarity to the belief, as one woman put it, that "the city was where evil lurked from all corners" and that "if you went to the city you were asking for trouble."[18] The young women were completely unprepared for urban life and, as some explained, their parents could not help because they themselves did not know what life in the city was like. The advice the girls received included warnings about taking rides from strangers and reminders to walk in groups, to look after their money, and to be home before dark. Parents warned about getting into "bad company" that might be found at theatres, dance halls, and "wild parties." Some of the parental advice was rather vague, including admonitions "not to get lost in the city." This was a directive to avoid non-Mennonite people on their time off, as such company was seen as sinister, offering an occasion for young daughters to be lured away from Mennonite circles. The women also received vague warnings about the men in the households. Although very rarely talked about, some of the women hinted that there were instances in which they had to deal with "improper advances" from men in their workplaces. Parents reportedly agonized over their inability to guard their daughters from the dangers of "sexual impurity" and bodily harm, and they were greatly relieved by the appearance of the girls' homes.

Mennonite girls' homes in western Canada may well have grown from the vision and example of Anna Thiessen, a young Mennonite woman from Herbert, Saskatchewan. While doing mission and relief work in Winnipeg, Anna Thiessen was the first to notice and respond to the plight of the Mennonite working girls. Daughter of a blacksmith and lay minister, and the oldest of thirteen children, Anna was eleven years old when she arrived in Canada in 1903. The Thiessens were affiliated with the Mennonite Brethren (MB) Church, a branch of Mennonites heavily influenced by German pietistic movements and emphasizing proselytization. Serious-minded, conscientious, and independent even as a young girl, Anna's goal was to become a missionary in India. However, in 1915, when she was invited by the MB Church to serve in Winnipeg, she decided this would be as much a "mission field" as would India. According to Anna's sister, "at that time, the Mennonites looked upon the whole city as a place where gospel was not known."[19]

In the city, Anna Thiessen worked mostly with women and children of the German-speaking immigrant population. During her first years in Winnipeg, Anna made home and hospital visitations, and distributed clothing and other aid. While meeting the urgent physical needs of the newcomers, she encouraged spiritual conversion and entry into the fledgling local mission church. She helped to establish a German language Saturday School, a Sunday school, a Christian Young Peoples Association, and a "Ladies' Fellowship," where Bible lessons were combined with practical skills such as knitting or sewing. But the first influx of Mennonite immigrants in 1923 brought a dramatic change in the primary focus of the city mission. The needs of the Mennonite immigrants were compelling. Anna Thiessen saw their plight first-hand on the train platforms and in Immigration Hall, where city residents came to solicit domestic help, and she began translating between the Winnipeggers and the parents contracting their daughters' employment. She especially noted the vulnerability of the many orphaned and widowed women who in some cases would scarcely be missed if they disappeared in the city. She collected the employers' addresses so that she could check on the girls. And, to as many of the young women as she could, Thiessen gave the address of her own small, rented suite and invited them to visit her on their half days off. Her small rooms soon became a favourite meeting place for Mennonite domestics, the first chapter in the creation of the Mennonite girls' homes in Canada.

In her book, *The City Mission in Winnipeg* (1955), Anna Thiessen described her urgent concern for the protection of the Mennonite working girls, her determination to formalize aid for them, and her long struggle to acquire adequate residences and official church support for a girls' home in Winnipeg.[20] In 1925 the Mennonite Brethren Church administration formally assigned Anna Thiessen to work with the Mennonite working women in addition to her other tasks, and it provided a small budget to help her rent additional space for this purpose.[21] Anna's rented rooms began to function very much like other women's hostels supported by government or private agencies – as employment centres and "homes" providing shelter between placements, company, solace, and advice. Her work was noted by other groups of Mennonites. In 1926, the other major branch of Mennonites in North America, the General

Conference (GC) Mennonite Church, assigned a couple to the task of providing a home in Winnipeg for the young working women affiliated with the GC Mennonites. These two homes became part of the Winnipeg experience of thousands of young women over a thirty-year period. In other large cities, such as Vancouver, Saskatoon, and Calgary, similar homes sprang up to assist Mennonite working girls. Though numbers are impossible to verify, they were clearly high – of the 20,000 Mennonites who immigrated to Canada in the 1920s, virtually all of the families had women (mothers, sisters, aunts, or cousins) who entered domestic service for a period of time.

After moving from a series of rented rooms and rented buildings, Anna Thiessen's Mary Martha Home found its permanent home at 437 Mountain Avenue, and the parallel Ebenezer Home was located at 605 Bannatyne Avenue. While the Mennonite girls' homes in Winnipeg saw a few short-term houseparents and various assistants over the years, they were shaped mostly by the great energy and vision of two long-term matrons: Anna Thiessen, who ran the Mary Martha Home from 1925 until the mid-1940s,[22] and Helen Epp, who dedicated twenty-seven years to the Ebenezer Home, until it closed in 1959.

The matrons of the girls' homes protected the young working women in very practical ways. Instead of being isolated, vulnerable individuals, they were now connected under the umbrella of an agency. The matrons set standards for the employers to meet, and made employers accountable to them for how they treated the young women. Besides screening

Young women arriving at the Mary Martha Home in the 1930s

the places of employment, the matrons watched for mistreatment. Often they accompanied girls on their first day of work in order to assess the home and meet their new employer. So that the young women would be able to gather together at the girls' homes each week, both Epp and Thiessen insisted that the employers give the maids Thursday afternoon and evening off.[23] According to Thiessen's sister, Martha Schulz, Anna even lobbied city officials for a bylaw making time off for maids on Thursdays a requirement. These were all critical initiatives at a time when there were no formal labour laws protecting domestic servants.

Other protective measures the matrons took were to refuse to place a maid in situations that they considered substandard. This included cases where employers expected maids to sleep in damp, unfinished basements; where the workload was clearly unreasonable; or where an employer was "stingy" with food. Martha Schulz (who served as matron of the Mary Martha Home in the late 1940s) told of how she refused to place a Mennonite maid in the home of the Speaker of the House in the Manitoba legislature because he offered the girl a "closet room" after escorting her through an elaborate home with several unoccupied guest bedrooms. Other "unacceptable situations" would include a maid being expected to serve alcohol at late-night parties or being exposed to other "bad influences." As well, the matrons put an end to the expected practice of employers coming to the homes to "pick out" their own maid. Finding this humiliating to the young women, they matched the girls with the requests according to information they acquired from interviewing both parties. In an environment in which domestic service was seen as the lowliest kind of employment, these actions were not very popular. While it was middle- and upper-class women who were often at the forefront of social reform movements fighting for improvements in labour conditions and labour laws, they exhibited far less enthusiasm for extending these privileges to the women labouring in their own kitchens.

The girls' homes also addressed spiritual and social needs. On Thursday afternoons crowds of young women from throughout the city walked or travelled by streetcar to the homes, where they visited together, ate their bagged lunches, sang songs, caught up on the news, and participated in Bible study. Ladies' Fellowship groups at the local churches were organized to accommodate the young women's time off. The matrons organized birthday dinners and encouraged churches to hold special Easter and Christmas celebrations at a time when the working girls could be there. In their retrospectives the women expressed great appreciation for these efforts. The girls' homes were, as many said, an "oasis" during a very difficult time.

From Refuge to Hiring Hall

The process by which the girls' homes gained community support grew out of the gender relations in the Mennonite families and churches. In Winnipeg, as in several other cities, the Mennonite girls' homes were initially founded by women, but it was male church leaders who quickly became the decision makers and owners. All of the homes ran on a shoestring, with the main financial strategy being "klein Arbeit" (small work), by which a great many minute contributions – on the scale of pennies and dimes – added up to the required amounts in groceries, rent, and mortgage payments. The women staying in the homes between jobs paid small amounts for rent and meals, while others spent time between their intense work schedules doing hand-work for sale at church bazaars to raise their small donations. The day-to-day burden of making ends meet fell on the houseparents, or matrons, who worked tirelessly at fund-raising, budgeting, and collecting donations.

Initially, Anna Thiessen helped Mennonite working girls as a part of her city mission mandate. But, frustrated by how little she could do on her own, she organized an appeal for official support from the church administration. With official church involvement the initiative changed from one of "women helping women" to one governed by the male leadership and having the entire community's involvement. The effect of this was to keep the women connected to the church and their families in a way that was consistent with the traditional, patriarchal social system, rather than to encourage the kind of independence and "sisterhood" that sometimes developed amongst other groups of female domestic servants.

Most effective in Anna Thiessen's appeal for community support was her argument that the girls' homes served a spiritual cause. She emphasized what people already believed – that urban life was dangerous and that the young women were being sent out into the "darkness of the city" without physical and spiritual protection. Throughout the 1930s, Anna Thiessen presented long, impassioned reports on the girls' homes at the annual meetings of the Mennonite Brethren Church, where she was conspicuously the only woman reporting to the all-male delegates. For example, at the 1933 meeting in Dalmeny, Saskatchewan, she warned that "the Lord entrusted your daughters and your sisters [to us]. Should we pass by indifferently? No, the danger exists that many of them would be lost in the currents of the world. Our main purpose is to win them for the Lord. A large number of the girls that come and go in the home were delivered from the shackles of the evil one and added to the church."[24] During the same meeting, a male colleague of Anna's reiterated that the

Mary Martha Home was "a very important branch of the mission whose real significance we will recognize, if some day we should be without it ... Imagine, some 250 noble souls, virgins, our daughters, 'dumped' into a large city by conditions beyond their control, without the home!"[25]

The protective function of the girls' homes was readily appreciated. In order for them to serve as a strong link to Mennonite teaching and values, imagery was carefully chosen to communicate the spiritual concepts they were to inculcate. The Ebenezer Home was named after a biblical story in which Samuel built a stone monument, called an Ebenezer, to celebrate how God delivered the Israelites from the hands of their enemies, the Philistines. The Ebenezer, then, was a powerful symbol of God's presence and help in a crisis situation. The Mary Martha Home was named after the New Testament story that tells of Jesus' visit to the home of two sisters, where he found Mary to be a model of devotion and Martha to be a model of service. Dorcas, another biblical personality held up to the women, was a woman known for her modesty and good works. From her example, the women learned that "the one who fills her time with good works is protected from evil."[26] These biblical symbols evoked devotion and service to the point of sacrifice, virtues that were certainly modelled by both Anna Thiessen and Helen Epp.

To this idea about the religious role of the girls' homes was added the argument that the girls, too, would serve a "mission"; they would be a light in the dark world of the city and "ambassadors" of Christ and of the Mennonite community among non-Mennonites. The matrons and visiting conference pastors assigned to lead the weekly Bible studies in the girls' homes impressed upon the young women that it was God who sent them to the city. The Ebenezer women were often reminded by their minister of the importance of their good behaviour in the homes: "You are an open book, read by many. That's how you have to live."[27] Similarly, Anna Thiessen wrote:

> It is surely not a matter of chance that the Lord sent our Christian girls into the big cities to serve in the homes of those we would not reach otherwise. Some of these homes do not wish to have repentance and holiness preached to them; therefore the preachers and missionaries turn to the poor who are more approachable. And now our sisters are entering the homes of the wealthy, the influential, and the professional people of our country as servants. Their quiet, Christian diligence presents the message of the Cross in a powerful sermon.[28]

It is important to note that the girls' "mission" was defined very specifically. It was to display a "quiet Christian diligence." Significantly, besides "the message of the cross," this would present the message of the groups' virtue and their respectability as Canadian citizens – a reputation that the Mennonites were concerned to perpetuate. The girls' mission, then, was not based on the notion of seeking the conversion or church attendance of their employers (Mennonite church services were almost exclusively in the German language throughout this period); rather, it was to perform the very important function of community ambassadors, building up the positive public image required of any immigrant group wishing to find a point of entry in Canadian society.

In 1934, at the annual general meeting of the MB Church in Winkler, Manitoba, a special evening service was dedicated to the topic of the girls' homes. This time, in a lengthy, compelling oration, Anna Thiessen compared the girls' home experience to a school. The "tears of homesickness" were the "tuition" the girls paid, the "administrator" was the "Lord Jesus Christ," and "those for whom we work and serve" were the "teachers." The employers' homes were the "classrooms" where the girls studied the different "disciplines" – "washing dishes, taking care of the clothes, attending to children, serving at the table, speaking the English language well, and answering the telephone politely."[29] Much like the "mission" imagery, by equating the young women's maid experience with getting an education in the arts and sciences of domesticity, Anna Thiessen elevated the lowly occupation. As she said of service in her 1937 report, "be it ever so low, so simple, so insignificant [it] receives dignity and honor, because it is a part of the program of our heavenly Father."[30] Elevating the women's work in this way likely had the dual effect of guarding the dignity of the women and soothing the consciences of those who found it unsettling to send their daughters to the city.

As the endorsement of the churches became more secure, the community's confidence in their daughters' safety in the city grew. The girls' homes even encouraged young women into domestic service who otherwise might not have gone. Rather than protecting or rescuing young women from the work, the matrons were helping them find work, advertising their services in the newspapers, taking calls, and matching employers with workers. The matrons played the role of employment brokers, and the girls' homes fulfilled the dual roles of refuge and hiring hall.

This did not happen without expressions of dismay. As the numbers of young Mennonite girls streaming to the city in search of work grew during the 1930s, Thiessen's reports at the annual church meetings included attempts to discourage the influx. In 1936, at the meeting in Waldheim, Saskatchewan, Anna offered the admonition, "Some have to work, but some come out of pure curiosity. Often I wish that the mothers would not send their daughters into the city at such an early age. They depend so much on this home, thinking that all will be well there."[31] At the meeting the following year, she warned:

> In most of the homes where the girls are serving, there are temptations of all kinds: tickets to the theatre are offered, or money is left on any spot in the house to lead the girls into temptation. There is much smoking, dancing and drinking; the masters go after all kinds of amusements and live in all kinds of devilry. The city life is for some very magnetic, and so many unsaved girls come into the city to seek a place of service. We do not only see the houses in which they work as our field, but also to win the unsaved girls is our aim. Repeatedly, we have been overwhelmed with respect to the tremendous responsibility that rests upon us when the young girls come so delicate and so young. Many of them are in need of parental care. Parents should not send their daughters too early and not too young into the life of the city and its attractions.

Nevertheless, she came to the conclusion that "the Lord needs us ... What no minister can do from the pulpit or through his visits ... God-fearing girls can do through piety and a quiet walk. These means the Lord can use in His service."[32]

Certainly the "service" the young women were providing was multiple. The belief that young women domestics performed an important mission for their own families and communities was especially strong in the Ebenezer Home. Noting that the most-often stated reason for sending the women to the city to work was the travel debt, Helen Epp established the practice of collecting the young women's monthly earnings directly instead of having them sent home to parents, where more immediate priorities often prevailed. The earnings were passed from the girls' home to C.F. Klassen, collector of the travel debt for the Canadian Mennonite Board of Colonization, who made regular visits. Apparently, while some parents initially protested, in time Epp was praised for this initiative.[33]

The campaign to achieve community support for the girls' homes was very successful. However, it brought some unexpected results. Besides bringing financial contributions, church endorsement meant that decision making for the girls' homes became the official responsibility of the usually all-male boards to whom the matrons were expected to report. It also meant the appointment of church ministers to oversee the spiritual welfare of the women connected to the homes.

The ministers assigned to the girls' homes usually attended the Thursday evening gatherings, where they led Bible studies. Visitors of both homes remember sermons on moral living and on being a witness in the homes where they worked. At these Bible studies the women also discussed how to handle stressful times of year, such as religious holidays, when cultural and religious differences were most evident. And they reviewed moral points about their outward appearance (e.g., whether or not they should use makeup or buy the latest fashions). All aspects of the everyday work world came under scrutiny. Mary Heidebrecht remembered lengthy debates with her friends on whether or not it was justifiable to press employers for permission to wear short-sleeved uniforms (which some considered immodest) on very hot days – a relevant topic, as many of the girls were annually accompanying their employers to their summer cottages, where, in their long-sleeved, black uniforms, they were expected to do the heavy work of cooking and washing without the amenities of electricity or running water.[34]

While the attention of the church administrators helped to broaden the base of support, still, their financial contributions were only partial, and the "klein Arbeit" continued throughout the decades the homes operated. For instance, in the early years, the Mennonite Brethren Church contributed $20 a month to the Mary Martha Home for the rent of the building. The home's operating budget for the entire year, June 1928 to June 1929, totalled $2,605.70. More than half of the amount came from the working women themselves ($1,324.97), $1,040.73 came from "friends," and only $240 (for the rent) came from the church administration. (This was in addition to the $40 a month the conference was paying Anna Thiessen for her general work with the city mission.)[35]

Still, that the homes were approved and supported by the churches was comforting to the parents of the young women. They could read about the activities of the homes in detailed reports appearing regularly in such Mennonite church papers as *Zionsbote, Mennonitische Rundschau*, and *Der Bote*. The homes' reputation as a "mission" also contributed towards the women developing a sense of pride in their work. This was of considerable value because in their daily work environment they endured the vivid symbolic reminders of their lowly, separate status – the uniforms, the bells they answered to, the separate quarters in which they ate and slept. Agatha Isaak, who had worked for the same family for thirty-seven years, said, "They used to say I was like one of their family. And yet I wasn't." She recalled how, even on a visit after her retirement, the lady was reluctant to have her sit together with her in the parlour. Another woman, who had worked for an especially "uppity-up lady," remembered receiving instructions "not to say one extra word – just what I had to say." In such a context, the girls' camaraderie and their sense of being "ambassadors" in the city contributed to their self-esteem and, as they said, helped them to feel like "more than just maids." [36] This attitude was well expressed in a poem written by one of the young women:

> Though I work as a servant / For meagre reward,
> Lose my bloom in a lowly place / In a stranger's house and service;
> Though nightly my needle / Works my fingers raw,
> My heritage and honour is: "I am a servant of the Lord.[37]

This conception of the Mennonite domestic servants as missionaries and community ambassadors was sometimes reinforced by employers' responses. One account, surviving in a scrapbook made by Anna Thiessen, is a lengthy Winnipeg newspaper article with the headline, "Margaret Makes Good." In it Kathleen Strange speaks in glowing terms of the Mennonite maid whom she hired through the Mary Martha Home: "In a very short space of time I had come to look upon her as an invaluable adjunct to our family life. Never, in all my housekeeping experience, had I known a more capable, conscientious and amiable young maid." The writer goes on to tell how, in just eight short years, Margaret had succeeded in saving enough money to buy property of her own and had "retired" from domestic service. She exclaims: "As the years went by I confess I almost came to hope that Margaret would remain with me for ever! I could hardly conceive of our household without her (I am pleased to say that she has since been replaced by another young Mennonite girl equally as good!)."[38] In 1937 Anna Thiessen reported to the church conference that these sentiments were widespread, pointing out that "many a favourable witness one hears about the girls," and, while at first girls waited for jobs, "today the women wait for the girls."[39] Apparently, newspaper ads of the day calling for domestic servants sometimes included the note "Mennonites preferred."[40]

Such public endorsement was of great value to the Mennonite newcomers who had so recently been impressed by the lesson in Russia that friends in high places of government were not enough and that the support of their fellow citizens and neighbours could be essential to survival. Shades of the persecution they suffered in the destruction of Czarist Russia were felt during the Second World War years, when the Mennonites became the target of some of the virulent anti-German sentiment due to their language and their objection to serving in the military. In southern Alberta, where two Mennonite churches were burned down during those years, the impact felt by the domestic servants was reported by Annie Martens: "Much friendliness has been shown us here till the outbreak of the Second World War. After that, the hate against Germans could be plainly noticed, and we also had to suffer. Having at first shown us great trust, this now changed radically to mistrust ... Even our Ministers, who had punctually visited and served us in German before, were now strictly forbidden to do so."[41] For the Mennonite immigrants as a group, then, it was a very genuine and practical consideration to build up and maintain a good reputation in order to gain status within, and acceptance into, Canadian society. At the time, the women working in the cities were recognized as playing an influential part in this important work.

The community's endorsement of the girls' homes brought new expectations and strong pressures for the young women to perform well. On the whole, the women exhibited an unusually strong sense of obligation and responsibility, coupled with a respect for their parents. As one said, "Those years we didn't speak up to our parents ... They needed help and that was the way it was."[42] One woman mentioned how her mother always emphasized a cheerful outlook, admonishing her never to complain or feel sorry for herself. However, it was not unusual to get "difficult places" where the women had to face hard-driving, "bossy" employers or work at all hours of the day and night. Mennonite domestics were slow to identify the work demands as unreasonable. This may have been, in part, because they were concerned that the employer, the girls' home matron, their family, or their peers would think they were not trying hard enough. On the whole, it was commonly thought that, if the work really was too hard, then bringing it to the employers' attention or seeking improvement would not help. If the situation became especially difficult, then the solution was to quit quietly and find another place. But hard work in itself was generally not considered a good enough reason to leave employment, and sometimes a girl would bear considerable hardship before mentioning it to the girls' home matron. The dilemma the young women sometimes felt may be attributable to the dual role of the girls' homes, as matrons increasingly became "mediators," with responsibilities to the young women but also to their employers.

Changing Times and the Closing of the Girls' Homes

While listening to these women's personal stories and interpretations of their experiences, I was impressed by the differences between those who went to Winnipeg to work in the 1920s and 1930s and those who went in the 1940s and 1950s. It is quite clear that in the 1920s and 1930s the primary factor in the move to the city was economic. Prepared by the devastation and loss they had experienced in Russia, the Mennonites were exhibiting a classic "immigrant mentality," where individual needs and aspirations were necessarily put aside in order to succeed, where gratitude for whatever they had superseded discontent, and where the feeling of being at the "bottom of the ladder" provoked humility and a strong work ethic. Despite their distrust of the city and their reluctance to have their daughters work there, parents accepted the situation as an emergency measure. The girls' homes helped parents to make that decision and to feel better about it. As for the women, they "grew up fast," shouldering the responsibilities and proving themselves capable. Even though they did not know where the city work would eventually lead, they took it on with courage and displayed the resilience, diligence, and often self-abasement that were the qualities looked for in good servants.

The women who worked in Winnipeg in the 1940s and 1950s described a much less difficult situation. By then, in most cases the travel debts had been paid and the family farm established. The women were more likely to be working in Winnipeg for more personal objectives. Working in the city also became easier when older sisters and friends had paved the way, establishing a pattern and reporting that the city and the maid work "wasn't so bad." This impression spread quickly amongst the girls, who walked the streets day and night, cautiously, but without fear, often travelling many miles by foot in order to save streetcar fare.

At the time, Winnipeg was a small fraction of its present size and, according to many of the women, was not nearly as dangerous as today. While many were "shaking in their boots" when they first came to Winnipeg, for some of the girls the city was already familiar because of previous monthly shopping trips. Also making city life less formidable was the growing Mennonite community in North Kildonan, just north of Winnipeg. Small acreages were bought by widows with their children, families who lost their farms during the 1930s, and others who were inexperienced in large-scale agriculture. Many of them subsisted on market gardens and poultry, while others travelled to the city centre to find work in construction or to take odd jobs.[43] As Mennonite churches and other institutions took root in Winnipeg in the late 1930s and early 1940s, significant Mennonite networks developed.

In these decades, the women were less apprehensive about taking work in the city. Though they had seen some women get "stuck in it," most of them thought of domestic work as "a stepping stone," an occupation for a time. While the women did not complain about maid work, most were quick to take other opportunities when they arose. During the Second World War years, many were willing to take on the more difficult, lower paying assembly-line work in order to have the freedom of evenings and weekends off. This attitude, typical of that of domestic workers in general, was largely what brought an end to the "maid" phenomenon in Canada and elsewhere; because of the universal problems with the occupation (the loneliness, low social status, hard work, long hours, and lack of freedom), women changed to other employment when possible.[44] In fact, the 1950s, with the mechanization of housework and new concepts of domesticity (which created the single-handed "housewife"), marked the practical demise of the live-in-maid phenomenon. While some of the Mennonite working girls switched to housework by the day, and others took up employment in the kitchens or laundries of hospitals and nursing homes, the majority turned to factory work, usually in sewing factories, where for weeks and months on end they would sew the same small portion of one type of garment. Instead of an hourly wage they usually started with piece work, which, until they learned to work at top speed, gave them meagre compensation for their efforts. Of the women I interviewed, Annie Dyck worked for over thirty years in sewing factories. Erica Voth traded domestic service for work in a factory making caps for army uniforms, while Katie Peters worked in a bindery inspecting tickets, and Nettie Warkentin worked for thirty-four years in a coffee and tea factory at such tasks as filling tea bags. The tedious, fragmented tasks of the assembly line, which took place during long days (8:00 AM to 6:00 PM) that were frequently without coffee breaks, were performed with the same diligence and care as was the housework.

The key difference was that several of the women described their work in the city during the 1940s and 1950s as an opportunity to improve their own rather than their family's situation. They pointed out that they were not forced to go to the city to work, that it was their own idea. Some women even expressed a motivation to escape hard work at home. Domestic work was known to be lighter and higher paying in the city than in the country. Some women chose to work in the city because it was less lonely than working in the isolation of southern Manitoba farms. Katie Loewen, for one, described herself as having been "socially starved" in the country.[45] In Winnipeg there was more opportunity for a young woman to have friends her own age through the girls' homes and the churches. Another positive aspect of city domestic work was that it meant adventure, growing up, and a chance to learn new things. One woman said that at first she thought some of the customs in the homes were rather "crazy" but that, later, she thought they were "actually quite nice." She said that she learned a lot about other people: "how they think, how they bring up their children, and so on."

Unlike in the 1920s and 1930s, when the women were usually working for their families' needs, in the years that followed they were often more free to save for their own goals. Some women saved money for their own education – often an English course, a sewing course, missionary or Bible studies, or professional training in teaching or nursing (which were also accepted as appropriate work for women). Until the 1940s and 1950s, however, it was the exceptional girl who graduated from high school or earned a teaching certificate. Most either "didn't have a chance" or found that higher education was not encouraged. As one woman explained, at that time there were other priorities for Mennonite women, such as learning homemaking skills.[46] Most hoped to get married and have families of their own, and this is generally what happened. The majority of the young women came from the countryside, did domestic service for several years between their mid-teens and early twenties, and returned to their rural communities to marry and establish their own family farms after which, in many cases, they retired to the city. Maid work gave them training in running a household, so they "didn't need to learn after marriage." Indeed, amongst themselves some of the women would joke that after marriage the domestic service continued but without wages or time off!

By mid-century the women's move to the city to work had changed from an emergency measure to an accepted pattern. Even when the economic need lessened, they continued to go there. Parents' attitudes slowly changed from fear or suspicion of the city to familiarity and confidence in urban Mennonite connections. The imagery of the girls' homes as mission stations continued to be perpetuated by some observers, despite the growing numbers of "day workers" diversifying into various types of employment. At the 1944 annual meeting of the MB Church, Cornelius Peters's report on the Vancouver City Mission work insisted:

> The home of the girls is, as before, a mission station. The two sisters, Tina Lepp and Mary Thiessen, serve in the home. Formerly it was a mediation centre for those who sought work in the city in the homes, today it is a center where the girls who work by the hour or by day stay for the night ... The mission spirit has not changed. The same as before, the Word is still the nurture for the soul, light on their faith path, as guide-line for the walk.[47]

But, even while the young women and their parents were becoming more comfortable with the city, voices of protest were gaining prominence, calling for a return to tradition. Fearful images overpowered the positive imagery of the maid experience as one that provided an education and mission field. At the 1942 annual meeting of the MB Church,

"Sister H.S. Rempel" of the Saskatoon Girls' Home requested intercessory prayers, warning: "We deeply acknowledge that we live in a city surrounded with much danger. There are lurings on every hand, especially for the young inexperienced girls."[48] At the meeting in 1943, Jacob Thiessen, a minister connected with the Vancouver Girls' Home, expounded that he, together with his wife and the two women running the home, "would greet that day with joy, when no daughter of our people would ever, ever have to tread the glare-ice of the city anymore!"[49] The year before, he had addressed parents with the plea, "Don't send your daughters to the city unless you are in dire straits."[50]

By the 1940s and 1950s people in the churches were beginning to be less sympathetic to the "condition" of the Mennonite working girls. They began to suspect that the girls' homes were changing from a "refuge" and a "mission" to simply a cheap place to board. Class divisions became apparent as some of the newcomers achieved a measure of prosperity. The women felt that some of the "better-off" Mennonites began to look down on the working girls. Indeed, in the 1942 meeting of the MB Church, Jacob Thiessen's address to the delegates expressed a growing sense of class consciousness: "May the hour soon come when none of our people can be found in Vancouver, or any other large city, except for a few missionary companions. I am anxious at the thought of a Mennonite 'proletariat' in the city. May the Lord guide us back into a quiet country life, and help us to serve Him in simplicity."

In this climate, in the late 1950s the Mennonite girls' homes came to an abrupt close. Both the Mennonite Brethren and the General Conference Mennonite Church administrations made the decision to withdraw their affiliation and financial support, effecting the closure of girls' homes in Winnipeg in 1959 and in Vancouver, Saskatoon, and Calgary shortly after that. It is noteworthy that, even though the churches had only contributed a small fraction of their support, they had the power to close and sell the homes and reallocate the assets without even consulting the matrons running and living in them. Today, the hurt and disappointment comes out as these women note that the homes were still fulfilling ongoing as well as new needs, especially with the new wave of post-Second World War Mennonite immigrants. Anna Thiessen's sister, Martha Schulz, who had served as matron from 1945 until she married in 1951, described the closure of the Mary Martha Home: "Most of the girls were more established in their way of life in the '40s. So many of them had church connections, and were not so lonely. My question was, when do we consider it a mission work? When there are 60 and 80 and 200 coming? We seem to go by numbers ... I really was quite often torn. I didn't have an answer."[51] In a similar retrospective, Helen Epp's sister noted that the closure "just shows [how] these men don't know nothing about the girls [or their] needs. The decision was made by the Conference, and that was it."[52] Nevertheless, at the time the women made no notable protest, keeping the peace and submitting quietly to those in authority over them.

The church decisions were especially difficult for the women serving as matrons in the homes because the closures meant losing their only residence and livelihood. By that time, because of failing health, Anna Thiessen had been living in the Mary Martha Home on a stipend of twenty dollars per month for about ten years in a supportive role to a series of matrons. At the annual meeting of the MB Church in 1959, the motion to sell the Mary Martha Home was coupled by one to provide Anna Thiessen with a retirement pension of fifty dollars per month from the proceeds.[53] Fortunately, by the time the house was actually sold in 1962, she also received a Canada Pension. Helen Epp, on the other hand, was not immediately offered the retirement pensions typically given to church missionaries. Nor was she eligible for Canada Pension. According to her sister, Helen felt "quite defeated" by the General Conference Mennonite Church's decision to close the Ebenezer Home. One of Helen's sisters, Ida, recalled bringing the situation to the attention of church

Former domestics visiting house parent Helen Epp in her retirement

representatives, who reportedly conceded that she was entitled to some pension. Ida emphasized, "They even said she was a missionary just the same as any other missionary that goes out, and she is entitled to have a pension. But she didn't know about it." Eventually, Helen Epp did receive a fifty-dollar-per-month pension from her church conference. This supplemented her main support, which was her and her sister's employment in domestic day work, which continued for more than twenty years after the home closure. That Helen Epp was right in foreseeing the ongoing need for the girls' home was evident when Mennonite women of the post-Second World War immigration repeatedly turned up at the door of her small house in North Kildonan asking whether it was the place where they could stay.[54]

While finances and declining need were the official reasons given for the abrupt closures of the homes, other factors were also at work. The young women had gone from "missionaries" and "ambassadors" of the community in hard times to aspiring students and independent working women after the community debts were paid. The closure of the girls' homes was an assertion of the male leadership, reclaiming men's functions as providers and communicating a clear call to the young women to return to hearth and home. They were also a statement about Mennonite aspirations. Community reputation, which had previously been enhanced by the girls' homes, was now perceived to be negatively affected by them, for the homes had become a symbol connecting the community with a place in society it wished to rise above, and a chapter in its story that it wished to leave behind.

Conclusion

How do the women interviewed for this chapter evaluate their experiences as they look back on them now? Many must have felt, as one woman expressed it, "My life turned out very different from what I expected!" Yet most insist that they appraised the situation and either chose that life themselves or found their own ways to make "something good of it." One informant declared, "It didn't do anybody any harm. I think it made people out of us!" Others called it "a good learning experience" and a time when "we learned to stand on our own feet." Typically, they report, "I got used to it," and "they were good years, no matter how hard it was sometimes." Many of the women looked back on their experience with a resoluteness and, often, a kind of resignation, "taking it" as their "lot." For instance, in response to whether or not domestic work was a factor in her never marrying, Katie Enns responded, "No, some things just were not meant to be." Another, Anna Harder, admitted that it was a very lonely life, "But, well, I came to here, I wanted it like that, I have to take it like it is. Nothing to say anymore ... Now I have to be pleased with it as it is." Elizabeth Friesen said, "It wasn't for us to decide, 'What will I do?' There wasn't money to think about that." Another, when asked if she had any regrets, said, "No. That's the way it should be for me ... You can't turn your life this way or that way."

When these women reflect on their experiences as domestic servants they note that their hard work and frugal habits paid debts, built savings, and contributed towards prosperity. Indeed, most of the women I visited are today solidly middle class. One declared, "I never, never would have dreamt that I would ever live in a house like where I used to work for people!" In many cases the women's homes today resemble those of their past employers. Several women mentioned that they adopted things they learned in their workplaces – for example, new recipes, "English" manners, and new styles of table setting, serving, and home decor. These acquired styles and customs have since become traditions in many Mennonite homes.

The voices of these now elderly Mennonite women are expressions of an immigrant experience at once common to countless others and uniquely their own. Their language and attitudes fit uncomfortably into familiar, contemporary categories. Were the female leaders in the girls' homes movement social reformers or champions of women's rights? Were the working women victims, whose youth and futures were sacrificed for the benefit of the larger group? Were Mennonite women "silent" and "passive" or did they actively shape their futures? As the religious and self-abasing elements of their discourse becomes embarrassing and even incomprehensible to their own children and grandchildren, we risk projecting onto them our contemporary values and ideologies. But by actively preserving their stories, perhaps we can learn to listen to and understand these voices on their own terms, in their own terminology, and to reconstruct more authentically the women's own experiences.

This chapter shows that the decades when great numbers of Mennonite immigrant women worked as urban domestic servants in the Canadian West were an important time of transition. The long-held principles of separation from, and non-conformity to, the world were expressed by earlier Mennonite immigrants through their rural block settlements and distinctive language, culture, and, in some cases, dress. But this was more difficult to achieve by the 1920s.

Still, group membership held an importance for these Mennonites that is often foreign to their contemporary descendants. This was a time when the threat of excommunication held great power in the Mennonite churches. It was a time when the often-expressed fear of "losing the children" (likely a vestige of the broken families in the war) made some segments of the group extremely protective of the German language and Mennonite religio-cultural traditions, driving such incredible feats as the early establishment of a network of private education institutions in Canada even during the difficult decades of resettlement. This urgency is well expressed in Cornelius Peters's report on the Vancouver Girls' Home at the 1944 annual meeting of the MB Church. He described the Mennonite working girls as "off-splits, wandering, that had to be sought and nurtured if they should not suffer damage." They were members "scattered in the city," who needed to be "gathered" with "much love and patience" into a "united fellowship." [55]

Mennonite immigrants responded to this challenge by evoking old, familiar religious traditions to mediate their new experience in Canada. Newcomer Mennonite women were channelled into domestic service by forces inherent in Canadian society as well as by the community's unique conceptualization of the women's work as a "mission" to their families and to their employers in the city. Community leaders cooperated in this process in order to protect the reputation of the community; retiring community debt took precedence over guarding female purity and piety. At the time, the women's work as domestics was framed within the context of two overarching purposes: their service to others and their devotion to God. The women were taught that their labour as domestics was important, bringing the light of the gospel into the city while expressing and developing virtues of forbearance, diligence, and honesty. The sudden withdrawal of support for their work and the ensuing silence in the official historical accounts about their contribution is noted by the women today with both puzzlement and dismay. Today the story can be seen in the context of Canadian colonization of immigrant populations and the construction of class hierarchies. But at the time the male leadership in the communities likely saw it as their own failure to protect their daughters and to preserve Mennonite values. For them, then, it was not a very proud chapter, which may explain why it has been ignored in the official histories.

Girls' homes had a protective and rescuing function, even as they served as "hiring halls," ushering the women onto new and threatening ground. They were an important conduit of Mennonite cultural and religious values and facilitated "belonging." The transition in the late 1950s of the girls' homes from an important branch of the Mennonite mission effort to a somewhat embarrassing vestige of a past immigration experience coincides with the increased security of the Mennonite community in Canada. The girls' homes illustrate a conflict felt more widely by immigrant groups and visible minorities in Canada – the tension between the dual imperatives to manage public perception of the group (usually requiring a certain degree of conformity) and to retain cultural distinctiveness and identity.

That the women in this study see the major value of their maid experience as preparation for their role as wives and mothers shows that city work, with all its newness, also reinforced traditional roles and values. Yet, while the girls' homes were apparently successful in maintaining group cohesiveness and in reserving a traditional place in Mennonite society for returning daughters, the experiences the women brought back to "hearth and home" had a significant and lasting effect on their communities. Women who worked as domestic servants contributed a crucial point of entry into Canadian life for the Russian Mennonite immigrants of the 1920s. They helped to construct a positive, non-threatening public image of the group leading to wider social acceptance, and they facilitated the gradual breakdown of cultural barriers to urban life and to the language, mores, and social structures of their adopted home.

Notes

1 Frank H. Epp, *Mennonite Exodus: The Rescue and Resettlement of the Russian Mennonites Since the Communist Revolution* (Canadian Mennonite Relief and Immigration Counsel, 1962), 19.

2 The Mennonites owned more than three million acres in south Russia at the time of the Revolution. See Frank H. Epp, *Mennonites in Canada, 1920-1940* (Toronto: Macmillan, 1982), 140-1.

3 CPR debts were incurred by more than 13,000 of the Mennonite immigrants. See Epp, *Mennonites in Canada*, 384.

4 The interview project was supported by grants from the Manitoba Heritage Federation and the Provincial Archives of Manitoba (PAM) Oral History Grants Program. The tapes and 170 pages of interview outlines are identified as the CMBSC Oral History Project, 1987, and are held at PAM and the Centre for Mennonite Brethren Studies in Canada, Winnipeg, Manitoba.

5 See Epp, *Mennonites in Canada*, 474-5; J.A. Toews, *A History of the Mennonite Brethren Church* (Fresno, CA: Board of Christian Literature, General Conference of Mennonite Brethren Churches, 1975), 157, 206; E.K. Francis, *In Search of Utopia: The Mennonites in Manitoba* (Altona, MB: Friesen, 1955), 215, 248, 267; Henry C. Smith, *The Story of the Mennonites* (Berne, IN: Mennonite Book Concern, 1941), 710-1.

6 See Marlene Epp, "The Mennonite Girls' Homes of Winnipeg (1925-1959): A Home Away from Home," *Journal of Mennonite Studies* 6 (1988): 100-14; Frieda Esau Klippenstein, "'Doing What We Could': Mennonite Domestic Servants in Winnipeg, 1920s to 1950s," *Journal of Mennonite Studies* 7 (1989): 145-66; Leo Driedger, *Mennonites in Winnipeg* (Winnipeg: Kindred, 1990). See also Cornelius Krahn, "Research on Urban Mennonites," *Mennonite Life* 23, 4 (October 1968): 189-92.

7 Unlike factory work, domestic service was considered to be employment in the "private" realm and, thus, was not covered by labour laws addressing minimum wage, maximum work days, or child labour. Live-in domestics with grievances had no forum for protest beyond leaving their place of employment. This was difficult to do, as it also meant giving up their place of shelter until another situation could be found. The public perception was that homeless women outside the protection of a family roof were most likely to turn to prostitution, and prostitution brought with it unwanted pregnancy, which, in turn, led to infanticide or abortion – thus the link between domestic service and these notorious vices. See Christine Stansell, *City of Women: Sex and Class in New York, 1789-1860* (New York: Knopf, 1986); Veronica Strong-Boag, *The New Day Recalled: Lives of Girls and Women in English Canada, 1919-1939* (Toronto: Copp Clark Pitman, 1988), 55-6; David Katzman, *Seven Days a Week: Women and Domestic Service in Industrializng America* (Oxford: Oxford University Press, 1978); and Donna Van Raaphorst, *Union Maids Not Wanted: Organizing Domestic Workers, 1870-1940* (New York: Praeger, 1988).

8 Varpu Lindstrom-Best, *Defiant Sisters: A Social History of Finnish Immigrant Women in Canada* (Toronto: Multicultural History Society of Ontario, 1988).

9 Stansell, *City of Women*, 155-68.

10 Roxanna Ng, "The Social Construction of 'Immigrant Women' in Canada," in *The Politics of Diversity: Feminism, Marxism and Nationalism*, ed. Roberta Hamilton and Michele Barrett (London: New Left, 1986), 270.

11 In Winnipeg, the first hostel for domestic servants was the "Girls' House of Welcome," which was founded by Octavia Fowler, opened in the late 1890s, and operated until the early 1930s. See PAM, Immigration Branch Records, MG4 D1 vol. 138. See also Marilyn Barber "The Servant Problem in Manitoba, 1896-1930," in *First Days, Fighting Days: Women in Manitoba History*, ed. Mary Kinnear (Regina: Canadian Plains Research Centre, University of Regina, 1987), 101.

12 Some 1.6 million immigrants arrived in Canada between 1911 and 1921, and 1.2 million arrived from 1921 to 1931. See Gerald Friesen, *The Canadian Prairies: A History* (Toronto: University of Toronto Press, 1984), 248.

13 In this chapter I refer to the Mennonite working women as "women" and "girls" interchangeably. This reflects the women's own discourse: in their reminiscences they consistently refer to themselves and their mostly teen-aged friends as "girls."

14 See Epp, *Mennonite Exodus*, 186-202, the chapter on acquiring land. See also p. 198 for a map showing location of the mentioned Manitoba towns.

15 Nettie Warkentin interview, CMBSC Oral History Project, 1987, Winnipeg, Centre for Mennonite Brethren Studies in Canada.

16 Epp, *Mennonites in Canada*, 384-5.

17 Not until the late 1940s, after huge individual and collective effort on the part of the Mennonite community and after the Canadian Pacific Railway cancelled interest fees of about a million dollars, was the travel debt finally liquidated. For more on the challenge of the travel debt, see Epp, *Mennonite Exodus*, 281-95, 335-48.

18 Martha Schulz interview, CMBSC Oral History Project, 1987, Winnipeg, Centre for Mennonite Brethren Studies in Canada.

19 The Mennonite Brethren Church established a local mission church in Winnipeg with twenty-two members in 1913. See Epp, *Mennonites in Canada*, 189.

20 Anna Thiessen's book, *Die Stadtmission in Winnipeg*, was translated into English by Ida Toews and republished as *The City Mission in Winnipeg* (Winnipeg: Centre for Mennonite Brethren Studies, 1991).

21 In the 1920s Anna Thiessen's wage was forty dollars per month, dipping to thirty dollars per month in the 1930s. In 1949, her failing health was recognized and she received twenty dollars per month plus room and board to remain in the home in a supportive role to new matrons. See Annual Report of the Northern District Conference of Mennonite Brethren Churches, Coaldale, Alberta, 1949, 161.

22 Anna Thiessen continued to live at the Mary Martha Home after medical problems prompted her to give up her role as matron in the early 1940s. She stayed until the home was closed in 1959. For more information on Anna Thiessen and Helen Epp, see Neoma

Jantz, "Sister to Many: Anna Thiessen (1892-1977)," in *Women Among the Brethren,* ed. Katie Funk (Wiebe Hillsboro, KA: General Conference of Mennonite Brethren Churches, 1979), 118-28; and Eric Rempel, "Eben-Ezer Girls' Home, Winnipeg (1926-1959)," unpublished paper (Winnipeg: Mennonite Heritage Centre, 1977).

23 Linda Kealey (1987), "Women and Labour during World War I: Women Workers and the Minimum Wage in Manitoba," in Kinnear, *First Days, Fighting Days*, 76-99. Minimum wage legislation came in 1920 during a period of intense labour and reform activity. Kealey notes that, unlike the waitresses and other service workers, domestic servants did not benefit from Minimum Wage Board decisions. Household workers were specifically excluded from its jurisdiction. See also Thiessen, *City Mission in Winnipeg,* 65.

24 Annual Report of the Northern District Conference of Mennonite Brethren (MB) Churches, Dalmeny, Saskatchewan, 1933, 65.

25 Ibid., 66.

26 Thiessen, *City Mission in Winnipeg,* 78.

27 This was expressed by Helen Epp's sisters Ida Friesen and Aganetha Epp, CMBSC Oral History Project, 1987, Winnipeg, Centre for Mennonite Brethren Studies in Canada.

28 Thiessen, *City Mission in Winnipeg,* 75.

29 Annual Report of the Northern District Conference of MB Churches, Winkler, Manitoba, 1934, 95.

30 Ibid., 1937, 87.

31 Ibid., Waldheim, Saskatchewan, 1936, 39.

32 Ibid., Winkler, Manitoba, 1937, 87.

33 Aganetha Epp and Ida Friesen interview, CMBSC Oral History Project, 1987, Winnipeg, Centre for Mennonite Brethren Studies in Canada.

34 Mary Heidebrecht interview, CMBSC Oral History Project, 1987, Winnipeg, Centre for Mennonite Brethren Studies in Canada.

35 Annual Report of the Northern District Conference of the MB Churches, 1929, Herbert, Saskatchewan, 123.

36 Susan Schmidt and Helen Warkentin interview, CMBSC Oral History Project, 1987, Winnipeg, Centre for Mennonite Brethren Studies in Canada.

37 Thiessen, *City Mission in Winnipeg,* 71.

38 Strange, Kathleen, "Margaret Makes Good," article from a Winnipeg newspaper, in scrapbook of Anna Thiessen, Winnipeg, Centre for Mennonite Brethren Studies in Canada, n.d.

39 Annual Report of the Northern District Conference of the MB Churches, Winkler, Manitoba, 1937, 87.

40 Personal Communication, LaVerna Klippenstein, September 1995.

41 Annie Martens, "Report on the Condition of the Serving Girls in Calgary," in Annual Report of the Alberta Conference of MB Churches, Coaldale, Alberta, 1943, 23.

42 Mary Peters interview, CMBSC Oral History Project, 1987, Winnipeg, Centre for Mennonite Brethren Studies in Canada.

43 Epp, *Mennonites in Canada,* 189.

44 Genevieve Leslie, "Domestic Service in Canada, 1880-1920," in *Women at Work, 1850-1930,* ed. Janice Acton et al. (Toronto: Canadian Women's Educational Press, 1974), 857.

45 Katie Loewen interview, CMBSC Oral History Project, 1987, Winnipeg, Centre for Mennonite Brethren Studies in Canada.

46 Susan Schmidt interview, CMBSC Oral History Project, 1987, Winnipeg, Centre for Mennonite Brethren Studies in Canada.

47 Annual Report of the Northern District Conference of MB Churches, Coaldale, Alberta, 1944, 91.

48 Ibid., Winkler, Manitoba, 1942, 130.

49 Annual Report of the Alberta Conference of MB Churches, Coaldale, Alberta, 1943, 26.

50 Annual Report of the Northern District Conference of MB Churches, Winkler, Manitoba, 1942.

51 Martha Schulz interview, CMBSC Oral History Project, 1987, Winnipeg, Centre for Mennonite Brethren Studies in Canada.

52 Ida Friesen and Aganetha Epp interview, ibid.
53 In the minutes of the Manitoba Conference of the MB Church, Winnipeg, 1959, 39.
54 Aganetha Epp and Ida Toews interview, CMBSC Oral History Project, 1987, Winnipeg, Centre for Mennonite Brethren Studies in Canada.
55 Annual Report of the Northern District Conference of MB Churches, Coaldale, Alberta, 1944, 90.

CHAPTER 9

Negotiating Sex and Gender in the Ukrainian Bloc Settlement

East Central Alberta between the Wars

FRANCES SWYRIPA

By the time Maxim Pylypczuk became a cause célèbre in the local Anglo-Canadian press for the brutal murder of his twenty-year-old wife near Pakan in the heart of the Vegreville bloc in east central Alberta in 1912, the criminal reputation of Ukrainian immigrants was well established.[1] According to the stereotype that persisted until the Second World War, Ukrainians beat their wives, drank to excess and ended up in bloody brawls, stole without conscience and engaged in senseless litigation, and figured disproportionately in the country's penitentiaries and insane asylums. This image – popularized and sensationalized in articles, editorials, fiction, and countless discussions of the "immigrant problem" – reflected, in part, the reality of Ukrainian peasant cultural baggage and the volatility that often goes with being uprooted.[2] But it also reflected Anglo-Canadians' concerns for the moral fibre of their nation, and it was based as much on anti-Ukrainian prejudice as on hard data and research. Anxious to blend in and be accepted, successive generations of Ukrainian Canadians preferred simply to ignore the issue of crime in their community rather than to draw attention to it by subjecting the Anglo-Canadian stereotype to serious scrutiny. Recently, however, that stereotype has been challenged. Ukrainian-Canadian criminal behaviour has also begun to be examined within the dual context of the Old World peasant culture, patriarchal and materially poor, and the emerging Prairie frontier culture that nurtured it.[3]

This chapter uses Crime Investigation Files, compiled by the Department of the Attorney General in Alberta between 1915 and 1929, to continue the process of exploring how Ukrainian men and women in the

Vegreville bloc negotiated issues of sex and gender between the wars.[4] Carnal knowledge, rape, seduction, indecent assault, and wife-beating charges – which formed only a minority of the 1,500 cases to involve Ukrainians in these years – reveal the extent to which attitudes and behaviour imported from Ukrainian villages in Galicia and Bukovyna were retained, redirected, or submerged under the influence of the Canadian legal system.[5] A combination of isolation, ignorance, fear, and physical force would have prevented most victims of domestic violence and sexual assault from bringing their problems before the courts to be solved by Anglo-Canadian notions of abstract justice. But in those instances in which charges were laid, whether by women themselves or by their male relatives, individuals on both sides of the dispute had an ambiguous relationship with the state institutions and laws of their adopted homeland. If they sometimes welcomed outside intervention and saw the courts as an ally, they more frequently tried to adapt and manipulate an often inflexible law to their own ends. Above all, Ukrainians of both sexes tended to turn to mainstream structures for the resolution of their problems only after their informal community-based structures had failed.[6]

Criminal activity represents the irregular and never shows people at their best. Moreover, all parties to a dispute that reaches the attention of the authorities naturally structure their stories to promote and protect their own best interests. The first observation cautions the historian against stereotyping Ukrainians in inter-war Alberta on the basis of the Crime Investigation Files located in the Department of the Attorney General. The second warns of potential problems with using this material as a historical source. The teenager who thought she had strained herself lifting and did not know she was pregnant until consulting a doctor some five months later is perhaps plausible; her seducer, she said, "told me he was trying not to have any children."[7] Less believable is the uncle who claimed ignorance of the condition of the niece in his care until the doctor informed him the day she delivered a full-term baby, and one suspects that he wanted to defend himself from both criticism for inaction and rumours that he had fathered the child.[8] Other problems with the material have nothing to do with the credibility of the actors. Sentences like: "He inserted his penace [sic] into my private parts," and "You told my learned friend that you called your sister a hoar [sic]," question the literacy skills of the police and court officials creating the written record.[9] Incompetent or biased interpreters intruded more seriously on proceedings. Pressed by the judge to get an alleged rape victim to recount her experience in detail, one interpreter insisted that "pregnant" was "rather a hard word" to translate.[10] A witness's imperfect English, especially without a translator, further complicated the Court's efforts to arrive at the truth. It put the plaintiff at a decided disadvantage when she lacked the vocabulary either to describe her sexual assault or to understand the precise meaning of terms like "intercourse."[11]

Regardless of such limitations, the sworn statements and testimony of the principals in a case, their families, and neighbours registered what people either believed was the truth or wanted others to believe was the truth and, thus, how they ordered and perceived their world. Furthermore, while the files under examination constituted official records generated and maintained by the Anglo-Canadian establishment, the actions they documented differed significantly from liquor-related offences that arose from government agents or police officers campaigning against illicit stills.[12] Indecent assault, carnal knowledge, seduction, rape, and wife-beating charges were initiated by Ukrainians against other Ukrainians. As women acted on their own behalf, or as husbands and fathers spoke for wives and daughters, they defined what Ukrainians – and not mainstream society – considered important, morally or legally right and wrong, and in need of "justice." In presenting their claims, they furnished inadvertent but valuable insights into the functioning and mindset of the rural Ukrainian bloc settlement as peasant tradition jostled with the values of industrialized North American society.

Emigration and education had not yet alienated Ukrainians from centuries-old rituals and superstitions that governed life and conditioned peasant attitudes and behaviour.[13] For example, despite the modernity on Ukrainian farmsteads that was signalled by the telephone and Eaton's catalogue, belief in magic survived. A woman contaminated her neighbour's well with dead chickens and rotten eggs, she explained, because its owner had changed himself into a mouse and stolen a sack of her grain, then turned into a horse and ridden off with it.[14] The complainant in a seduction trial testified that, when she rejected the suggestion of the father of her child that she induce a miscarriage by jumping off the hayloft, he instructed her to tie red string around her wrists and legs and she would escape unharmed.[15] In another incident, a farmer dragged his wife of thirty years off the wagon into the bush, tied her up, and struck her – demanding to know where she had learned "those mysterious things," and threatening to rape her with a stick if she did not confess "how your sister learned you to be a witch." This accusation of witchcraft appeared to arise from a power struggle within the marriage, for the man later complained that for nine months "since our trouble commenced" his wife had been "very angry" and "against my will."[16] Finally, a recent immigrant denied any responsibility for a schoolgirl's pregnancy. "How did you get that way?" he demanded, "Did you take a magnet off me?"[17]

A late night fracas in an Edmonton rooming house, in which a female resident struck a visitor from Smoky Lake with a poker, reveals the survival of magic in another context – continued belief in the potency of a curse. When the case reached court, the judge was astonished to learn that the man considered his assailant's exclamation, "Lightening [sic] strike you here," to be swearing and to constitute part of his injuries.[18] A squabble over a haystack in a long-standing property dispute near Chipman saw a son actually charged with assaulting his father not only by hitting him on the nose but also by calling him "dirty names." "Nick," the father explained, "called me a thief ... he said also your mother is a *hour* [whore]."[19] A curse or name-calling was particularly inflammatory if it involved sexual prowess or impropriety. In a second violent altercation over hay, which was stored on land the complainant's wife had rented to the accused, the woman's husband admitted to taunting the man, but only after "he called me a balled [sic] headed prick."[20] When several men called a woman "filthy names" on her return from the toilet at a country dance, her brother leapt to her defence. Whether to emphasize his chivalry or to justify losing the ensuing brawl, he explained that "if I could have got a fence post I would have got the best of it ... It was not right that he called my sister a dirty fool" (her testimony specified "whore" and "dirty son of a bitch").[21] But an image of retiring womanhood relying on male initiative and gallantry to defend its honour would be a misreading of Ukrainian peasant society. Women not only appreciated the power of a curse, but also, quite literally, fought their own battles. This was clearly demonstrated when a Fort Saskatchewan-area farm wife took a club to her neighbour after she ran into her yard yelling, "You blind woman without ovaries."[22]

Yet Old World beliefs and practices faced competition from new values, reflecting the impact of immigration and Anglo-Canadian influences. The changing world view of Ukrainian women entailed a reassessment of both their self-image and their rights as human beings. According to folklorist Robert Klymasz, the folk songs composed by Ukrainian immigrant women in Canada – a sensitive barometer of popular opinion – shifted from "balladic outpourings" to become "more outspoken in [their] opposition to the woman's traditionally subordinate position in the Ukrainian family and community."[23] One folk song in particular – rife with anglicisms and preserved in the collective memory of its unknown creator's female contemporaries – revealed how some women internalized and interpreted female emancipation as a Canadian concept. The author describes how her husband beat her, how she eventually had enough, and how she ran away to a woman friend who "knew the law real well" and immediately called the police. Now, she is enjoying herself while her husband languishes in jail: "And when he comes out he'll know that he should show respect for a *lady*!"[24] Too few original sources exist either to reconstruct the process by which individuals who were physically and linguistically cut off from mainstream society learned about Anglo-Canadian notions of womanhood and womanliness or to determine precisely what Ukrainian immigrants understood by "lady." But Alberta's Crime Investigation Files reinforce the message of the anonymous folk song through offering evidence of a handful of women who refused to endure further physical abuse. Equally significantly, these women perceived the Canadian justice system not as an alien interloper in the Ukrainian community or in their lives, but as an ally to enlist on their behalf. When assaulted by her husband at the breakfast table, a Vilna woman testified, "I told him for to be careful with the knife or I will put him in the Court for that." Undeterred by his threat to kill her on his release from jail if she did, she had a charge laid.[25] After her husband beat her with a broom handle and knocked her to the floor while she was nursing her baby, another wife matter-of-factly testified, "as soon as I could get up I went and phoned the Police."[26] The actions of these two women reflected the influence of the Canadian environment, but they also drew on established practices in their homeland. Ukrainian women in Galicia, for example, also took steps to escape intolerable situations, initiating the great majority of inter-war petitions requesting the Greek Catholic Church to dissolve unhappy marriages.[27]

Ukrainian men, more exposed to the Anglo-Canadian world through work, also exhibited new values. Some – like the defendant in a seduction trial who declared he would not marry the girl because she could not read or write – were clearly status conscious and upwardly mobile.[28] The expectant mother in another seduction case testified that the father of her child promised to marry her if she went first to the nearby Methodist mission "to learn to cook and talk."[29] Other men absorbed less savoury prejudices of Anglo-Canadian society. Fisticuffs erupted at Star Church, for example, after the accused asked the complainant what "he meant by spreading the story around that he, accused, was a half breed and that his sister was a nigger."[30] But if Ukrainians quickly identified and disparaged those beneath them in Canada's emerging ethnic hierarchy, freely using racial taunts, a domestic dispute between a well-known moonshiner and his wife shows they were more circumspect when it came to those above them. The confrontation occurred in front of several witnesses, including a non-Ukrainian neighbour who had reluctantly come to the house at the entreaty of the distraught wife. One of the Ukrainians present testified that the accused "throwed the bread and meat" at his wife and said he was prevented only by the presence of Bob Coleman from throwing more. Her husband's exact words, the woman recalled, were: "If it was not for this Englishman here I would show you how I'd fix you."[31]

Canadian attitudes had a more positive impact as well. While Ukrainian parents were criticized by Anglo-Canadians and the Ukrainian pioneer intelligentsia alike for their apathy towards education – particularly with regard to girls destined for matrimony – more than one father objected to the marriage of a pregnant daughter on the grounds that she was too young or still in school.[32] Girls themselves seemed to think that schooling was important. The girl who supposedly took a magnet off her seducer had been attacked on the way home from a concert at the local school. Before he knocked her down, she told the court, "Panko said he wanted to marry me and I said I don't want to get married because I am a scolar [sic] yet." One of the most telling instances of new values, or at least of female rebellion against traditional roles and parental expectations, involved a young woman who poisoned her father's cattle by putting lye in their feed because she was angry that he had accused her of stealing twenty dollars. She had worked for nine years, she explained. Her father had taken all her wages and given her nothing for her wedding, so she wanted to see him with nothing too.[33]

The co-existence of Old World and New World value systems clearly indicates that the Vegreville bloc remained an immigrant society in transition. After some thirty years in Canada, Ukrainians had discarded much but not all of their peasant past. Certain observances, as the puzzled lawyer for a youth charged with seduction learned, were tenaciously kept. His client, even when arrested, wanted to marry the underaged girl but was prevented by her mother, who "would not permit the marriage during a Russian [sic] holiday season" (she proved perfectly amenable once the pre-Christmas Lenten period had ended).[34] The religious calendar joined the agricultural, or seasonal, calendar in ordering the Ukrainian world. Time was measured and events pinpointed not by the dates and months demanded by Canadian courts and modern urbanized society, but by the yardsticks of pre-industrial Christian communities. One girl recalled that the hired hand who seduced her had begun to work for her father "about Ruthenian New Year;" a second recalled that her rapist left her father's employ "after the spring work."[35] Others testified that sexual intercourse had occurred "about a week after the Ruthenian Easter," "during shooting time, I don't remember what month," "on the church holiday (Safat)," "two weeks before St. Peter holiday," "when people were putting the potatoes in."[36] Parents first suspected something wrong "about the time we were digging potatoes"; "about two weeks after the Russian [sic] Xmas"; during "spring work they were ploughing and seeding."[37] That Ukrainians adhered to the Julian calendar and not the Gregorian (which they identified as "Polish," underlining how the old country continued to define the outside world) further complicated matters for a legal apparatus intent on establishing time and place.[38]

From the perspective of the female victim of a sex crime, inability to furnish the type of precise information the law required could be disastrous. In the case of the young woman whose uncle disclaimed all knowledge of her pregnancy, the police found there was insufficient evidence to proceed with the seduction charge:

> No further proof can be got as to the complainant's age, she does not possess a birth certificate, just her own statement that she is twenty in September coming ... complainant cannot give any definite time or date as to when her marriage with the accused was to take place ... she cannot speak one word of English and has no idea what month week or day the intercourse took place, denies having intercourse with any person except the accused.[39]

Sometimes, without the village priest to keep the peasants' records for them, the upheaval of emigration and pioneering meant that events like the birth of a baby had never been registered or were subsequently forgotten. Such negligence had significant repercussions in seduction and carnal knowledge cases, in which the alleged victim's age was crucial. One investigating officer did his best. The girl's father, he wrote, testified that "he really did not know how old Yowdoha was, but he stated that he has been in Canada since 1899 and that after a little while his girl Annie was born and three years afterwards Yowdoha was born. According to Land Office statistics ... [X] ... filed on his farm in 1901 and he had one daughter, and three years afterwards would give him Yowdoha, and this would make the girl just about 15 years in a few more months."[40] A judge threw out a seduction charge after the fifteen-year-old girl, the eldest of ten children, admitted on cross-examination to prior intercourse with the accused, thus ruling out either chastity or rehabilitation. Defence counsel's attempt to trip up the mother over her daughter's age, however, shows how much the act of moving half way around the world defined people's lives. The woman remembered neither the date nor the time of year of her marriage some twenty-five years earlier, but she knew exactly how old her daughter was "because I came to Canada in 1903 and she was born two years later."[41]

Nowhere were two not always compatible value systems more visible than in Ukrainian-Canadian attitudes towards marriage. Twenty of twenty-five seduction charges formally read "under promise of marriage," and a good proportion of carnal knowledge and rape cases also involved a promise of marriage on the part of the accused. If the girls' versions of events are to believed, it was this guarantee, or understanding, that convinced them to agree to sexual intercourse. Many subsequently described their hesitancy, shame, fear, incomprehension, or confusion at the act itself. In other respects, their response serves as a reminder of the need to approach past phenomena within their proper cultural context rather than within that of the historian's particular society. These girls saw themselves not as violated children, but as young women ready for marriage. One twelve-year-old described how the accused had had intercourse with her when she went to his place: "We had arranged to get married next year, after Xmas we were to be married the accused said. I was satisfied ... I like the accused and would like to get married to him. I think that we can make a good home."[42]

While this girl was exceptionally young, the files under review confirm that early marriage for girls was accepted and normal among Ukrainians in the Vegreville bloc.[43] Statistical findings support this. Through the First World War one-third of Greek Catholic brides in the area married at sixteen or younger, and fully three-quarters were under twenty. (During the same period, in Alberta as a whole, only one-third of brides were under twenty.) In the early 1920s a massive shift benefited the seventeen-to-nineteen age group in particular, so that at mid-point in the decade some two-thirds of the girls were marrying in their late as opposed to their mid-teens.[44] But while delayed marriage signified changing attitudes, sex crimes cases showed that tradition persisted. Well into the 1920s, as girls agreed to arranged marriages or marriage to men they scarcely knew, economic considerations and parental pressure, rather than love and free choice, were the major determinants in conjugal unions. One would-be groom (whom his prospective bride had never seen) arrived at her parents' house at ten o'clock at night with his witness, who would testify that the man "was going to look at the girl and if he like that girl he was going to marry her." Presumably he liked her, for he proposed and proceeded to have intercourse in the upstairs bedroom after she accepted. "Everybody wanted us to get married," the girl later explained, adding, "I wouldn't have had connection with him if he hadn't promised to marry me." When the man failed to appear for the wedding, charges of seduction were laid. The preliminary hearing prompted a change of heart, and he agreed to the match, only to discover that the girl had also reconsidered. "I don't see what is the use of me getting married to him," she declared under cross-examination, "if he said he would give me a licking every day."[45]

Her resolute stance shows that Ukrainian girls did not simply stand by as others decided their future, nor did they simply acquiesce in family and community expectations; rather, they developed a range of strategies to negotiate power and to control their own destiny. Some refused to have sexual relations without a wedding ring on their finger; others spurned the offer of marriage that accompanied sexual assault or was extended after pregnancy resulted. "I don't want to marry him," one pregnant young woman protested, informing the court that the man had proposed when a charge of carnal knowledge loomed. Either external pressure or the social and economic consequences of single motherhood outweighed her resistance, however, as the pair eventually wed.[46] A second pregnant girl apparently valued independence over respectability conferred by a husband, taking no action until seven months after her sexual assault because "I was working in Vegreville and did not want to lose my position."[47]

Most striking in the depositions and testimony of the female "victims" of sex crimes is a calculating practicality designed to look after their own best interests, reflecting the cultural significance of land and material goods as a sign of security and status. A sixteen year old who had successfully resisted the sexual advances of the man charged with her abduction, telling her Edmonton employer he had come to take her home to the farm, made her priorities clear. "He bought me a hat," she told the court:

> I was perfectly willing to stop with him if he let me alone. He did not promise to give me any money if I kept quiet. He was going to use the money to buy a farm when we got married. I told him if he would buy a farm we would get married, and he paid a deposit of $60 on a farm. He told me he had paid the deposit. After we went home [to Radway] he came to my father and said he had bought a farm and after Easter we would get married. He wanted to get married while we were at the hotel [in Edmonton] and I said not till you have a farm and then we will be married, after Easter. I did not have a good time in Edmonton. I was all played out.[48]

The couple had known each other for approximately six weeks. In another case, the woman's age – she was twenty-nine – and the fact that she was physically handicapped undoubtedly influenced her decision to accept a stranger's lure:

> The people I was working with were away and he told me to come to have a look at his place and told me he would give me ½ his farm if I married him. When he asked me to go to his place I got ready and went to his place and after I looked at his place I agreed to get married with him and in the evening he asked me to go to bed with him. I told him that after I am married to him I will go to bed with him, but he insisted that I was his now and I had to go to bed with him. He said that we could go the next day to Mundare and get married ... I told him I would go to bed after he married me and gave me half the farm ... I could not fight with him as I have only one arm.[49]

The next morning the man cancelled the marriage as his son opposed signing over the land to the woman. Apparently her handicap was also a factor, for she retorted, "I told him why did you bring me here? You saw I was a cripple you were at my place twice." Economic reality obliged her to accept the thirty-one dollars offered as conscience money; she knew she would lose her housekeeping job, she said, "because I left the children alone and they would cry."

If carnal knowledge, seduction, indecent assault, and rape cases show Ukrainian girls acting in their own interests, the men involved were equally motivated by selfish concerns. Besides the substantial offer of land or the easy promise of marriage, inducements to win consent to intercourse ranged from clothes, ribbons, oranges, and candy to a trip to the movies.[50] But money, with five cents the base rate, seemed the preferred incentive and pacifier. After an unsuccessful attempt at penetration, one girl testified, her assailant gave her a nickel "to buy something with."[51] Confronted by the mother of the seventeen year old he had seduced and impregnated, a neighbouring farmer reputedly retorted: "We don't owe you anything as I paid you, five cents each time I did it."[52] A hired hand charged with carnal knowledge of a girl under fourteen not only disputed the complainant's chastity, claiming she had admitted to being with "other boys" who had paid for her favours, but also implied that any obligations on his part had been discharged because "after business I gave her a dollar." The investigating officer saw the incident differently. "The girl states," he wrote in his report, that "the accused after ravishing this child laid a dollar bill on her leg and told her not to tell her parents or anyone."[53] The givers of such gifts clearly regarded acceptance as both a contract for services and payment for services rendered. In the men's minds – and more than one defence counsel adopted the same position –

it also absolved them of any future moral or legal responsibility.[54] The threat of discovery, however, could raise the value of the transaction from the man's point of view. A girl who struggled free of her captor's drunken fondling in her brother's livery barn was offered five dollars to keep quiet. She refused and ran to tell her family.[55]

The number of private bargains amicably struck, or not exposed by court cases involving pregnancy, will never be known. Nor will the attitudes of the intended or actual recipients of the ribbons and nickels before everything exploded and they felt compelled to present themselves in the most positive light possible. Casual sex was perhaps the only way for girls to acquire money and goods independently of the family. Certainly, the instance of a woman accosted by her neighbour early one morning while she was feeding the pigs suggests that females placed their value somewhat higher than the males who sought them out. She begged the man to leave her alone because she was tired. "I told him that even if he paid me $10 I would not do it [consent to intercourse]." An hour later her married daughter arrived to help clear the garden: "I told her while we were cutting the cabbages, I told her I am tired. She asked me what is the matter, and I said I don't know whether to tell you or not. Then I told her that [accused] was abusing me. That is the reason I am tired. I told her that he promised to buy me a shawl and my daughter began to laugh."[56]

On at least one occasion the male aggressor in a sexual assault enlisted his superior knowledge of Canada, and Ukrainian immigrants' perverted image of a "fri kontri" (free country) in which no restrictions applied,[57] to subdue a reluctant partner. In tackling his neighbour, a recent immigrant out fencing while her husband was in Edmonton, the would-be rapist explained that this was Canada and he could do as he wanted. His assault had serious economic consequences for the needy couple, who rented their farm, as the woman's fear of staying alone subsequently prevented her husband from seeking outside work.[58] Recent immigrants were not alone in having their ignorance of the new homeland exploited or in feeling uncertain about their rights. In 1926 a woman confined to the farm since her arrival in Canada and her marriage thirteen years earlier was twice waylaid by a neighbour on the public trail that crossed his parents' property. After the first encounter, she testified,

> I was very scared and ashamed ... I thought I would forgive him for his act and would not mention it to anybody. I was unable to speak English and in a new country and did not know the language and did not wish to make trouble at home or have the public laugh at me. When I got home from the

> store I was shaky and nervous at my work ... The next day my husband said there was something the matter with me as I was shaky and looked different but I was afraid to mention anything as I thought he would beat me and I would suffer for the rest of my life.[59]

Despite her shame and fear, this woman proved no passive victim. On the second occasion she told her attacker "to go to Hell" and "hoped the lightening [sic] would strike him dead." She also informed her husband (the record does not say if he did, in fact, beat her) as well as the culprit's mother (who said she should have pulled his eyes out). And when neither of them gave her satisfaction, she took matters into her own hands:

> After he ran after me the second time I knew that he would bother me in the future right along and I would not stand for it. When I saw that my husband was not taking this matter very seriously, I started to talk amongst the neighbours and to get advice what was the best thing to do and if it was the law in Canada that a man could attack anybody he likes and I was advised to report the matter to the police, that if a man does anything like that he will be punished and the following day my husband went to make a complaint ... I told all the neighbours I met about this trouble, since which all the women who were using this path avoid it or use it when they have somebody with them.[60]

This woman's story raises several important issues. First, it says much about women in her position, unfamiliar with Canadian law and prey to unwanted attentions. Second, for she was not unique in making her case public, it illuminates how Ukrainians in the rural bloc settlement dealt informally with illicit sexual liaisons and their consequences. Last, it offers insight into how the various parties in a grievance mobilized and actively involved the community in settling or arbitrating their disputes.

Immigrant women – isolated on the homestead, often illiterate in their own language, for the most part certainly illiterate in English – were at a decided disadvantage when it came to seeking outside help or "justice." Victims of domestic violence especially could not look to their husbands to initiate proceedings or to guide them through an unfamiliar and often bewildering legal apparatus. The plight of the woman beaten for being a witch, for example, reached official attention only because her daughter wrote an aunt, asking her to tell the police.[61] One would expect the Canadian-born or -raised generation to be more skilled in dealing with the outside world, but the bloc and farm also isolated adolescents. As late as 1928 a nineteen year old did not know her postal address; queried to ensure she appreciated the gravity of an oath, another girl knew only that the Bible was a book; a third girl, tricked by her seducer into believing that the piece of paper she signed properly married them, defiantly insisted that she knew what weddings were, she had been to them.[62] Notwithstanding such "enlightening" agencies as the public school, or even the Ukrainians' own churches, the female world was often circumscribed.

In addition, a rural and pioneering lifestyle that took men from the farm and parents from the house sent children into lonely pastures, and featured foot traffic along country roads at trails that left them vulnerable. Eight rape cases involved women whose husbands were away working; three girls had been babysitting younger siblings while their parents went to the store, to church, or visiting; two girls had been out fetching the cows; and two had been walking home from a dance. Three incidents occurred at community functions. At least one man proposed a liaison precisely because the woman's husband would be away and they would have "all kinds of chances."[63] Males exploiting long- or short-term parental absences constituted the largest group of accused malefactors in carnal knowledge cases (eight). This pattern tempers the image of women's isolation, as wives accompanied husbands on their journeys, but it reinforces the perils facing daughters left at home. The hired hand figured conspicuously in every type of sex offence; virtually all other defendants were well-known neighbours.

If neighbours began the trouble, neighbours also participated in its publicity and resolution. When the woman who balked at being accosted on the footpath complained to the young man's family, they urged her not to talk about the affair so as not to be publicly mortified for raising "that kind of boy." This presumably referred to his age, as the woman's husband later chided him that "it was not right for a young boy to go after an old woman" (she was thirty-three). The husband had also preferred to suppress the matter and deal with the young man privately, and he was upset when his wife went over his head to seek advice from the neighbours. That she broadcast his reluctance to take action, causing him to lose face and be sharply lectured on his duty, he found particularly galling. Neighbours were thus viewed in two lights: one supportive and desirable, the other interfering, censorious, constricting. Often the two roles overlapped. One husband's perceived public humiliation triggered a fight with his wife when he returned home from church and ordered his visiting sister-in-law to leave because "she had been telling the neighbours that I had not been with my wife for 6 months that I ran away from her." The wife declared her sister would stay, and announced that she herself – likely in a bid to rally community opinion – had publicized their situation.[64]

That the community was prepared to intervene and take sides in domestic disputes is indicated by a letter to the attorney general requesting the early release of a husband jailed for beating his wife. The man, his lawyer wrote, was a farmer and property owner with several head of livestock and thirty-five acres of grain. Incarceration would be ruinous, "a more serious loss to the country" than the husband's correction, for even if guilty he was "not a criminal in the ordinary sense." The lawyer elaborated:

> From what I could gather the quarrel ... arose over the unchastity or suspected unchastity of [the wife], and her behaviour with two other men of that settlement, which may not be justification for him evoking the plea of the unwritten law, but in these farming communities sometimes things are done in a passion, and with outsider's influences, more particularly in a case of this kind, are brought to bear on the wife to have the husband incarcerated and out of the way for a couple of months.[65]

Ignoring the lawyer's sexism to focus on his primary complaint – meddling "outsiders" – the truth is that these anonymous individuals were really "insiders," friends and neighbours and fellow Ukrainians. Moreover, the ethnic community they represented would determine if and when the real outside – the Anglo-Canadian law – became involved in its affairs. After a Radway couple were charged with confining their severely handicapped son in a chicken coop, for example, the local teacher (himself Ukrainian) pleaded with the attorney general to deny the rumour he had been the one to notify the authorities.[66] The ethnic community also expected Anglo-Canadian law to do right by it. Although admittedly not an impartial observer, the lawyer consulted by a father whose daughter's seducer had his conviction quashed on a technicality twice wrote the attorney general to say he had been sought out by concerned individuals from the district. Persistent rumours about no retrial, they had cautioned, were having "a rather disquieting effect on the neighbours."[67] In a second case, news that a Copernick-area youth had taken advantage of his parents' absence to sexually assault a girl stopping at the house on her way home from school soon circulated locally, and, on his next visit, the Greek Catholic priest was approached for advice. Meeting with several men after church, he advised them "not to have such matters hushed up," and the girl's mother was told. When insufficient corroboration brought a stay of proceedings, the girl's family continued to campaign for justice through both the legal system and community opinion, prompting the youth's lawyer to threaten the mother and grandmother with a damage suit if they persisted in making "bad statements" about his client, whose reputation in the community had suffered as a result. The grandmother was particularly irresponsible and provocative, boasting that she "could lay any charge she wanted" against the youth "because it did not cost her anything."[68]

Community sanctions and opinion could exert immense pressure. A Chipman-area teenager seduced by the hired hand said nothing because "I was afraid and he told me to keep quiet because people would be laughing and I would not be able to go out anywhere amongst people ... he told me if Father found out he would not let me go anywheres, and people would be laughing at me and Father was liable to kill me." Finally convinced that the people were indeed talking about her, the girl agreed to run away with the man.[69] Shame and fear of "a licking" (which often proved well founded) deterred many girls from telling their parents about unwanted intercourse until pregnancy forced the issue. An attacker's threats to "tell father" – or to "kill me," "shoot me," "cut my head off" – were equally effective silencers. Yet someone told someone, for rumours and gossip flourished as an underground grapevine turned a secret act between two people into public property.

Frequently, a parent or husband first learned of a problem from this grapevine. An Andrew-area father "never thought" his hired hand had anything to do with his daughter "until I heard some of my neighbours talking," whereupon he took the pregnant girl to a doctor.[70] The threshing crew, a witness in a seduction trial recalled, had joked with the accused about his girlfriend's condition. According to the investigating officer, the witness knew "Nettie ... was pregnant having been told by [X] who informed me that Mrs [Y], Nettie's sister, had told his wife."[71] A Vermilion-area husband remained ignorant of his seventeen-year-old wife's antics while he was away threshing until he heard gossip "in the settlement" several months later and confronted her. The police opposed a criminal charge, citing the wife's history of misconduct, and one suspects that the woman – who claimed she could not produce her torn skirt as evidence because the cow had eaten it – professed rape to extricate herself from a voluntary romance during her husband's absence.[72] Another husband, who admitted he was "awful mad" and "spoke rough to her" on finding out, learned of his wife's attempted rape at a dance; again, "the people were talking."[73] More than a year after intercourse began, a charge of rape with consent extorted by threats or fear of bodily harm was laid when a woman's husband returned to Smoky Lake from working elsewhere and "heard the people talking" about his wife and the accused. Although sufficiently desperate to have written her husband to come home, the woman had not dared say why because he was "bosh" and she was afraid he would beat her.[74]

The most explicit indication of what "the people talking" actually meant comes from outside the Vegreville bloc. The wife of a Coalhurst miner belatedly initiated a criminal charge against the couple's boarder, she explained, after a neighbour woman told her the man had announced in the Ukrainian hall (probably a labour temple) that "he was doing business with me." Another meeting goer confirmed this. The accused, he testified,

> said right in front of people, he was up on the platform, there was about 25 people there, and he said he had business with Mrs [X]. He said before the people he had had the same with that woman just as if she was his wife. I do not know why he said this. No one asked him to say it. I heard that speech. There was reading of rules and these say we should do right and we were talking about, and [accused] said he did that. The society objected to his conduct and was against that business. He said he have that business with that woman. He meant he had sexual intercourse. He said "she is no good anyway. I have the business with her." He said "*Maeiu*," the proper word to express sexual intercourse. Everybody knew what it meant.[75]

The implications of community went much deeper than a forum for gossip, rumour, and bragging about sexual exploits or even the mobilization of public opinion in resolving personal disputes. As people tried to sort out their problems, both "injured" and "guilty" parties formally involved friends, relatives, and neighbours in enforcing communal standards. This was particularly true of sexual liaisons and the shame and embarrassment, loss of reputation, or unwanted pregnancy that either attended or ensured discovery. In fact, it would appear that physical relationships outside marriage became rape, seduction, carnal knowledge, or indecent assault – that is, "sex crimes" to be decided by the Canadian courts – only when Ukrainians' private system of justice failed. With respect to a pregnant daughter, marriage presumably represented the ultimate form of justice, and in an unknown number of instances a wedding would have been arranged, amicably or otherwise. If need be, a seduction charge could be brandished to help convince a recalcitrant young man that matrimony was preferable to a trial and perhaps jail.[76] But not all girls or their parents saw marriage as the answer. One pragmatic father objected to his daughter marrying the father of her child because the nineteen year old, his former hired hand, had "no home of his own ... was a lazy useless fellow and would not be able to support a wife."[77] When marriage, for whatever reason, was rejected, Ukrainians turned to the community, soliciting its cooperation to correct the wrongs of sexual transgressions.

In such situations, whether giving redress or absolution, justice was understood as concrete and personal; it was not dispensed by a fine or prison term imposed by the courts in the name of a nebulous Crown. To Ukrainians in the Vegreville bloc justice in a "sex crime" meant a "settlement," or monetary compensation, negotiated between the male perpetrator and his female victim (or her parents or husband) either directly or with neighbours and friends as intermediaries. Numerous agreements were undoubtedly struck without being recorded. But unless the male refused to consider this option, the settlement process had to break down before what was perceived as a problem of the Ukrainian community to be resolved by the Ukrainian community was handed over to mainstream society for solution according to its rules. Those rape, seduction, carnal knowledge, and indecent assault cases in which a settlement was broached, or even purportedly reached, reveal a set of values at odds with Canadian society and the Canadian legal system.

While Canadian law defined a whole series of sexual irregularities as criminal offences to be prosecuted by the Crown on society's behalf, privately, Ukrainians treated them like civil offences, with restitution being made directly to the victim. Moreover, in taking or threatening legal action, the injured party in a "sex crime" seemed to assume that the Canadian courts would also treat the matter as a civil suit and dispense material compensation. When their neighbour, who was subsequently charged with rape, originally came to settle, a Smoky Lake farmer told his nineteen-year-old wife that "she knew what he had done to her and ... what to do to him. If he had done very bad she could go to court and sue him."[78] Rape charges were dismissed against a Wahstao man on the grounds that the seventeen-year-old girl was known to be prostituting herself in the district; according to the investigating officer, the accused had had intercourse with her on several occasions "and this time she was put in the family way and wanted him to pay her some damages."[79] There is evidence that the perpetrators of "sex crimes" also construed any wrongdoing on their part in a civil rather than a criminal light. "I didn't kill anybody. I am not going to Gaol," an Edmonton meatpacking plant worker quoted her seducer as saying when she confronted him with her pregnancy and he refused to settle.[80]

Even when couched in terms of innocent and wronged womanhood, the notions of "damage" and "damages" bore a price tag, reducing women to male or family property. Aided by an English-speaking accomplice who posed as a detective, the Smoky Lake poolroom operator tricked a local woman into intercourse. "He said if I did not go with him," she explained, her fugitive husband "would be catched ... and then who would give bread to me and my children." Hearing gossip on his return from the Drumheller mines, the husband refused to sleep in the conjugal bed until he "knew what was true," and he informed the poolroom operator that "money could not settle it, as it had spoiled my wife." Yet he accepted the $500 offered.[81] In another case, the Attorney General's Office recommended dropping charges against an itinerant beggar accused of raping a farm wife while her husband skinned a cow a hundred yards away. The woman was strong and the man crippled; he had readily admitted to intercourse (and paying five dollars); and the woman's husband had admitted rejecting thirty dollars to keep quiet because he "would not settle it up for less than $500 for my shame."[82] Last, the girl who had rebuffed her attacker's offer of marriage because she was still in school was blunt about her priorities, even on cross-examination. On discovering her pregnancy, she stated, she had demanded "$500 to get my honor. He said he wouldn't give me anything because he didn't have nothing and I said if you won't pay $500 you'll pay me $1000 later." A letter entered as evidence of blackmail had promised to "go further" (presumably a criminal charge) if the man refused to settle. Something of the girl's plight, and the practical considerations motivating her actions, can be gleaned from her comment: "I told him to give me a living or get married because I had no place to stay."[83]

This girl moderates the image of women as male or family property, ignored and irrelevant as fathers or husbands bargained over "damage" and "damages." At times those most personally affected by the exposed sexual relationship participated actively in the settlement process, being consulted directly, being allowed to accept or reject the payment offered, and taking the initiative. And in representing themselves, they gave their own estimates of their worth. The girl jilted at the altar after being seduced by the stranger she had just agreed to marry testified that she was offered $500 to keep quiet. Under cross-examination her brother denied all knowledge of her demanding $3,000 if the accused refused to marry her or telling him that the family wanted $3,000 in lieu of a marriage.[84] Pressed by a hostile defence, a Bellis farm girl employed as a waitress in Edmonton refused to confess to asking for money in return for dropping a seduction charge against the man she found out was married; counsel suggested she had wanted $2,000 to settle the matter.[85]

When an affair became public and a guilty man attempted to buy absolution or the silence of his victim and her kin, and they, in turn, demanded money as restitution or the price of keeping quiet, the female's value moved well beyond the nickels and candy secretly proffered at the time of intercourse. On both sides the sums quoted were no longer five or ten, but hundreds and thousands of dollars. Particularly if he opposed marriage, an expectant father took the initiative in a financial settlement in order to avoid a criminal charge of seduction, and, not unnaturally, he placed a high value on his freedom. The father of one young man convinced the pregnant girl and her parents to accept $500 because he "did not want any Court"; they proceeded with the case when the money failed to materialize.[86] A man who accosted a girl on the road home from a dance and play at Opal Hall tried to settle for $500, her brother-in-law testified, but she refused.[87] Visited by his pregnant neighbour and her brother, the youth, whose initial advice had been to induce a miscarriage by jumping off the hayloft, told the girl not to cry: "I'll be at your place tomorrow evening and I'll make a settlement everything quiet and good."[88] For their part, an alleged seducer's or rapist's victim and her family were not above using the threat of court action to extract a financial settlement. One father asked the youth responsible for his daughter's pregnancy if "he wanted to settle without going to lawsuit."[89] A young man tried for carnal knowledge stated that, after the woman fled the neighbourhood to avoid giving false testimony, her husband accused him "amongst the people" of running away with her and "wanted to make a settlement with me without going to court."[90]

But much more than a piece of blackmail or spur-of-the-moment response to discovery, a financial settlement represented an accepted mechanism for rectifying the wrongs of illicit sexual liaisons. The deliberate presence and involvement of "witnesses," who did not simply verify the agreement reached but first participated in its negotiation, attests to the formal and public nature of the settlement process. Although he rejected monetary compensation in favour of marriage for his pregnant daughter, the courtroom testimony of one father suggests how well the procedure and rules of the settlement process were understood in the Ukrainian bloc. It also highlights the central, mediating role of the third party, mistakenly identified by the court as the accused's "lawyers." The man had come with his two witnesses, the father stated:

> Q. Was anything said about sexual intercourse with the girl? A. There was no use in talking to stir up the matter. Q. What matter were you settling? A. I simply took it for granted that we knew because he came down and wanted

> settlement. I took it for granted that we knew what we were talking about ... Q. Were you willing to discuss any settlement by money? A. No ... Q. Did he suggest it? A. No he never suggested it. Q. Did either of his lawyers [sic]? A. His witnesses said he wanted financial settlement.[91]

Known to both parties and representing one of them, a witness was nevertheless not necessarily chosen for any expected partiality, which suggests that greater importance was attached to status and respect. One witness said he had to drag out of the accused what exactly it was that he was supposed to settle with the farmer in question. When informed of the sexual advances made to the farmer's fourteen-year-old daughter, he agreed to mediate – making the offer of fifty dollars (which the accused considered appropriate), while the man himself "stayed in the bush" outside the house.[92] In another case, the local blacksmith – who declined the accused rapist's request to mediate ("I told him I could not be a judge in anything") – also had not known what he was being asked to settle. The alleged victim in this instance, a woman only two years in Canada, was the sole person to appear ignorant of a financial settlement and its mechanism. She had not understood what her assailant and his witness meant by damages or wanted by a settlement, she said, and she had told them that there had been no damage apart from her dress. The witness, she continued, offered her and her husband ten dollars, saying it was better "to pay you poor people than some rich people getting it," and he advocated a settlement "to save court" and to "save spending money on lawyers." Yet neither the woman nor her husband were innocents. Under cross-examination they vigorously denied prosecuting for money, and the husband specifically denied telling anyone that the accused "would pay me for every day I lost work"; but the woman had already testified that her husband initially went to the local Justice of the Peace to sue her attacker.[93]

Although certainly thinking of his "client" in discouraging legal action, the above witness also showed disdain for a foreign and rapacious Canadian judicial system. Other Ukrainians seemed anxious to involve the Canadian legal establishment (if not Canadian law) in the settlement process. Still others, voicing doubts about the wisdom or legality of what they were doing, recognized that their idea of justice contravened Canadian practices and attitudes. The man who futilely hoped five dollars would buy the silence of the girl he assaulted in the livery barn testified at his rape trial that her father had immediately rushed out to demand $200 to settle; the father, likely realizing this harmed his case, contradicted him in rebuttal.[94] The husband, who refused to settle for less than $500 for "my shame," ultimately decided to consult a lawyer about accepting the sum he negotiated.[95] The Smoky Lake man and local poolroom operator who had tricked his wife into intercourse jointly consulted a lawyer after the poolroom operator said he could not afford the $1,000 the husband wanted and suggested four town lots instead. But the pair told the Anglo-Canadian attorney, who innocently advised taking out a $500 mortgage, only that the one owed the other money. "I thought it over," the husband testified in self-justification, "and thought that I ought not to settle it myself because there was a law in Canada. I took the mortgage from him because it would be good evidence for me."[96]

One case saw Ukrainians not only using the Canadian legal establishment to legitimize the settlement process but also attempting to gain the active cooperation of members of that establishment in ignoring the law on "sex crimes" in order to seek monetary restitution for the injured party. Going with his witness to confront the neighbour boy who had impregnated his deaf and mute daughter, an Andrew farmer turned down $150 as insufficient to cover the hospital bill during the girl's confinement, and he refused to consider a revised $250 settlement until consulting his son in Edmonton. Under urging from the son, whom the accused also asked to mediate "so as not to take the case to Court," the two parties did not settle privately but met "in Mr. Crump's office" to draw up an agreement. According to the son, the young man "put down $700 there," upon which, the father testified, "Mr. Crump's clerk said I must sign a paper so that I must not say anything more about this case among the people." The police summary of the young man's subsequent trial for carnal knowledge, while identifying different individuals, revealed the extent of the collusion of the lawyers:

> On advice [accused] received, he made settlement with the ... family for $700 and received an agreement drawn by R.G. Adams, that they would not prosecute him for this offence. He later found that he had received bad advice, he then started legal proceedings to regain his money and had received judgment when it was blocked and the above charge laid against him. For the defence, S.H. Bahlay and R.G. Adams, sworn, stated, the ... family and [accused] had come to them to draw an agreement that the ... family would not prosecute. This was done, $700 being amount of this, Adams received $400 and Bahlay $50 for their services.[97]

More commonly, the Canadian legal establishment took a dim view of Ukrainians' attempts to resolve "sex crimes" according to their own definition of the nature of the offence and rules for restitution. An exchange of money represented not justice but an attempt to thwart it, and it was not to be condoned. When, for example, the lawyer for a man charged with seduction entered a not-guilty plea, saying the matter had been settled when his client gave the girl $200, the judge refused to allow the case to be settled out of court.[98] And charges of rape laid by a young widow working as a chambermaid in Edmonton were dismissed after she essentially admitted to bringing the charge because she feared pregnancy and was after a settlement ("What can I do? I have got to work every day. I have ... two children to support"). She did not help her cause by interjecting "How much?" when defence counsel asked if she wanted money or to send the man to jail.[99]

One last point concerning Ukrainians' use of Canadian law with regard to sexual offences merits mention. The alleged rape victim who claimed the cow had eaten the evidence raises the issue of false charges, made either to hide a voluntary relationship or for some other reason. The handful of cases in which a false charge was proven or greatly suspected reveals a willingness by families and husbands to exploit their daughters and wives for revenge or material gain. A local furore over whether a young wife had died from mistreatment by her husband provoked the investigating officer (not privy to the community's secrets) to describe the affair as "a typical Galician case, where the father-in-law ... tried to get ... [the husband] into trouble for some petty grudge he bore him."[100] The judge threw out a carnal-knowledge case in which the defence argued that the girl's mother had let her sleep with the accused, the hired hand, so that he would not quit and demand his wages. Only some six months later, when the man was pressing her parents for the $600 owed him, did they seek to have him charged.[101] A second carnal-knowledge charge was dismissed under suspicions of a frame-up over debts the girl's grandfather owed the accused; her uncle had also tried to bribe the examining physician.[102]

Finally, one false charge exploded in its instigator's face to turn a wife's nightmare into a celebration of her liberation. Furious that his neighbour had him jailed overnight after he drunkenly took the man's car joyriding, the woman's husband accused the man of raping her. She told a convincing story and the neighbour was convicted. But her conscience pricked her, and she soon confessed to perjury under pressure from her husband, who had beaten her when he came home from jail and threatened to keep beating her until she agreed to the rape scenario. The woman's revised statement poured out the story of three years of misery during which she endured her husband's violent rages, drunken rampages, and petty tyrannies:

> I bought a band for my hair and paid 25 cents for it, and when I put it on the next day my husband grabbed me by the head and tore the band off and put it in the stove, and I cried, my heart was so sore, and he told me to stop crying but I couldn't, and he then took a strap and struck me over the shoulders and back with it, and there was a witness to this and he left six great bruises on me. One time I was with him in the car driving, and he was mad and quarreling, and he speeded up the car to about 25 miles an hour and then pushed me out of the car onto the road, and I had my right shoulder terribly hurt, and my shoulder and arm pain me still, and sometimes I can hardly use it. On that same occasion I had a front tooth knocked out but he took me to a dentist and had another one put in, and it isn't paid for yet.[103]

She then described her attempt to run away between the preliminary hearing and the trial to avoid lying in court, but she had no money to go farther than Mundare, where her husband found her three days later. Trusting his promise to always treat her well if she testified to rape, she returned home. After the trial, however, her domestic situation worsened:

> My husband was always afraid of what might happen to him over the … case, and he told me that [accused] might take away the farm from us, and he asked me to sign it to his father so we couldn't lose it … I signed the paper, and now I guess the father has the farm, but he didn't pay anything for it. I was terribly unhappy and my husband was beating me all the time, and we had not much to eat, and I had no clothes, and my heart was sore, and I had to do the work on the farm. I worked in my bare feet and had no clothes to wear, I drove the drill and the binder, and worked like a man, and I was thin and sick, and when we threshed I had to sell the wheat which I hauled to Vegreville, and I paid the thresh bill, and I couldn't stand it any longer and I took some wheat to town and got $80 and that night I left and came to Edmonton. I hated to leave the kiddies as I love them, but I couldn't take them with me as I had no money, and I was afraid my husband would follow me and kill me, and I got work in a house in Edmonton … One week after, I saw Billy Elock the policeman and I told him all about my husband and [his accomplice] and what they did to [accused], and I told him how my husband had beat me and how he would kill me if he could, and I asked him to help me.[104]

The woman concluded with a declaration touching in its simplicity and sense of release. Her solicitor, she said, had read her statement; she understood it, would swear to its truthfulness, and had made it of her own free will. "I am happier now and I have gained 42 pounds since I left home … and that is only six weeks ago yesterday."

Most certainly, countless disputes highlighting sex and gender in the Ukrainian bloc settlement of inter-war Alberta never reached the Canadian courts to be arbitrated by the law of the new homeland. Those that did, entering the realm of Canadian legal history as official "criminal cases," comment at length on not only the interaction of Ukrainian immigrant and Canadian concepts of justice, but also on the transitional world the bloc's residents inhabited. Men and women confronted with domestic violence or sexual irregularities were prepared to seek help from the Canadian judicial system, but they looked first to their own community to air their grievances and solve their difficulties. While women, both old and young, were often shown to be the naive and impotent objects of male aggression, they equally often proved to be shrewd and forceful defenders of their own interests.

Acknowledgment

This chapter is reprinted with the permission of the Canadian Plains Research Center. The article first appeared in *Prairie Forum* 20, 2 (Fall 1995): 149-74.

Notes

1 In March 1912, the Pylypczuk case received extensive coverage in the *Vegreville Observer*, the *Edmonton Journal*, and the *Edmonton Bulletin*.

2 See, for example, Reverend Charles W. Gordon (Ralph Connor), *The Foreigner* (Toronto: Westminster, 1909); W.G. Smith, *A Study in Canadian Immigration* (Toronto: Ryerson, 1920); and Charles Young, *The Ukrainian Canadians: A Study in Assimilation* (Toronto: Thomas Nelson and Sons, 1931).

3 See Gregory Robinson, "Rougher Than Any Other Nationality? Ukrainian Canadians and Crime in Alberta, 1915-29," *Journal of Ukrainian Studies* 16, 1-2 (Summer/Winter 1991): 147-79; see also his "British-Canadian Justice in the Ukrainian Colony: Crime and Law Enforcement in East Central Alberta, 1915-1929" (MA thesis, University of Alberta, 1992).

4 Cases involving Ukrainians form only a small part of the Crime Investigation Files. These files are housed in the Provincial Archives of Alberta (Acc. 72.26) and one may gain access to them through an alphabetical surname index (Acc. 72.82) that identifies the accused, the locality, and usually the nature of the offence. The great majority of Ukrainian cases focus on the Vegreville bloc; smaller numbers originated in Edmonton, followed by mining communities like Drumheller and the Crowsnest Pass. Crimes against morality and/or persons (dominated by assault) and crimes against property together accounted for two-thirds of all Ukrainian cases; liquor-related offences came next. Although these are public records, to protect the privacy of the individuals and families concerned, no names appear in either the text of the chapter or the notes.

5 Christine Worobec, "Temptress or Virgin? The Precarious Sexual Position of Women in Postemancipation Ukrainian Peasant Society," in *Russian Peasant Women*, ed. Beatrice Farnsworth and Lynne Viola (New York and Oxford: Oxford University Press, 1992), 41-53, uses court documents and folk songs to examine a sexual double standard and women's subordinate position in late nineteenth-century Russian Ukraine. There is no comparable study of Western Ukrainian territories, which contributed the bulk of immigrants to Canada.

6 There is a growing body of historical literature, drawing heavily on court records, that examines how gender has affected the treatment of women by the Canadian legal system. Much of it deals specifically with sex crimes. The two major monographs are Constance Backhouse, *Petticoats and Prejudice: Women and Law in Nineteenth-Century Canada* (Toronto: University of Toronto Press and Osgoode Society, 1991); and Karen Dubinsky, *Improper Advances: Rape and Heterosexual Conflict in Ontario, 1880-1929* (Chicago and London: University of Chicago Press, 1993). See also, for example, Carolyn Strange, "Patriarchy Modified: The Criminal Prosecution of Rape in York County, Ontario, 1880-1930," in *Essays in the History of Canadian Law*, vol. 5, ed. Jim Phillips et al. (Toronto: University of Toronto Press, 1994), 207-51; Joan Sangster, "'Pardon Tales' from Magistrate's Court: Women, Crime, and the Court in Peterborough County, 1920-50," *Canadian Historical Review* 74, 3 (1993): 161-97; Karen Dubinsky, "'Maidenly Girls' or 'Designing Women': The Crime of Seduction in Turn-of-the Century Ontario," in *Gender Conflicts: Essays in Women's History*, ed. Franca Iacovetta and Mariana Valverde (Toronto: University of Toronto Press, 1992), 27-66; and, on the Prairies, see Terry Chapman, "Sex Crimes in the West, 1890-1920," *Alberta History* 35, 4 (1987): 6-21; and "'Till Death Do Us Part': Wife Beating in Alberta, 1905-1920," *Alberta History* 36, 4 (1988): 13-22. A smaller number of studies look at the impact of ethnicity and gender on the Canadian legal system. They include Backhouse, *Petticoats and Prejudice*; Carolyn Strange, "Wounded Womanhood and Dead Men: Chivalry and the Trials of Clara Ford and Carrie Davis," in Iacovetta and Valverde, *Gender Conflicts*, 149-88; and Karen Dubinsky and Franca Iacovetta, "Murder, Womanly Virtue, and Motherhood: The Case of Angelina Napolitano, 1911-1922," *Canadian Historical Review* 72, 4 (1991): 505-32.

7 72.26/2931, carnal knowledge under 18, Vermilion 1919. The case was never tried, the judge concluding that conviction was impossible, and the couple (who were cousins) eventually married.

8 72.26/6621, seduction under promise of marriage, Edson 1925; the young woman was a recent Polish immigrant, the accused Ukrainian. In a separate case (72.26/5921, assault, Edson 1924), the uncle successfully charged a neighbour with assault after a verbal confrontation ended in violence; the Polish bridge builder had told the accused to stop saying publicly that he was going to send for the police because the uncle was living with his niece as man and wife.

9 72.26/4956, rape (amended to carnal knowledge) over 14 under 16, Leduc (Dnipro) 1922; and 72.26/5329, assault occasioning actual bodily harm, Lethbridge 1923.

10 72.26/3928, rape, Edmonton 1921.

11 To describe her actual seduction one girl switched from English to an interpreter; 72.26/3878, seduction over 14 under 16, Carvel 1920. See also 72.26/1562, procuring a miscarriage, Meanook 1917 (the parties' Ukrainian origins are not certain); 72.26/3928, rape, Edmonton 1921; 72.26/4491, seduction under promise of marriage (over 16 under 18), Edmonton 1921; and 72.26/6442, seduction under promise of marriage, Edmonton 1924 (where one witness called the young woman German, but the court interpreter, identified as "Nick Sowchuk – Russian," was definitely Ukrainian).

12 The best discussion of policing Ukrainians for moonshine is Robinson, "British-Canadian Justice in the Ukrainian Colony," 138-73.

13 Samuel Koenig, "Ukrainians of Eastern Galicia: A Study of Their Culture and Institutions" (PhD thesis, Yale University, 1935), is a good English-language introduction to nineteenth- and early twentieth-century Ukrainian peasant beliefs and customs. On the survival and adaptation of Old World beliefs and rituals in Canada, see, for example, Robert Klymasz, *Svieto: Celebrating Ukrainian-Canadian Ritual in East Central Alberta through Three Generations* (Edmonton: Alberta Culture and Multiculturalism, 1992); and Rena Hanchuk, "The Word and Wax: Folk Psychology and Ukrainians in Alberta" (MA thesis, University of Alberta, 1990). More generally, see Orest Martynowych, *Ukrainians in Canada: The Formative Period, 1891-1924* (Edmonton: Canadian Institute of Ukrainian Studies, 1991), 91-100.

14 72.26/6537, placing poison in wells, Vermilion 1925.

15 72.26/6088, seduction under promise of marriage (over 16 under 18), Mundare 1924.

16 72.26/2250, assault causing actual bodily harm, Andrew (Wostok) 1919. The man was acquitted, even though the daughter testified that her mother could barely walk when her parents arrived home.

17 72.26/7427, seduction over 16 under 18, Leduc 1926. Convicted and jailed when he could not pay the fine, the young man faced deportation until his uncle (who guaranteed his employment and good behaviour), a local "deputation of Ukrainians" to their MLA, and the Attorney General's Office intervened. Ottawa agreed to delay action for a year, despite the seriousness of the crime and the man's undoubted guilt.

18 See transcript (file incomplete) in 72.26/7531, assault occasioning actual bodily harm, Edmonton 1927.

19 72.26/3608, assault, Chipman 1921; see also 72.26/3607, unlawfully wounding, Chipman 1921.

20 72.26/3895, assault causing grievous bodily harm, Mundare 1921.

21 72.26/7589, common assault, Tofield (Holden) 1927.

22 72.26/5936, assault causing actual bodily harm, Fort Saskatchewan (Dalmuir) 1924.

23 Robert B. Klymasz, *Folk Narrative among Ukrainian-Canadians in Western Canada* (Ottawa: Museum of Man and Nature, 1973), 24.

24 Recorded in Shortdale, Manitoba, 1963; ibid., 24-5.

25 72.26/3539, assault wife and threaten to kill her, Vilna 1921. Found guilty, the man was ordered to leave town and find work elsewhere, away from his wife.

26 72.26/5659, assault and beat wife occasioning actual bodily harm, Tofield (Holden) 1921.

27 See the archives of the Consistory of the Greek Catholic Church in Lviv, Ukraine (Tsentralnyi derzhavnyi istorychnyi archiv Ukrainskoi respublyky, Lvivskyi viddil, fond 201, opys 2a). Some 200 files deal with the validity and dissolution of marriages in which both partners were living, approximately another 100 deal with the dissolution of marriages where one partner – usually the husband, who had disappeared during the Great War or military campaigns that followed – was presumed dead.

28 72.26/3422, seduction under promise of marriage (under 21), Vegreville 1920. The case was dismissed because of insufficient corroboration, but only on the promise of marriage.

29 72.26/4212, seduction under promise of marriage (under 21), Bellis 1921. The judge justified his not guilty verdict by noting that the witnesses appeared ignorant of the case, that as intercourse had first occurred in a room where the girl's sister and brother-in-law were sleeping he doubted she had tried to resist, and that the complainant had sworn an affidavit saying the accused was not the father of her child. On the latter point, the girl insisted she thought she was signing marriage papers and only said another man was her baby's father because the accused promised to marry her if she did.

30 72.26/4429, wounding, Star 1922. For attempts to slur Ukrainian women by insinuating sexual relationships with "Chinamen," see 72.26/2909, wounding, Radway 1920; and 72.26/1316, rape, Edmonton 1918.

31 72.26/6238, assault wife with intent to do grievous bodily harm, Viking (Bruce) 1924. A stay of proceedings was entered to allow the wife to lay a common assault charge, which could be dealt with summarily.

32 See, for example, 72.26/298, seduction over 14 under 16, Radway 1916; 72.26/907, seduction over 14 under 16, Chipman 1917; 72.26/1268, seduction, Vermilion 1917; and 72.26/4018, carnal knowledge over 14 under 16, Smoky Lake 1920. The father of a pregnant daughter crippled since falling and hurting her back as a child did not think the young woman was "fit to be married, or to have children"; 72.26/3412, carnal knowledge, Bruderheim (Egremont) 1920.

33 72.26/6906, wilfully place poison, to wit, lye in such a position to be easily partaken of by cattle, Spedden 1925.

34 72.26/7020, seduction under promise of marriage (over 16 under 18), Leduc (Calmar) 1925.

35 72.26/907, seduction over 14 under 16, Chipman 1917; and 72.26/2523, carnal knowledge over 14 under 16, Vegreville 1919.

36 72.26/372, carnal knowledge under 14, Fort Saskatchewan (1915-6); 72.26/1428, carnal knowledge over 14 under 16, Bruderheim 1917; 72.26/3422, seduction under promise of marriage (under 21), Vegreville 1920; 72.26/4956, carnal knowledge over 14 under 16, Leduc (Dnipro) 1922; 72.26/5783, rape, Smoky Lake 1922; and 72.26/6088, seduction under promise of marriage (over 16 under 18), Mundare 1924.

37 72.26/2523, carnal knowledge over 14 under 16, Vegreville 1919; 72.26/4956, carnal knowledge over 14 under 16, Leduc (Dnipro) 1922; and 72.26/6536, carnal knowledge, Andrew 1924.

38 72.26/907, seduction over 14 under 16, Chipman 1917; 72.26/4212, seduction under promise of marriage (under 21), Bellis 1921; and 72.26/6088, seduction under promise of marriage (over 16 under 18), Mundare 1924. From outside the Vegreville bloc, see 72.26/2129, assault occasioning actual bodily harm, Lethbridge (Staffordville) 1919; and 72.26/4816, indecent assault, Blairmore (Bellevue) 1922.

39 72.26/6621, seduction under promise of marriage, Edson 1925; insufficient evidence led to a stay of proceedings.

40 72.26/639, carnal knowledge under 14, Wostok 1916. See also 72.26/6475, carnal knowledge under 13, Chipman 1925; and 72.26/7427, seduction over 16 under 18, Leduc 1926.

41 72.26/3878, seduction under promise of marriage (over 14 under 16), Carvel 1920; see also 72.26/5976, seduction over 14 under 16, Vegreville 1924.

42 72.26/1140, carnal knowledge under 14, Vegreville 1917.

43 Six carnal knowledge cases involved married women. Of the remaining complainants, eleven were under 14, five over 14 under 16, one under 16, two under 18, and two over 20; four had no age given. Eight alleged seduction victims were over 14 under 16, one was under 14, nine were over 16 under 18, six were under 21, and one was 29. The great majority (18/27) of rape charges involved married women; of the remaining complainants, one was under 12, one was 14, two were 15, one was under 16, one was under 18, one was 18, one was 19, and one had no age given. Two indecent assault cases concerned wives; of the unmarried, two were 14, one was 17, and two had no age given.

44 For a fuller discussion of marriage patterns in the Vegreville bloc, based on the parish registers of the Basilian Fathers in Mundare, see Frances Swyripa, *Wedded to the Cause: Ukrainian-Canadian Women and Ethnic Identity, 1891-1991* (Toronto: University of Toronto Press, 1993), 83-8.

45 72.26/6416, seduction under promise of marriage (under 21), Leduc 1925.

46 72.26/2931, carnal knowledge under 18, Vermilion 1919; see also, for example, 72.26/1084, carnal knowledge over 14 under 16, Wostok 1916.

47 72.26/116, indecent assault, Vegreville (Wahstao) 1915.

48 72.26/2085, abduction, Radway (Edmonton) 1918. See also, for example, 72.26/2523, seduction under promise of marriage (over 16 under 18), Vegreville (Kaleland) 1919, in which the economic status of the youth and his family appeared to influence the girl's decision making; and 72.26/7110, seduction under promise of marriage (over 16 under 18), Vegreville 1925, where the chambermaid tricked by the Anglo-Canadian cook at Prince Edward Hotel into believing she was married testified that "he said he had a place in Vancouver and ... would sign it over in my name if I became his wife."

49 72.26/6414, seduction under promise of marriage, Mundare (Hilliard) 1925.

50 See, for example, 72.26/1084, carnal knowledge over 14 under 16, Andrew (Sunland) 1917; 72.26/2280, attempted rape, Smoky Lake 1919; 72.26/2532, carnal knowledge under 14, Daysland 1915; 72.26/3878, seduction over 14 under 16, Carvel 1920; 72.26/4212, seduction under promise of marriage (under 21), Bellis 1921; and 72.26/4956, rape, Leduc (Dnipro) 1922.

51 72.26/5215, carnal knowledge, Vegreville (Mundare) 1923; the accused was found guilty of indecent assault.

52 72.26/3656, seduction under promise of marriage (under 21), Vegreville 1920.

53 72.26/5130, carnal knowledge under 14, Tawatinaw (Nestow) 1923.

54 Some men took steps to guard against unpleasant consequences, giving the woman "pills" at the time of intercourse, for example, or promising "medicine" if/when she became pregnant. See 72.26/5783, rape, Smoky Lake 1922; 72.26/6088, seduction under promise of marriage (over 16 under 18), Mundare 1924; 72.26/4491, seduction under promise of marriage (over 16 under 18), Edmonton 1921; and, although the parties' Ukrainian origins are not certain, 72.26/1562, procuring a miscarriage, Meanook 1917.

55 72.26/8220, attempted rape, Smoky Lake 1928; the man was found guilty of indecent assault.

56 72.26/4862, attempted rape (amended to indecent assault), Bellis 1922. On the recommendation of the agent of the attorney general, no charges were preferred. He argued that the evidence did not substantiate the information laid, that the parties did not think things would go as far as they had, that the witnesses were unreliable.

57 The Ukrainian peasant immigrant's understanding of "fri kontri," particularly as it was perceived by the Ukrainian immigrant intelligentsia, is discussed in Swyripa, *Wedded to the Cause*, 67-8.

58 72.26/8457, attempted rape, Opal 1928.

59 72.26/7176, carnal knowledge thereby committing rape, Waugh 1926.

60 Ibid. At the subsequent trial, on the advice of the judge who stated it was the only way to construe the evidence, a jury found the boy not guilty.

61 72.26/2250, assault causing actual bodily harm, Andrew (Wostok) 1919.

62 72.26/8522, rape, Lamont (Eldorena) 1928; 72.26/6088, seduction under promise of marriage (over 16 under 18), Mundare 1924; and 72.26/7110, seduction under promise of marriage (over 16 under 18), Vegreville 1925.

63 72.26/4862, attempted rape (amended to indecent assault), Bellis 1922.

64 72.26/2567, assault causing actual bodily harm, Leduc (Bulford) 1919. On the order of the Attorney General's Office charges were not preferred. This was due to the written request of the wife, whose letter contained the following: "Since the date in question my said husband has treated me well, and we have settled all our outstanding differences."

65 72.26/1113, assault (wife beating), Boian 1917.

66 72.26/7610, failure to provide the necessities of life, Radway 1927. The teacher claimed to know "nothing about the child or anything about the family affairs except what I have learned through the papers," which suggests that he was perhaps himself an "outsider" or not native to the district.

67 72.26/4696, seduction under promise of marriage (over 16 under 18), Vegreville (Kaleland) 1922.

68 72.26/7649, carnal knowledge under 14, Bruce 1927. This was not the only instance in which the priest played an active role in bringing sexual impropriety into the open; see also, for example, 72.26/4696, seduction under promise of marriage (over 16 under 18), Vegreville (Kaleland) 1922.

69 72.26/907, seduction over 14 under 16, Chipman 1917.

70 72.26/5625, carnal knowledge under 14, Andrew 1923.

71 72.26/7427, seduction over 16 under 18, Leduc 1926.

72 72.26/277, rape, Vermilion 1915; no information was laid.

73 72.26/8091, attempted rape, Edwand 1927.

74 72.26/5783, rape, Smoky Lake 1922. Due to the weakness of the evidence to convict, a stay of proceedings was ordered.

75 72.26/4414, carnal knowledge, Coalhurst 1922; both parties seemed anxious not to proceed and the charge was dropped. "Maiu" literally means "I have"; witnesses in the documents also use "iebaty" for intercourse, which corresponds to the English "to fuck."

76 See, for example, 72.26/4696, seduction under promise of marriage (over 16 under 18), Vegreville (Kaleland) 1922.

77 72.26/5625, carnal knowledge under 14, Andrew 1923; after hearing the witnesses for the prosecution, the accused changed his plea to guilty. One police inspector disapproved of the marriage that caused a seduction charge to collapse, complaining that "the ends of justice have been defeated" and insisting that the youth be forced to repay the money wasted bringing him back from British Columbia; 72.26/7020, seduction under promise of marriage (over 16 under 18), Leduc (Calmar) 1925.

78 72.26/2280, rape, Smoky Lake 1919; the wife refused the thirty dollars offered and demanded seventy-five dollars instead.

79 72.26/4739, rape, Bellis (Wahstao) 1922. According to the crime report, after the girl miscarried her mother told a relative that they had only been playing a joke on the accused about getting her pregnant.

80 72.26/6442, seduction under promise of marriage, Edmonton 1924. Although the complainant was identified as German, the accused as Austrian and Roman Catholic, and the court interpreter as Russian, Anglo-Canadian ignorance of central and eastern Europe casts the two men's identities into doubt. From their surnames, the interpreter was most certainly Ukrainian, the accused perhaps so.

81 72.26/3500, carnal knowledge, Smoky Lake 1920.
82 72.26/5172, rape, Smoky Lake 1923.
83 72.26/7427, seduction over 16 under 18, Leduc 1926.
84 72.26/6416, seduction under promise of marriage (under 21), Leduc 1925.
85 72.26/3365, seduction under promise of marriage (over 16 under 18), Edmonton 1920.
86 72.26/5335, seduction under promise of marriage (under 21), Calmar 1922. See also, for example, 72.26/1316, rape, Edmonton 1918; the seventeen year old, separated from her husband, who charged her Serbian rooming-house employer with rape, testified that the man's court interpreter (also Serbian) had offered her money not to proceed with the case.
87 72.26/5042, rape, Opal 1923. In his own defence the man said that the girl had offered him whisky at the dance and promised "something more" if he walked her home; he was acquitted.
88 72.26/6088, seduction under promise of marriage (over 16 under 18), Mundare 1924.
89 See, for example, 72.26/2931, Vermilion, carnal knowledge under 18, 1919.
90 72.26/6729, carnal knowledge, Vegreville 1925; the guilty verdict was overturned on appeal and a stay of proceedings entered. See also 72.26/667, rape, Redcliff 1917; the miner testified that on the night he allegedly raped his landlord's wife her husband promised to say nothing in return for $500.
91 72.26/3422, seduction under promise of marriage, Vegreville 1920. See 72.26/3656, seduction under promise of marriage (under 21), Vegreville 1920, for an example of a mother deliberately taking witnesses to confront the man responsible for her daughter's pregnancy and to arrange a settlement.
92 72.26/5500, attempted rape (amended to attempted indecent assault), Eldorena 1923. News of the assault had apparently not reached the girl's father, for he seemed not to know what the witness had come to settle.
93 72.26/8457, attempted rape, Opal 1928.
94 72.26/8220, attempted rape, Smoky Lake 1928.
95 72.26/5172, rape, Smoky Lake 1923.
96 72.26/3500, carnal knowledge, Smoky Lake 1920.
97 72.26/6536, carnal knowledge, Andrew 1924; the man was found guilty.
98 72.26/6416, seduction under promise of marriage (under 21), Leduc 1925.
99 72.26/3928, rape, Edmonton 1921.
100 See 67.172/599, inquest files, Myrnam 1914.
101 72.26/2523, seduction under promise of marriage (over 16 under 18), Vegreville (Kaleland) 1919.
102 72.26/6840, carnal knowledge under 14, Leduc (Conjuring Creek) 1925.
103 72.26/6729, carnal knowledge, Vegreville 1925.
104 Ibid.

CHAPTER 10

"Abundant Faith"

Nineteenth-Century African-Canadian Women on Vancouver Island

SHERRY EDMUNDS-FLETT

African-Canadian women who lived on Vancouver Island during the nineteenth century have been all but forgotten. Although residents of the Island from 1858 onward, the provincial historical record provides few references pertaining to them. As a small beginning towards correcting the oversight, this chapter will examine the activities of Black women within the private and public spheres. Its premise is that, bound by an intimate network of family/kinship ties and community obligations, the private and public lives of Vancouver Island's African-Canadian women could not be separated.

The focus on the lives of middle-class English- and French-Canadian women within Canadian women's history[1] has expanded in recent years to include the experiences of working-class and immigrant women.[2] There have been two major studies of First Nations women's history concentrating on the interaction of Native women and fur trade company employees.[3] Although the importance of race/ethnicity along with class and gender has been acknowledged by Canadian feminist historians, very little has been written about women who are not of European origin.[4] As Gail Cuthbert Brandt pointed out, "the history of black women and women of other races remains a largely unexplored field."[5]

Generally, the lives of African-Canadian women have been reduced to being mere illustrations, or "add-ons," within feminist history. Fortunately, within the last few years, the restoration of Black women to their rightful place in Canadian women's history has begun. Dionne Brand's book, *No Burden to Carry: Narratives of Working Women in Ontario, 1920s to 1950s*, was the result of an oral history project she initiated in 1988 under the sponsorship of the Immigrant Women's Job Placement Centre in Toronto. About twenty-five Black women over the age of sixty were the focus of the project. Most of these women were born in Canada, the majority in Ontario. Their families had come to Canada between the 1830s and 1860s. They discussed their lives from the 1920s through to the 1950s, decades, as Brand notes, "which seem to be missing in the historical record of Black life in Canada."[6] Suzanne Morton, in her article "Separate Spheres in a Separate World: African-Nova Scotian Women in Late 19th Century Halifax County," examines the impact of the ideology of separate spheres upon the lives of Black women in Halifax County, Nova Scotia, during the latter part of the nineteenth century. She describes how at the same time that the doctrine of separate spheres was used to exclude Black women from White society it offered them protection and empowerment within the Black community. Morton notes that in most African-Nova Scotian households in the county, there was no separation of work and home.[7]

Focusing on African-Canadian women in Southern Ontario during the 1850s and 1860s, Shirley J. Yee, in "Gender Ideology and Black Women as Community-Builders in Ontario, 1850-1870," describes the crucial role they played in establishing Black community organizations in a new land. Like Morton, she found that there was little distinction between the public and private lives of the women she studied. However, the institutions they built were based upon the doctrine of separate spheres.[8] *We're Rooted Here and They Can't Pull Us Up: Essays in African Canadian Women's History,* a significant collection of articles, concentrates primarily on African-Canadian women in Nova Scotia and southwestern Ontario. Sylvia Hamilton, in "Naming Names, Naming Ourselves: A Survey of Early Black Women in Nova Scotia," surveys some of the contributions made by enslaved, Loyalist, Maroon, and refugee women within the Black community and the wider society. The article "'The Lord Seemed to Say "Go"': Women and the Underground Railroad Movement," by Adrienne Shadd, is part of a larger work in progress about the experiences of Black women fleeing slavery on the Underground Railroad and coming to Canada West. Profiling Harriet Tubman, whose basis of operation was St. Catharines, Ontario, Shadd looks at how countless other women helped fugitive slaves once they reached Canada. Peggy Bristow's "'Whatever You Raise in the Ground You Can Sell It in Chatham': Black Women in Buxton and Chatham, 1850-65," is also part of a larger work in progress. Her discussion centres around African-Canadian women living in Chatham, the commercial centre of Kent County, and on the all-Black farming settlement of Elgin in Buxton.

These women worked to improve their own lives and to "uplift the race." The career of Mary Miles Bibb Cary is outlined by Afua P. Cooper in her article "Black Women and Work in Nineteenth-Century Canada West: Black Woman Teacher Mary Bibb." Mary and her husband Henry Bibb moved from Boston in 1850 to Sandwich, Canada West, where Henry published *Voice of the Fugitive* and Mary established and taught in a school for Black children. After the school closed due to lack of funds, the Bibbs moved to Windsor in 1852, where Mary opened up a second and possibly third school. A fervent abolitionist, Mary Bibb helped to found the Windsor Anti-Slavery Society. The remaining two articles in this important collection, Dionne Brand's "'We Weren't Allowed to Go into Factory Work until Hitler Started the War': The 1920s to the 1940s," and Linda Carty's "African Canadian Women and the State: 'Labour Only, Please,'" are concerned mainly with the twentieth century. Using the oral histories published in their entirety in *No Burden to Carry*, Brand points out that the wages of Black women were essential for family survival. They worked within the home, on family homesteads, and in domestic work, but it wasn't until the Second World War "opened things up" that African-Canadian women were tenuously employed in industry. As Carty states, race and class shaped opportunities for African-Canadian women. She analyzes the relationship between Black women and the Canadian government by examining federal immigration policies in the years after the Second World War as well as West Indian domestic labour.

The emphasis on larger African-Canadian communities in central and eastern Canada is continued in the general histories about Black people written by Robin W. Winks, James W. St. G. Walker, and Daniel G. Hill. In *The Blacks in Canada: A History*, published in 1971, Winks surveys African-Canadian history from slavery in New France to the civil rights movement of the 1960s.[14] Concentrating primarily on the nineteenth century, he does not give an adequate account of Black people in the twentieth century. Although he provides his readers with a wealth of primary and secondary documentation, Winks frequently interjects his own opinions into the text, which suffers as a result. James W. St. G. Walker's detailed study, *The Black Loyalists: The Search for a Promised Land in Nova Scotia and Sierra Leone, 1783-1870*, allows him to examine more fully the Black Loyalist community in the Maritime province of Nova Scotia and Sierra Leone.[15] *The Freedom Seekers: Blacks in Early Canada*, by Daniel Hill, is a popular account of Black people who lived primarily in Toronto and southwestern Ontario during the first part of the nineteenth century. Hill is a prominent member of the African-Canadian community in Toronto, and his study is full of family photographs and other details that indicate his personal connection with his subjects.[16] Marginalized in all of these accounts are the unique contributions African-Canadian women made to their communities, as gender is missing "as a fundamental category of analysis."[17]

The only major scholarly works on African-Canadian history in British Columbia have been the BA (1949) and MA (1951) theses of James Pilton (UBC).[18] He examines the 1858 migration of about 300 residents of California to Victoria, the Fraser River goldfields, and, later, to Saltspring Island, concentrating on the interaction of the new settlers with the dominant White society. With its focus on the public sphere, Pilton's narrative makes little reference to women and children. Although not directly about Black women in British Columbia, Keith Ralston's article, "John Sullivan Deas: A Black Entrepreneur in British Columbia Salmon Canning," does give some insight into the life of Fanny Harris, a native of Hamilton, Canada West, who had married John Sullivan Deas in Victoria.[19] Crawford Kilian's popular account, *Go Do Some Great Thing: The Black Pioneers of British Columbia*, is heavily based upon the research of James Pilton and the newspaper indexes of the Vancouver City Archives and the British Columbia Archives. Although Kilian interviewed third generation descendants of some early African-Canadian families in the province, his timeframe remains largely the same as Pilton's – from 1858 to 1871. Like Winks, his examination of Black life in the era between the First and Second World wars is cursory. Furthermore, *Go Do Some Great Thing*, like the other general histories of African Canadians, does not adequately address the role of women.[20]

The African-Canadian population of British Columbia was never enumerated at more than 1,000 until the 1961 census. During the nineteenth century, approximately 300 Black people lived on Vancouver Island and neighbouring Saltspring Island, with the majority residing in Victoria. Studying this small but important community would illuminate some of the differences and similarities between it and other nineteenth-century African-Canadian communities. More specifically, a grassroots approach would yield detailed information about the province's early Black women and their lives, where they lived, their relationships with family, and their organizational efforts within both the Black community and the wider society. This chapter, which is part of a larger work in progress on African-Canadian women in British Columbia from 1858 to 1960, begins to address the important gap caused by the "absence of studies on the west."[21]

The first African-Canadian women known to have settled on Vancouver Island arrived from San Francisco in the spring of 1858. Prior to the advent of the California gold rush in 1848, the state's Black population numbered less than fifty. According to the 1850 census, there were 962 people of African descent in California. By 1852, these numbers had more than doubled.[22] Attracted by the promise of material prosperity, Black men and women from all over the United States and the West Indies had settled there even though their basic rights were not secure. In 1850, the Civil Practice Act was passed, barring Blacks from testifying against Whites. Two years later, the Fugitive Slave Act took effect. Any Black person suspected of being a slave could be arrested and returned to owners in other states without being allowed to give testimony on his/her own behalf. Black businesses and landowners were expected to pay state taxes but were not allowed to vote. Conditions worsened in 1858. During that year, Archy Lee, a nineteen-year-old slave, was held for deportation to Mississippi under the Fugitive Slave Act. Bill 339, "which sought to restrict and prevent the immigration to and residence in California by people of African descent" was introduced in the state legislature.[23] Schools in San Francisco became segregated when the board of education asked Sarah Lester, daughter of Peter and Nancy Lester, to leave the public high school and attend the city's only Black school.[24] In a series of three assemblies, San Francisco's Black community debated whether or not to emigrate. At one meeting, held on 14 April 1858 at the AME Zion Church, possible destinations (such as Panama and Mexico) were discussed. However, Vancouver Island was finally selected due, in part, to news of the Fraser River gold rush.[25] The first party of emigrants departed on 20 April 1858. The *San Francisco Daily Evening Bulletin* editorial of 21 April 1858 stated that "the sixty-five yesterday went off in the Commodore and are now pushing up towards the north, bearing their lares and penates to find new homes. It is said that if the attempt to make a settlement on Vancouver Island should prove abortive, a number who favour P. Anderson's proposition for a settlement in Sonara, Mexico, will make an attempt in that direction. Whatever may be their destiny, we hope the coloured people may do well."[26]

On Sunday, 25 April, the ship docked in Victoria's harbour. Upon arrival, the settlers rented a large room from a local carpenter and spent the evening worshipping and praising God. A couple of days later, the Anglican minister Reverend (later Bishop) Edward Cridge called on them in the morning and extended an invitation to attend church, a sign of respectability for the emigrants.[27] He asked the new residents why they had left San Francisco to come to Victoria. Various people told him about the injustices they laboured under in California and that they were "much encouraged by the privileges they would enjoy [on Vancouver Island]."[28] Nancy Lester, in the only known existing letter from that period written by a Black woman who settled on Vancouver Island, told her friend abolitionist William Still that "it seems to be a Providential provision for us who are so oppressed ... that ere long we may find a home for our children in the right place." She spoke of the hospitable reception that the group that had left at the end of April received from Governor James Douglas. Some newspapers in California were "taunting the coloured people" who were leaving to come to Vancouver Island. "However," Nancy Lester stated, "our enemies are never willing that we should emigrate to a place where we will be benefitted."[29]

It is difficult to know exactly how many Black women migrated to Vancouver Island during those early years and who they were.[30] Their invisibility is due, in part, to their classification in the historical record as wives, mothers, and daughters. Women were present, however, in all phases of settlement from the initial party of sixty-five onwards. As Reverend Cridge described in his diary, some men had brought their wives and children with them from California while others came ahead to prepare a home. Others hoped to earn enough money in the Fraser River gold mines to buy family members out of slavery and bring them to the Vancouver Island colony.[31] Some women came as domestic servants; others came on their own, with sisters or aunts.

Information about these women is not easily extracted from a single body of documents. For instance, included in Pilton's MA thesis appendices is an undocumented list of Black British Columbians. The few married women noted were identified solely by their husbands' surnames, and only one single woman was listed. Identifying these early African-Canadian settlers involved merging discrete details from various sources to create a coherent picture. Drawing upon census, church, cemetery, and court records, along with will and probate files; birth, marriage, and death records; newspapers and oral histories, a list of 179 women living on Vancouver Island from 1858 to 1901 was compiled.

Almost half the women on the list emigrated from the United States between 1858 and 1860. Before they had moved to California, most first generation women had lived in cities in the eastern states of Massachusetts, Pennsylvania, Delaware, New Jersey, New York, and Maryland. Others were from southern states such as Kentucky, Missouri, and Florida. A few came from Canada West. One woman was born in Puerto Rico.

The majority of women were involved in long-lasting, stable marriages interrupted only by the death of a spouse. Their adherence to the separate spheres doctrine was facilitated by the fact that most either aspired to or were part of the middle class. Many were married to business or tradesmen who achieved relative economic prosperity due, in part, to the California and Fraser River gold rushes. This afforded them the opportunity to stay at home and work within the family. Victoria Clanton (nee Richard) was one such woman. The Richard family was part of a nucleus of families who moved to California from Florida and then later to Vancouver Island.[32] Victoria's aunt, Sophia Everton, had also come from the southern States. She lived next door to the Clantons and Richards on Topaze Avenue for many years.[33] Born in Jacksonville, Florida, Victoria married Robert Thompson Clanton on Boxing Day, 1866, at St. John's Anglican Church, Victoria.[34] The Clantons became moderately wealthy and influential within the Black community. Robert owned a clothing store in the 1870s.[35] He later worked as a bookkeeper at M.R. Smith and Company's Crackery Factory – an African-Canadian-owned business in Victoria, still operating in 1901. Victoria Clanton worked at home, giving birth to five children, with one dying at birth and another shortly thereafter.[36]

The number of married women with families employed in paid work is not readily apparent, as there is no census data for the early years of settlement on Vancouver Island. Only an informal household census exists, which was conducted by the Victoria Police Department in 1871, prior to British Columbia joining Confederation.[37] Two parent households enumerated in the 1881 and 1891 census rarely list mothers/wives as having an occupation other than homemaker or housewife.[38] An exception to this was Adelina Phelps, who was listed in the 1881 census as married to Edward Phelps. She was a nurse and mother of four children whose ages ranged from eight to eighteen years old. The absence of recorded occupations for married African-Canadian women with families does not necessarily mean that they did not do waged work. As part of the household economy, their contributions to the family income, such as taking in boarders or piece work, were often invisible. For example, Corinthia Alexander, wife of Thomas Alexander, was an "excellent dressmaker [who] made dresses for a lot of well-known women."[39] Yet the 1891 census does not list an occupation for her. Probate files hint at other sources of income for married women with children. Mary Barnswell, wife of James Barnswell and mother of ten children, "despite her lack of formal education, was sought out by Victoria businessmen and politicians who valued her intelligence and sound judgement."[40] In his will, sixty-five-year old Columbus Jones gave her "all [the] household furniture chattels and personal effects including the picture 'my dog.'"[41]

Adherence to the doctrine of separate spheres and working within the home offered Black women a measure of protection and respectability within the African-Canadian community. Racism remained overt, especially during those early years of settlement, due, in part, to an influx of White Americans from California. P.A. Bell, editor of *Pacific Appeal*, an African-American newspaper from San Francisco, stated that "there [was] as much prejudice and nearly as much isolation in Victoria as in San Francisco."[42] A group of White Americans attempted to segregate schools and churches, but this failed. However, Black people were denied access to various public facilities, such as barbershops, pubs, hotels, and theatres. Segregation of social engagements was often enforced by threats of physical violence to any Black person who attended. In one particular instance, during a benefit concert for the Royal Hospital on 25 September 1861, a package containing one pound of flour was thrown on Mifflin Gibbs, his pregnant wife Maria, Nathan Pointer, and his daughter for sitting in the dress circle.[43]

In general, first generation employed married women were also childless. One of these women was Sarah Jane Douglas, who married Wellington Delaney Moses on 14 December 1858. Reverend Cridge noted in his diary that Moses had been married before but had lost his wife and four children.[44] Together, Sarah and her husband ran a boarding house in James Bay. In 1861, Lady Franklin, wife of the explorer Sir John Franklin, and her niece Sophia Cracroft stayed at their establishment. According to Sophia, they were very glad to get the lodging, "the very best in [Victoria] and really very tolerable – the landlady giving up her own room above for me."[45] Sophia reported that Sarah Moses had "the reputation of being a first rate cook."[46] In a patronizing description that speaks of the racial and class exclusiveness underlying the notion of separate spheres, she stated that Sarah Douglas Moses was "a queer being, wear[ing] a long sweeping gown without crinoline – mov[ing] slowly and h[ad] a soft sort of stately way (in intention at least) which [was] amusing. Sometime (Mrs. Moses) t[ied] a coloured handkerchief round her head like the American negroes (she was from Baltimore) but on that Sunday, she wore a sort of half cap with lace falling behind, her hair being long enough to be parted. The language of both (Sarah and her husband) was very good."[47] Obviously, to Sophia, Sarah's aspirations to genteel womanhood were doomed to failure because of her race.

In her diary, Sophia records Wellington Moses's praise for his wife's excellent housekeeping.[48] His words give no indication that their marriage was troubled. A year later, in September 1862, Sarah Douglas Moses was arrested for attempting to commit suicide. She had jumped into James Bay at the foot of their boarding house stairs. Crying for help, Sarah was pulled out by a passerby; then she again attempted to throw herself in. Locked up in the city jail for twenty-four hours before being released, she blamed her husband's recent elopement with another woman for her failed suicide attempt.[49] Although no written evidence actually documents his infidelity, Wellington Moses did leave Victoria around this time to work as a barber in mining camps in the present-day British Columbia Lower Mainland. He later became a storeowner and resident barber of Barkerville.[50] Listed as a widower in the 1881 census, Wellington Delaney Moses died there in 1890. His will makes no mention of Sarah. His assets were left to a woman living in San Francisco and the children of his executors.[51] Sarah Douglas Moses left Victoria shortly after her suicide attempt, visiting San Francisco on 29 November 1862.[52] It would appear that she resided there for a period of time, as the *Elevator*, an African-American newspaper operating out of San Francisco, listed letters received for her by its office in October 1868 and in July of the following year.[53]

At least twenty-six of the 179 identified women were widowed before the age of fifty.[54] Needing to support themselves and other family members, most of these women lived in Victoria. Like their sisters elsewhere in Canada and the United States, they found work in the service sector as domestics, laundresses, and cooks.[55] Often a widow would have more than one occupation in her lifetime. Catherine Gant was listed in the 1871 household census as a clothier. In the 1881 census, her occupation was nursing. In her oral history, Ada Matilda Barnswell Alexander said that Catherine Gant was employed as a cook.[56] Other women, such as Mary Jane Hamilton, Phillis Randall, and Adelina Phelps, ran boarding houses and took in single men and women as lodgers.[57] Mary Ann Bailey, after the death of her husband Madison in August 1893, advertised in the *Victoria Daily Colonist* want ads for "the care of a couple of children: a comfortable home provided."[58] Widows like Sarah Smith, who took over her husband's steam bakery after his death, or Ella Cooness, who inherited the sizable estate of John Giscome, were rare.[59] Only one identified widow, Julia Travis, owned property in her own right prior to marriage.

Julia Travis was an extraordinary woman. In 1853, as Julia Hernandez, she left Jacksonville, Florida, with her sister Mary to join other family members who had arrived in California the year before. According to Delilah Beasley in the *Negro Trail Blazers of California* (1919), "when the Fraser River gold excitement reached California, the [sisters] decided to go to British Columbia and cook, at a wage of a hundred dollars a week."[60] Julia must have prospered, since she was listed in the Government Gazette as owning a portion of five acres on Pioneer Street in Victoria.[61] She married Augustus Travis at Christ Church Cathedral on 10 May 1860. One of her witnesses was her niece, Emma Segee, who came to live with her aunts in Victoria in order to attend school.[62]

Life did not treat Julia Travis very kindly in her later years. Tragedy struck the Travis household repeatedly. Augustus Sr., Julia's husband, died sometime before 1881, since the census for that year listed her as a forty-six-year-old widow, no occupation given.[63] Her eldest son William died of consumption at only thirty-two years of age at her home in 1894.[64] His brother Augustus Jr. died in 1909 after being shot by a policeman in Idaho.[65]

Even though she had been continually employed as a cook and laundress – jobs of low pay and status – Julia Travis was still an influential woman within the Black community. Witnessing wills as "Julia Travis, property owner," she was also active in the Anglican and Reformed Episcopalian Churches.[66] After her death on 2 May 1911, Julia Catherine Travis was interned in a plot beside the stately grave of Bishop Cridge.[67] This burial location would seem to be an indication of the great respect Julia Travis had earned in her lifetime.

With the majority of married, single, or widowed women living within city limits, only a small number worked alongside their husbands on family homesteads. One of these, Sylvia Stark, was the only woman from the list of 179 clearly identified as having been born a slave.[68] Her three siblings were owned by one man and her father, Howard Estes, by another. A very religious family, the Estes attended church regularly. In 1849, Howard Estes went to California to earn the money necessary to buy his family's freedom. When they were all free, the Estes bought forty acres of land in Missouri, but night visits by the Ku Klux Klan convinced them to travel overland by covered wagon to California in 1851. Sylvia met Louis Stark in California, and they married in Placerville on 24 September 1855.[69]

Married for only three weeks, Sylvia wanted to leave her husband and his "sullen and unpredictable moods." But he persuaded her to stay. Although they came from different backgrounds, the racism they both experienced made Sylvia decide to stay in the relationship with her husband. Children started coming early: two were born prior to the family's

1860 emigration to Vancouver Island with Sylvia's father, mother, and brother. Five more children were born when the Starks settled on Saltspring Island after first buying property in Saanich, outside Victoria.

The Stark family members worked hard to clear their land. During the flu epidemic of 1862, Louis came down with smallpox. While he lay delirious for several days, Sylvia milked fourteen cows, looked after pigs, and did the work inside the house.[70] Her life on the farm was lonely; she missed the company of other women. Sylvia Stark's religious faith was a source of comfort, helping her survive the hardships of her life, which included a turbulent marriage.[71] Sylvia Stark continued to live on Saltspring Island with her son Abraham after the rest of the family moved to the Cranberry District near Nanaimo during the 1870s.[72] She stayed until her death in 1944.[73]

Most young, unmarried African-Canadian women living on Vancouver Island were daughters of first generation women. As girls, they attended the "Ladies College," or "Girls' Collegiate School," better known as Angela College.[74] Sophia Cracroft described in her diary how "the unmistakable descendants of negroes in Mrs. Woods' little school

Mrs. Sylvia Stark, aged 92

of 30 [studied] side by side with the English and American girls." A fractious group of White Americans who wanted segregated classrooms threatened to withdraw their children from school. Bishop Cridge stood firm, however, and the Anglican schools remained integrated.[75] Black children and youth continued to study in integrated classrooms, often garnering praise for their efforts. On 30 June 1874, a decade later, during the city school midsummer examinations, young Joanna Pointer acquitted herself with some acclaim. The *Daily British Colonist* reported that she had won the prize for general studies and sang the national anthem solos "most effectively."[76]

Prior to marriage, a number of these young women were enumerated as living with their parents or a widowed mother. Employed mainly as dressmakers, servants, or waitresses, they contributed to the family income. Sixteen-year-old Ada Matilda Barnswell, daughter of James and Mary Barnswell (who boarded at her parents' residence), was a dressmaker at Mrs. Crabbs's in Victoria.[77] A few also became nurses or teachers. Emma Stark Clark, who completed her education when the family moved to the Cranberry District, was teaching at the North Cedar school in 1874, "at the starting salary of $40.00 a month."[78] At the family home on Vancouver Street, Sarah Lester gave "instruction on the piano."[79] Under the pseudonym Violet, Emma Segee wrote articles for the *Pacific Appeal*.[80]

Many first-generation women and their daughters were involved in local churches. In contrast with California, a separate African-Canadian church was not established in British Columbia because the new emigrants decided that, because they did not want to be marginalized, it was better not to form "a distinct Church organization."[81] This push for integration came from the desire to be part of the democratic tradition that provided equal access to institutions, services, and the political process – rights denied in the United States. Some families became members of the Anglican and, later, Reformed Episcopalian Churches led by Bishop Cridge.[82] Others were Methodist, Baptist, or Presbyterian.[83] African-Canadian women on Vancouver Island were actively involved in community building, as were other nineteenth-century Black women. "Not only did they consider their roles as wives and mothers important, but they also felt that they had as equally as important duties outside the home, the most significant of which was their duty to work for the general improvement of society and especially the uplifting of the race."[84] Although there is only direct evidence of Nancy Lester's ties to the abolitionist movement, women such as Sarah Pointer, Maria Gibbs, Sydna E.R. Francis, Julia Ann Booth, and Nancy Lester herself were married to men with a history of involvement in the movement.[85] African-Canadian women from Vancouver Island publicly supported the Pioneer Rifle Corps, a volunteer militia made up of Black men. At one event, Sarah Amelia Pointer gave a speech and presented a silk flag sewn by the women to the Rifle Corps.[86] Two years earlier, the women had presented $100 to the company to help with operating expenses.[87] The Committee of Coloured Ladies, as they called themselves, held a donation party on New Year's Eve, 1863, and raised money for ex-slaves in the United States. A letter sent by Emily Allen, president of the committee, to Hannibal Hamlin, vice-president of the United States, requested that the draft for £86 14s 9d. sterling be sent to Beaufort, South Carolina, for the benefit of the contrabands. In the same letter she mentioned $170 sent to the City of Philadelphia for the same purpose.[88] The women cooked for and participated in the annual Emancipation Day celebrations and acted in dramas at the Pioneer Hall.[89] Some belonged to the Janisaries of Light, a fraternal order composed of both Black men and women that took care of ailing members by donating money raised from membership dues and subscription fees.[90] Women were also involved in individual acts of kindness. The *Daily British Colonist* reported that "Mrs. Lester donated Fruit, Vegetables, Eggs to the BC Protestant Orphans' Home."[91] They often took children or seniors into their homes or nursed them through illnesses. Catherine Gant and her husband William, for the three years prior to his death, supported a White child who had been

Barnswell residence, 293 Johnson Street, Victoria

abandoned by its mother.[92] Corinthia Alexander and her sister-in-law Georgina Pierre helped John Lomax, who died at ninety-eight years of age on 17 February 1893. Both women were given bequests in his will.[93]

The deep commitment to the community among Vancouver Island's African-Canadian residents was reflected in their family and kinship networks.[94] Most women married within the Black community in Victoria. Five families – the Carters, Alexanders, Clantons, Barnswells, and Spotts – were related to nearly every other Black family who lived on either Vancouver Island or neighbouring Saltspring Island.[95] During the nineteenth century, first generation women and their descendants lived in close proximity to each other in Victoria's Johnson and Yates Street Wards, in Saanich, and on Saltspring Island. They often inhabited the same houses for generations.[96]

Marriage or residence outside the local community, rare until the 1880s and 1890s, usually took place in another West Coast Black community located in or around Vancouver, Seattle, Portland, or San Francisco.[97] Lucinda Alexander married William Mortimer and was living in Vancouver when her brothers James and Edward drowned while ice skating on 19 February 1890.[98] Emily Gant moved to Walla Walla, Washington, and married Lewis Greenaway, resident of that city, on 29 November 1880.[99] Theodosia, daughter of Sydna and Abner Francis, married a Thomas Green in Portland, Oregon, on 4 September 1873.[100] Sisters Sarah and Joanna Pointer both moved to San Francisco. Sarah married William H. Carter there at the Bethel African Methodist Episcopalian Union Church on 27 January 1869, moving back to Victoria in the 1890s.[101] Widowed Joanna White lived at her parents' residence until she married Lee Darrington and moved to Seattle before the turn of the century.[102] The majority of married African-Canadian women in the colony of Vancouver Island worked primarily within the private sphere. Single, widowed, or married but childless women were mainly employed as domestics, laundresses, seamstresses, cooks, nurses, and teachers. They participated in integrated worship services and educated their children in integrated schools. Their public efforts were largely directed towards "betterment of the race." A sense of commitment existed among the members of Vancouver Island's African-Canadian community, and this was reflected in its marriage and settlement patterns. Rarely, until the 1880s and 1890s, did these women and their descendants marry or move outside the local Black community. Intimately connected through family/kinship ties and community obligations, the interwoven private and public spheres of British Columbia's early African-Canadian women could not easily be separated.

Acknowledgments

I would like to thank the following people: Allen Seager, my senior supervisor, for his encouragement; Veronica Strong-Boag for her comments on an earlier draft of this paper; Robin Fisher; Roderick Barman; the reference staff at the Provincial Archives of British Columbia; the Cloverdale Library Genealogical Section; Andrew McBride of Vital Statistics, Ministry of Health; Afua Cooper for her critical analysis; Suzanne Morton for sending me a copy of her paper; Kathleen MacDonald; the staff at Ross Bay Cemetery; Victoria City Archives; Karen Alexander Hoshal; Lois Akam; Peggy Phillip; Myrtle Holloman; Norman Alexander; the late Barbara Slye; my mother Shirley Edmunds; my father-in-law the late Arnold Flett; my husband Glenn Flett for his patience; and the Holy Spirit from whom all things come. Finally, I would like to dedicate this chapter to our good friend Ronald Clifford Grant, 1953-91. The grandson of James Grant, who received the Military Cross for bravery in action during the First World War and a "lifer," Gypsy initiated this project by saying "tell them something about us."

Notes

1 For example: Veronica Strong-Boag, *The New Day Recalled: Lives of Girls and Women in English Canada, 1919-1939* (Toronto: Penguin, 1988); Alison Prentice and Susan Mann Trofimenkoff, eds., *The Neglected Majority: Essays in Canadian Women's History*, 2 vols. (Toronto: McClelland and Stewart, 1977 and 1985); Clio Collective, *Quebec Women: A History* (Toronto: Women's Press, 1987); Carol Lee Bacchi, *Liberation Deferred? The Ideas of the English Suffragists, 1877-1918* (Toronto: University of Toronto Press, 1983); Linda Kealey, ed., *A Not Unreasonable Claim: Women and Reform in Canada, 1880-1920s* (Toronto: Women's Press, 1979).

2 For example: Franca Iacovetta and Mariana Valverde, eds., *Gender Conflicts: New Essays in Women's History* (Toronto: University of Toronto Press, 1992); Barbara K. Latham and Roberta J. Pazdro, eds., *Not Just Pin Money: Selected Essays On The History of Women's Work In British Columbia* (Victoria: Camosun College, 1984); Gillian Creese and Veronica Strong-Boag, eds., *British Columbia Reconsidered: Essays on Women* (Vancouver: Press Gang Publishers, 1992); Joy Parr, *The Gender of Breadwinners: Women, Men, and Change in Two Industrial Towns, 1880-1950* (Toronto: University of Toronto Press, 1990); Joan Sangster, *Dreams of Equality: Women on the Canadian Left, 1920-1950* (Toronto: McClelland and Stewart, 1989); Bettina Bradbury, "The Family Economy and Work in an Industrializing City: Montreal in the 1870s," in *Canadian Historical Association Historical Papers* (1979); Bettina Bradbury, "Pigs, Cows and Boarders: Non-Wage Forms of Survival Among Montreal Families, 1861-1891," *Labour/Le Travail* 14 (Fall 1984): 9-46; Ruth Roach Pierson, *"They're Still Women After All": The Second World War and Canadian Womanhood* (Toronto: McClelland and Stewart, 1986); Janice Acton et al., eds., *Women at Work, Ontario 1850-1930* (Toronto: Canadian Women's Educational Press, 1974); Marjorie Griffith Cohen, *Women's Work, Markets, and Economic Development in Nineteenth Century Ontario* (Toronto: 1988); Veronica Strong-Boag and Anita Clair Fellman, eds., *Rethinking Canada: The Promise of Women's History* (Toronto: Copp Clark Pitman, 1986); Alison Prentice et al., *Canadian Women: A History* (Toronto: Harcourt, Brace and Jovanich, 1988); Jean Burnet, ed., *Looking into My Sister's Eyes* (Toronto: Multicultural History of Ontario, 1986); Varpu Lindstrom-Best, *Defiant Sisters: A Social History of Finnish Immigrant Women in Canada* (Toronto: Multicultural History Society of Ontario, 1988).

3 Sylvia Van Kirk, *Many Tender Ties: Women in Fur-Trade Society in Western Canada, 1700-1850* (Winnipeg: Watson and Dwyer, 1980); Jennifer S.H. Brown, *Strangers in Blood: Fur Trade Company Families in Indian Country* (Vancouver: UBC Press, 1980).

4 For instance: Tamara Adilman, "A Preliminary Sketch of Chinese Women and Work in British Columbia, 1858-1920," in *Not Just Pin Money: Selected Essays on the History of Women's Work in British Columbia*, ed. Barbara K. Latham and Roberta J. Pazdro (Victoria: Camosun College, 1984), 53-78; Mary Yee, "Chinese-Canadian Women: Our Common Struggle," in *British Columbia Reconsidered: Essays on Women*, ed. Gillian Creese and Veronica Strong-Boag (Vancouver: Press Gang Publishers, 1992), 233-43.

5 Gail Cuthbert Brandt, "Postmodern Patchwork: Some Recent Trends in the Writing of Women's History in Canada," *Canadian Historical Review* 62, 4 (December 1991): 468.

6 Dionne Brand, *No Burden to Carry: Narratives of Black Working Women in Ontario, 1920s to 1950s* (Toronto: Women's Press, 1991), 30-1.

7 Suzanne Morton, "Separate Sphere in a Separate World: African-Nova Scotian Women in Late 19th Century Halifax County," *Acadiensis* 22, 2 (Spring 1993).

8 Shirley J. Yee, "Gender Ideology and Black Women as Community-Builders in Ontario, 1850-1870," *Canadian Historical Review* 75 (1994): 73.

9 Sylvia Hamilton, "Naming Names, Naming Ourselves: A Survey of Early Black Women in Nova Scotia," in *We're Rooted Here and They Can't Pull Us Up: Essays in African Canadian Women's History*, coord. Peggy Bristow (Toronto: University of Toronto Press, 1994), 13-40.

10 Adrienne Shadd, "'The Lord Seemed to Say "Go"': Women and the Underground Railroad Movement," in *We're Rooted Here.*

11 Peggy Bristow, "'Whatever You Raise in the Ground You Can Sell It in Chatham': Black Women in Buxton and Chatham, 1850-65," in *We're Rooted Here.*

12 Afua P. Cooper, "Black Women and Work in Nineteenth-Century Canada West: Black Woman Teacher Mary Bibb," in *We're Rooted Here.*

13 Dionne Brand, "'We Weren't Allowed to Go into Factory Work until Hitler Started the War': The 1920s to the 1940s," and Linda Carty, "African Canadian Women and the State: 'Labour only, Please,'" in *We're Rooted Here.*

14 Robin Winks, *The Blacks in Canada: A History* (London: Yale University Press, 1971).

15 James W. St. G. Walker, *The Black Loyalists: The Search for a Promised Land in Nova Scotia and Sierra Leone, 1783-1870* (New York: Africana, 1976).

16 Daniel Hill, *The Freedom Seekers: Blacks in Early Canada* (Agincourt, ON: Book Society of Canada, 1980).

17 *We're Rooted Here*, 6-7.

18 James Pilton, "Early Negro Settlement in Victoria" (BA Thesis, University of British Columbia, 1949), and "Negro Settlement in British Columbia 1858-1871" (MA thesis, University of British Columbia, 1951).

19 Keith Ralston, "John Sullivan Deas: A Black Entrepreneur in British Columbia Salmon Canning," *BC Studies* 32 (Winter 1976/7): 64-78. Deas, who canned salmon at the mouth of the Fraser River for seven years, died in 1880 at forty-two years of age, in Portland, Oregon. Fanny, left widowed with seven children, ran a boarding house in Portland. She later married Edward Warren. Falling on hard times, Fanny was listed in 1905 as living by herself in a rooming house in Portland.

20 Crawford Kilian, *Go Do Some Great Thing: The Black Pioneers of British Columbia* (Vancouver, BC: Douglas and McIntyre, 1978).

21 Introduction, *We're Rooted Here*, 11.

22 Rudolph Lapp, *Blacks in Gold Rush California* (London: Yale University Press, 1977), 49-50.

23 F.W. Howay, "The Negro Immigration into Vancouver Island in 1858," *Transactions of the Royal Society of Canada,* Section 11, 1935, 145.

24 Lapp, *Blacks in Gold Rush California*, 169-71.

25 James Pilton, "Negro Settlement," 28.

26 *San Francisco Daily Evening Bulletin*, 21 April 1858, as cited in Pilton, ibid., 33. Copy in the British Columbia Archives and Records Service (BCARS).

27 For a discussion of respectability and the Black elite in Halifax during the last half of the

nineteenth century, see Judith Fingard, "Race and Respectability in Victorian Halifax," *Journal of Imperial and Commonwealth History* 2, 2 (May 1992): 169-95.

28 Reverend Edward Cridge Diary entry dated Thursday, 6 May 1858, BCARS.

29 Nancy Lester to William Still, "San Francisco June 4, 1858," William Still, Correspondence of the American Negro Historical Society Papers (gift of Leon Gardiner), Historical Society of Pennsylvania, Philadelphia, Pennsylvania.

30 The number of Black people who settled initially on Vancouver Island ranges from 300 to 800 in various accounts. Winks states that "in 1923 one of the noncommissioned officers of the [Pioneer Rifle Corps], Corporal [Samuel John] Booth, told the City Archivist of Vancouver, J.S. Matthews, that the proper figure was 600." See Winks, *Blacks in Canada*, 286, n. 43.

31 Cridge Diary, Friday, 14 May 1858.

32 Delilah Beasley, *The Negro Trail Blazers of California* (New York: Negro Universities Press, 1969), 106.

33 Clarissa Richard, Victoria Clanton's mother, is buried beside her sister in Ross Bay Cemetery, Victoria, British Columbia. City of Victoria, Parks Department, Ross Bay Cemetery Records, p. 128, permit 1717. The tombstone inscription reads "Clarissa Richard Died August 4, 1890 aged 80 years. Also her sister Sophia Everton, January 1907, aged 80 years." Plot and row numbers F13 and E20.

34 Clanton Family Tree courtesy of Mel Clanton. In the possession of author.

35 Greater Victoria Police Archives, Charge Book, 13 August 1870, reports that Robert Clanton's clothing store was broken into by a person or persons unknown. The goods stolen included: "12 Baltic shirts, 6 pairs of grey drawers and 5 lambs wool undershirts."

36 BCARS Will and Probate Files, call no. 1052, 5 June 1915. Her will mentions sons Robert Wendell and Frederick Sumner Clanton and daughter Clarissa (Clanton) Besselleu. Ross Bay Cemetery, "Clanton – infant daughter of R.T. Clanton, 19 days old born Victoria, died there July 16, 1883, buried July 19, 1883 4 pm. No officiating clergy, Hayward Undertaker, G13 W13." "Clanton-R.J., still born, Victoria born and died, July 18____? buried July 19, 3:30 pm, no officiating clergy, no undertaker, G Block 13 W13 p. 60."

37 BCARS, GR 428, vol. 1, 104. The population totals in Victoria were "1615 White men, 1197 White women, 141 Native men, 219 Native women, 181 Chinese men, 30 Chinese women, 128 Black men and 89 Black women."

38 B-390, British Columbia, 1881 Census, Victoria, Yates Street Ward.

39 Kilian, *Go Do Some Great Thing*, 156. She was the daughter of Thomas Whiting and Ann Elizabeth Pierre. Her father, a tailor, owned and operated his own tailoring and dye business in Victoria for many years.

40 Ibid., 160.

41 BCARS, GR 1052 3539, Will of Columbus Jones, dated 23 January 1886.

42 *Pacific Appeal*, 6 February 1864, 3.

43 *Colonist*, 1 October 1861. The charges against Ryckman, the White man who had thrown the flour, were dismissed. Mifflin Gibbs, however, was convicted of assault and fined five pounds for striking Ryckman.

44 Anglican Church Archives, Victoria, BC Christ Church Cathedral, "Marriage" folder 3, 19. Emily Allen, another Black woman living in Victoria, was her witness.

45 Sophia Cracroft, *Lady Franklin Visits the Pacific Northwest*, ed. D.B. Smith (Victoria: Provincial Archives of British Columbia, 1974), 60.

46 Ibid.

47 Ibid.

48 Ibid.

49 *Victoria Colonist*, 23 September 1862. BCARS GR 848, vol. D, Police Charge Books, 138-9.

50 BCARS, Wellington Delaney Moses, Account Books.

51 B-389, 1881 Census District no. 188, Cariboo District and Richfield, Barkerville, Lightning. BCARS, Probate File, call no. 436, 25 July 1890.

52 *Pacific Appeal*, 29 November 1862, "Strangers." A microfilm copy of *The Appeal* can be found in BCARS.

53 *Elevator*, San Francisco, California, Friday, 16 October 1868, 2; and Friday, 30 July 1869, 2.

54 Some of these women included Mary Jane Hamilton, Didamia Copeland, and Catherine Gant. See probate file of husband, Harriet Staff, Mrs. Baldwin, Louisa Booth, Julia Travis, Fanny Deas, Mrs. Ford, Sarah Hobbs, Sophia Page, Adelina Phelps, Mary Cecilia Spotts (daughter of Ann and Thomas Pierre), Sylvia Stark, Rosa Hayes, Ignore Jessie McMillan, Amanda Scott, Mary Stewart, Joanna Pointer White Darrington, Sydney E.R. Francis, and Phillis Randall.

55 Jacqueline Jones, *Labor of Love, Labor of Sorrow: Black Women, Work and the Family, From Slavery to the Present* (New York: Vintage, 1985), 98-9.

56 BCARS GR 428, vol. 1, 62-3; B-390 BC 1881 Census, Victoria B, Johnson Street Ward; BCARS, Sound and Moving Image Division, no. 1308:1, Ada Matilda Barnswell Alexander Oral History Tape.

57 Mr. Hamilton died in 1864. Mary Jane Hamilton is listed in both the 1881 census and the 1891 census as a housekeeper. One of Phillis Randall's boarders, John Banks, died of alcohol poisoning at her house.

58 *Victoria Daily Colonist*, Wednesday, 20 September 1893, 2.

59 In 1891, John Giscome, a wealthy member of the Black community who made his money mining, was listed as living with Mary Jane Hamilton. A decade later, his housekeeper, Ella Cooness, wife of Stacey Cooness, inherited his estate, which was worth $22,252.66. BCARS, John Robert Giscome, Probate File, "Schedule A, Affidavit."

60 Beasley, *Negro Trail Blazers*, 122.

61 Province of British Columbia, *Government Gazette*, Victoria, Vancouver Island, 7.

62 Emma regularly attended Bishop Cridge's Sunday school, as noted in his attendance book. She "remained in BC for seven years, when she returned to Marysville, California, where she married [a] Mr. Washington and was given a position as the first coloured public school teacher in that city." See Beasley, *Negro Trail Blazers*, 122.

63 B-390, BC Census, Victoria, Yates Street Ward. However, page 76 of the *1882-1883 BC Directory* lists Julia Travis as doing washing and ironing out of her home.

64 Anglican Church Archives, Victoria, British Columbia, Reformed Episcopalian Church, Death Register.

65 *Victoria Times*, 3 May 1909, 16. "Sad Death: Former Resident of Victoria Shot by a Policeman in Idaho ... Travis and a friend who worked on the train had after quitting work been playfully scuffling. A policeman interfered and as Travis attempted to get away, the policeman drew a revolver and shot him. The officer is under arrest and public sentiment ran so high against him that there was talk of lynching him. This occurred on April 27th."

66 BCARS, 1052, no. 378, "Will of Andrew Samuel Booth," 20 August 1894. Andrew Booth was the son of Julia Ann and Samuel Booth. His father Samuel had sailed from New York to the Isthmus of Panama, then to California by mule, and later settled in Victoria.

67 Ross Bay Cemetery tombstone inscription, "George Edward Keithley, born February 9, 1858 Sacramento California. Died February 11, 1912 Victoria BC." Plot and row numbers F25 and W20.

68 BCARS, Add MSS 91, Marie Wallace, "Sylvia Stark's Story," 3. Sylvia Stark, the daughter of Hannah and Howard Estes, was born in Clay County Missouri in 1839.

69 From a conversation with M. Holloman, granddaughter of Sylvia Stark, October 1991. Notes in possession of author. See Wallace, "Sylvia Stark's Story." Notes in possession of the author. Sylvia Stark's mother, Hannah Estes, did not want her to marry Louis Stark. Sylvia did marry him, however, wearing a wedding gown she made herself of white brocaded satin. She also wore white satin slippers.

70 Wallace, "Sylvia Stark's Story," notes. In possession of Myrtle Holloman.

71 As Reverend Ebenezer Robson, who visited the Starks, noted in his diary, Louis was not as religious as Sylvia. See BCARS, Ebenezer Robson, "Diary," Sunday, 22 December 1861.

72 *Daily Colonist*, Sunday, 27 October 1968, 3. This is where Louis Stark met his death in 1895. After a seam of coal had been found running through his property, Louis refused to sell. He was subsequently found dead at the bottom of a mine shaft. The family said he was murdered. BCARS, Saltspring Correspondence, Willis Stark to James H. White,

2 November 1932. "Father was all alone on his farm and only his dead body to show he had been murdered by someone."

73 B-390 1881 Census, District 191, Vancouver Cowichan/Saltspring Island. Trouble had continued to exist in the marriage of Louis and Sylvia Stark. In his will, Louis stated that his wife "was bequeathed the sum of one dollar in lieu of dower because she (had for) some years since without cause left (his) bed and board. Consequently [she was] not entitled to any of his property." See BCARS, GR 1052, no. 6810, "Will of Louis Stark," 1.

74 Boys went to a similar institution, where Mr. Woods was the principal.

75 Cracroft, *Lady Franklin Visits the Pacific Northwest*, 10.

76 *Daily British Colonist*, Wednesday, 1 July 1874.

77 *1892 British Columbia Directory*, 522.

78 Jan Gould, *Women of British Columbia* (Saanichton, BC: Hancock, 1975), 107.

79 *Victoria Gazette*, 23 December 1859.

80 In her first letter to the *Appeal*, dated "July 27, 1863 Victoria, V.I.," she expressed the desire "if capable, to assist in the swelling its literary merit ... [and that she was] happy to become an occasional contributor."

81 BCARS, Cridge Diary, 6 May 1858; although decades later, in 1891, the Puget Sound Conference of the AME Church was organized, "composed of the Seattle Church, and those in Tacoma, Roslyn, Franklin, Spokane; Portland and Salem, Oregon; and Victoria, Wellington, and Saltspring Island, British Columbia." Esther Hall Mumford, *Seattle's Black Victorians: 1852-1901* (Seattle: Ananse, 1980), 155.

82 BCARS, Add MSS 320, vol. 8, folder 12, Cridge Papers Congregation List, c. 1860-1, 2. Included in this undated list were Madison F. Bailey and his wife Mary Ann as well as Washington and his wife (unnamed) who was described by Sophia Cracroft as having excellent manners and being very light in colour. Alexander and Mary Jane Hamilton as well as Mifflin and Maria Gibbs were also part of Cridge's congregation, along with Gibbs's partner Peter Lester, his wife Nancy, and their two daughters. Augustus and Julia Travis and Emma Segee were also on this list. Initially, a vocal minority consisting of White members of Cridge's congregation complained about "perspiring Ethiopians" sitting next to them in the pews and advocated for a separate section in the church for Black people. See *Victoria Gazette*, 24 August 1858. This did not occur. However, a battle over segregation did take place in the Congregationalist church between Reverend William F. Clarke, a staunch anti-slaver, and Reverend Matthew Macfie. Clarke conducted integrated worship services while Macfie stated he would separate Blacks from Whites. The Colonial Missionary Society failed, at first, to give an opinion on the matter, which undermined Clarke's position. Clarke resigned and returned to Canada West. See P.H. Reid, "Segregation in British Columbia," the Committee on Archives of the United Church of Canada, *Bulletin 16* (1963), 4-15.

83 These women included Clarissa Richard, Mary Ceasar, Mary Carter, Mary Christopher, Ann Gwyne, Julia A. Matthews, Adelina Phelps, Sarah Ann Wheeler, and Sydney E.R. Francis. Amanda Scott was listed as agnostic in the 1891 census. See T6292 1891, BC Census, City of Victoria, Yates Street Ward; but her obituary in the *Victoria Times* said that she was a founder of the First Methodist Church. See *Victoria Times*, 9 September 1919, 26.

84 Beverly Guy-Sheftall, *Daughters of Sorrow: Attitudes Toward Black Women, 1880-1920* (Brooklyn, NY: Carlson, 1990), 162.

85 Lapp, *Blacks in Gold Rush California*; Mifflin Wistar Gibbs, *Shadow and Light: An Autobiography, with Reminiscences of the Last Century* (Washington: N.p., 1902).

86 *Chronicle*, 15 March 1864.

87 *Colonist*, 9 January 1862.

88 *Victoria Daily Chronicle*, 10 July 1863.

89 *Daily British Colonist*, Tuesday, 4 July 1874, and BCARS Oral History Tape, Ada Barnswell Alexander.

90 The Janisaries of Light were mentioned in Ada Alexander's oral history as an exclusively female organization. This is not the case. In Victoria, both men and women belonged to Columbia No. 3 Temple. However, Royal City Temple No. 4 in New Westminster appears to be composed totally of men. The Grand Lodge of the Janisaries of Light was located in

California. See BCARS, "Janisaries of Light," Minute Book, Royal City Temple No. 4, 4 November 1878 - 4 August 1880; Tuesday, 18 November 1879; and *Daily Colonist*, "The Janisaries of Light," Friday, 3 January 1879.

91 *Daily British Colonist*, Wednesday, 8 July 1874.

92 *British Colonist*, Tuesday, 27 August 1867, 2.

93 BCARS, John Lomax Will, dated 27 January 1893, "I give and bequeath all my real and personal estate not hereby disposed of unto my trustee upon trust to permit Mrs. Pierre the wife of John T. Pierre senior of the said City of Victoria during her life to receive the rents and profits of or if she desires to occupy and enjoy my house and the furniture and household effects therein and the piece of land whereon such house stands ... And from and after her decease I direct my trustees to assure the said lot with the house and furniture unto Juinta [Corinthia] the wife of Thomas Alexander her heirs and assigns."

94 Sharon Harley, "For The Good of Family and Race: Gender, Work, and Domestic Roles in the Black Community, 1880-1930," *Black Women in America: Social Science Perspectives* (Chicago: University of Chicago Press, 1990), 172. "The elevated social status denied black domestic workers and laundresses by the larger society and even some members of the black community could be found by them in their families and neighbourhoods."

95 Karen Alexander Hoshal wrote for her daughters an excellent family history of the Alexanders. A copy of this story can be found in the Saanich Pioneer Museum, Saanich, British Columbia.

96 For example, the Pierre family lived at 22 Pioneer Street for at least thirty years, as did the Gants at 125 Blanshard Street and the Lesters at 93 Vancouver Street.

97 These women included Louisa Christopher, daughter of Lucinda and Augustus Christopher, who married George Green, jailer of New Westminster, some time in the 1880s; Emily Turner (Portland); Fanny Deas (Portland); Harriet Freeman (Seattle); Henrietta Barnswell Carter (Vancouver, BC); Maria Stark Wallace (Vancouver BC); and so on.

98 Ada Alexander's oral history tape, BCARS GR 1327, reel no. B2373 13/1890, "Inquest in the Deaths of James and Edward Alexander," T-6428, 1901, BC Census District No. 1, Burrard, Vancouver City.

99 *Daily Colonist*, Tuesday, 23 December, 1880.

100 *Elevator*, 13 September 1873, 3.

101 Ibid., 29 January 1869, 3; BCARS GR 1304, "Probate File of Nathan Pointer."

102 *1892 BC Directory*, 470-1; "Quarter Century Club," *Cayton's Weekly*, Seattle, WA, vol. 2, no. 4, Saturday, 7 July 1917, 4.

CHAPTER 11

Marriage, Family, and the Cooperative Ideal in Saskatchewan

The Telfords

ANN LEGER-ANDERSON

"You, who meant so much to him, and gave him strength for so many years, must feel his loss especially keenly."[1] "You were very close together."[2] "You were indeed a 'both' – a partnership, and it must be hard to pick up and go along alone."[3] "I will always think of the way he and you stood up during the dark days of the 'hungry thirties' ... [It was refreshing] to see ... you and John face up to the problems and never allow yourselves to become embittered."[4] Such comments, evoking the image of a close-knit, dedicated couple, appear in letters of condolence written to Gertrude S. Telford after her husband John M. Telford's death in November 1963 at the age of eighty-five. Also noted was the couple's steadfast shared commitment to principle: "It is no wonder you were both in the vanguard of our movement. Your ideals have been ahead of your times always."[5] These words, referring to decades of involvement in the Saskatchewan Co-operative Commonwealth Federation (CCF), the democratic socialist predecessor of today's New Democratic Party, caught the very essence of the Telfords: their commitment to an ideal. That ideal, which they shared with so many women and men of their generation, can be summed up in one word: "cooperation."

What cooperation meant in practice – how it, as ideal and principle, affected the attitudes, perceptions, and behaviours of its advocates – varied. This chapter examines what cooperation meant in the lives of Gertrude S. and John M. Telford. Of especial interest is their marriage and family life as it emerges from the records deemed appropriately public and hence available for others' scrutiny: the Telford manuscript collections, their respective autobiographical accounts, and an oral history audiotape interview with their daughter, Margaret Thomas.[6] For the researcher interested in the intimate details of the familial, the private, the Telford manuscript collections are frequently disappointing. But they are also telling indicators of what was permissible to note, to give "voice" to. The contents suggest the conventional norms that informed their sort, the constraints and expectations of Victorian and Edwardian Canada, with an emphasis upon the "reserved" – a disinclination to reveal the private. The selection is illustrative, too, consciously or not, of the conviction that service to others and efforts to make the world a better one made up the observable behaviours that counted in one's life and in the historical record. The two autobiographical accounts present a different sort of challenge. We are given narratives of "his" and "her" lives, not merely of "his" and "her" marriages. Each spouse reveals little about the other or about the family unit. Each writes largely about the self – his or her family history, his or her activities, his or her children. This "separateness" contrasts sharply, and strikingly, with the "both," the close-knit relationship perceived by friends. It is as though each spouse, when writing for posterity, chose to draw a boundary and treat the self as private space, to construct a "room of one's own," a place free of intrusion and accommodation.[7]

These sources can be fruitfully used, providing us with insights into many aspects of the lives and times of the Telfords and their pursuit of the "cooperative ideal." The Telford marriage itself comes to life, albeit like a partially completed jigsaw puzzle with tantalizing openings for which no pieces can be found. (And sometimes family life itself is revealed.)[8] We are able to explore the Telfords' understanding of appropriate gender roles and relationships, note the operation of constraints, and glimpse the inner dynamics of their marriage. Given the Telfords' commitment to the ideal of cooperation, the complex issue of "marital power" is of particular significance. As students of family sociology have demonstrated, it is difficult to achieve a fruitful understanding of how couples balance differing interests and make decisions.[9] The Telford marriage provides some revealing insights into the nuances of adjustment and accommodation.

Exploration of the Telfords' relationship contributes to our knowledge in several areas of current interest. It adds to our understanding of marriage and family in the Canadian past.[10] It relates to women's history, to gender history, and to "men's history" (the exploration of the private side of the lives of men).[11] Study of the Telfords also enlarges our understanding of the life experiences of a stratum of Canadian society that is crucial to effective institutional functioning but often receives less attention than is warranted and is often difficult to research: the middle-rank leaders in public and community affairs who are women and men of favoured ethnicity, culturally attuned, well-educated, and middle class. (Indeed, within the local context, these individuals might often be better described as upper-middle class.) Important, too, is the religious connection, in this case the evangelical Protestantism that was such a crucial formative influence for many Anglo-Canadians. As for the Telfords, their contributions were shaped by the discourse of cooperation as it was understood by Ontario-born liberal evangelical Baptists with a Social Gospel orientation.

Who, then, were the Telfords? And what can their lives reveal to us of the once powerful discourse of cooperation and its operation in people's lives? It was on 15 June 1944 that the CCF, the major expression in Canadian politics of cooperation, won the Saskatchewan election, making the "wheat province" the first seat of a democratic socialist government in North America. Gertrude S. and John M. Telford, who were then middle-aged and well-known local community leaders and party activists, looked forward to furthering the principle of cooperation through continued devoted service to the CCF. Gertrude Telford, who described herself with false modesty as an "ordinary Canadian," was, in fact, better known than her husband – quite a rarity in 1944.[12] Her pinnacle as party activist, however, had nearly been reached, her hopes for service soon to be dashed. In contrast, her husband was beginning his upward climb as a loyal and commended CCF public servant. Gertrude Telford did remain a loyal supporter and eventually became a respected policy advisor. In the meantime, she sought other activities, including involvement in such influential women's organizations as the local and provincial Councils of Women.

The Telford marriage, which spanned five decades, was one in which the wife and mother had not only extensive interests outside the home, but also interests that sometimes went beyond conventionally accepted public boundaries for women. Unquestioned was Gertrude Telford's involvement in church work and women's organizations. Here she challenged no norms within her circle. In fact, such participation had become commonplace, even expected, in the worlds of middle- and upper-middle-class English Canada. (Such involvement could also serve as a "substitute career" for an ambitious and energetic woman with an acquiescent husband.) This wife and mother, however, had greater ambitions: paid employment, a graduate university degree, and political engagement. All challenged conventional norms, and her political interests raised several issues about the limits of women's sphere in the 1930s and 1940s. She wanted more than an auxiliary role, which had itself only recently become relatively acceptable, preferring "masculine" options like policy maker and candidate. Such "deviant" behaviour presented a special challenge to the CCF, whose impressive egalitarian discourse was frequently at odds with its (male and female) members' conventional gender expectations.[13]

Gertrude Telford's pursuit of her many and varied interests, like that of a few other women, not only challenged notions (widely shared by both women and men) about what was fitting and proper for women to do, but also raised questions about how much personal freedom was appropriate for a married woman (questions that became even more pressing when she was the mother of young children). In a marriage like that of the Telfords, the sine qua non was the husband's acknowledgment of his wife's relative autonomy. To examine the relationship of Gertrude and John is to take a step towards better understanding one type of marital restructuring that was occurring during the early decades of the twentieth century as North American couples, so diverse with regard to class, ethnicity, religion, culture, and region, responded to changing norms. Their marriage was not an example of the new-style marriage that was so often an object of media attention in metropolitan centres, its hedonistic lifestyle and sophisticated consumerism sharply contrasting with the emphasis that old-style marriage placed upon duty and responsibility.[14] Moreover, their marriage only partially fit the description of new style companionate, or partnership, marriage noted by family sociologists of secular orientation.[15]

Gertrude and John had an earnest, purposeful marriage that commingled Protestant Victorian-Edwardian moral idealism and commitment to service. At its best, such a marriage may be considered from the perspective of a type of Christian marriage – one that has been described as "a permanent union in which the personalities of husband and wife attain enhanced expression and development."[16] This definition denotes loving concern for the other and mutual self-sacrifice – a supportive and intimate interrelationship. It speaks of an enhancement of personality quite distinct in nature from the glorification of untrammelled self-expression or self-absorbed individual fulfilment. To attain such idealized intimacy is, indeed, a difficult, if not impossible, task, even among the most devoted of mortals. But the Telfords' generation was one that attempted to realize ideals. And, significantly, the ideals and principles affirmed in this type of marriage were regarded as having general and universal validity. In fact, they informed conceptions as to what constitutes proper relationships not only in the private sphere, but also in the public sphere.

These values were held by many women and men in North America, including that inter-denominational group of Protestants known as Social Gospelers. These people were committed to liberal theology and to social as well as individual salvation.[17] The American scholar Janet Forsythe Fishburn has emphasized the importance of the family model to Social Gospel spokesmen. "All the Social Gospel men drew their vision of the mutual self-sacrifice and cooperation in a well-ordered society from the Victorian family idea," she contends. "The family, as the most nearly Christianized institution of the social order, set the pattern for personal and social relations ... [in] a fully realized democracy."[18] Among these Social Gospelers were Baptists like the American Walter Rauschenbusch, who rose to international prominence in the early twentieth century. As for the contentious issue of women's status, which was being debated in this era of the "new woman," Social Gospelers considered their Christian religion as affirming a high position for women. "The spirit of Christianity," wrote Rauschenbusch, for example, had elevated the female sex, "and our women are now free and our equals."[19]

Socialists, including Laurence Gronlund, the man whose 1884 book title, *The Co-operative Commonwealth*, expressed the ideal so often cherished by dissidents in an era of exploitative capitalism, were also inclined to affirm the family ideal. "Like so many of the utopians, Gronlund found in the ethics of the family relationship his norm for social relations in the larger community. Self-love and regard for others would be reconciled in devotion to the larger good."[20]

When privileging "family virtues" in the public sphere, writers like Rauschenbusch and Gronlund rarely questioned conventional assumptions about the complementarity of the sexes and the linkage of woman and home; rather, this complementarity was affirmed, and an idealized family life characterized by loving relationships served as a model.[21] Gronlund's position well illustrated the limited revisioning of woman's place in the restructured world of the cooperative commonwealth. He, like socialists generally, espoused, in principle, economic independence for women but shied away from domestic reconstruction and affirmed the sexual division of labour in his cooperative commonwealth. The socialist family ideal, indeed, was frequently indistinguishable from the bourgeois family ideal. For these socialists, however, the abolition of capitalism was essential to the realization of what was, in their eyes, a perfect set of arrangements in which the husband would be the provider, the wife the homemaker. As Gronlund put it: "We emphatically hold, that it is the husband's province to provide for the necessities of his family (much more so in the coming Commonwealth where it will be so much more easy to do it) and that the wife has done her full share of the common labor, when she manages her household properly."[22] Free from financial worries and niggling economies, the wife would, indeed, be queen in her home.

Not surprisingly, male socialists rarely considered how the principle of cooperation might challenge conventional norms of domesticity. The conventional parameters of that discourse have been well delineated by the Canadian scholar David Laycock: "Co-operation signified both more and less than an amalgamation of answers to questions of justice, ethical behaviour, proper limits to power, social organization, and so on."[23] This ideal, about which they spoke in glowing generalities, was to be implemented in the public sphere, where it would be fully realized only after the difficult and extensive restructuring of the political economy. In the domestic economy, however, such upheaval and drastic rearrangement was unnecessary – and unwanted – and even unnatural. Some women, and the occasional man, disagreed. Socialist-feminist women in English Canada, for example, sometimes spoke about the need for a domestic restructuring that included more equitable relationships and sharing of tasks.[24]

Organized farm women who gave voice to an all-encompassing ethos of cooperation – "'The co-operative movement is a mode of life, a spiritual and mental atmosphere'" – sometimes briefly acknowledged the need for greater cooperation and partnership within the home.[25] Even so, cooperation, whether understood from a religious or a secular perspective (or the not uncommon blend of both), most often left conventional norms intact in the private sphere. It was against those norms that the Telford marriage was tested.

That marriage, which was to be "a permanent union" for half a century, began on 4 December 1912 when the couple was married at Nassau Street Baptist Church in Winnipeg. John, who was then thirty-four years old, had journeyed there from Roland, Manitoba, where he was pastor. Gertrude, almost twenty-six, had travelled from rural Saskatchewan where she had been teaching school. After the brief ceremony and a celebratory restaurant dinner with friends, the newlyweds left for Roland, a small community south of Winnipeg. A few weeks later, they moved to Weyburn, Saskatchewan.[26]

The newly married couple did not know each other well. They had spent little time together in friendship or courtship. Two weeks in Roland during the summer of 1912, recalled John, "were about the only courting days we ever had."[27] They had met early in 1910 while students at McMaster University (then in Toronto), and in April, three months after their chance encounter at a skating rink, they became engaged. John was then studying for the ministry and would soon leave for western Canada, where Baptist pastors "were desperately needed."[28] Gertrude was an undergraduate. What they were able to learn about each other during those few months occurred in the regulated settings that then still largely governed relationships between the young men and women of British Ontario. For Gertrude and John those settings were the institutional structure provided by university and church. Family and local community had been left behind in rural Ontario.[29]

It is easy to imagine their mutual attraction in these early months of 1910. Both were pious Baptists who had made the pilgrimage to the central Canadian Baptist citadel of learning, McMaster University, and, as students, experienced crucial, and similar, formative experiences. McMaster, sometimes unfairly disparaged as "'a little school for Baptists,'" provided a good four-year bachelor's degree program as well as theological training and some graduate work.[30] Students there were exposed to diverse points of view. Only its small theological faculty was required to subscribe to regular Baptist tenets, and by 1911 McMaster's (predominantly male) student body of nearly 300 included many non-Baptists. Moreover, McMaster, certainly no intellectual backwater, was experiencing the impact of new, and controversial, currents then emanating from the University of Chicago, a centre of Baptist liberalism in North America.[31] Both John and Gertrude were caught up in the winds of change, which were both theological and intellectual. For example, at the time John was preparing for the Baptist ministry two able proponents of the "higher criticism" of the Bible were teaching at McMaster. These men understood the Bible as conditioned by history and culture and spurned literal interpretation.[32] McMaster, hence, offered John an environment that provided a liberal theological answer to his doubts about orthodoxy. (He also witnessed first-hand a major round in the emerging modernist-fundamentalist controversy that was to drive him from the pulpit and eventually split the Baptists.)[33]

For Gertrude, her daughter recalled, McMaster had been "an eye-opener."[34] A new world opened up. As an Arts student Gertrude was introduced to the challenging perspectives of the fledgling social sciences. She found sociology especially interesting, and she learned from her McMaster mentors about the innovative approaches taught them at the University of Chicago. The new sociology was a heady blend of ethics, religion, and science, and it was reformist in orientation. It was a sociology that drew upon empirical investigation and historical perspective in order to understand and ameliorate social problems. And, so important, this sociology was not only compatible with Christianity, it was its handmaiden.[35] Gertrude's McMaster experiences may have reshaped her Christianity, but they did not shatter her faith. Like John, she questioned orthodox verities and even attended occasional Unitarian services. But the Baptist faith, liberally interpreted, remained her home, and she continued to hold to her dream of becoming a foreign missionary after graduation.[36]

Not only the classroom was important to Gertrude's development. Also significant was the Young Women's Christian Association (YWCA), of which she became president. Student YWCAs were influential and popular organizations. A small minority of university students were female (often of evangelical background), and such young women found in the student YWCAs a "'place of their own'" in which an attractive model of activist Christian womanhood was set forth. "Canadian women students were exhorted to heed 'the call to service,'" Diana Pedersen has written. They were given "an invitation to dedicate their lives to Christian social service and the 'regeneration' of society."[37] The foreign missionary, to which Gertrude aspired, had long been held up as "the ideal career model for budding professionals." Although ordination was, of course, out of the question, Gertrude's attraction to the mission field is understandable. As Pedersen explains, to be a foreign missionary "opened up possibilities of independence, travel, and adventure … otherwise inaccessible to young middle-class women, while … allowing them to appear, both to others and to themselves, appropriately respectable and self-sacrificing."[38]

Besides reinforcing her career goal, the YWCA affected Gertrude in other ways. Its approach to religion reinforced her liberal evangelicalism, with its critical historical approach to the Bible (which she loved to study) and its doctrinal reinterpretation. Her YWCA involvement certainly added to her knowledge of social issues. In 1910 student YWCAs refocused their concerns, and mission-study classes began to investigate Canadian social conditions.[39] The studies used in this class included those of the increasingly prominent James Shaver Woodsworth, a Methodist minister of Social Gospel orientation and superintendent of All People's Mission in Winnipeg, "a settlement house *cum* social-welfare agency" located in heavily immigrant-populated North End Winnipeg.[40] Gertrude herself led a popular study class in a discussion of Woodsworth's *Strangers within Our Gates* (published in 1909), and, over a half century later, she remembered this as having been "a very, very convincing book."[41] Her remark, which is not elaborated, raises questions for the reader today. The book, a major expression of the rapidly mounting concern among Anglo-Canadians about the immigrant flood from continental Europe, displays the ambivalence that was then so common. Appalled by the conditions in which the immigrants lived, Woodsworth called for their amelioration, but he was also worried about the preservation of Anglo-Canadian culture.[42] In later years Gertrude, on the one hand, demonstrated tolerance for, and empathy towards, people of many backgrounds, but, on the other hand, she affirmed the importance of eventual assimilation.

Through the student YWCA, then, Gertrude reinforced the new reform-oriented preoccupation with social conditions and the religious liberalism that was so captivating for questioning minds of her generation. Also important for her development was the emphasis that student YWCAs placed upon organizational skills. Here she found "a supportive female environment for the acquisition of experience in public speaking, fund-raising, and conducting business meetings."[43] The McMaster YWCA seems to have played an important role in shaping Gertrude's adult world view and in providing her with needed skills. Pedersen concludes her discussion of the student YWCAs as follows: "Further examination may yet reveal that the evangelical commitment to usefulness, service, and self-sacrifice helped to shape the work experience of the first generations of college women and the character of the emerging female professions."[44] It is also likely that, for young women like Gertrude, the YWCA shaped their ventures into the world of politics, which was then on the verge of opening up to women.

McMaster University played an important role in the lives of both Gertrude and John. They were groomed for their futures and for each other. Both were deeply committed Baptists of liberal orientation. Still valid for them at this time was the experiential religion and individual salvation of orthodoxy, but they also embraced the increasingly influential Social Gospel with its more liberal theology and its call for social salvation. That position, held by a minority of Baptists, was well summarized in a *Canadian Baptist* editorial: "'It is the duty of the Church to preach the Gospel of the divine love and mercy, and along with it add simultaneously the Gospel of a better day.'"[45] Both had a strong commitment to service, and, in early 1910, both were seriously considering their futures. As John's seminary days drew to a close and he prepared to enter the regular ministry, he was likely aware how useful an asset a wife of the right sort – a woman of faith who could share his burdens and strengthen his ministry – would be to his career. Gertrude's dream had recently been crushed. She had so desperately wanted to become a missionary in India and was likely anticipating a future among her Baptist sisters working with the Telugus on the east coast of India. (Interestingly, had she gone, she would have been, as she so often was, atypical. Few of the Baptist female missionaries had an Arts degree from McMaster.)[46] But her physician refused to issue the requisite health certificate. "I was so shocked," recalled the elderly widow in *Memories*, "but that winter I met John Telford, a young theolog at McMaster, and within 3 months we were engaged."[47] Her long-sought objective unobtainable, she was suddenly presented with the next best option for a devout evangelical Protestant young woman, and she chose it. If not a missionary, then a minister's wife.[48] Both were mature adults. Gertrude had just turned twenty-three and John was nine years older, and they were both single people living within a heterosexist cultural milieu that placed a premium upon marriage and family life.[49] Meeting each other at such a crucial time in their lives must have seemed providential. And the fact that, after just three months, they committed themselves to enter into what was expected to be a lifelong marriage suggests how welcome each was to the other.

They complemented one another in many ways. Gertrude, an excellent student and leader, had a practical yet helpful and kindly nature. John was a modest, gracious man, humorous and fun-loving, more easy-going than Gertrude, and he had no difficulty making friends. As to their backgrounds, each knew and, as young adults, had fled Ontario rural life.

Both were relatively mature, autonomous individuals who had largely made their own way and decided the direction of their own lives – a pattern more common among men than among women. Both, though, had retained family connections, although (again in contrast to the norm) John's were more extensive than Gertrude's. Not all was similar in their backgrounds. When we consider childhood and adolescence (which we glimpse through selective accounts of memories), we see that there were important differences between them. Apparently, John's childhood had been far more secure and happy than Gertrude's, and the presence of many siblings as well as both parents provided him with a close and extensive family network that she, an only child brought up by grandparents, never had.

John was nine years older than Gertrude, having been born in 1878, the eighth of thirteen children in a family of English stock and Presbyterian faith who lived on a farm close to Valens Corners (near Galt). His mother he remembered as a hardworking, uncomplaining woman who bore her trials in quiet calm. His sister, Jean, to whom he was very close, grew up to be an independent woman who largely made her own way and loved to teach and travel. At age sixteen John left the farm for British

Columbia where, for five years, he worked at a variety of jobs. He was never far from family, though, as Jean and brother George were already there. He apparently never jettisoned the upright life of the rural Victorian Ontario of his boyhood. He did, however, put behind him his Presbyterian background, as did his brother and sister. Undergoing the conversion experience so central in evangelical Protestantism, he, like George, followed sister Jean into the Baptist fold. Then, encouraged by her and local Baptist pastors, he decided to become a minister. He returned home, prepared for university entrance at Woodstock College (a Baptist institution), and, after two years of working in mission fields, he went to McMaster. John found his studies arduous and demanding, but he was able to complete them, and he graduated in 1910. He was already thirty-two years old.[50]

His future wife was then twenty-three. Born in 1887 in the Simcoe area, Gertrude Sarah Steinhoff was of English and Pennsylvania-German stock. Her mother soon died from tuberculosis, however, and her father placed baby Gertrude in the care of grandparents. Freed from family obligations and his wife's opposition, he was now free to go to McMaster to study for the Baptist ministry, and he was ordained in 1892. Given the demands of the ministry, his peripatetic life, and the rarity of a father-headed single-parent family, it is not surprising little Gertrude remained with his parents.[51]

Her life on their farm was difficult. "I really had an unhappy childhood," she wrote in her laconic style.[52] Her grandmother's temperament was disagreeable, even cruel, and at age fourteen Gertrude desperately wanted to run away from home. Her grandfather dissuaded her from doing so, telling her he would help her to stand up against her grandmother. School provided an attractive escape from family realities. She loved to read and study and she did very well, her achievements as well as the encouragement of teachers likely bolstering her sense of self-worth in difficult circumstances. That her entry into adulthood was traumatic is suggested by the sketchy picture Gertrude provides in *Memories* concerning several crucial events that followed one upon another. On her sixteenth birthday she suffered a "terrible breakdown" that lasted three months. Then, in a jumbled sequence of events briefly related, came the long-awaited conversion experience that sealed her religious commitment – "When I was eight years of age, I made up my mind that I would be a Christian" – and with it membership in the Simcoe Baptist Church as well as a visit to her father. She also made plans for her future, deciding to attend McMaster, and began to teach school so she could earn money. Able and determined, she succeeded in realizing her ambitions.

She graduated in 1911 with first-class honours in Classics, which she had loved since her schooldays, but also well versed in Bible studies and the exciting new field of sociology.[53] A success story, indeed, that calls to mind her sense of identification with the girls in *Rebecca of Sunnybrook Farm* and *Anne of Green Gables*: "These delightful stories appeal to me much the same way [as *Little Women*]. In each a lonely hearted plucky little girl goes to live with strangers. Both Rebecca and Anne have numerous difficulties in their own impetuous natures and in the frowning correction of elderly Aunts, but each triumphs in growing into capable winsome womanhood."[54]

Both John and especially Gertrude deviated from stereotypical norms of Victorian and Edwardian Canada. And both also had "role models" that likely affected their notions of appropriate "gendered" behaviour, particularly for women. During Gertrude's formative years positive "significant others" in her life appear to have been more often male than female. (Accounts suggest that the most positive female influence within the family was Aunt Edie, a young schoolteacher.) Her father was largely absent from her life, but two men did serve as role models and supportive figures. One was her grandfather. "She loved him dearly," her daughter recounted. Though bad-tempered, he was kind to Gertrude and, as noted, helped her to stand up to her grandmother. She often talked to him and preferred his "men's talk" to the "women's talk" at home, an early indication of Gertrude's interest in the "public sphere."[55] The second male role model was Dr. Thompson, "a very wonderful teacher," who taught her Classics in high school, and not only encouraged her to attend university but also helped her prepare for entrance examinations. He was also influential in another way, for he provided, indirectly, a socialist perspective. Gertrude recalled: "It was known that he was a socialist, although he never mentioned such a thing in high school. But I can look back now and see that in his teaching of Latin and Ancient History he did interpret some things in the light of socialism."[56]

Gertrude, then, had a set of experiences that gave her a more positive view of men and the "masculine" world than that held by many women. What was to happen, though, when she had to deal with a husband in the intimate relationship of "a permanent union" and accommodate herself to the cultural pressures that dictated female subordination within the institution of marriage? Moreover, how would she cope when she was catapulted, by her mate's decision, into an alien environment?

And what about John? What were the implications of marriage for him? The household at Valens Corners had contained strong, positive female personalities. They – and especially his sister Jean, whom he described as "independent" and "ambitious" – likely contributed to his willingness to consider marrying a talented, ambitious woman like Gertrude. But how would he, as her husband, accommodate his wife's efforts to realize her talents and ambitions?

This new phase of their educations soon began. Before their marriage Gertrude had taught school in rural Saskatchewan so that she could repay education debts, and she hated it. Two short stories she wrote at that time are thinly disguised personal accounts of her sense of isolation from all she valued. In one she writes, "All the lonesomeness of the big lonesome prairie, all the longing for companionship, all the heartache for loved ones far away, seemed to close in."[57] In the other, she describes her fictional character Margaret as "often driven to the verge of distraction by the commonplaces of her surroundings," the preoccupation of her neighbours with "the weather, the crops and the neighbors." And she ponders how unattractive Margaret has become – "How much she herself must have lost in that nicety of polish that can come only from the brush of intellect with intellect! Would Donald notice the difference in her? She must look old and faded after such a year." The earnest and serious Gertrude reappears, however, in a telling conclusion: "But then it wouldn't matter so much if she had really accomplished anything."[58] Commitment to service and constructive self-sacrifice were far superior to attractive appearance and sophisticated behaviour. These priorities were ever her twin lodestars, and they were important in shaping her decisions and her responses to John's (perhaps not always wise) decisions.

Gertrude's unwanted return to Saskatchewan occurred within a few weeks. That her new husband knew of her dislike of the province is revealed in *Recollections*: "In those days immediately following our arrival in Roland Gertrude constantly proclaimed her happiness in being out of Saskatchewan, and vowed she never wanted to see it again." Only a month after their marriage, however, John accepted the position in Weyburn, close to where she had taught. It was, he wrote, "rather an unkind trick to play on a bride."[59] It is quite understandable that the still fledgling minister would jump at the first opportunity to escape an entry-level rural parish, but John's attempt at facetiousness, which grates on our contemporary sensibility, barely cloaks the reality: the new husband made the decision on his own, thus asserting his presumed male prerogative in making crucial decisions that would permanently affect his wife and their life together.

Like the ideal helpmate so central in the traditional image of Christian marriage, Gertrude followed her husband – and made the best of it. Weyburn was "a broader field of labor," wrote John in 1913. "We believe that God is leading us to a larger opportunity for service."[60] Then, and later, this was their raison d'être. "When we were married in 1912 we attempted really to do Christian work," wrote his wife.[61] And so they did – for half a century. That Gertrude sometimes chafed at the restraints of a dutiful life is certain, as in comments written in the early 1920s when praising the suitability for girls of "splendid Wild Animals [sic] stories" that acted as "a great safety valve." Who has not felt, she asks, "the call of the wild life of freedom?" "Who has not felt the chaffing of restraint?" But she concludes: "Only in ones [sic] reading can one break away." Daily life and service imposed restraints. "Our lives are bound about by social laws and codes and if we would truly serve our fellow-men and make the most of our own lives we must observe these codes."[62] If John ever experienced such a sense of constraint, he never expressed it. Indeed, as a male, his relatively greater freedom of action combined with his moderate ambitions and (in some respects) easygoing personality lessened the likelihood of such reactions.

As the newlyweds began their life together, they faced the challenge of putting ideals into action – implementing what they understood to be the cooperative ideal of Christianity and living in accordance with their Christian ideal of marriage with its emphasis upon mutuality (while not infrequently exercising the Christian virtue of forbearance).[63] Whether the contemporary debates about the nature, demands, and expectations of marriage directly affected the Telfords is unknown, and it is clear that the hedonistic currents then surfacing in contemporary North American culture ran counter to everything in which they believed. Both Gertrude and John were encapsulated by a liberal evangelical Christian culture within which woman, and even man, was a helpmate, and each sought the other's welfare. Each, recalled daughter Margaret, had real love and concern for the other.[64]

This love for each other was expressed in several ways. As for John, his love for Gertrude came to entail at least partial supportive acceptance of her autonomy. John-the-young-minister had been mildly sensitive to women's inferior position.[65] John-the-fiancé-and-new-husband had certainly been aware that Gertrude was not only talented but also more ambitious than the average Edwardian Canadian woman. Whether he ever thought about the "problems" her talent and ambition might create for him in the future is another matter. (He may have had an inkling of what lay in store, however, when Gertrude toyed with the notion of being an "assistant pastor" during the brief time they were in Roland.)[66] In daughter Margaret's view, when it came to be essential, John made a timely accommodation. The marriage would have collapsed, she believed, had he been unwilling to back Gertrude's later public life strongly. On the whole, she noted, her father accepted the fact that his spouse was his intellectual superior, even though he sometimes found it wounding.[67]

Gertrude, in turn, attempted to avoid hurting him. This required tact, resourcefulness, and an understanding and acceptance of John's expectations (and of social constraints as well). Historical perspective, drawn from both religious and secular sources, helped her to adjust to (sometimes painful) contemporary realities. The Baptist tradition that was so important to her had a more egalitarian ethos than did most variants of Christian tradition, but what had this meant for women? In the early 1930s Gertrude began to address this issue. In 1934 she reminded her Baptist sisters of their heritage: a tradition of "equality," "democracy," "mutual responsibility and co-operation." And for Gertrude, ultimately this entailed equality between the sexes.[68] Three years earlier, in what is apparently her first public acknowledgment of gender inequities, she had asserted that equality of men and women "is a great ideal that we are striving to attain."[69] Secular historical forces were also leading the way to women's equality. Like so many of her contemporaries, Gertrude Telford believed that materialist aspects of historical evolution were providing essential foundations for the improvement of women's status. The "machine," she wrote, "has given women freedom to develop outside the home." And further, it was also "giving us a fine ethical type of marriage based upon mutual love, respect and responsibility."[70] In the here and now, however, in the imperfect world that had so far evolved, one dealt with irritants, difficulties, and obstacles.

A major problem was finances – an issue that is among the most serious causes of family tension and upset.[71] In the case of the Telfords, John's inept handling of family finances caused difficulties. Gertrude had little voice in making major decisions about how John's salary would be spent, and, as daughter Margaret remembered it, her mother was not prepared to fight over the issue of John's money management. In this regard, Gertrude acknowledged her spouse's need to retain control over decision making in an area that he considered to be of pre-eminent importance. Since she doubted his capacity for wise financial management, her acknowledgment of his authority suggests an acquiescence to the conventional norm of female subordination.[72] Poor spending habits began at the outset of their marriage. John's accounts ledger, for example, indicates that their first household was set up in rather a grand style for a fledgling Baptist pastor and his wife and that money was spent rather heedlessly. Expenditures of over $600 for household furnishings nearly match his annual income of slightly more than $900.[73]

Poor financial management, of course, could have advantages, which Gertrude may well have recognized. Insufficient family income, while raising doubts about the adequacy of the male provider, was the only "legitimate" reason for a middle-class married woman to work outside the home. Gertrude, then, could use it to justify her periodic forays into the workforce, while believing that there were other equally, perhaps even more, valid reasons for such participation. It was only in the 1940s, though, that she explicitly stated her views about the importance of paid work for married women. Earlier, in 1937, she had gone no further than to note rather cryptically: "As homes are organized today the husband is, in the vast majority of cases, bearing the burden of providing for the material needs of the family."[74] A few years later she endorsed the idea of the working wife, using an argument that blended duty, responsibility, partnership, and cooperation: "If she [the wife] is awake to her joint responsibility for the home she will feel the necessity for making financial contribution to that home particularly if the husband's pay cheque is insufficient to meet the family's needs." Disappearing was the old partnership of husband and wife as it existed in the agricultural economy: in the modern world "a wife's contribution to the economy of the home is narrowed and restricted."[75] But Gertrude then moved beyond her preoccupation with partnership and cooperation to concern herself with women's freedom: "No woman can be free so long as she's economically dependent upon a man no matter how kind or generous that may be."[76]

Whether Gertrude rethought her own position on working wives or finally decided to speak out, her views are indicative of a woman who was willing to question conventional notions. And, as we shall see, her own forays into employment displayed her increasingly independent spirit. Her efforts, it should be noted, were not always sufficient to keep the Telford family financially solvent. Sometimes her periodic contributions had to be supplemented by gifts and loans from relatives. In 1942 she calculated the total: "I've turned more that [sic] $3000 in earnings into the home since we were married and Aunt Edie has given us probably $2000 more – nearer $3000 I think."[77] (Whether financial assistance came also from John's side of the family is not known.) In the traditional role of male provider, John definitely fell short.

Besides recurring financial problems, the Telfords were beset by family and career crises. Adding to the difficulties they faced during their first twelve years of marriage were the frequent moves necessitated by their search for material security and a niche in the world. This odyssey took them from Manitoba, where they remained for just a few weeks, into the communities of Saskatchewan, the province that became their permanent home. In little more than a decade they moved four times – to Weyburn, Yorkton, Melville, then Pelly. "Starting afresh was becoming common," John remembered thinking in 1924. A final move – to Regina – came two decades later.[78]

The Telfords' four-year sojourn in Weyburn, which began in early 1913, initially appeared to be an auspicious move, at least from John's perspective. Weyburn, located in the southeastern part of the province, had been a rapidly growing community. It had many new buildings and modern amenities and now, with a bustling population of 5,000, was on the verge of becoming a city. John's church, Calvary Baptist, was newly self-supporting and promised what was so important to both Telfords: "a larger opportunity for service."[79] There was at least one feature that was likely attractive in Gertrude's eye. The new charge, unlike the one in Roland, provided a small comfortable parsonage. It was needed, as Gertrude soon became pregnant.

Then tragedy struck. Within thirteen months death twice robbed them of newborn infants: "Ruth," born on 28 October 1913, was likely a premature or stillborn birth; "Margaret Jean," born on 20 November 1914, lived a few weeks.[80] A barely slit veil of silence shrouds the sorrowing couple. John's *Recollections* simply noted their deaths and burials in the city cemetery and did not name them. Gertrude, in *Memories*, briefly mentioned the two newborns and named them in a telling distortion of memory. Her writing down the name "Ruth," although no name had been officially registered, reads as the poignant reminder of a moment some sixty years past when the expectant parents had chosen a name for their joyously anticipated firstborn. As for the second infant, she wrote of "Jean," although the actual name was "*Margaret* Jean."[81]

How they coped with this dual tragedy so early in their marriage can be glimpsed only in the historical record. Even given the then devastatingly high infant mortality rates, two losses so close together would have been excruciatingly painful experiences. There were precious few months for recovery – either of Gertrude's physical health or their mutual emotional stability and mental equilibrium. John did remember the people's "sympathy" and "kindness" in those "sad days,"[82] but they quite likely felt terribly adrift. They were newcomers in a small and isolated city. No favourite family members or long-standing close friends were present during either tragedy, and it is most unlikely that any new close friendships had as yet been made when "Ruth" was lost. Given the pervasive apotheosis of motherhood, Gertrude as grieving wife/mother would presumably receive more attentive sympathy than would her spouse as husband/father. She was, however, somewhat of an anomaly in Weyburn – a woman with a university degree – and, besides, she did not make friends as easily as did her husband. Moreover, both were in a distinctive – and distancing – position because of her and John's status as "the minister and his wife."

And what about the Telfords' own soul-searching? When in her seventies, Gertrude expressed her dislike of the not uncommon belief that responsibility for death lay in divine hands: "These things are not the will of God," she wrote.[83] What she – and John – thought about this difficult question at the time we do not know. Nor do we know whether the loving God of the Telfords' liberal theology made it easier either to adjust to this dual tragedy so early in their marriage or to avoid recriminations. Decades later, Gertrude blamed the "human bungling" of physicians who were "not always wise."[84] Is it also possible that she (or John) had somehow considered her responsible? Had she perhaps done something wrong, or neglected guidelines, or had too little information? Was her history of ill health somehow responsible? Did fault for the deaths lie in conditions and, therefore, in John's hands? It had, after all, been his decision to move to Saskatchewan where medical care was grossly inadequate even by the standards of the day; high maternal and infant death rates attested to this. In fact, the province had an above-average infant mortality rate in an era during which it (like the maternal mortality rate) was far higher than it is now. In 1915, the year Margaret Jean died, there were 1821 deaths, and numbers subsequently increased. Many of these infant deaths were preventable even then, and, in the face of mounting pressures, the Saskatchewan government finally acted, promoting the dissemination of information about known causes of infant mortality as well as instruction in proper methods of infant care.[85] Whether or not the lack of such knowledge on the part of the mother or her physician was responsible, the deaths of the two Telford infants had occurred. And Gertrude Telford, it should be noted, had given birth in far better circumstances than most women, many of whom gave birth in the deplorable conditions depicted in Nanci Langford's chapter. She did give birth at home (then still the norm), but it was a relatively comfortable urban home, not a primitive, isolated homestead, and, as was common among urban middle-class women, she was attended by a physician.[86] This was in Saskatchewan, however, with its grossly inadequate facilities (by Toronto standards), and John had been the one who had made the decision to move there.

Whatever the recriminations, the Telfords did not have the option that couples often consider today as they struggle to come to terms with the loss of a child: divorce. Given the sensibility of the 1910s, it would have been an inconceivable way to deal with remorse and grief, even if the couple in question had not consisted of a devout Baptist pastor and his equally devout wife. Accommodating such a loss, however, was certainly difficult, even when, as in the case of "Ruth," the parents would not have witnessed the death of a lively baby.[87] Compounding pressures for the Telfords after that initial tragedy was Gertrude's almost immediate second pregnancy. How anxious they must have been. That Gertrude and John were under stress during the summer of 1914 is suggested when we read of their taking a delayed "wedding trip" to Vancouver, "made possible" Gertrude recalled, "only through the generosity of John's brother Dr. Robert who sent us a hundred dollars."[88] That Gertrude's Aunt Edie accompanied them may indicate the need Gertrude had for the support of a beloved relative,[89] and they likely spent much time with John's relatives who had moved to British Columbia. The trip was, at best, a very brief respite from their woes.

To add to their difficulties, the Great War had begun while they were still in Vancouver, and it soon turned into a long and brutal conflict. Canada's participation in that war served to test the nature of the cooperative spirit of the Telford relationship, for Gertrude and John took opposing positions. John was but one of many Baptists – men and women who had identified with the peace tradition within their church and looked favourably upon the early twentieth-century peace movement – who found themselves in a quandary when war came. Like most, he concluded that the Allies were upholding principle against the Kaiser's onslaught, and they reluctantly supported the war as a tragic necessity.[90] In contrast, Gertrude refused to abandon the pacifism she had espoused since the Boer War, when her grandfather told her, in response to her questions, that the local boys marching off to fight might be killed. She remained an avowed pacifist throughout the Great War, and in Weyburn she came to be regarded, according to her daughter, as "quite beyond the pale."[91] On the question of Canada's participation in the Great War, then, husband and wife were able to agree to disagree, but they left no record of how they resolved an issue that was a potentially explosive one, given John's prominent position in a community that enthusiastically endorsed the Canadian war effort. One can suggest, however, that on a public issue that involved a matter of conscience and unswerving commitment to principle, especially given the Baptist heritage of ambivalence towards war, John felt compelled to acknowledge his wife's autonomy.

While accommodating their differences around war, Gertrude and John had to cope with the second tragedy, Margaret Jean's death in late 1914. For the Telfords, 1915 is a missing year – a year of grief that was to be forever buried in their minds. The following year saw a very active Gertrude Telford. As was to happen in later crises, she sought to absolve grief and alleviate disappointment through work – a tonic taken by many people – and one that accorded well with her ethos, which placed service to others foremost. She made her initial foray into the labour force, working as a substitute teacher at Weyburn Collegiate, her paycheque a welcome addition to the family income since the wartime decline in Baptist finances meant a lower salary for John.[92] Church work, always of importance in her life, also occupied Gertrude, and it even provided her with a welcome opportunity to escape the confines of Weyburn. In early 1916 she was able to visit the West Coast, travelling to Vancouver to attend the second annual meeting of the Board of Women's Work of the Baptist Union of Western Canada.[93] (Interestingly, although concerned about women's status in the Baptist Church, she was apparently uninterested in the provincial effort to secure women's suffrage, which was then in the final stages of victory.) After her return, she became involved in the Weyburn Baby Conference held 7 to 9 August 1916. This clinic, the second to be held in the province, was an example of the new provincial effort to reduce infant and maternal mortality. It was without question an exceedingly painful experience for Gertrude, and, in fact, she was involved only because of an emergency. The original organizers, she recalled, "were unable to act due to absence and accident and the organizing devolved upon the unwilling shoulders of the writer."[94] Seen from that perspective, her involvement was another expression of her commitment to serving others, in this case, helping to prevent the tragedy of needless infant deaths. Meanwhile John was kept busy with his two charges.[95] No better antidote than work.

At the end of this busy year the Telfords were preparing to leave Weyburn for another small Saskatchewan city: Yorkton. John had been invited to preach at the First Baptist Church there, and he was then asked to serve as the new minister. Whether Gertrude had a voice in John's decision to go to Yorkton is unknown – and unlikely, given what we know about decision making in the Telford family. John simply wrote: "The invitation was accepted."[96] Yorkton, which was 151 miles northeast of Weyburn, appeared to be a positive move. The Baptist church was a bigger one, their home was more commodious, and the community was larger. And, besides, nearby were wooded areas, a pleasant relief from the unrelentingly open prairie that Gertrude so disliked. Again, pastor and wife set out to do their "Christian work," wholeheartedly devoting themselves to the local church and community, and becoming leaders in the work of the Yorkton Social Services Council. John became district organizer for the Victory campaign while the spouses continued to agree to disagree about the war.[97]

There was joyous celebration, too. In June 1917 Gertrude Telford delivered a healthy baby girl, who was given Gertrude's favourite name, Margaret. The Telfords were now truly a family in their eyes and in those of their peers, for only a few cosmopolitan North Americans at the time considered a marriage complete without children. The residents of a small city like Yorkton, like most people, and like the Telfords' faith, privileged the family. Their happiness was darkened, though, as John's mounting difficulties with his congregation over his liberal understanding of the Baptist faith shattered hopes of a secure future in the church.[98] His ministerial career ended as the new decade neared. Already uneasy about the recurring fundamentalist-modernist controversy among Baptists, and doubtful about the future of the Baptist denomination in the West where its members were relatively few in number, scattered, and divided, John concluded that accepting one of the invitations he received to minister to another congregation was not the answer. He also briefly considered pursuing his Christian commitment by undertaking work in the nondenominational YMCA, but he then rejected it because he felt out of touch with boys.[99] He opted instead for a totally different career path and decided to become a lawyer, doing so in the old-style apprentice system then nearing its end.

Since both spouses discuss the momentous issue of John's career shift in 1919, we can examine the dynamics of the decision-making process in their marriage as recalled in their respective reminiscences. That emphases vary, that sometimes differing versions of events are found, should not be surprising, and it suggests not only distinctive perspectives but also the peculiarities of memory. There is a striking similarity between the accounts, however: neither says anything about what must have been a wrenching aspect of the shift – the jettisoning of John's career-based Christian service. To leave the ordained ministry, which required a special sense of vocation and commitment to enter, could not have been an easy choice even given John's frustrations with his congregation.

How John initially got the idea of becoming a lawyer is remembered differently by each spouse. In Gertrude's version a lawyer friend of John's suggested he study law and told him about the Melville law firm (run by friends), which needed another person in the office.[100] As John remembered it, he approached two lawyer friends about the possibility of studying law, was encouraged to do so, and was referred to the Melville firm.[101] Regardless of the truth of the matter, does Gertrude's version hint at her reluctance over the venture, while John's version shows his need to see himself as the actor, the initiator? The differing recollections of the decision-making process are quite interesting. Here the critical moment came when John was invited to study law at the law firm in Melville. Gertrude's recollection is brief: "Well, John came home from Melville, came in the front door and said, 'Well, see your lawyer husband, we'll go to Melville.'"[102] John fills in details:

> When in the office with Mr. McKim a phone call came from Gertrude informing me that two or three letters had come for me ... [which offered him positions as pastor]. It appeared to me at that moment that the opportunity of making a clean break with it all had come ... I hinted such a step to Gertrude, who pretty well understood my feeling. A quite definite arrangement had been made with Mr. McKim ... At home again the next few days we re-thought the whole affair. Our plans were fully made to make the final break. We did.[103]

In such a crucial matter – making a major change of career when a middle-aged man with family responsibilities – John indicates that he and Gertrude engaged in extensive discussion. It is clear, however, even in his account, that he was the major, and perhaps sole, decision maker. He had already "a quite definite arrangement" before he and Gertrude "re-thought the whole affair." Gertrude certainly seems to have regarded his announcement when he arrived home as final, but her extremely laconic writing style may possibly hide some genuine reconsideration.

John's "career crisis" is an example of how the "cooperative spirit" was affected by the weight of patriarchal tradition. Gertrude deferred, willingly or not. Practical realities and conventional assumptions together reinforced traditional patterns that placed the ultimate decision-making authority in male hands. The choice was a crucial one, the sort that involved serious issues of balancing of interests, exercise of authority, and power relationships, and in which the decision would greatly affect each individual spouse, the partnership, and the family unit.[104] In this "career crisis" issue, what was at stake was the future of the "breadwinner," the "male provider." Extensive discussion and consultation with the wife/mother/homemaker might occur, and this appears to have been as far as exercise of the ideal of cooperation was taken when John decided to go into law. The man controlled. The woman's task was to support and encourage. John's wife performed her expected duty: "Gertrude stood by my side. 'Anything and anywhere,' she said. I felt strong."[105]

To Melville the Telford family went. The small town twenty-seven miles southwest of Yorkton became their home from January 1920 until September 1924. Initially they had financial difficulties, and Gertrude made another of her periodic forays into paid work to augment family income. For this, her second temporary job, she had to leave home, which was most unusual behaviour for a married woman with a small child, and it hints at the severity of the Telfords' financial problems. Taking baby Margaret with her, she went to British Columbia where John's relatives lived and teachers were needed. She earned "something over $600" – a welcome addition to the family coffers – by teaching a session of school. Subsequently, their finances gradually improved. As John's knowledge of the law, and his contribution to the firm, increased, his income went up. Also, the Telfords received help from Gertrude's Aunt Edie, who sent them a good-sized sum – $500 – towards a future home. Unfortunately, after the Telfords purchased their home John found out he would be forced to seek permanent employment elsewhere because lawyers had become too plentiful in Melville.[106]

In the meantime, however, John had accomplished his goal. During these Melville years he was very busy, working by day in the law firm, then reading law until midnight, but he successfully met the challenge of becoming a lawyer despite the fact that he was already a middle-aged man. In *Recollections*, he recalled his initial feelings about the new undertaking: "Here I was near the age of 42, a home to keep, a wife and child to provide for. Starting once again at the bottom. How I mustered the courage to take the plunge I do not know." He then gave credit to his wife-cum-helpmate: "Gertrude was standing by my side. Never did she flinch or falter. So we started on together. Without this it never could have been done."[107] But done it was, and soon their future appeared full of promise. Their family increased when a second daughter, Mabel, was born in 1921. (She, like Margaret, would live to maturity.) Their church life, always so important to them, was far more satisfactory than it had been in Yorkton. In their new locale Baptists were few in number, so the Telfords, who in any case disliked artificial Protestant denominational boundaries, participated in the Melville Union Church, with its diverse membership. John was also able to keep his hand in the ministry and quite enjoyed working as a relief minister, free from the demands of a regular pastorate. Gertrude's familiar church tasks continued as she became active in the Sunday school and the Ladies' Aid and Missionary Society.[108] "We were happy and contented," wrote John.[109] Gertrude corroborated his assessment (albeit with qualification): "in many, many ways those were happy years."[110]

Then came another major readjustment. In October 1924 they moved again – this time to Pelly, fifty miles northeast of Yorkton as the crow flies, and close to the Manitoba border, an isolated Saskatchewan village of a few hundred people where a position had opened up in the Pelly branch of a Yorkton law firm. Its small businesses served the local agricultural community, and the train stopped there twice daily. Pelly was little more than a decade old, a village with town pretensions and the absence of most urban comforts, an enclave of British and Canadians surrounded by a countryside dominated by European immigrants.[111] The move was another horrific shock for Gertrude, who was once again cast in the role of faithful helpmate. Many decades later, in *Memories*, she wrote: "It took me a while to become accustomed to a village ... But I learned to like Pelly very, very much."[112] Her love of Pelly was evident in a comment she made in 1941: "I have loved its beauty and the courteous kindly people with a passionate devotion."[113] In 1924, however, she had hated John's decision to move there but had remained silent. John recalled: "I did not realize ... that Gertrude so greatly disliked facing life in a small frontier town. She said nothing ... My thoughts were so intently on the new life ahead that I never thought of liking or disliking the place in which we were to live."[114]

From John's perspective, that of a family man embarking upon a new profession in middle age, the only important matter was the opportunity to pursue his career and to be able to function as male provider. Gertrude's awareness of his critical need of employment and his lack of other options may have contributed to the (likely wise) veil of silence that cloaked this talented and well-educated woman's initial intense dislike of yet another move and, what was even worse, relocating to a place like Pelly. One wonders whether she, or John, having moved so frequently during the first twelve years of their marriage, had any inkling that this tiny isolated village would be their home for two decades.

As before, the Telfords settled quickly into their new locale and soon rose to positions of community leadership, but now their primary identification was that of village-lawyer-and-wife. Expected – and expecting – to serve the community, they became very active in local affairs. Still committed to "Christian work" as liberal Protestants, they kept separate from the small local group of conservative Baptists (John declining their invitation to serve as pastor), instead becoming active in the Pelly congregation of the liberally oriented United Church of Canada, the denomination then being established as a result of (primarily) the merger of most Methodists and many Presbyterians. Each served in accordance with their talents. Organizationally minded John initially helped with fund-raising for the proposed church building and, later, undertook a variety of tasks. Gertrude, always the educator, handled the Sunday school and became leader of Canadian Girls in Training and Golden Keys, both of which sought to mould Christian girlhood. In time, their daughters also became active, and each served as organist.[115] During their many years in Pelly the Telfords also served their fellows in numerous community tasks, and John undertook a public role, as befitted his gender and professional status, serving as a village councillor and overseer.[116]

Until the early 1930s John's salary was a good one, and Gertrude and the girls were able to enjoy the material comforts and amenities then available to a successful village lawyer and his family. That these were far below the 1920s urban standard of middle-class comfort goes without saying. The house in which they lived for most of their years in Pelly was quite nice by village standards. "Markham Cottage," which they purchased and enlarged, had been built by a well-to-do English couple on an attractive acreage. Its domestic technology was not up to urban levels, but Gertrude now had a large garden. She had always loved the orchards and gardens of Ontario and was finally able to enjoy the pleasures of cultivating her own domestic garden. Prosperity also allowed John to purchase one of the automobiles that were becoming so attractive, especially to the middle classes outside urban centres. His first car was a Model T Ford, and it was followed by two other Fords, a Model A, and then, shortly before financial catastrophe struck, a 1930 Model B. The Telford family could now enjoy greater mobility – so long as the dreadfully poor roads were passable. And John was ready for a jaunt. Automobile ownership, it should be noted, opened up a new area of possible contestation about decision making and marital power as questions arose about who would drive the family car and who would decide where, and when, to drive.[117]

Whatever the struggles, if any, over use of the family Ford – the records are silent – the Telfords possessed a major symbol of 1920s consumerism, and one that most people could not yet afford. The improving material circumstances of the Telfords in the latter 1920s, however, were made bittersweet by tragedy. On 22 May 1927, John "Jackie" Lyman, the Telfords' three-day-old baby, died. He had been their eagerly awaited son. "Truly now late in life our family was complete – a son was born," Gertrude wrote decades later in her heartrending account, "The Happiest Day of My Life." In it she described her elation, then remarked how "kind" the doctor had been to allow her son to remain with her and described how she felt with him by her side – the "greatest of all joy." "And so the day passed," she wrote. "And night fell and peace descended on the earth. One day of perfect happiness. My son, my only son died early Sunday morning aged three days."[118] His death she considered another testament to "human bungling." John wrote nothing about his son's death in *Recollections*, although, as noted, he did mention briefly the loss of his first- and second-born infant daughters. Even in 1962, his grief was seemingly too deep to break the silence. The one glimpse we have of John's feelings is his purchase, at a time when the family could ill afford the expense, of a small tombstone. It was a final memorial to the son they never raised and was symbolic of an excruciatingly difficult period in their lives. Coping with "Jackie's" death meant not only dealing with a third infant death but also coming to terms with a family that would likely always be in a sense "incomplete," as a son was not only desperately wanted but also was considered an essential part of a complete family. Gertrude and John, after all, were middle-aged parents, and, at age forty, Gertrude was nearing the end of her child-bearing years. And, to add to their burden, they needed the strength to console and support two little daughters, six-year-old Mabel and ten-year-old Margaret, in a time of tragedy.

Our glimpses of the Telfords' family life and of Gertrude's and John's relationship during their two decades in Pelly suggest an active nurturing household. Although terribly disappointed by the absence of a son in the family, Gertrude and John never saw their daughters as somehow "second-best." They were loving parents wanting the best for Margaret and Mabel, who were, recalled the elder daughter, "treasured children."[119] They sought to provide the two girls with a culturally and intellectually stimulating environment suffused by the liberal evangelical ethos, and they encouraged them to develop their talents and interests. Despite their straitened economic circumstances during the worst of the Great Depression, the doting parents were determined to secure the best possible futures for their girls and were adamantly committed to ensuring university educations should their daughters want them.

About the specifics of Gertrude's – or John's – actual child-rearing methods, the records are silent. Given today's growing interest in fatherhood, one cannot help but wonder how active a father John was and whether his fathering role was as secondary in the parenting process as was common among so many middle-class families during the 1920s and 1930s. One wonders, too, whether he was more present as a father in Pelly village, where work and home were barely separated and his schedule less demanding, than in Melville.[120] As for Gertrude, one wonders what pressures this only child, now a highly educated woman, felt as she sought to be a good mother in small – and remote – communities. That her views and behaviours as a mother were shaped by the proliferating advice literature emanating from the metropolitan centres appears certain, given her education, her involvement in the baby clinics and Saskatchewan Homemakers' Clubs (SHC), and occasional statements in CCF literature.[121]

Another interesting question is that of the family dynamics of the Telford household, one about which the record provides occasional hints. Family relationships appear to have been affected by the sharply different temperaments of the two daughters. The elder, Margaret, was more docile and even-tempered than was Mabel, and, given the glimpses we have, there is no reason to question her description of Mabel as a somewhat headstrong sort who was "agin things." Mabel also disliked her mother's absences, recalled Margaret, who was herself apparently not bothered by them and who, as a young teenager, helped out at home when necessary.[122] Perhaps age as well as temperament explains the different reactions. Mabel was likely about ten years old when the absences increased, for in the early 1930s Gertrude Telford was very active as provincial president of the SHC (and then she undertook a major CCF commitment). No more is revealed, however.

What we are able to glimpse of Gertrude's and John's lives together in Pelly tells us more about Gertrude than it does about John. As for Gertrude, wife/mother/homemaker, there is something of a deliberate, almost desperate, quality in her drive and determination to engage in additional tasks after her infant son's death. To occupy herself with her beloved church work was seemingly not enough to alleviate the pain, and she now attempted to realize a long-desired personal goal while also extending her service commitments.

Gertrude Telford

She decided that the time had come to attain what had been her dream for nearly two decades: a master's degree in sociology from McMaster University. She was able to make use of a correspondence program (far more unusual then than now) that had been established at her alma mater, and for her thesis she conducted a community study of the neighbouring rural municipality of Livingston. She received her degree in 1931, enjoying the distinction – and attention – of being the first woman to receive a degree from the newly relocated McMaster, now in Hamilton. In this era Gertrude Telford's accomplishment was commendable. Few women in Canada had even a bachelor's degree. Moreover, she was a middle-aged woman, wife of a professional man, and mother of a young family – for such a woman, a graduate degree was an extraordinary accomplishment. John himself played a supportive role. In fact, he did not merely acquiesce in her decision to study for her master's, but he also actively cooperated in the final stages. He pitched in to help, even staying up all night to type the final copy. Together they drove to Ontario for the convocation – the drive itself being an adventure, given the wretched state of the roads – and made it quite a celebration, taking a long-deserved holiday and visiting relatives.[123]

In the meantime Gertrude Telford's service-oriented ethos had prompted her initial interest in the well-respected SHCs. They were already widespread in the province when she helped to organize one in Pelly in 1926. Following her infant son's death, she became more fully involved, participating in district work, and then in 1930 she was chosen provincial president, a post she held until 1934. As president she headed an organization with extensive outside links, the provincial SHC being affiliated with the Federation of Women's Institutes of Canada, the largest organization of rural women in the Dominion. It, in turn, had international connections.[124] Gertrude was now very much involved in a prominent institutional expression of respected and approved "women's work" that privileged homemaker and mother. Rather ironically, it was Gertrude's foray into this "women's work" that first took her away from home on frequent occasions – a pattern that would continue for the rest of the Pelly decades.

Beginning in 1934, after she finished her stint as president of the non-partisan SHC, Gertrude became involved in the "man's world" of politics. She did so in tandem with John, and the work they did on behalf of the CCF was the major cooperative effort of their lives together. Looking back upon the 1930s, John recalled that he and Gertrude had expended their energies and what money they could spare "with no regrets" for a cause "we could not, dare not, give up."[125] The Telfords' interest in dissident politics had roots that predated the CCF, going back to at least the Yorkton years, when John had attended a Progressive convention. In the 1921 federal election, however, it was Gertrude who voted for the voice of agrarian protest, the Progressives, while John opted for the Liberal candidate. And so they cancelled each other's vote, an event that she later described as "funny." Subsequently, Gertrude supported the Progressives and campaigned for Milton Campbell, who remained the Progressive MP for Mackenzie federal constituency during the 1920s.[126]

The Progressives, who were short-lived as a political force, had been but one of the dissident voices in the 1920s, and these grew in strength with the onset of the Great Depression. Then, in Calgary in 1932 came the founding convention of the Co-operative Commonwealth Federation. It has been aptly described in a recent popular history as "a loose coalition of farm, labour and socialist groups, the culmination of several decades of effort by scattered and fragmented progressive groups to win a voice for farmers, workers, the poor and the elderly."[127] The following July saw the assembling in Regina of some 130 delegates at the first national convention, where the Regina Manifesto, the CCF policy statement, was approved. Its focus was the political economy, its objective "the establishment in Canada of a Co-operative Commonwealth in which the principle regulating production, distribution and exchange will be the supplying of human needs and not the making of profits."[128] Its ideal world was one of freedom, equality, justice, and peace, where cooperation, not competition, would be the ruling principle in all spheres of life.

The CCF became the focal point of the Telfords' lives. Gertrude, John, and their daughters (Margaret, in particular) devoted themselves to the cause. They, like many activists, saw the CCF as "applied Christianity." It was the Social Gospel in action, the instrument for realizing the cooperative ideal, the essence of the Christian message with its emphasis upon the Fatherhood of God and the brotherhood of man. The Telfords were ever ready to serve, their contribution being a cooperative sharing of complementary abilities and interests. John's strength was in his organizational skills and his knowledge of law. He assisted the Pelly constituency in various ways and did extensive work on the local level for the 1944 campaign. During the Pelly years, Gertrude was a more prominent CCFer than her spouse, who sometimes helped her. (Although not always – she had, for example, planned to attend the 1933 Regina convention but had to stay home because of her daughter's illness.)[129] There were few hats that Gertrude Telford did not wear as she sought an influential voice in the party. She was one of the earliest local organizers, and the Telford home was the local "CCF hotel" for several years. She was involved in the provincial-level organization, attending her first provincial convention in 1936; she was elected chair in 1942, and she also served as a member of the provincial council and executive. Always the educator, she worked hard to make the CCF summer camps a reality, devoting most of her attention to managing the Crystal Lake camp, 1937-42, assisted by John and their two daughters. And she wrote political pamphlets, study lessons, stories, plays, skits, radio broadcasts, and election appeals. She also wanted something barely within reach of a woman in the 1930s: elective office. In the 1938 provincial election she ran as the CCF candidate in Pelly constituency. She lost, but gained experience and made a good showing, and she looked forward to victory in the next election. Her hopes were dashed.[130]

That story is linked with the political culture of her era. Given her commitment to service, ambition, and testing boundaries, it is not surprising that Gertrude Telford sought to be a leader and decision maker. However, she confronted a political culture that welcomed only those women who accepted a subordinate position as auxiliary workers and left leadership to men.[131] The CCF, as was often true with third parties, attracted more activist women than did the established parties. Even so, women were a minority – numbering twenty-one out of a total of 131 delegates at the 1933 convention, for example.[132] The lengthy Regina Manifesto itself only briefly noted women, calling for a labour code that would include "equal reward and equal opportunity of advancement for equal services, irrespective of sex."[133] This inattention mirrored societal apathy, and, in its practices, the CCF was more likely than not to frown upon women who stepped out of their auxiliary role.

Gertrude Telford's responses expressed her "mentalité." Although becoming more concerned about women's rights issues over the years, she never identified with feminism, regarding it as too "intense" and as pulling men down: this was at odds with her paramount values of partnership, cooperation, conciliation, and gradualism.[134] In the political sphere her ideal was women's equal partnership, and she considered women as well as men to be responsible for the inequitable status quo. Women had to make the effort to become full-fledged citizens and strive for acceptance. In 1938 her campaign flyer had stated: "I feel profoundly that women have been shirking responsibility, that they have not been taking their fair share of the difficult task of governing the country." Then, shifting ground, she argued that their representation was "a matter of common justice." Moreover, as legislators, they would contribute "that good judgement, that knowledge of detail of management that makes for successful homes."[135] In 1941 she found out just how unfairly things could be stacked against women. She confidently sought the nomination in Pelly constituency for the provincial election that was expected to be called the following year, but unexpected opposition gave the nomination to a last-minute rival – and male – candidate. "The whole attack was made on the *Woman*," she wrote, and then noted "a second feature of the attack but under cover is that it was a nationalist move by the Ukranians [sic]."[136] Numerous episodes of unjust treatment of CCF women followed, and nearly two decades later, she wrote sorrowfully: "There was a time when many of us thought the CCF was to be the answer to women's dream of justice and equality."[137] She had herself been a woman of perseverance, and time and again she had swallowed her resentments; she did not dwell upon her disappointments but negotiated the circumstances as best as she could.

When practising the "art of the possible," Gertrude Telford was also one of the small minority of women forging atypical relationships with men. What may rightly be called her political career entailed deportment that ran counter to the stereotypically conventional notions of gender roles and relationships held by middle- and upper-middle-class English-Canadians, and she posed a challenge that differed from that of being an "absent mother." Now she was not merely involved in an expanded world of "women's work," which required periodic trips away from home as had been the case when she served as president of the SHC; rather, she acted within the public world of men and dealt with male associates on a fraternal basis. She liked to discuss issues with them; in fact, even as a farm girl this politically oriented woman had preferred "men's talk." Gertrude not only campaigned for, but also became a friend of, Milton Campbell, and, during the 1930s, after his move to Ontario, they corresponded, their letters filled with discussions of politics and current events.[138] She also became a campaigner for, and friend of, a later MP in Mackenzie federal constituency, the CCFer Sandy Nicholson. Within the provincial CCF she counted among her friendships one with Carlyle King, which was based upon a shared understanding of the CCF cause.[139] Such departures from convention – long hours of political discussion, work relationships, and friendships with men – was accepted by John, though one suspects the "cooperative spirit" was sometimes sorely tested on both sides. He seemingly preferred socializing with "the ladies" to talking about politics and public affairs. He did, however, recognize his spouse's partial autonomy, and apparently she was the one who made the decisions affecting her political career. That she had come to think of herself as a potential candidate is suggested in a letter written to Carlyle King prior to the federal election of 1945: "While one is considering these large questions, one must consider all possibilities."[140] The context suggests that she had in mind political considerations.

John's recognition of Gertrude's partial autonomy was one thing. Adjustment of conventional household arrangements to facilitate her political aspirations, however, was another. The cooperative ideal was implemented in their domestic economy in a gingerly and minimal fashion – one that entailed no significant restructuring of duties. Like the vast majority of men, progressively oriented or not, John looked upon most household chores as "women's work." Gertrude, who occasionally expressed her views on the subject, found it praiseworthy when, in special circumstances, men helped out or took them over. That this was rare is suggested by her vivid memory of prominent CCF leader J.S. Woodsworth and candidate Judge Stubbs doing the dishes during their three-day stay at the Telfords' when the 1933 federal by-election campaign was underway. She also commended the men for doing their share of housekeeping tasks at Crystal Lake. Regular assistance, however, was not to be expected, and in conciliatory fashion she excused them from regular duties because they were already "so busy."[141] How, then, given her belief that all aspects of life should be governed by the principle of cooperation, could that principle be applied to household tasks? Her solution was illustrated in a skit she wrote, entitled "Co-operation in the Work of the Home." This skit, which appears to be loosely based upon experiences in the Telford household, depicts a restructuring of household tasks that frees the mother to take an enjoyable job and add to the family income. It is, however, the teenage son and daughter who take on the household chores. "Dad" is portrayed as too busy to help out.[142] As for "Dad" in real life, John infrequently did more than the "heavy" chores normally considered to be "men's" domain although he was described by a neighbour as a man able to "shift for himself."[143] Gertrude appears to have done all she could to make sure he did as little "shifting" as possible, making arrangements so that his comfortable routine was minimally disturbed by her absences from home after the late 1920s. The Telfords' eldest daughter, Margaret, helped with Mabel's care, and both girls cooked. Looking after the two girls, then, was not an onerous task for John, especially with his law office and neighbours nearby. In contrast, Gertrude was busy day and night with her double load, and wrote of "the extreme hard work that we knew in a small town, where ones [sic] day began often enough at five in the morning and ended at twelve at night."[144] She worked quickly and without fuss, and kept the house neat and clean, recalled daughter Margaret, but she was often very tired.[145] In an economical fashion, then, she sought to provide for her own family the clean and comfortable home that was so important a part of a proper physical environment, the material domestic space that would assist the creation of a generation fit for cooperation.

Although willing to hand over mundane household chores, if only she could find someone to do them, during the Pelly years, Gertrude did not consider as desirable any drastic restructuring of her central role as homemaker and mother. The first was a sort of necessary evil; upon the second she placed a premium. And her public statements, a mirror of private convictions, were common currency. In them were familiar phrases: "the maker and sustainer of the home – the mother";[146] "a woman's first responsibility and privilege is in making a home and caring for her children."[147] Clichés they were, but such phrases distilled the essence of the discourse of motherhood so pervasive from the late nineteenth century into – and beyond – the mid-twentieth century. The words suggested the power and authority that, in this discourse, were ideally part of what was construed as woman's rightful sphere. Gertrude Telford's affirmation of this position is well illustrated in her skit on cooperation in the home, for woman-as-mother-and-homemaker has the responsibility for calling family members together to deal with a problem, and she presides over the discussion.

In fact, woman as mother/homemaker/wife had a central role to play in the creation of the cooperative commonwealth. Gertrude, and like-minded advocates of cooperation, gave a new twist to conventional assumptions. Now the "queen of the home" (as she would have been styled in the nineteenth-century discourse of domestic ideology that was being modernized) was responsible for advancing the principle and practice of cooperation. Of greatest importance was the mother's duty to raise children who would become well-adjusted adults, instilling in the next generation a sense of purpose and capacity for self-expression and service – qualities essential for the creation of the socialist society that was cooperation writ large.[148] So important in Gertrude's eyes was cooperation and its inculcation in children that in the 1950s she endorsed day-care facilities, in part because in them children would have additional opportunities to learn how to cooperate with others.[149] Her second reason was that they allowed the mother greater freedom. How much she had revised her other views is uncertain. For most, if not all, of her life, she did affirm a set of notions that accorded largely with convention. Woman as mother/homemaker/wife properly focused upon her children's development, nurtured her husband, and created a wholesome material and ideological environment – one that was comfortable, attractive, healthful, and harmonious. Now, though, it was done in the name of cooperation.

This was a new twist to familiar notions, and one that used a secular vocabulary, the spiritual having become implicit for those of liberal Protestant bent like the Telfords.

As we have seen, the implementation of cooperation within the home, as Gertrude Telford understood it, entailed several behaviours. A central feature was the economic partnership of wife and husband, the importance of which has been noted.[150] In the early 1940s she once again had the opportunity to play the role of financial rescuer for the family. Initially the Pelly years were prosperous, as noted, but the "dirty thirties" became ever more a grim reality in their lives as John's income dwindled, and the advent of the Second World War brought no economic upturn. Then a crop failed. In 1942 economic pressures heightened for the Telfords because Mabel now decided that she wanted to go to McMaster. She, like Margaret, was then working in Ottawa, but, unlike her older sister, who graduated from the University of Saskatchewan in 1938, she had never attended university. Mabel had left Pelly at the first opportunity, taken a business course in Regina, and worked there before moving to Ottawa.[151]

Gertrude, now fifty-five years old, went back to work. This time it was a two-year absence, and in a distant city – Ottawa. Canada's capital had several advantages. It was there that she had connections, jobs were available, and her beloved daughters would not be far away (Margaret in the capital, Mabel in Hamilton). Letters written in November 1942 shed light on her decision. Earlier Gertrude had wanted to move east with John, but, as she lamented in a letter to her friend Milton Campbell, "Mr. Telford has always opposed the idea of our moving Eadt [sic] and naturally I would not stay in the East if he were determined to stay in the West."[152] Her departure, as a temporary solution to insurmountable problems, was another matter, as she wrote to Margaret: "It is a terrible wrench for me to leave home … but we are getting deeper and deeper into debt and the business is falling away, so there is nothing for me to do but try to get us on our feet again … Dad is fairly pushing me to get work. Poor darling he worries so. It is just terrible to have to leave him but we will make the best arrangements we can for his comfort."[153] Whether from habit, necessity, or conviction, Gertrude seemingly felt obliged to make all arrangements and to ensure that her husband would be properly cared for. John seems to have been passively "uncooperative" at this critical time in the life of the Telford family.

Besides undertaking the responsibility to ensure John's comfort, Gertrude had the task of finding suitable employment, and she called upon her Ottawa friends, Campbell, Nicolson, and M.J. Coldwell, for assistance. Unable to get a definite job offer, she decided, nevertheless, to leave for Ottawa.[154] Finally, in December she got a job that provided sufficient income, although she had to settle for a low-level temporary white-collar position. Ironically, the job this registered Christian pacifist found was available because of wartime demands. She worked for the Department of National Defence, processing special assistance requests on the Dependents Board of Trustees, remaining there until mid-1944.[155]

This Ottawa interlude cast Gertrude in an anomalous position that quite deviated from several norms and doubtless led to many raised eyebrows in the community. For a woman in her mid-fifties with an able-bodied professional husband to move thousands of miles from home to seek paid employment was most unusual. Even to rationalize her departure and lengthy absence as a domestic responsibility – shoring up family finances and assisting daughter Mabel's education – was problematic given the still pervasive familial discourse, for it subverted assumptions about the husband's/father's pre-eminent role as provider. Her workforce presence was itself an issue. Although the growing need during 1942 for women workers (whose numbers doubled during the war) led to escalating patriotic appeals directed towards women, they were first targeted to young single women, then childless married women, then, finally, to married women with children. They stopped short of middle-aged wives with professional husbands, who were seen only as volunteer workers.[156] As a lifelong Christian pacifist, Gertrude Telford would, of course, have spurned pleas to fill a newly created job in war industry or to take over a man's job to release him for military service even if they had been deemed suitable for women in her social position. Ironically, the war created jobs, and the possibility of employment served as a lure despite her pacifism and her anomalous status as a desirable worker. Certain other developments also made feasible her employment in the Dominion capital. Barriers against married women's employment in the federal civil service were temporarily lowered during the war,[157] and in July 1942 income tax laws were amended so that the husbands of most working wives could continue to claim their full married status exemption.[158]

Our occasional glimpses of Gertrude in Ottawa from late 1942 until mid-1944 provide an image of a woman in action, as always, busy with her not always pleasant job and in contact with a variety of people. There were acquaintances and friends, likely fellow CCFers. She was often with the invalided Nora Coldwell, wife of the Saskatchewan MP and CCF parliamentary leader. Nora was one of her few close woman friends and confidants, a woman who shared the political interests so important to Gertrude. Daughter Margaret was there, too, working as a secretary for Sandy Nicholson, who was now national treasurer of the CCF as well as an MP.[159] As for John, except for one extended trip to Ottawa, he stayed in Pelly where for a time he shared the house with renters who prepared his meals.[160]

Then came 15 June 1944. The last major phase began in the lives of the Telfords, and they relocated to Regina. (So devoted were they that they offered their Pelly home to the new government for use as a health-care facility.) The CCF victory in Saskatchewan promised unprecedented opportunities to serve their beloved cause, and a close friend like CCF MP Sandy Nicholson acknowledged the strength of that dual commitment in his letter to Gertrude: "I hope that you and Mr. Telford will both have an opportunity to give equally important leadership in Regina in the years to come."[161] When this letter was written in late November, Gertrude's expectation of equal service had been effectively dashed by the gender expectations of the era. She had used her network of connections to explore possibilities, initially hoping to work for the CCF government itself in the new Department of Social Welfare.[162] However, she ran afoul of convention. Not only was employment of both spouses too unconventional to contemplate, but there was also opposition to married women's employment. In fact, the CCF government itself amended the Public Service Act during the following year to prohibit the employment of married women as civil servants. Even though that policy was subsequently changed because of protests at the provincial convention, the CCF government again showed its colours when it failed to object to the exclusion of women from what was otherwise an innovative measure in Canada, the provincial Bill of Rights.[163] The "problem" of Gertrude was temporarily settled when she was given employment at party headquarters in Regina. Her duties, however, were not well defined. Initially she was little more than a glorified secretary, and Carlyle King sympathized: "I don't see that your time, energy, and ability should be wasted on answering phones and doing other minor office jobs."[164] She did remain at party headquarters until September 1946 and was involved with leadership camps as well as the organization of CCF clubs.[165]

For John it was a happier time as he came into his own at age sixty-six, a loyal CCFer receiving due reward for services he – and Gertrude – had rendered for over a decade. John was appointed clerk of the Executive Council and became legal advisor in the department for which his spouse so much wanted to work, the Department of Social Welfare. He also became chief electoral officer. (In 1951 he received another sort of honour, appointment as King's Counsel.) John Telford, who remained active until poor health forced his retirement in 1957, loved these years during which he strove to advance the CCF vision: "I count it the greatest privilege of my life to have been so closely associated with Tommy Douglas for twelve years," he wrote. About his retirement celebrations he said: "These two functions are highlights of my life. No one can ever wish for more than to receive such honor from those with whom he has for years been associated in the tasks of his office."[166]

At the time of John's retirement the Telfords had lived in Regina for thirteen years. It had been a period of relative and well-earned ease, marked initially by renewal of the Telfords' relationship upon Gertrude's return from Ottawa. "John and I tease each other saying that we are having our second honeymoon," she wrote in July 1945.[167] They were then living in two rooms, for housing was very difficult to find in crowded postwar Regina, and one, or both, had turned down Gladys Strums's proposal to enter into a "Co-operative Household": "Would you like to live with the Strums on a Co-operative Household arrangement? We're hoping so, and are trying to close a deal on a cozy little bungalow."[168] Cooperative life could go too far even for the Telfords! Housework for Gertrude was minimal. The two rooms required little care, and besides, Gertrude had a heavy work schedule that left her little time for domestic chores. "We have dinner downtown at noon so I haven't much bother with the meal at night," wrote Gertrude in late 1944. "I am so frightfully busy I just cant [sic] manage more."[169] Household duties were also eased by urban comforts: "Mr. Telford and I are enjoying our work in the City very very much, living is so easy here," she wrote several months later. "We have two large, bright comfortable rooms with all the modern conveniences."[170]

Busy as they were, the Telfords still had time for a social life, and they continued to be active in the church. Now, though, they were able to return to the Baptist fold, going to the large centrally located First Baptist Church where Tommy Douglas, the CCF premier, and other Social Gospel Baptists went. Even with all her activities, however, Gertrude felt somewhat isolated, and in the spring of 1945 she confided to Nora Coldwell: "I still miss you very greatly. There is of course not anyone in Regina with whom I can discuss all our work as fully and freely and completely as I did with you."[171] Nora was that rarity in Gertrude's life, a political soulmate. John did not provide the intellectual comradeship she craved, and, as recent arrival in the provincial capital and extremely busy worker at party headquarters, she had no intimate friendships. (Her daughter, in fact, recalled her mother as a woman who had few close friends, although she was usually surrounded by people, and she suggested that some found her mother "formidable.")[172] The following year saw another irritant. John's gout (or arthritis), which had plagued him since the Melville years, flared up, and they had to curtail their usual round of activities. "Really it is most annoying," she complained in early 1946. "Usually we have such fine times going to lectures, etc. etc., but this winter nearly all that has had to be omitted."[173] (Why Gertrude could not go to them on her own is not explained.) His illness also meant more work at home. Already busy at the office, Gertrude complained that now she "had all the housework to do since John has been sick."[174] (During this period, at least, John did engage in some domestic labour.)

Then came September 1946. After her departure from CCF headquarters, Gertrude Telford's life took an abrupt turn, though she retained close ties with the party as wife of an active loyal CCF public servant and as an "elder stateswoman." Her ambition and commitment to service centred far more fully upon church and community involvement (including prominent work with the Council of Women, both local and provincial), as had been the case during the first phase of the Telford marriage. It was now John's turn to take political centre stage until his retirement in 1957. By the early 1960s age and illness had taken its toll upon both Telfords, and soon after John's death in 1963 Gertrude was forced to curtail her activities because of ill health. (She died in 1978 in Edmonton.) A life of service had ended. M.J. Coldwell put it well when he spoke of the Telfords' "determination ... [to] live their lives in the service of good causes and their fellow citizens."[175] That ideal, the spirit of cooperation, exemplified what their basic commitment – the Christian ethical ideal – was all about.

Their life of service had been lived, by chance, in Saskatchewan, where opportunity had beckoned to thousands upon thousands from many quarters of the globe in the early twentieth century. John, it would appear, came to identify more strongly with the province than did Gertrude. Although she developed attachments to particular localities, Gertrude continued to look East, and she viewed paeans to the rural community with scepticism. "Our settlement," she wrote in a personal brief to the Royal Commission on Agriculture and Rural Life in 1953, "has been mainly with the idea of accumulating sufficient surplus to be able to move to a more affable climate or to a centre of population where more of the amenities of life were to be found." "The natural trend is to the larger community."[176]

How unexpected the twists and turns in their lives of "Christian work," from Baptist ministry to the secular world – a legal career for John, women's organizations for Gertrude, the CCF for both. And at the end, their most basic commitment led to yet another departure. They broke from their deeply rooted Baptist connection in order to honour their socially oriented liberal religious beliefs. The rapidly spreading conservatism among Baptists left them adrift. For whatever reasons they did not shift membership to the United Church of Canada, that bastion of liberal Protestantism which served as the religious shelter for so many CCFers and was their church during the Pelly years. John's funeral service was at the First Baptist Church, but at the time of his death he was not even a nominal Baptist. In her quest for a new religious home, Gertrude had initially considered Quakerism, but there was no well-established group of Quakers in Regina, and she joined the Unitarians. (For John this was not a viable alternative.)[177] How unexpected the journey to realize their commitment to the Christian Social Gospel message of "cooperation" that was so central in their lives.

That commitment made their relationship a particular type of marriage. As numerous studies demonstrate, factors such as class, education, ethnicity, religion, environment, and technology interact in complex ways to shape and reshape notions, practices, and relationships within the institution of marriage. Marriages are diverse – over time and at any given time in history. The Telfords and their ilk were well educated, middle- and upper-middle-class "old stock" Canadians whose marriages and lives were strongly influenced by liberal evangelical Protestant culture, often in its British Ontario cultural guise. For such individuals, and for other moral idealists, Gertrude S. Telford's description of an ideal marriage was indeed apt: "A fine ethical type of marriage based upon mutual love, respect and responsibility."[178] In *The New Day Recalled* Veronica Strong-Boag has noted features of good marital relationships and asserts: "Marriage blessed with a sense of mutual regard and common purpose could prevail over bad times and less than perfect spouses."[179] How well this applies to the Telfords.

Strong-Boag also states: "A shared commitment to religion and politics strengthened many a couple."[180] This "shared commitment," as we have seen, was paramount in the Telfords' marriage, and their lives demonstrated how that commitment called forth ongoing adjustment and accommodation. In a sketch prepared for the fiftieth anniversary of his university class, John wrote the following about his spouse: "Gertrude is the same bright, intelligent and ambitious person as in those early days, and many of life's struggles have been made smooth by her cheerful cooperation throughout the years, and her ambition and resourcefulness."[181] Two references to his spouse's ambition in one sentence is telling. It was his major accommodation in the marriage to acknowledge that ambition.

Within the Telford marriage a balance of interests had been struck and maintained within the confines of the "acceptable," as it was then defined. Gertrude Telford, like the vast majority of women, contended that woman's primary responsibility was to home and children. Like her CCF cohorts, she acquiesced in a gendered division of domestic labour that, at best, allowed for a minimal restructuring of conventional household arrangements.[182] She also accepted, or acquiesced in, ultimate male control in such crucial areas as career decisions and financial management. But female subordination had its limits for Gertrude. She had her own space, unlike so many women in her era. She was able to enjoy partial autonomy and so participate more fully in the public sphere than most women. In her world of work outside the home it was politics that, above all, interested her, and her involvement meshed with John's. In this "men's world" Gertrude and John came far closer than they did in their marriage to a true partnership in which they lived out the spirit of cooperation, their differing talents and abilities complementing each other. As for their marriage, "marital power," as perceived from a 1990s egalitarian perspective, was decidedly unbalanced. As exemplars of socialism Saskatchewan style, which emphasized cooperation, the Telfords had a relationship that contained an element of the cooperative spirit. It was, however, an example of cooperation as understood and practised in particular historical circumstances. As Joan Sangster has shown, women of the Canadian left were largely caught up in that era's pervasive notions about womanhood, marriage, and home.[183] Gertrude S. Telford dwelt in a world in which one lived in accordance with "the art of the possible." For her, as for the Alberta women studied by Eliane Leslau Silverman, life had many constraints. Gender and culture ultimately triumphed over education and ambition.[184]

Acknowledgments

Earlier versions of portions of this chapter were presented as follows: "The Telfords: Marriage and the Co-operative Ideal," Western Canadian Studies Conference, Banff, 17 February 1990; "Infant Death – A Research Note: Glimpses of a Family Tragedy," Women in Alberta and Saskatchewan History, Workshop 4, Edmonton, 13 August 1994. I would like to thank Randi Warne and Laura Macleod at UBC Press for their helpful critiques of the previous draft of this chapter.

Notes

1 M.C. Shumiatcher to G.S. Telford, Regina, 11 February 1963, folder 31.12, R-334, Telford Papers, Saskatchewan Archives Board (SAB), Regina. The items in the extensive manuscript collection at the SAB relating to the Telfords were deposited over several years. The materials have been kept separate (as received) in order to maintain an accurate provenance, and the result of this is a somewhat unwieldy collection. For the sake of simplicity I have used one general label: Telford Papers. For accuracy, the reference number for each of the two major subdivisions is used: R-334 and R-382. Within each subdivision folders are separately labelled.

2 Gerald and Velma (?) Ward to G.S. Telford, Lancaster, NB, 31 March 1963, folder 31.12, R-334, Telford Papers.

3 Barbara and George Cadbury to G.S. Telford, Toronto, 28 February 1963, folder 31.12, R-334, Telford Papers.

4 Milton Campbell to G.S. Telford, London, Ontario, 12 February 1963, folder 17, R-334, Telford Papers.

5 Irma Douglas to G.S. Telford, n.d., folder 31.12, R-334, Telford Papers. Telford usually signed her name as Gertrude S. Telford when acting in a public capacity. Her maiden name was Gertrude Sarah Steinhoff.

6 Margaret Thomas, interview by Georgina Taylor, 20 August 1981, R-8153 to R-8157, tape recording, "Saskatchewan Women in the Co-operative Commonwealth Federation," Saskatchewan Sound Archives Program, SAB. Thomas also wrote a brief family history sketch for St. Philips/Pelly History Book Committee, *History Coming Alive: R.M. of St. Philips, Pelly and District*, 2 vols. (Regina: Focus [a division of Bridgens], 1988).

7 John's is longer, more detailed, with disproportionate attention given to his childhood, youth, and young adulthood: John M. Telford, *Recollections of Seven Decades*, mimeograph, spiral-bound (Regina: Self-published, 1962). A copy of *Recollections* is available at the Prairie History Room, Regina Public Library. Gertrude's is short and general, though more evenly covering her life: Gertrude S. Telford, *Memories*, mimeograph, spiral-bound (Edmonton: Self-published, 1976). A copy of *Memories* is available at the SAB: folder 31.11, R-334, Telford Papers. That each spouse may well have a separate marriage is recognized. For example, in *The Future of Marriage* (New York: World Publishing, 1972) Jesse Bernard concluded, after a survey of the sociological literature on marriage, that two marriages existed, his and hers. The same conclusion was reached in studies like Phyllis Rose's 1983 analysis of prominent English literary couples, *Parallel Lives: Five Victorian Marriages* (New York: Knopf, 1983).

8 Occasional manuscript collections do allow for extensive reconstruction of marriage and family life. An excellent recent example is Katherine M.J. McKenna, *A Life of Propriety: Anne Murray Powell and Her Family, 1755-1849* (Montreal and Kingston: McGill-Queen's University Press, 1994). An extremely rich manuscript collection at the SAB, that of Violet and John McNaughton, has been examined by Georgina Taylor. Usually, however, researchers confront quite limited documentation. What such sources reveal, however, are telling indicators, as noted, and serve as essential building blocks for that important task: a more richly textured reconstruction of history – one that includes voices small as well as big.

9 The issue of marital power per se and the question of decision making in marriage have, in the past, received more attention in the United States, where sociology developed earlier. For a useful discussion, see Maximiliane E. Szinovacz, "Family Power," in *Handbook of Marriage and the Family*, ed. Marvin B. Sussman and Suzanne K. Steinmetz (New York: Plenum, 1987), 651-93. This chapter contrasts sharply with a major reference work of the previous generation: Harold T. Christensen, ed., *Handbook of Marriage and the Family*, Rand McNally Sociology Series, ed. Edgar F. Borgatta (Chicago: Rand McNally, 1964). The term "power" does not appear in the index and only a few references are found under "decision making." Power and decision-making issues are noted briefly in occasional essays. In contrast, too, is the recently published Pauline G. Boss, et al., eds., *Sourcebook of Family Theories and Methods: A Contextual Approach* (New York and London: Plenum, 1993). It has numerous index references under "decision making" and "power." An especially helpful essay discusses how the emergence of a feminist perspective has contributed to greater attention to power and

inequitable power relationships within marriage: See Marie Withers Osmond and Barrie Thorne, "Feminist Theories: The Social Construction of Gender in Families and Society," 591-623. A recent Canadian feminist analysis is Ann Doris Duffy's "Struggling with Power: Feminist Critiques of Family Inequality," in *Reconstructing the Canadian Family: Feminist Perspectives*, ed. Nancy Mandell and Ann Duffy (Toronto and Vancouver: Butterworths, 1988), 111-39.

The initial attempt to study the issue of marital power predates the resurgence of feminism. One early example dates back to 1932: H. Rodman, "Marital Power and the Theory of Resources in Cultural Context," *Journal of Comparative Family Studies* 3 (1932): 51-69. The "classic" study is Robert O. Blood and Donald M. Wolfe, *Husbands and Wives: The Dynamics of Married Living* (N.p.: Free Press of Glencoe, 1960). It stimulated further investigation, including numerous articles in *The Journal of Marriage and the Family*. Oft-cited ones include (in chronological order): Constantina Safilios-Rothschild, "Family Sociology or Wives' Family Sociology? A Cross-Cultural Examination of Decision-Making," 31 (May 1969): 290-301; Constantina Safilios-Rothschild, "The Study of Family Power Structure: A Review, 1960-1969," 32 (May 1970): 539-52; Dair Gillespie, "Who Has the Power? The Marital Struggle," 33 (August 1971): 445-58; Denise B. Kandel and Gerald S. Lesser, "Marital Decision-Making in American and Danish Urban Families," 34 (February 1972): 134-8. The May 1972 issue was devoted to the debate over family power. By the time this spate of articles appeared many researchers were concluding that attempts to study marital power issues, including the matter of decision making, raised difficult methodological and theoretical problems. James L. Turk, for example, whose 1970 doctoral dissertation dealt with measurement of power, concluded that a better alternative might be to examine process. See "Who Has the Power?" in *Marriage, Family and Society: Canadian Perspectives*, ed. S. Parvez Wakil, with F.A. Wakil (Toronto: Butterworths, 1975), 237-55. Other articles published during the 1960s and early 1970s include two by David Heer in *Marriage and Family Living*: "The Measurement and Basis of Family Power: An Overview," 25 (May 1963): 133-9; and "Husband and Wife Perceptions of Family Power Structure," 24 (February 1964): 65-7. Helpful orientations include R. Centers, B.H. Ravens, and Aroldo Rodrigues, "Conjugal Power Structure: A Re-examination," *American Sociological Review* 36 (April 1971): 264-78; and Ronald E. Cromwell and David H. Olson, eds., *Power in Families* (New York: Sage, John Wiley, 1975). Canadian contributions include Merlin B. Brinkerhoff and Eugen Lupri, "Theoretical and Methodological Issues in the Use of Decision-making as an Indicator of Conjugal Power: Some Canadian Observations," *Canadian Journal of Sociology* 13 (1978): 1-20; Merlin B. Brinkerhoff and Eugen Lupri, "Conjugal Power and Family Relationships: Some Theoretical and Methodological Issues," in *The Canadian Family*, ed. K. Ishwaran (N.p.: Gage, 1983), 202-19; and Emily M. Nett, "Marriage and the Family: Organization and Interaction," in *Courtship, Marriage, and the Family in Canada*, ed. G.N. Ramu (Toronto: Macmillan, 1979), 59-77.

As is evident, interest in family power issues reached a zenith in the first few years of the 1970s, then waned. A parallel development was the emergence of feminist-oriented critiques of power relationships in marriage, some rooted in Marxist-based analyses. These were frequently part of extensive analysis, and devaluation, of conventional marriage. Such critiques served to bring about some reconsideration of power issues in "mainstream/malestream" sociology. Also utilized as an analytical approach in examination of gendered power relationships, including marriage, is deconstructionism. See, for example, the utilization of Michael Foucault's analysis in Karen Anderson, *Chain Her by One Foot: The Subjugation of Women in Seventeenth-Century New France* (London and New York: Routledge, 1991).

10 There is far less research on the Canadian family, past or present, than on the American family, although some excellent work is available. Most is contemporary sociological analysis. The classic study of the Canadian family is Frederick Elkin, *The Family in Canada: An Account of Present Knowledge and Gaps in Knowledge about Canadian Families* (Ottawa: The Vanier Institute of the Family, 1964). It is an indispensable introduction to the state of research and knowledge in the early 1960s and clearly illustrates the paucity of knowledge about the history of Canadian families. As Canadian sociology and family studies developed, a variety of works with a contemporary focus became available. Included are S. Parvez Wakil, ed., with F.A. Wakil, *Marriage, Family and Society: Canadian Perspectives* (Toronto:

Butterworths, 1975); K. Ishwaran, ed., *The Canadian Family* (N.p.: Gage, 1983); and Margrit Eichler, *Families in Canada Today: Recent Changes and Their Policy Consequences*, 2nd ed. (Toronto: Gage, 1988). The sociologist Emily N. Nett has emphasized the need to study the Canadian family from a historical perspective. In 1988 her *Canadian Families: Past and Present* (Toronto and Vancouver: Butterworths, 1988) appeared. Nett produced an expanded and updated second edition in 1993. Subsequent to my own examination of available relevant material there appeared the following useful articles: Emily M. Nett, "Family Study in Canada during Sociology's Shifts from RC to PC to DC," *Canadian Review of Sociology and Anthropology/Revue canadienne de sociologie et d'anthropologie* 34, 1 (February 1997): 93-9, along with Emily M. Nett's "Response to Bonnie Fox's Comment 'Another View of Sociology of the Family in Canada,'" 385-408.

Historians have also begun to study Canadian marriage and family issues. See, for example, Peter Ward, *Courtship, Love and Marriage in Nineteenth-Century English Canada* (Montreal and Kingston: McGill-Queen's University Press, 1990); and James G. Snell, *In the Shadow of the Law: Divorce in Canada, 1900-1939* (Toronto: University of Toronto Press, 1991). A wide-ranging compilation is Bettina Bradbury, ed., *Canadian Family History: Selected Readings* (Toronto: Copp Clark Pitman, 1992). Articles that provide a helpful quantitative portrayal of the Canadian family from a historical perspective include Ellen Gee, "Female Marriage Patterns in Canada: Changes and Differentials," *Journal of Comparative Family Studies* 11 (Autumn 1980): 457-73; Ellen Gee, "The Life Course of Canadian Women: An Historical and Demographic Analysis," *Social Indicators Research* (1986): 263-83; Ellen Gee, "Marriage in Nineteenth Century Canada," *Canadian Review of Sociology and Anthropology* 19 (1982): 311-25. A useful historiographical article is Cynthia R. Comacchio's "Beneath the 'Sentimental Veil': Families and Family History in Canada," *Labour/Le Travail* 33 (Spring 1994): 279-302.

Often relevant American studies include Stephanie Coontz, *The Way We Never Were: American Families and the Nostalgia Trap* (New York: Basic, 1992); John Demos, *Past, Present and Personal: The Family and the Life Course in American History* (New York and Oxford: Oxford University Press, 1986); Michael Gordon, ed., *The American Family in Social-Historical Perspective*, 2nd ed. (New York: St. Martin's, 1983); and Steven Mintz and Susan Kellogg, *Domestic Revolutions: A Social History of American Family Life* (New York and London: Free Press, 1988). Of some use for comparative purposes in terms of the history of marriage is John R. Gillis, *For Better, For Worse: British Marriages, 1600 to the Present* (New York and Oxford: Oxford University Press, 1985).

11 Relevant contributions in men's history, albeit American ones that need to be used cautiously, include Robert L. Griswold, *Fatherhood in America: A History* (New York: Basic, 1993); Margaret Marsh, "Suburban Men and Masculine Domesticity, 1870-1915," *American Quarterly* 40 (June 1988): 165-86; William Marsiglio, "Contemporary Scholarship on Fatherhood: Culture, Identity, and Conduct," *Journal of Family Issues* 14 (December 1993): 484-509; E. Anthony Rotundo, "American Fatherhood: A Historical Perspective," *American Behavioral Scientist* 29 (1985): 7-25. See also Peter N. Stearns, "Fatherhood in Historical Perspective: The Role of Social Change," in *Fatherhood and Families in Cultural Context*, ed. Frederick W. Bozett and Shirley M.H. Hanson (New York: Springer, 1991), 28-52. The history of Canadian fatherhood is now beginning to attract researchers. Of especial relevance is Cynthis Comacchio, "'A Postscript for Father': Defining a New Fatherhood in Interwar Canada," *Canadian Historical Review* 78, 3 (September 1997): 385-408.

12 She was not the only CCF woman to be better known than her spouse. Gladys Strum and Louise Lucas were two other such women.

13 Problems facing women in the post-suffrage political left are the focus of Joan Sangster's *Dreams of Equality: Women on the Canadian Left, 1920-1950* (Toronto: McClelland and Stewart, 1989). See also Georgina Taylor, "'The Women ... Shall Help to Lead the Way': Saskatchewan CCF-NDP Women Candidates in Provincial and Federal Elections, 1934-1965," in *"Building the Co-operative Commonwealth": Essays on the Democratic Socialist Tradition in Canada*, ed. J. William Brennan (Regina: Canadian Plains Research Centre, University of Regina, 1984), 141-60; and "Equals and Partners? An Examination of How Saskatchewan Women Reconciled Their Political Activities for the Cooperative Commonwealth Federation

with Traditional Roles for Women" (MA thesis, University of Saskatchewan, 1983). For discussion of difficulties facing women in all political parties, see Sylvia B. Bashevkin, *Toeing the Lines: Women and Party Politics in English Canada* (Toronto: University of Toronto Press, 1985); and Linda Kealey and Joan Sangster, eds., *Beyond the Vote: Canadian Women and Politics* (Toronto: University of Toronto Press, 1989).

14 Elaine Tyler May, an American scholar, was among the first to undertake a scholarly study of changing attitudes about marriage. See her *Great Expectations: Marriage and Divorce in Post-Victorian America* (Chicago and London: University of Chicago Press, 1980). For Canada see Snell, *In the Shadow of the Law.*

15 Ernest W. Burgess and Harvey J. Locke, *The Family: From Institution to Companionship* (New York: American, 1945). The changing nature of marriage is noted in several of the studies already cited. "Companionate" marriage is used here to describe a marriage relationship in which the spouses treat each other as companions. (The term was also sometimes used in the early twentieth century to refer to a marriage of voluntary childlessness or a trial marriage.)

16 Ibid., 731.

17 The basic study of the Social Gospel in Canada remains Richard Allen, *The Social Passion: Religion and Social Reform in Canada, 1914-1928* (Toronto: University of Toronto Press, 1973). But see also Michael Gauvreau, *The Evangelical Century: College and Creed in English Canada from the Great Revival to the Great Depression* (Montreal and Kingston: McGill-Queen's University Press, 1991), especially 183-4, 259, 341-2 (notes).

18 Janet Forsythe Fishburn, *The Fatherhood of God and the Victorian Family: The Social Gospel in America* (Philadelphia: Fortress, 1981), 23-4, 28.

19 Walter Rauschenbusch, *Christianity and the Social Crisis* (New York and London: Association, 1907), 134.

20 Stow Persons, "Introduction," in Laurence Gronlund, *The Co-operative Commonwealth in Its Outlines: An Exposition of Modern Socialism* (Boston: Lee and Shepard, 1884 [reprint, Cambridge: Belknap, 1965]), xx.

21 Fishburn, in fact, argues that Rauschenbusch "opposed the possibility of change in the family or in the spheres of marital responsibility" (24). In contrast is Susan Curtis's contention that Rauschenbusch "adopted a twentieth-century mode of family relationships based on cooperation, companionship, and accessible parents." She also suggests that neither he nor his spouse "tried to dominate the other in the domestic or professional sphere." See Susan Curtis, *A Consuming Faith: The Social Gospel and Modern American Culture*, ed. Thomas Bender (Baltimore and London: Johns Hopkins University Press, 1991), 112. That Rauschenbusch had a more liberal orientation on women-related issues than is often assumed is also suggested in William D. Lindsey, "The Social Gospel and Feminism," *American Journal of Theology and Philosophy* 13, 3 (September 1993): 195-210. Lindsey discusses Rauschenbusch as well as Shailer Mathews, both of whom were Social Gospelers of Baptist background (although Lindsey fails to note the Baptist connection). Mathews, however, was significantly more liberal than Rauschenbusch; the differences are indicative of the range of Baptist opinion at the time.

22 Gronlund, *Co-operative Commonwealth*, 187.

23 David Laycock, *Populism and Democratic Thought in the Canadian Prairies, 1919 to 1945* (Toronto: University of Toronto Press, 1990), 119, 128. The focus upon the "public" in the male discourse of cooperation was both explicit and implicit, as speeches and essays clearly indicate and as scholarly discussions suggest.

24 Janice Newton, in her excellent examination of women's rights and the Canadian left in the pre-suffrage era of the twentieth century, has found evidence of such concerns among a few women associated with the pre-First World War Canadian left. It seems clear, however, that proposals like those being made by some American feminists or socialist-feminists for reorganization of domestic work had little impact, and, in any case, these proposals were likely to call for the socialization of domestic labour. See Janice Newton, *The Feminist Challenge to the Canadian Left, 1900-1918* (Montreal and Kingston: McGill-Queen's University Press, 1995).

25 Alice Hollis, quoted in Cheryle Jahn, "'Class, Gender and Agrarian Socialism': The United Farm Women of Saskatchewan, 1926-1931," *Prairie Forum* 19 (Fall 1994): 195.

26 Winnipeg Free Press, n.d., clipping, folder 31.10, R-334, Telford Papers; G.S. Telford, *Memories*, 21, 29; J.M. Telford, *Recollections*, 97-8.

27 J.M. Telford, *Recollections*, 97. Few details remain concerning their two-year engagement period.

28 Ibid., 79, 97; G.S. Telford, *Memories*, 23. Church congregations were then proliferating as the newcomer population rapidly increased. In 1914 the Baptist Union in the West reported that there were 253 churches in the four western provinces. See Walter C. Ellis, "What the Times Demand: Brandon College and Baptist Higher Education in Western Canada," in *Canadian Baptists and Christian Higher Education*, ed. G.A. Rawlyk (Kingston and Montreal: McGill-Queen's University Press, 1988), n. 29, 123.

29 This era, however, did see changes beginning to occur, but at present developments are more fully documented for the United States. (Ward, *Courtship, Love and Marriage*, focuses upon the nineteenth century.) Beth L. Bailey describes a shift from courtship to dating in *From Front Porch to Backseat: Courtship in Twentieth Century America* (Baltimore and London: Johns Hopkins University Press, 1988). See also Ellen K. Rothman, *Hands and Hearts: A History of Courtship in America* (New York: Basic, 1984). Both need to be used cautiously, for they are general American studies.

30 Charles M. Johnston, *McMaster University*, vol. 1: *The Toronto Years* (Toronto and Buffalo: University of Toronto Press, 1976), 74, 75, 122. A general survey provides some interesting comparative statistics for McMaster. Arts and Science enrolment for 1911-2 was 177 students, and of this total 50 students, or 28 percent, were female; this was double the percentage of female enrollment in 1901-2 (17 women in the Arts and Science total enrolment of 126). See Appendix 2, "Enrollment in Canadian Universities in Census Years, 1861-1911," in Robin S. Harris, *A History of Higher Education in Canada, 1663-1960* (Toronto and Buffalo: University of Toronto Press, 1976). A short account of Moulton College is available: Alfreda Hall, *Per Ardua: The Story of Moulton College, Toronto, 1888-1954* (N.p.: Moulton College Alumnae Association, 1987).

Johnston's two-volume work takes an institutional approach. There are as yet no studies for McMaster that explore student life and the "gendering" of education, as do some recent accounts of other Ontario institutions. See, for example, Lynne Marks and Chad Gaffield, "Women at Queen's University, 1895-1905: A 'Little Sphere' All Their Own?" *Ontario History* 78 (December 1986): 331-49; Jo LaPierre, "The Academic Life of Canadian Coeds, 1880-1900," *Historical Studies in Education/Revue d'histoire de l'éducation* 2 (Fall 1990): 225-45; and relevant essays in Paul Axelrod and John G. Reid, eds., *Youth, University and Canadian Society: Essays in the Social History of Higher Education* (Montreal and Kingston: McGill-Queen's University Press, 1989). A good general picture of early twentieth-century Ontario universities and of student life and culture is found in A.B. McKillop, *Matters of Mind: The University in Ontario, 1791-1951* (Toronto: University of Toronto Press, 1994), chaps. 8-10.

31 The University of Chicago opened its doors in 1892, its initial funding coming from the industrial magnate and devout Baptist, John D. Rockefeller. William Rainey Harper, president from 1892 until his death in 1906, was a renowned Baptist educator and sought to make the institution "a major centre of advanced learning, as well as contribute to the improvement of society through providing knowledge and action needed for the solution of social problems." He succeeded. "The prestige of the new university and its position in the forefront of the movement to marry Christianity, science, and social improvement, gave its graduates a special *cachet*." See Steven J. Diner, "Department and Discipline: The Department of Sociology at the University of Chicago, 1892-1920," *Minerva: A Review of Science, Learning and Policy* 13 (Winter 1975): 515, 530, 552. (Italics in original.)

Johnston notes that the University of Chicago "was in the forefront of the campaign in the United States to subject Scripture to exhaustive analysis and to adapt the church to 'modernity.'" And he also notes: "Given the university's Baptist heritage and its swift emergence as a leading institution in the United States, not to mention the presence there of Professor Foster, it naturally became one of McMaster's favourite graduate schools." See Johnston, *McMaster University*, vol. 1: *The Toronto Years*, 93. See also chaps. 5, 6, passim, for general discussion. And see G.A. Rawlyk, "A.L. McCrimmon, H.P. Widden, T.T. Shields, Christian Higher Education, and McMaster University," in *Canadian Baptists and Christian*

Higher Education, ed. George A. Rawlyk (Montreal: McGill-Queen's University Press, 1988), 31-62.

32 Johnston, *McMaster University*, vol. 1: *The Toronto Years*, 96-102.

33 J.M. Telford, *Recollections*, 72, 76-7.

34 Thomas, interview by Taylor.

35 On the McMaster faculty were A.L. [Abraham Lincoln] McCrimmon and W.J.A. Donald, former students at the University of Chicago, where the world's first independent department of sociology had been established in 1892. Under the direction of Baptist minister and educator Albion B. Small, the department became an influential force in the development of North American sociology. Small's "prime interest" was to use scientific knowledge to improve society. See Diner, "Department and Discipline," 517, 523. The liberal Baptists of Chicago and McMaster, who believed in the compatibility of sociology and Christianity, affirmed the stance of Charles R. Henderson (social reformer, scholar, and University of Chicago chaplain), who had written in 1899: "'To assist us in the difficult task of adjustment to new situations ... God has providentially wrought out for us the social sciences and placed them at our disposal.'" (Quoted in ibid., 524.)

McCrimmon joined the McMaster faculty in 1904 after completing the requirements for the master's degree in economics and sociology at Chicago, and he remained there until his death in 1935. Initially appointed to a position in political economy, he offered a course that covered topics like trade unionism, labour economics, trusts, and doctrines of socialism. He also developed a sociology course. However, conspicuously absent from his reading list was *Principles of Sociology*, which was written by the prominent Social Darwinist, Herbert Spencer. Becoming interested in the new "rural sociology," McCrimmon began to direct theses that examined how the churches might help to ameliorate social conditions in rural south-central Ontario. See Johnston, *McMaster University*, vol. 1: *The Toronto Years*, 114, 123-4; vol. 2: *The Early Years in Hamilton, 1930-1957*, 56.

McCrimmon's many interests included the "woman question," and one wonders whether he influenced Gertrude's thinking. In 1915 his book, *The Woman Movement*, was published (Philadelphia: Griffith and Rowland). It is a lengthy exposition based upon extensive reading, and it discloses his own ambivalent thoughts about what women's nature and capacities really were. Gertrude's personal copy of the book, as attested to by her signature, is in a collection that was given to the University of Regina Library after the death of her son-in-law, Lewis H. Thomas. Unfortunately, no date accompanies her signature. The book itself appears almost unused, and marked passages are found only in the first few chapters, which are mainly informative sections about women's history and status in ancient civilizations and about suffrage movements in the Western world. One also wonders whether the presence of academic women at Chicago shaped McCrimmon's attitudes and his receptivity to students like Gertrude, who eventually fulfilled her goal of completing a master's degree in sociology. (Between 1892 and 1920, 32 percent of the master's degrees [twenty-two] and 11 percent of the doctorates [six] went to women. See Diner, "Department and Discipline," 547.)

W.J.A. Donald, a McMaster alumnus who then studied political economy at the University of Chicago, soon joined McCrimmon. No additional information is provided about him. Johnston, *McMaster University*, vol. 1: *The Toronto Years*, 114. It is interesting to note that Gertrude gave the name Donald to a character in one of the short stories she wrote while teaching school in Saskatchewan.

36 G.S. Telford, *Memories*, 22-3; G.S. Telford to Dr. A. Hoffer, 14 March 1962, copy, folder 32.1h, R382, Telford Papers. Her attendance at Unitarian services was likely related to the arrival of Reverend T.T. Shields at Jarvis Street Baptist Church, "Canada's premier Baptist church." He was then on his way to becoming a major figure among the emerging "fundamentalist" forces. See Leslie K. Tarr, *Shields of Canada: T.T. Shields (1873-1955)* (Grand Rapids, MI: Baker, 1967), 47.

37 Diana Pedersen, "'The Call to Service': The YWCA and the Canadian College Woman, 1886-1920," in *Youth, University and Canadian Society*, ed. Axelrod and Reid (Montreal and Kingston: McGill-Queen's University Press, 1989), 187.

38 Ibid., 198. See also Myra Rutherdale, this volume, 32-59.

39 Ibid., 199.

40 Allen Mills, *Fools for Christ: The Political Thought of J.S. Woodsworth* (Toronto: University of Toronto Press, 1991), 36. Woodsworth was superintendent from 1907 until 1913. He then became director of the Canadian Welfare League, and, in 1916, he was named head of the Bureau of Social Research (ibid., 39). During these years his orientation became increasingly secular, and Mills contends that by the early 1920s Woodsworth is best described as "a free-thinking deist and humanist rather than a social gospeller, even a radical one" (ibid., 92). Remaining, however, the firm moralist who sought a better world, he became, as historian Kenneth McNaught suggests in the title of his 1959 biography, *A Prophet in Politics: A Biography of J.S. Woodsworth* (Toronto: University of Toronto Press) and was a major figure in the CCF.

41 G.S. Telford, *Memories*, 47.

42 Mills describes *Strangers within Our Gates, or, Coming Canadians* (Toronto: F.C. Stephenson, c. 1909) as "perplexing and frustrating," but he thinks that recent assessments of it as "a work of nativism, Anglo-Canadian nationalism, and near-racism" are too extreme. See Mills, *Fool for Christ*, 42-50. *My Neighbor: A Study of City Conditions, A Plea for Social Service* (Toronto: Toronto Missionary Society of the Methodist Church, 1911), writes Mills, is even more emphatic about the need for integration, but then Woodsworth shifted. By 1913 he "stated his abandonment of the Anglo-Canadian ideal" (ibid., 50, 62).

43 Pedersen, "'The Call to Service,'" 196.

44 Ibid., 207.

45 *Canadian Baptist*, 30 July 1914, as quoted in John S. Moir, "*The Canadian Baptist* and the Social Gospel Movement, 1879-1914," in *Baptists in Canada: Search for Identity amidst Diversity*, ed. Jarold K. Zeman (Burlington: Welch, 1980), 155.

46 This was the main base of operations for Canadian Baptists. See A.A. Scott, *Beacon Lights: A Sketch of the Origin and Development of Our Mission Stations in India*, rev. ed. (Toronto: Canadian Baptist Foreign Mission Board, 1922), 21. In a section on "Missionary Personnel," 187-210, Scott lists all those who had served or were serving as of 1922 and provides brief biographical sketches. Forty-seven men and ninety-eight women are listed. Out of all the women (regardless of marital status), only twelve appear to have graduated from, or received some education at, McMaster (including two who had gone to Moulton College). Five women on the list appear to be medical doctors who were badly needed in the mission fields. Slightly over half of all the women were unmarried throughout their missionary careers.

A brief account of Baptist women missionaries and the female missionary societies that supported them is H. Miriam Ross, "Shaping a Vision of Mission: Early Influences on the United Baptist Woman's Missionary Union," in *An Abiding Conviction: Maritime Baptists and Their World*, ed. Robert S. Wilson, 83-107 (Hantsport, NS: Lancelot, 1988). For recent scholarly investigations of women's missionary work in the two largest evangelical Protestant denominations, see Rosemary Gagan, *A Sensitive Independence: Canadian Methodist Women Missionaries in Canada and the Orient, 1881-1925* (Montreal and Kingston: McGill-Queen's University Press, 1992); and Ruth Compton Brouwer, *New Women for God: Canadian Presbyterian Women and India Missions, 1876-1914* (Toronto: University of Toronto Press, 1990).

47 G.S. Telford, *Memories*, 23, 68.

48 She could envision being an assistant pastor. See my endnote 66. At the time there was some discussion about the possible use of women as deaconesses and pastors' assistants. In 1916 a formal proposal was made. It was one of several proposals made in a five-year program for the Baptist Union of Western Canada. See Margaret E. Thompson, *The Baptist Story in Western Canada* (Calgary: Baptist Union of Western Canada, c. 1974), 149. During this era the ordination of women was not accepted in Canadian Baptist circles, but it did occasionally occur in the United States, at least among Free Will Baptists.

49 Marriage was considered the norm, although approximately 11 percent of the population did not marry in this era. See Ellen M. Gee, "The Life Course of Canadian Women: An Historical and Demographic Analysis," *Social Indicators Research* (1986), 189. In this article, she has calculated the median age at first marriage for women in Gertrude's cohort, 1881-90, as 25.1. (Gertrude was just short of twenty-six when she married. Gertrude was also close to the median of 27.1 for first birth, but, in contrast, she last gave birth at age forty, far above

the median age of 36.3.) See Gee, "Life Course," table 6, 196. The age difference between Gertrude and John was greater than was commonly found. One calculation, for example, sets 4.4 years as the median difference between husband and wife at time of first marriage for Canadian women whose birth period was between the 1880s and 1900s. See Roy H. Rodgers and Gail Witney, "The Family Cycle in Twentieth Century Canada," *Journal of Marriage and the Family* 43, 3 (August 1981): 729. In Ward's discussion of nineteenth-century Canada, he writes that in nine out of ten cases a man in his late twenties or early thirties married a younger woman, the average difference in age being eight years. See Ward, *Courtship, Love and Marriage*, 58.

50 G.M. Telford, *Recollections*, 14, 45, 47, 76-7.

51 G.S. Telford, *Memories*, 14-5. Reverend Steinhoff served in several small churches in Canada and the United States, his frequent moves suggesting that Gertrude's mother had correctly concluded that he was not really "fitted for it."

52 Ibid., 15.

53 G.S. Telford, *Memories*, 14-5, 19-23, 39, 68; mementos, unidentified clippings, folder 31.10, R-334, Telford Papers.

54 "Books," c. 1922, 2pp. mimeograph, folder 31.10, R-334, Telford Papers. The books to which Telford refers are classic stories read by generations of girls, and still available today. The original publication of each is as follows: Louisa May Alcott, *Little Women, or Meg, Jo, Beth and Amy* (Boston: Roberts Brothers, 1868); Kate Douglas Smith Wiggin, *Rebecca of Sunnybrook Farm* (New York: Houghton Mifflin, 1903); and Lucy Maud Montgomery, *Anne of Green Gables* (Boston: L.C. Page and Co., 1908).

55 G.S. Telford, *Memories*, 15, 20, 22.

56 Ibid., 47. She also notes the influence of Edward Bellamy. See n. 76.

57 Gertrude Steinhoff, "Robins's Message," unidentified newspaper clipping, n.d., folder 31.10, R-334, Telford Papers. She expressed her dislike for the flat, open prairie landscape in "A Saskatchewan Beauty Spot," *Canadian National Railway Magazine*, June 1931, 29, folder 31.6, R-334, Telford Papers. Only when she saw the water, hills, and trees in the Crystal Lake area, after six years on the prairies, did she feel comfortable: "And never shall I forget the feeling of relaxation that came over me."

58 Gertrude Steinhoff, "Billy," n.d., 5pp. handwritten, folder 31.10, R-334, Telford Papers.

59 J.M. Telford, *Recollections*, 98.

60 Unidentified newspaper clipping, n.d., folder 30.10, R-334, Telford Papers.

61 G.S. Telford, *Memories*, 69.

62 G.S. Telford, "Books."

63 Burgess and Locke, *The Family*, 731.

64 Thomas, interview by Taylor.

65 This sensitivity occasionally surfaced in the small collection of handwritten sermons in folder 30.3, R-334, Telford Papers. Most revealing is "The Fall" and the outline notes for it. The outline suggests he was considering several approaches to dealing with the matter of the role and responsibility of Eve: "Adam blamed Eve – not *question of sex/shift responsibility* – cowardly?/No one ever sins *alone*" (italics in original). In the sermon itself Eve is barely mentioned, and the serpent gets all the blame.

66 An invitation card for a series of sermons for young people at the Baptist Church, Roland, Manitoba, has printed at the bottom "J.M. Telford, Pastor." This has been changed, in pencil, to read "Mrs. J.M. Telford, Asst. Pastor." See folder 30.4, R-334, Telford Papers.

67 Thomas, interview by Taylor.

68 G.S. Telford to Women's Missionary Society, First Baptist Church, Regina, 7 June 1934, copy, 30.5, R-334, Telford Papers.

69 *Melville Canadian*, 23 September 1931, clipping, folder 32.2, R-382, Telford Papers. The statement was made in an address she gave at the Melville United Church.

70 G.S. Telford, *What Happened to David Jones*, c. 1939, 17, folder 32.3a, R-382, Telford Papers.

71 See, for example, the discussion of an extensive survey in Philip Blumstein and Pepper Schwartz, *American Couples: Money, Work, Sex* (New York: William Morrow, 1983). The subject is also discussed in several of the studies on family/marital power cited in n. 9.

72 Thomas, interview by Taylor.

73 See Day Book, folder 30.1, R-334, Telford Papers. Major expenditures for household furnishings are itemized on pages 45 and 98. (In *Recollections*, however, John wrote, "we began to gather our furniture piece by piece" [98].) On pages 81 to 86 are found salary entries up to 14 May 1917. His initial salary at Roland was $900 per year. The Weyburn-McTaggart income levels vary. For example, he received from Weyburn $966, May-December 1913. His January-December 1915 salary for Weyburn was $862.10.

74 Letter to "Dear Homemakers" (Saskatchewan Homemakers' Clubs), 7 September 1937, copy, folder 32.1a, R-382, Telford Papers.

75 G.S. Telford, "The Meaning of Socialism in the Life of the Individual. Lesson 9, Part 1, for C.C.F. Clubs," c. 1945, 4pp. typescript, copy, folder 30.1, R-334, Telford Papers.

76 G.S. Telford, "C.C.F. Broadcast," c. 1945, typescript, folder 4.2, R-334, Telford Papers. She may well have derived this view from Edward Bellamy's *Looking Backward, 2000-1887*. This classic utopian socialist novel, written by an American, circulated widely in North America for many decades after its publication in 1889, and it appeared regularly on recommended reading lists in socialist circles. According to G.S. Telford, *Memories*, 47, Gertrude read it at the rural Ontario home where she boarded during her first teaching job. It "convinced me more than ever of socialism," she wrote. In Bellamy's future world, where cooperation, not competition, reigned, and where peace and plenty had replaced his era's conflict, brutality, and poverty, women and men alike participated in productive labour. (The women, however, were largely depicted as paragons of Victorian womanhood.) It is not known whether Gertrude Telford read Charlotte Perkins Gilman's *Women and Economics: A Study of the Economic Relation between Men and Women as a Factor in Social Evolution*, which circulated for some decades after publication in 1898 (Boston: Small, Maynard and Company). Among the major themes of this American feminist was the importance of women's economic independence.

77 G.S. Telford to Margaret Telford, 6 November 1942, folder 31.18, R-334, Telford Papers.

78 J.M. Telford, *Recollections*, 109.

79 This was the same church in which Tommy Douglas, the first CCF premier of Saskatchewan, served during the early years of the Great Depression.

80 J.M. Telford, *Recollections*, 101

81 G.S. Telford, *Memories*, 33.

82 J.M. Telford, *Recollections*, 101.

83 G.S. Telford, "Buying for a Son," n.d., 2pp. handwritten, folder 32.2, R-334, Telford Papers.

84 Ibid.

85 In 1912 the ratio of infant deaths (those deaths under five years of age) to 1,000 live births was 101.58. Subsequent improvement was short-lived. In 1915 the rate was 89.5, but in 1916 the ratio shot up to 103.3. See Gertrude S. Telford, "The First Child Welfare Conferences in Saskatchewan," *Saskatchewan History* 4 (Winter 1951): 57.

86 Not until the Second World War era did even a slight majority of births occur in hospitals. See appendix, table A.12, "Percentage of births occurring in hospitals, 1931-1971," in Alison Prentice et al., *Canadian Women: A History* (Toronto: Harcourt Brace Jovanovich, 1988), 419. For a good introduction to changes in birthing practices, see Katherine Arnup, Andree Levesque, and Ruth Roach Pierson, eds., *Delivering Motherhood: Maternal Ideologies and Practices in the 19th and 20th Centuries* (London: Routledge, 1990).

87 Current research suggests the difficulties. See, for example, Joan Bordow, *The Ultimate Loss: Coping with the Death of a Child* (New York and Toronto: Beaufort, 1982); Therese A. Rando, ed., *Parental Loss of a Child* (Champaign, DE: Research Press, 1986); and John E. Scholwalter, et al., eds., *The Child and Death* (New York: Columbia University Press, 1983). That it is even more difficult today to suffer the loss of a child is suggested by Therese Rando, an American clinical psychologist who specializes in loss and grief issues: "Bereaved parents represent the worst fears of these other parents and they become the victims of social ostracism and unrealistic expectations as other parents attempt to ward off the terror generated within them by bereaved parents." They commonly "experience feelings of abandonment, helplessness, and frustration as reactions to their experiences with other parents." See Rando, *Parental Loss of a Child*, 38.

88 See handwritten entry, dated 11 November 1964, notebook leaves, folder 31.2, R-334, Telford Papers.

89 G.S. Telford, *Memories*, 32.

90 J.M. Telford, "In How Far Is Christianity Responsible for the Present European War?", 23 pages handwritten sermon, folder 30.3, R-334, Telford Papers.

91 Thomas, interview by Taylor. See also G.S. Telford, *Memories*, 36-7; and J.M. Telford, *Recollections*, 101.

92 G.S. Telford, *Memories*, 30; Thompson, *The Baptist Story*, 149.

93 A.T. Spankie, "The Story of Baptist Women's Missionary Work and its Purpose," chap. 14 in *Pioneering in Western Canada: A Story of the Baptists*, ed. C.C. McLaurin (Calgary: Self-published, 1939), 279.

94 Telford, "The First Child Welfare Conferences," 59. The first had been held in Regina.

95 Some glimpses of John Telford's years in the ministry are provided by items in folders 30.4 and 31.10, R-334, Telford Papers.

96 J.M. Telford, *Recollections*, 101.

97 Yorkton Press, 4 November 1919, clipping, folder 31.13, R-334, Telford Papers; Telford, "The First Child Welfare Conferences," 61.

98 J.M. Telford, *Recollections*, 101, 103; G.S. Telford, *Memories*, 34; Thomas, interview by Taylor, SAB; J.M. Telford, "My Birthday," dated November 1960, 5pp. typescript, folder 30.6, R-334, Telford Papers.

99 J.M. Telford, *Recollections*, 101.

100 G.S. Telford, *Memories*, 34.

101 J.M. Telford, *Recollections*, 102.

102 G.S. Telford, *Memories*, 34.

103 J.M. Telford, *Recollections*, 103.

104 Such issues are discussed in literature cited in n. 9.

105 J.M. Telford, *Recollections*, 102.

106 Ibid., 104; G.S. Telford, *Memories*, 30-1, 35.

107 J.M. Telford, *Recollections*, 104.

108 Ibid., 104-5; G.S. Telford, "Women's Missionary Society, United Church, Melville, Saskatchewan," n.d., 2pp. typescript, copy, folder 31.5, R-334, Telford Papers.

109 J.M. Telford, *Recollections*, 104, 106.

110 G.S. Telford, *Memories*, 34-5.

111 J.M. Telford, *Recollections*, 107-8; Thomas, *History Coming Alive*.

112 G.S. Telford, *Memories*, 30-40.

113 G.S. Telford to Clarence Fines, 12 June 1941, copy, folder 32.2, R-334, Telford Papers. In this letter she was expressing her anger at having lost the CCF nomination in Pelly because of political chicanery.

114 J.M. Telford, *Recollections*, 108.

115 Ibid., 104-10. For a general discussion of such activities and women's involvement in them, see Lucille M. Marr, "Church Teen Clubs, Feminized Organizations? Tuxis Boys, Trail Rangers, and Canadian Girls in Training, 1919-1939," *Historical Studies in Education/Revue d'histoire de l'éducation* 3 (Fall 1991): 249-67; and Lucille M. Marr, "Sunday School Teaching: A Women's Enterprise: A Case Study from the Canadian Methodist, Presbyterian and United Church Tradition, 1919-1939," *Histoire Sociale/Social History* 26 (November 1993): 329-44.

116 Over the years John was not only the village lawyer but also an agricultural implements dealer and secretary-treasurer of a local telephone company.

117 J.M. Telford, *Recollections*, 113; G.S. Telford, *Memories*, 44. See also the brief account of the Telford family during their Pelly years written by their daughter. See Thomas, *History Coming Alive*, vol. 2, 989-90. On the question of gender, decision making, and the automobile, see Katherine Jellison, "Women and Technology on the Great Plains, 1910-40," *Great Plains Quarterly* 8 (Summer 1988): 145-57. Gertrude Telford's later political involvement was apparently the impetus for her learning to drive. During the 1938 campaign her daughter recalled her "driving everywhere, often on impossible roads." See Margaret Thomas, "Telford, John M. and Gertrude," in *History Coming Alive*, vol. 2, 989.

118 G.S. Telford, "The Happiest Day of My Life," dated November 1963, 4pp. handwritten, notebook leaves, folder 31.2, R-334, Telford Papers. Jackie, her fifth infant, had been born at home with a physician in attendance. Data from the Canadian Census, 1941, show that 9.1 percent of "Ever-married Women" in her birth cohort 1887-96 had five "Ever-born" children; six or more children were borne by 31.7 percent in that cohort. See Gee, "Life Course of Canadian Women," table 5, 194.

119 Thomas, interview by Taylor, SAB.

120 Suggestive American accounts, indicative of the rising interest in the exploration of fatherhood and its history, include works cited in n. 11, especially Griswold's *Fatherhood in America*; and Ralph LaRossa and Donald C. Reitzes, "Continuity and Change in Middle Class Fatherhood, 1925-1939: The Culture-Conduct Connection," *Journal of Marriage and the Family* 55 (May 1993): 455-68. Both studies note the increasingly secondary status accorded the father in childraising, which paralleled the apotheosis of mothering, and the rise of concern about it.

121 For an excellent discussion, see the following recent book: Katherine Arnup, *Education for Motherhood, Advice for Mothers in Twentieth-Century Canada* (Toronto: University of Toronto Press, 1994). A useful portrayal of middle-class motherhood, one that concentrates on the interwar years, is Veronica Strong-Boag, *The New Day Recalled: Lives of Girls and Women in English Canada, 1919-1939* (Toronto: Copp Clark Pitman, 1988), chap. 5.

122 Thomas, interview by Taylor.

123 G.S. Telford, *Memories*, 23, 25; *Canadian Baptist*, n.d., clipping, folder 30.7, R-334, Telford Papers.

124 G.S. Telford, *Memories*, 40-1.

125 J.M. Telford, *Recollections*, 114.

126 G.S. Telford, *Memories*, 47; Thomas, interview by Taylor; J.M. Telford, "My Birthday." In 1930 Campbell was appointed to the tariff board.

127 Olenka Melnyk, *No Bankers in Heaven: Remembering the CCF* (Toronto and Montreal: McGraw-Hill Ryerson, 1989), 1.

128 Walter D. Young, *The Anatomy of a Party: The National CCF, 1932-61* (Toronto: University of Toronto Press, 1969), 304. *The Regina Manifesto*, which is reprinted in its entirety in Appendix A, was socialist in orientation and remained the CCF policy statement until the Winnipeg Declaration of 1956, a few years before the party was succeeded by the New Democratic Party. Much was susceptible to differing interpretations, however. For a time the party attracted extensive support in portions of English Canada, especially Saskatchewan, British Columbia, and Ontario. Young's book is a basic early study of the national CCF, which is analyzed in terms of being both a movement and a party. A good collection of essays is the previously cited Brennan, ed., *"Building the Co-operative Commonwealth."* As for the Saskatchewan CCF, the classic, though partially outdated, account is Seymour Martin Lipset, *Agrarian Socialism: The Co-operative Commonwealth Federation Saskatchewan: A Study of Political Sociology* (Berkeley: California Paperback Edition, 1971 1968 [orig. pub. 1950]). It might be noted that until 1935 the affiliating group in Saskatchewan retained its Farmer-Labour identification and that the provincial government of 1929-34, sometimes called the "cooperative government," had no connection with the CCF.

129 G.S. Telford, *Memories*, 48.

130 G.S. Telford, *Memories*, 47-58; J.M. Telford, *Recollections*, 114, 117-8. There is a brief discussion of Gertrude Telford's political career in Sangster, *Dreams of Equality*, 101, 104, 214. See also Betty L. Dyck, *Running to Beat Hell: A Biography of A.M. (Sandy) Nicholson* (Regina: Canadian Plains Research Centre, University of Regina, 1988), 81, 94. She ran against the incumbent Liberal Reginald J.M. Parker, the Minister of Municipal Services, who was responsible for direct relief – an unenviable position.

131 See n. 13.

132 *Leader-Post* list of delegates as cited in Sangster, *Dreams of Equality*, 247, n. 1.

133 Young, *Anatomy of a Party*, 309.

134 Thomas, interview by Taylor.

135 Campaign leaflet, folder 32.3c, R-382, Telford Papers.

136 G.S. Telford to Clarence Fines, 12 June 1941.

137 Gertrude S. Telford, "Women in Politics," *Western Producer*, 21 October 1959, clipping, folder 31.4; and "Women and Internationalism," c. 1933, handwritten, folder 22.7, R-334, Telford Papers.

138 In the Telford Papers there are several dozen incoming letters from the Campbells, mainly Milton, which span the period from 30 March 1933 to 1963. The 1930s letters were nearly always exchanged between Milton and Gertrude. From the mid-1940s on, he addressed most letters to both Telfords and discussed personal and political matters. His wife, Hazel, wrote occasional letters, usually to Gertrude; most concern personal, everyday matters. See folder 17, R-334.

139 See, for example, Carlyle King to G.S. Telford, Saskatoon, 25 February 1945, folder 32.1c, R-382, Telford Papers.

140 G.S. Telford to Carlyle King, 24 April 1945, copy, folder 32.1c, R-382, Telford Papers. In the letter she discussed possibly seeking the nomination in the Melville federal constituency after Louise Lucas had been forced to withdraw her candidacy because of terminal cancer.

141 "These Are the Builders," *Commonwealth*, 27 April 1949, clipping, folder 31.4, and scrapbook, passim, folder 3 (6), R-334, Telford Papers.

142 G.S. Telford, "Co-operation in the Work of the Home," n.d., 8pp. handwritten, folder 31.20, R-334, Telford Papers.

143 Winnifred Anderson to G.S. Telford, Glen Elder, Saskatchewan, c. 1943, folder 31.15, R-334, Telford Papers.

144 Telford to Nora Coldwell, Regina, 15 May 1945, folder 32.1c, R-382, Telford Papers.

145 Thomas, interview by Taylor.

146 G.S. Telford, "Statement," *Saskatchewan Homemakers' Clubs: Retrospect and Prospect; The Silver Cord and Golden Chain* n.p., n.d., 29, folder 22(7), R-334, Telford Papers.

147 G.S. Telford, "C.C.F. Broadcast," n.d., 7pp. typescript, folder 4(2), R-334, Telford Papers.

148 Gertrude Telford's views are expressed in several essays, addresses, and sketches. See, for example, two addresses to SHC Conventions: "Healthful Adolescence," notated June 1935, typescript, folder 31.13, R-334; and "The Underprivileged Child," n.d., typescript, folder 32.2, R-382, Telford Papers. Her lessons, which were prepared for study in CCF clubs, sometimes dealt with these matters. See typescript copies of "The Adolescent" and "The Child," c. 1945, folder 3(1), R-334, Telford Papers.

149 Letter to editor, *Chatelaine*, 1958, copy, folder 31.2, R-334, Telford Papers.

150 See Gertrude's endorsement of the idea of the working wife, earlier in this chapter.

151 G.S. Telford, *Memories*, 42-3; J.M. Telford, *Recollections*, 111-2, 115; Thomas, interview by Taylor. Straitened circumstances are suggested by the Telfords' use of very cheap typewriter paper and of odds and ends of business stationery.

152 G.S. Telford to Milton Campbell, Pelly, 10 November 1942, copy, folder 30.9, R-334, Telford Papers.

153 G.S. Telford to Margaret Telford, 6 November 1942, folder 31.18, R-334, Telford Papers.

154 Possible employment opportunities are discussed in letters from Milton Campbell, Ottawa, 31 October 1942; and from M.J. Coldwell, Ottawa, 2 November 1942, folder 32.1b, R-382, Telford Papers. Her decision to come East despite the lack of a job offer is indicated in her letter to Margaret Telford, Pelly, 6 November 1942, folder 31.18, R-334, Telford Papers.

155 Statement of Duties, folder 31.17, R-334, Telford Papers. A slightly different version is found in folder 31.8. She had to settle for Classification 1, although she had thought she might be qualified Classification 3. In June 1944 her income was listed as $1,380 (plus CLB). Workers, of course, were in special demand at the Department of National Defence. By 1 October 1940 there were, at National Defence Headquarters and District Headquarters, 593 civilian female employees working as clerks, typists, and stenographers, nearly all (509) in temporary civil servant positions. See Ruth Roach Pierson, *"They're Still Women After All": The Second World War and Canadian Womanhood* (Toronto: McClelland and Stewart, 1986), 95, 101-3.

156 Women's labour force participation went from 24.4 percent in 1939 to 33.5 percent in 1944, and actual numbers of full-time women workers doubled. See Pierson, *"They're Still Women,"* 9, 215. See (especially) chap. 1 for a discussion of the worker recruitment campaign.

157 The pre-war policy prohibiting such employment, which had been relaxed during the war,

was reaffirmed in late 1945, and these regulations remained in force for a decade. See ibid., 82-3, 258 (n. 97). That such prohibitions had not always been effective, at least in times of serious economic difficulties such as the 1930s, is suggested in Graham S. Lowe, *Women in the Administrative Revolution: The Feminization of Clerical Work* (Toronto and Buffalo: University of Toronto Press, 1987), n. 44, 198.

158 The July 1942 Amendment to the Income War Tax Act eliminated the provision that reduced a husband's married status exemption if his wife earned over $750. Now he was not taxed on any income up to $1,200, and his wife's income was not considered. A wife paid tax on any income greater than $660. These provisions changed considerably after the war. See Pierson, *"They're Still Women,"* 48-9. (In 1941 the average female clerical salary was $731, and the average female wage in the labour force was $490. See Lowe, *Women in the Administrative Revolution*, 145, table 7.1: "Average annual earnings for the total labour force and all clerical workers, by sex, and production workers in manufacturing, Canada, 1901-71.")

159 Dyck, *Running to Beat Hell*, 124-5.

160 J.M. Telford, *Recollections*, 115.

161 A.M. Nicholson to G.S. Telford, Ottawa, 29 November 1944, folder 32.1b, R-382, Telford Papers.

162 O.W. Valleau to G.S. Telford, Regina, 15 July 1944, folder 32.1b, R-382, Telford Papers.

163 Melnyk, *No Bankers in Heaven*, 77, 98-9.

164 Carlyle King to G.S. Telford, Saskatoon, 25 February 1945, folder 32.1b, R-382, Telford Papers.

165 G.S. Telford, *Memories*, 38. See Gladys Strum to G.S. Telford, Regina, 22 September 1944; Strum to Telford, telegram, Regina, 25 September 1944; Strum to Telford, Regina, 28 September 1944, folder 32.1b; and G.S. Telford to Margaret Telford, Regina, 4 July 1945, folder 32.1c, R-382, Telford Papers.

166 See J.M. Telford, *Recollections*, 117-8. When he retired the seventy-eight year old was feted by civil service and Cabinet personnel.

167 Telford to Nora Coldwell, Regina, 4 July 1945, copy, folder 32.1d, R-382, Telford Papers.

168 Gladys Strum to G.S. Telford, Regina, 28 September 1944, folder 32.1b, R-382, Telford Papers. Eventually the Telfords found an apartment, and, later, a bungalow. See G.S. Telford, *Memories*, 59.

169 G.S. Telford to Margaret Telford, 13 December 1944, folder 31.18, R-334, Telford Papers.

170 G.S. Telford to Nora Coldwell, Regina, 15 May 1945, folder 32.1c, R-382, Telford Papers. In *Memories* she described the accommodation in strikingly different terms: "we had most uncomfortable rooms in a house" (59).

171 Telford to Nora Coldwell, Regina, 15 May 1945, folder 32.1c, R-382, Telford Papers.

172 Interview by Taylor.

173 Telford to Nora Coldwell, Regina, 20 March 1946, copy, folder 32.1e, R-382, Telford Papers.

174 Telford to Nora Coldwell, Regina, 21 January 1946, copy, folder 32.1e, R-382, Telford Papers.

175 M.J. Coldwell to J.M. and G.S. Telford, Ottawa, 28 December 1962, folder 32.1h, R-382, Telford Papers.

176 G.S. Telford, "Personal Brief presented to The Royal Commission on Agriculture and Rural Life," November 1953, typescript, folder 27, R-334, Telford Papers.

177 In 1960 Mr. Telford had written: "I am Unitarian as opposed to Trinitarian. Other than that I feel that Unitarianism does not know where it is going or how to get there." See letter to sister Maud, Regina, 8 October 1960, copy, folder 30.9, R-334, Telford Papers. An illustration of Gertrude Telford's interest in the Quakers is found in a letter from Barbara Cadbury to G.S. Telford, London, England, 23 May 1962, folder 31.5, R-334, Telford Papers. As to her involvement with the Unitarians, see letter of appreciation sent to her on behalf of the Unitarians from Myrtle Surjek, Regina, 2 November 1971, folder 32.1i, R-382, Telford Papers.

178 G.S. Telford, *What Happened to David Jones*, 17.

179 Strong-Boag, *New Day Recalled*, 103.

180 Ibid., 102.

181 J.M. Telford to Class '08, McMaster, 3 May 1958, copy, folder 30.5, R-334, Telford Papers.

182 The accommodation made by Gertrude Telford has been briefly treated by Georgina

Taylor in her study of how twelve leading women activists reconciled public and private duties. See Taylor, "Equals and Partners?"

183 Sangster, *Dreams of Equality*, passim. See especially chap. 4.

184 Eliane Leslau Silverman, "Women's Perceptions of Marriage on the Alberta Frontier," in *Building Beyond the Homestead: Rural History on the Prairies*, ed. David C. Jones and Ian MacPherson (Calgary: University of Calgary Press, 1985), 61.

Bibliography

Acton, Janice. *Women at Work, Ontario 1850-1930*. Toronto: Canadian Women's Educational Press, 1974.

Adilman, Tamara. "A Preliminary Sketch of Chinese Women and Work in British Columbia, 1858-1920." In *Not Just Pin Money: Selected Essays on the History of Women's Work in British Columbia*, ed. Barbara K. Latham and Roberta J. Pazdro, 53-78. Victoria: Camosun College, 1984. Reprinted in *British Columbia Reconsidered: Essays on Women*, ed. Gillian Creese and Veronica Strong-Boag, 309-39. Vancouver: Press Gang Publishers, 1992.

Allen, Barbara. *Homesteading the High Desert*. Salt Lake City: University of Utah Press, 1987.

Allen, Judith A. "Introduction." *Rose Scott: Vision and Revision in Feminism*, 1-32. Oxford and Melbourne: Oxford University Press, 1994.

Allen, Richard. *The Social Passion: Religion and Social Reform in Canada, 1914-1928*. Toronto: University of Toronto Press, 1973.

Anderson, Kay J. *Vancouver's Chinatown: Racial Discourse in Canada, 1875-1980*. Montreal and Kingston: McGill-Queen's University Press, 1991.

Antoinetta, Carolina, and J.A. Van de Vorst. "A History of Farm Women's Work in Manitoba." MA thesis, University of Manitoba, 1988.

Armitage, Susan. "Through Women's Eyes: A New View of the West." In *The Women's West*, ed. Susan Armitage and Elizabeth Jameson, 9-18. Norman: University of Oklahoma Press, 1987.

Armitage, Susan, and Elizabeth Jameson, ed. *The Women's West*. Norman: University of Oklahoma Press, 1987.

Arnup, Katherine. *Education for Motherhood, Advice for Mothers in Twentieth-Century Canada*. Toronto: University of Toronto Press, 1994.

Arnup, Katherine, Andrée Lévesque, and Ruth Roach Pierson, eds. *Delivering Motherhood: Maternal Ideologies and Practices in the 19th and 20th Centuries*. London: Routledge, 1990.

Axelrod, Paul, and John G. Reid, eds. *Youth, University and Canadian Society: Essays in the Social History of Higher Education*. Montreal and Kingston: McGill-Queen's University Press, 1989.

Ayukawa, Midge. "Good Wives and Wise Mothers: Japanese Picture Brides in Early Twentieth-Century British Columbia." *BC Studies* 105 and 106 (Spring/Summer 1995): 103-18.

Bacchi, Carol Lee. "Divided Allegiances: The Response of Farm and Labour Women to Suffrage." In *A Not Unreasonable Claim: Women and Reform in Canada, 1880s-1920s*, ed. Linda Kealey, 89-108. Toronto: Women's Press, 1979.

______. *Liberation Deferred? The Ideas of the English Suffragists, 1877-1918*. Toronto: University of Toronto Press, 1983.

Backhouse, Constance. "Nineteenth Century Canadian Prostitution Law: Reflection of a Discriminatory Society." *Histoire Sociale/Social History* 18, 36 (1985): 387-423.

______. *Petticoats and Prejudice: Women and Law in Nineteenth-Century Canada*. Toronto: University of Toronto Press and Osgoode Society, 1991.

Bailey, Beth L. *From Front Porch to Backseat: Courtship in Twentieth Century America*. Baltimore and London: Johns Hopkins University Press, 1988.

Barber, Marilyn. "The Fellowship of the Maple Leaf Teachers." In *The Anglican Church and the World of Western Canada*, ed. Barry Ferguson, 54-66. Regina: University of Regina Press, 1991.

______. "The Servant Problem in Manitoba, 1896-1930." In *First Days, Fighting Days: Women in Manitoba History*, ed. Mary Kinnear, 100-19. Regina: Canadian Plains Research Centre, University of Regina, 1987.

Barman, Jean. *The West beyond the West: A History of British Columbia.* Toronto: University of Toronto Press, 1995.

Barron, F. Laurie. "Indian Agents and the North-West Rebellion." In *1885 and After: Native Society in Transition*, ed. F. Laurie Barron and James B. Waldram. Regina: Canadian Plains Research Centre, 1986.

Bashevkin, Sylvia B. "Independence Versus Partisanship: Dilemmas in the Political History of Women in English Canada." In *Rethinking Canada: The Promise of Women's History*, ed. Veronica Strong-Boag and Anita Clair Fellman, 2nd ed., 246-75. Toronto: Copp Clark Pitman, 1986.

______. *Toeing the Lines: Women and Party Politics in English Canada.* Toronto: University of Toronto Press, 1985.

Bauman, Paula. "Single Women Homesteaders in Wyoming, 1880-1930." *Annals of Wyoming*, 58 (1986): 39-53.

BC Studies. "Women's History and Gender History." A special double issue 105 and 106 (Spring/Summer 1995).

Beasley, Delilah. *The Negro Trail Blazers of California.* New York: Negro Universities Press, 1969.

Bennett, John W., and Seena B. Kohl. *Settling the Canadian-American West, 1890-1915.* Lincoln: University of Nebraska Press, 1995.

Blanchet, M. Wylie. *The Curve of Time.* Sidney, BC: Gray's, 1980.

Bliss, Michael. "Privatizing the Mind: The Sundering of Canada." *Journal of Canadian Studies* 26 (1991): 5-17.

Blumstein, Philip, and Pepper Schwartz. *American Couples: Money, Work, Sex.* New York: Morrow, 1983.

Blunt, Alison. *Travel, Gender, and Imperialism: Mary Kingsley and West Africa.* New York and London: Guilford, 1994.

Blunt, Alison, and Gillian Rose, eds. *Writing Women and Space: Colonial and Postcolonial Geographies.* New York and London: Guilford, 1994.

Bolt, Christine. *Victorian Attitudes to Race.* Toronto: University of Toronto Press, 1971.

Boutilier, Beverly. "Gender, Organized Women, and the Politics of Institution Building: Founding the Victorian Order of Nurses for Canada, 1893-1900." PhD thesis, Carleton University, 1994.

______. "Helpers or Heroines? The National Council of Women, Nursing, and 'Woman's Work' in Late Victorian Canada." In *Caring and Curing: Historical Perspectives on Women and Healing in Canada*, ed. Dianne Dodd and Deborah Gorham, 17-47. Ottawa: University of Ottawa Press, 1994.

Boyd, Lois. "Presbyterian Ministers' Wives: A Nineteenth-Century Portrait." *Journal of Presbyterian History* 59, 1 (1981): 3-17.

Bradbury, Bettina. "The Family Economy and Work in an Industrializing City: Montreal in the 1870s." *Canadian Historical Association Historical Papers* (1979): 71-96. Reprinted in *Interpreting Canada's Past: Volume II, After Confederation*, ed. J.M. Bumsted, 136-65. 2nd ed. Toronto: Oxford University Press, 1993.

______. "Pigs, Cows and Boarders: Non-Wage Forms of Survival Among Montreal Families, 1861-1891." *Labour/Le Travail* 14 (1984): 9-46.

Bradbury, Bettina, ed. *Canadian Family History: Selected Readings.* Toronto: Copp Clark Pitman, 1992.

Brand, Dionne. *No Burden to Carry: Narratives of Black Working Women in Ontario 1920s to 1950s.* Toronto: Women's Press, 1991.

Brandt, Gail Cuthbert. "Postmodern Patchwork: Some Recent Trends in the Writing of Women's History in Canada." *Canadian Historical Review* 72, 4 (1991): 441-70.

Brooks Sundberg, Sara. "A Female Frontier: Manitoba Farm Women in 1922." *Prairie Forum* 16 (1991): 185-204.

Brouwer, Ruth Compton. *New Women for God: Canadian Presbyterian Women and India Missions, 1876-1914.* Toronto: University of Toronto Press, 1990.

Brown, Jennifer. *Strangers in Blood: Fur Trade Company Families in Indian Country.* Vancouver: UBC Press, 1980.

Buck, Ruth Mateson. "Wives and Daughters." *Folklore* 9, 4 (1988): 14-5.
Buckley, Suzann. "Ladies or Midwives? Efforts to Reduce Infant and Maternal Mortality." In *A Not Unreasonable Claim*, ed. Linda Kealey, 131-49. Toronto: Women's Educational Press, 1979.
Burnet, Jean, ed. *Looking into My Sister's Eyes*. Toronto: Multicultural History Society of Ontario, 1986.
Burstyn, Joan N. *Victorian Education and the Ideal of Womanhood*. London: Croom Helm, 1980.
Bush, Julia. "'The Right Sort of Woman': Female Emigrators and Emigration to the British Empire, 1890-1910." *Women's History Review* 3, 3 (1994): 385-409.
Butler, Judith P. *Gender Trouble: Feminism and the Subversion of Identity*. New York: Routledge, 1990.
Canning, Kathleen. "Feminist History after the Linguistic Turn: Historicizing Discourse and Experience." *Signs: Journal of Women in Culture and Society* 19 (1994): 368-404.
Carter, Connie, and Eileen Daoust. "From Home to House: Women in the B.C. Legislature." In *Not Just Pin Money: Selected Essays on the History of Women's Work in British Columbia*, ed. Barbara K. Latham and Roberta J. Pazdro, 389-405. Victoria: Camosun College, 1984.
Carter, Sarah. *Capturing Women: The Manipulation of Cultural Imagery in Canada's Prairie West*. Montreal and Kingston: McGill-Queen's University Press, 1997.
______. "Categories and Terrains of Exclusion: Constructing the 'Indian Woman' in the Early Settlement Era in Western Canada." *Great Plains Quarterly* 13 (1993): 147-61.
______. "'A Fate Worse Than Death': Indian Captivity Stories Thrilled Victorian Readers: But Were They True?" *Beaver* 68 (1988): 21-8.
______. *Lost Harvests: Prairie Indian Reserve Farmers and Government Policy*. Montreal: McGill-Queen's University Press, 1990.
Cavanaugh, Catherine. "In Search of a Useful Life: Irene Marryat Parlby, 1868-1965." PhD thesis, University of Alberta, 1994.
______. "The Limitations of the Pioneering Partnership: The Alberta Campaign for Homestead Dower, 1909-25." *Canadian Historical Review* 74 (June 1993): 198-225.
______. "'No Place for a Woman': Engendering Western Canadian Settlement." *Western Historical Quarterly* 28 (1997): 493-518.
______. "The Women's Movement in Alberta as Seen through the Campaign for Dower Rights." MA thesis, University of Alberta, 1986.
Chapman, Terry. "Sex Crimes in the West, 1890-1920." *Alberta History* 35, 4 (1987): 6-21.
______. "'Till Death Do Us Part': Wife Beating in Alberta, 1905-1920." *Alberta History* 36, 4 (1988): 13-22.
Chaudhuri, Nupur, and Margaret Strobel, eds. *Western Women and Imperialism: Complicity and Resistance*. Bloomington: Indiana University Press, 1992.
Chong, Denise. *The Concubine's Children*. New York: Viking, 1995.
Christian, Timothy. *The Mentally Ill and Human Rights in Alberta: A Study of the Alberta Sterilization Act*. Report to the Alberta Law Foundation. University of Alberta Faculty of Law, 1973.
Clio Collective. *Quebec Women: A History*. Toronto: Women's Press, 1987.
Coates, Ken. "Send Only Those Who Rise a Peg: Anglican Clergy in the Yukon, 1858-1932." *Journal of the Canadian Church Historical Society* 28, 1 (1986): 3-17.
Cohen, Marjorie Griffin. *Women's Work, Markets, and Economic Development in Nineteenth-Century Ontario*. Toronto: University of Toronto Press, 1988.
Collis, Septima. *A Woman's Trip to Alaska*. New York: Cassell, 1890.
Comacchio, Cynthia R. "Beneath the 'Sentimental Veil': Families and Family History in Canada." *Labour/Le Travail* 33 (1994): 279-302.
Coontz, Stephanie T. *The Way We Never Were: American Families and the Nostalgia Trap*. New York: Basic, 1992.
Cooper, Carol. "Native Women of the Northern Pacific Coast: An Historical Perspective, 1830-1900." *Journal of Canadian Studies* 27, 4 (1992/3): 44-75.
Cran, Marion. *A Woman in Canada*. Toronto: Musson, 1910.
Creese, Gillian, and Veronica Strong-Boag, eds. *British Columbia Reconsidered: Essays on Women*. Vancouver: Press Gang Publishers, 1992.
Crosby, Marcia. "Construction of the Imaginary Indian." In *Vancouver Anthology: The Institutional Politics of Art*, ed. Stan Douglas, 267-91. Vancouver: Talon, 1991.
Curtin, Philip D. *The Image of Africa: British Ideas and Action, 1780-1850*. Madison: University of Wisconsin Press, 1964.

Curtis, Susan. *A Consuming Faith: The Social Gospel and Modern American Culture*. Baltimore and London: Johns Hopkins University Press, 1991.

Daenzer, Patricia M. *Regulating Class Privilege: Immigrant Servants in Canada, 1940s-1990s*. Toronto: Canadian Scholar's Press, 1993.

Davidoff, Leonore, and Catherine Hall. *Family Fortunes: Men and Women of the English Middle Class, 1780-1850*. London: Hutchinson, 1987.

Dawson, Carl A., and Eva R. Younge. *Pioneering in the Prairie Provinces: The Social Side of the Settlement Process*. Toronto: Macmillan, 1940.

Dean, Joanna. "Lady Aberdeen's Vision for Canadian Women: A Study of Evangelism, Liberalism and the Woman Question." MA essay, Carleton University, 1989.

DeBrou, David, and Aileen Moffatt, eds. *"Other" Voices: Historical Essays on Saskatchewan Women*. Regina: Canadian Plains Research Centre, University of Regina, 1995.

Demos, John. *Past, Present and Personal: The Family and the Life Course in American History*. New York and Oxford: Oxford University Press, 1986.

Dempsey, Hugh. *Big Bear: The End of Freedom*. Vancouver: Douglas and McIntyre, 1984.

Dickason, Olive. *Canada's First Nations: A History of Founding Peoples from the Earliest Times*. Toronto: McClelland and Stewart, 1992.

Douglas, Ann. *The Feminization of American Culture*. New York: Knopf, 1977.

Downey, Betsy. "Battered Pioneers." *Great Plains Quarterly* 12 (1992): 31-49.

Downs, Laura Lee. "If 'Woman' Is Just an Empty Category, Then Why Am I Afraid to Walk Alone at Night? Identity Politics Meets the Postmodern Subject." *Comparative Studies in History and Society* 35, 2 (1993): 414-37.

Driedger, Leo. *Mennonites in Winnipeg*. Winnipeg: Kindred, 1990.

Dubinsky, Karen. *Improper Advances: Rape and Heterosexual Conflict in Ontario, 1880-1929*. Chicago and London: University of Chicago Press, 1993.

______. "'Maidenly Girls' or 'Designing Women': The Crime of Seduction in Turn-of-the-Century Ontario." In *Gender Conflicts: Essays in Women's History*, ed. Franca Iacovetta, and Mariana Valverde, 27-66. Toronto: University of Toronto Press, 1992.

Dubinsky, Karen, and Franca Iacovetta. "Murder, Womanly Virtue, and Motherhood: The Case of Angelina Napolitano, 1911-1922." *Canadian Historical Review* 72, 4 (1991): 505-32.

Dubinsky, Karen, and Lynne Marks. "Beyond Purity: A Response to Sangster." *Left History* 3, 4 (Fall/Spring 1995/6): 205-20.

Duffy, Ann Doris. "Struggling With Power: Feminist Critiques of Family Inequality." In *Reconstructing the Canadian Family: Feminist Perspectives*, ed. Nancy Mandell and Ann Duffy, 111-39. Toronto and Vancouver: Butterworths, 1988.

Dunae, Patrick A. "Boys' Literature and the Idea of Empire, 1870-1914." *Victorian Studies* 24 (1980): 105-21.

Dyhouse, Carol. *Girls Growing Up in Late Victorian and Edwardian England*. London: Routledge and Kegan Paul, 1981.

Eichler, Margrit. *Families in Canada Today: Recent Changes and Their Policy Consequences*. Toronto: Gage, 1988.

Epp, Frank H. *Mennonite Exodus: The Rescue and Resettlement of the Russian Mennonites since the Communist Revolution*. N.p.: Canadian Mennonite Relief and Immigration Counsel, 1962.

______. *Mennonites in Canada, 1920-1940*. Toronto: Macmillan, 1982.

Epp, Marlene. "The Mennonite Girls' Homes of Winnipeg (1925-1959): A Home Away From Home." *Journal of Mennonite Studies* 6 (1988): 100-14.

Fabian, Johannes. *Time and the Other: How Anthropology Makes Its Object*. New York: Columbia University Press, 1983.

Fee, Margery. "The Native in Literature." In *Romantic Nationalism and the Image of Native People in Contemporary English-Canadian Literature*, ed. Thomas King, Cheryl Calver, and Helen Hoy, 15-33. Oakville, ON: ECW Press, 1987.

Fingard, Judith. "Race and Respectability in Victorian Halifax." *Journal of Imperial and Commonwealth History* 2, 2 (1992): 169-95.

Finkel, Alvin. "Populism and Gender: The UFA and Social Credit Experiences." *Journal of Canadian Studies* 27, 4 (Winter 1992-3): 76-97.

Finkel, Alvin, Margaret Conrad, and Veronica Strong-Boag. *History of the Canadian Peoples, 1867 to the Present*. Toronto: Copp Clark Pitman, 1993.
Fishburn, Janet Forsythe. *The Fatherhood of God and the Victorian Family: The Social Gospel in America*. Philadelphia: Fortress, 1981.
Flemming, Leslie A. *Women's Work for Women: Missionaries and Social Change in Asia*. Boulder: Westview, 1989.
Foster, Shirley. *Across New Worlds: Nineteenth-Century Women Travellers and Their Writings*. New York: Harvester Wheatsheaf, 1990.
Francis, Daniel. *The Imaginary Indian: The Image of the Indian in Canadian Culture*. Vancouver: Arsenal Pulp Press, 1992.
Friesen, Gerald. *The Canadian Prairies: A History*. Toronto: University of Toronto Press, 1984.
Fulford, Robert. "The Trouble with Emily." *Canadian Art* 10, 4 (1993): 32-9.
Gagan, Rosemary. *A Sensitive Independence: Canadian Methodist Women Missionaries in Canada and the Orient, 1881-1925*. Montreal and Kingston: McGill-Queen's University Press, 1992.
Gauvreau, Michael. *The Evangelical Century: College and Creed in English Canada from the Great Revival to the Great Depression*. Montreal and Kingston: McGill-Queen's University Press, 1991.
Gay, Peter. *The Cultivation of Hatred*. New York and London: Norton, 1993.
Gee, Ellen. "Female Marriage Patterns in Canada: Changes and Differentials." *Journal of Comparative Family Studies* 11 (1980): 457-73.
______. "The Life Course of Canadian Women: An Historical and Demographic Analysis." *Social Indicators Research* (1986): 263-83.
______. "Marriage in Nineteenth-Century Canada." *Canadian Review of Sociology and Anthropology* 19 (1982): 311-25.
Genovese, Elizabeth Fox. "Individualism and Women's History." In *Feminism without Illusions: A Critique of Individualism*, 113-38. Chapel Hill: University of North Carolina Press, 1991.
Gillis, John R. *For Better, For Worse: British Marriages, 1600 to the Present*. New York and Oxford: Oxford University Press, 1985.
Gordon, Deborah. "Introduction: Feminism and the Critique of Colonial Discourse." *Inscriptions* 3, 4 (1988): 1-5.
Gordon, Michael. *The American Family in Social-Historical Perspective*. New York: St. Martin's Press, 1983.
Gorham, Deborah. "From Bonavista to Vancouver Island: Canadian Women's History as Regional History in the 1990s." *Acadiensis* 28, 2 (Spring 1999): 119-25.
______. *The Victorian Girl and the Feminine Ideal*. London: Croom Helm, 1982.
Gowanlock, Theresa, and Theresa Delaney. *Two Months in the Camp of Big Bear*. Parkdale: Parkdale Times, 1885.
Granatstein, Jack. *Who Killed Canadian History?* Toronto: HarperCollins, 1998.
Green, Rayna. "The Pocahontas Perplex: The Image of Indian Women in American Culture." In *Unequal Sisters: A Multicultural Reader in U.S. Women's History*, ed. Ellen Carol DuBois and Vicki L. Ruiz, 15-21. New York: Routledge, 1990.
Griffiths, N.E.S. *The Splendid Vision: Centennial History of the National Council of Women of Canada, 1893-1993*. Ottawa: Carleton University Press, 1993.
Grimshaw, Patricia. *Paths of Duty: American Missionary Wives In Nineteenth-Century Hawaii*. Honolulu: University of Hawaii Press, 1989.
Griswold, Robert L. *Fatherhood in America: A History*. New York: Basic, 1993.
Guy-Sheftall, Beverly. *Daughters of Sorrow: Attitudes Toward Black Women, 1880-1920*. Brooklyn, NY: Carlson, 1990.
Haggis, Jane. "Gendering Colonialism or Colonising Gender? Recent Women's Studies Approaches to White Women and the History of British Colonialism." *Women's Studies International Forum* 13, 1/2 (1990): 105-15.
Hamer, David. *New Towns in the New World: Images and Perceptions of the Nineteenth Century Urban Frontier*. New York: Columbia University Press, 1990.
Hammerton, James. *Emigrant Gentlewomen: Genteel and Female Emigration, 1861-1914*. London: Croom Helm, 1979.

______. "Feminism and Female Emigration, 1861-1886." In *A Widening Sphere*, ed. Martha Vicinus, 53-71. Bloomington: Indiana University Press, 1977.

Hanchuk, Rena. "The Word and Wax: Folk Psychology and Ukrainians in Alberta." MA thesis, University of Alberta, 1990.

Hancock, Lyn, and Marion Dowler. *Tell Me Grandmother*. Toronto: McClelland and Stewart, 1985.

Harley, Sharon. "For The Good of Family and Race: Gender, Work, and Domestic Roles in the Black Community, 1880-1930." In *Black Women in America: Social Science Perspectives*, ed. Micheline R. Malson et al. Chicago: University of Chicago Press, 1990.

Harris, Cole. *The Resettlement of BC: Essays on Colonialism and Geographical Change*. Vancouver: UBC Press, 1997.

Harrison, J.F.C. *Late Victorian Britain, 1875-1901*. Fontana, 1990.

Hartmann, Heidi I. "The Family as the Locus of Gender, Class and Political Struggle: The Example of Housework." *Signs* 6, 3 (Spring 1981): 366-94.

Hill, Daniel. *The Freedom Seekers: Blacks in Early Canada*. Agincourt, ON: Book Society of Canada, 1980.

Hoff, Joan. "Gender as Postmodern Category of Paralysis." *Women's History Review* 3, 2 (1994): 149-68.

Holmes, P., and J. Roberts. *It Could Have Been Worse*. Toronto: Collins, 1980.

Hopkins, M. *Letters from a Lady Rancher*. Halifax: Goodread Biographies, 1981.

Horrall, S.W. "The (Royal) North-West Mounted Police and Prostitution on the Canadian Prairies." *Prairie Forum* 1 (1985): 105-27.

Houghton, Walter E. *The Victorian Frame of Mind, 1830-1870*. New Haven and London: Yale University Press, 1957.

Hume, Stephen. "The Spirit Weeps." In *The Norton Reader: An Anthology of Expository Prose* (shorter 8th ed.), ed. Arthur M. Eastman, 552-62. New York: Norton, 1992.

Hunter, Jane. "The Home and the World: The Missionary Message of U.S. Domesticity." In *Women's Work for Women: Missionaries and Social Change in Asia*, ed. Leslie A. Flemming. Boulder: Westview, 1989.

Iacovetta, Franca. "Manly Militants, Cohesive Communities, and Defiant Domestics: Writing About Immigrants in Canadian Historical Scholarship." *Labour/Le Travail* 36 (1995): 217-52.

______. "The Writing of English Canadian Immigrant History." *Canadian Historical Association*, Canada's Ethnic Group Series, Booklet No. 22. 1997.

Iacovetta, Franca, and Linda Kealey. "Women's History, Gender History and Debating Dichotomies." *Left History* 3, 4 (Spring/Summer 1995): 221-37.

Iacovetta, Franca, and Mariana Valverde, eds. *Gender Conflicts: New Essays in Women's History*. Toronto: University of Toronto Press, 1992.

Ishwaran, K. *The Canadian Family*. N.p.: Gage, 1983.

Jackel, Susan. *A Flannel Shirt and Liberty: English Emigrant Gentlewomen in the Canadian West, 1880-1914*. Vancouver: UBC Press, 1982.

______. "Introduction." In *Wheat and Woman*, ed. Georgina Binnie-Clark, v-xxxvii. Toronto: University of Toronto Press, 1979.

Jahn, Cheryle. "Class, Gender and Agrarian Socialism: The United Farm Women of Saskatchewan, 1926-1931." *Prairie Forum* 19, 2 (Fall 1994): 189-206.

Jalland, Pat. *Women, Marriage and Politics 1860-1914*. Oxford: Oxford University Press, 1986.

James, Louis. "Tom Brown's Imperialist Sons." *Victorian Studies* 18 (1973): 89-99.

Jameson, Elizabeth. *All That Glitters: Class, Conflict, and Community in Cripple Creek*. Urbana: University of Illinois, 1998.

______. "Women As Workers, Women As Civilizers: True Womanhood in the American West." *The Women's West*, ed. Susan Armitage and Elizabeth Jameson, 145-64. Norman: University of Oklahoma Press, 1987.

Jeffrey, Julie Roy. *Frontier Women: The Trans-Mississippi West, 1840-1880*. New York: Hill and Wang, 1979.

Jellison, Katherine. "Women and Technology on the Great Plains, 1910-40." *Great Plains Quarterly* 8 (1988): 145-57.

Johnston, Gordon. "An Intolerable Burden of Meaning: Native Peoples in White Fiction." In *The*

Native in Literature, ed. Thomas King, Cheryl Calver, and Helen Hoy, 50-66. Oakville, ON: ECW Press, 1987.

Jones, Jacqueline. *Labor of Love, Labor of Sorrow: Black Women, Work and the Family, From Slavery to the Present.* New York: Vintage, 1985.

Kaplan, Cora. *Sea Changes: Essays on Culture and Feminism.* London: Verso, 1986.

Katzman, David. *Seven Days a Week: Women and Domestic Service in Industrializing America.* Oxford: Oxford University Press, 1978.

Kealey, Linda. "Women and Labour during World War I: Women Workers and the Minimum Wage in Manitoba." In *First Days, Fighting Days: Women in Manitoba History*, ed. Mary Kinnear, 76-99. Regina: Canadian Plains Research Centre, University of Regina, 1987.

Kealey, Linda, and Joan Sangster, eds. *Beyond the Vote: Canadian Women and Politics.* Toronto: University of Toronto Press, 1989.

Kerber, Linda K. "Separate Spheres, Female Worlds, Woman's Place: The Rhetoric of Women's History." *Journal of American History* 75 (1988): 9-39.

Kieman, V.G. *The Lords of Human Kind: European Attitudes toward the Outside World in the Imperial Age.* Middlesex: Penguin, 1972.

Kilian, Crawford. *Go Do Some Great Thing: The Black Pioneers of British Columbia.* North Vancouver, BC: Douglas and McIntyre, 1978.

Kinnear, Mary. "'Do You Want Your Daughter to Marry a Farmer?': Women's Work on the Farm, 1922." *Canadian Papers in Rural History,* vol. 6, ed. Donald Akenson, 137-53. Gananoque: Langdale, 1988.

______. "Post-Suffrage Prairie Politics: Women Candidates in Winnipeg Municipal Elections, 1918-1938." *Prairie Forum* 16, 1 (Spring 1991): 41-58.

Kirsch, Gesa E. *Ethical Dilemmas in Feminist Research.* Albany, NY: State University of New York, 1999.

Klein, Laura F. "Contending with Colonization: Tlingit Men and Women in Change." In *Women and Colonization: Anthropological Perspectives*, ed. Mona Etienne and Eleanor Leacock, 88-108. New York: Praeger, 1980.

Klippenstein, Frieda Esau. "'Doing What We Could': Mennonite Domestic Servants in Winnipeg, 1920s to 1950s." *Journal of Mennonite Studies* 7 (1989): 145-66.

Klymasz, Robert. *Svieto: Celebrating Ukrainian-Canadian Ritual in East Central Alberta through Three Generations.* Edmonton: Alberta Culture and Multiculturalism, 1992.

Krahn, Cornelius. "Research on Urban Mennonites." *Mennonite Life* 23, 4 (1968): 189-92.

Kröller, Eva-Marie. "First Impressions: Rhetorical Strategies in Travel Writing by Victorian Women." *Ariel* 21, 4 (1990): 87-99.

Langford, Nanci. "'All That Glitters': The Political Apprenticeship of Alberta Women, 1916-1930." In *Standing on New Ground*, ed. Catherine A. Cavanaugh and Randi R. Warne, 71-85. Edmonton: University of Alberta Press, 1993.

______. "First Generation and Lasting Impressions: The Gendered Identities of Prairie Homestead Women." PhD thesis, University of Alberta, 1994.

LaPierre, Jo. "The Academic Life of Canadian Coeds, 1880-1900." *Historical Studies in Education/Revue d'histoire de l'éducation* 2 (1990): 225-45.

Lapp, Rudolph. *Blacks in Gold Rush California.* London: Yale University Press, 1977.

LaRossa, Ralph, and Donald C. Reitzes. "Continuity and Change in Middle Class Fatherhood, 1925-1939: The Culture-Conduct Connection." *Journal of Marriage and the Family* 55 (1993): 455-68.

Latham, Barbara K., and Roberta J. Pazdro, eds. *Not Just Pin Money: Selected Essays on the History of Women's Work In British Columbia.* Victoria: Camosun College, 1984.

Laycock, David. *Populism and Democratic Thought in the Canadian Prairies, 1919 to 1945.* Toronto: University of Toronto Press, 1990.

Leavitt, Judith Walzer. *Brought to Bed: Childbearing in America, 1750-1950.* New York: Oxford University Press, 1986.

Leger-Anderson, Ann. "Canadian Prairie Women's History: An Uncertain Enterprise." *Journal of the West,* 37, 1 (1998): 47-59.

Leslie, Genevieve. "Domestic Service in Canada, 1880-1920." In *Women at Work, 1850-1930*, ed. Janice Acton et al., 71-125. Toronto: Canadian Women's Educational Press, 1974.

Liddington, Jill, and Jill Norris, eds. *One Hand Tied Behind Us*. London: Virago, 1978.

Lillard, Charles. "Afterword: Listening to the Voices of the Coast." In *The Call of the Coast*, ed. Charles Lillard, 157-64. Victoria: Horsdal and Schubart, 1992.

______. "Foreword: What the Pinks Saw." In Kathrene Pinkerton, *Three's a Crew*. Ganges, BC: Horsdal and Schubart, 1991.

Lindgren, H. Elaine. "Ethnic Women Homesteading on the Plains of North Dakota." *Great Plains Quarterly* 9 (1989): 157-73.

______. *Land in Her Own Name: Women as Homesteaders in North Dakota*. Fargo: North Dakota Institute for Regional Studies, North Dakota State University, 1991.

Lindsey, William D. "The Social Gospel and Feminism." *American Journal of Theology and Philosophy* 13, 3 (1993): 195-210.

Lindstrom-Best, Varpu. *Defiant Sisters: A Social History of Finnish Immigrant Women in Canada*. Toronto: Multicultural History Society of Ontario, 1988.

Lorimer, Douglas A. *Colour, Class and the Victorians*. [Leicester]: Leicester University Press, 1978.

Lowe, Graham S. *Women in the Administrative Revolution: The Feminization of Clerical Work*. Toronto and Buffalo: University of Toronto Press, 1987.

McCallum, Margaret. "Prairie Women and the Struggle for a Dower Law, 1905-1920." *Prairie Forum* 18, 1 (1993): 19-34.

McClung, Nellie L. *Clearing in the West*. Toronto: Thomas Allen, 1935.

McCormick, Peter. "Regionalism in Canada: Disentangling the Threads," *Journal of Canadian Studies*, 24, 2 (Spring 1989).

McKenna, Katherine, M.J. *A Life of Propriety: Anne Murray Powell and Her Family, 1755-1849*. Montreal and Kingston: McGill-Queen's University Press, 1994.

McKillop, A.B. *Matters of Mind: The University in Ontario, 1791-1951*. Toronto: University of Toronto Press, 1994.

McKinlay, Clare Mary. "The Honourable Irene Parlby." MA thesis, University of Alberta, 1953.

McLaren, Angus. *Our Own Master Race: Eugenics in Canada, 1885-1945*. Toronto: McClelland and Stewart, 1990.

Macleod, R.C. *The North-West Mounted Police and Law Enforcement, 1873-1905*. Toronto: University of Toronto Press, 1976.

McManus, Sheila. "'Their Own Country': Race, Gender, Landscape, and Colonization around the 49th Parallel, 1862-1900." *Agricultural History* 73, 2 (Spring 1999): 168-82.

McPherson, Kathryn. "Was the 'Frontier' Good for Women? Historical Approaches to Women and Agricultural Settlement in the Prairie West, 1870-1900." *Atlantis: A Women's Journal* 25, 1 (Fall/Winter 2000).

Marks, Lynn, and Chad Gaffield. "Women at Queen's University, 1895-1905: A 'Little Sphere' All Their Own?" *Ontario History* 78 (1986): 331-49.

Marr, Lucille M. "Church Teen Clubs, Feminized Organizations? Tuxis Boys, Trail Rangers, and Canadian Girls in Training, 1919-1939." *Historical Studies in Education/Revue d'histoire de l'éducation* 3 (1991): 249-67.

______. "Sunday School Teaching: A Women's Enterprise: A Case Study From the Canadian Methodist, Presbyterian and United Church Tradition, 1919-1939." *Histoire Sociale/Social History* 26 (1993): 329-44.

Marsh, Margaret. "Suburban Men and Masculine Domesticity, 1870-1915." *American Quarterly* (1988): 165-86.

Marsiglio, William. "Contemporary Scholarship on Fatherhood: Culture, Identity, and Conduct." *Journal of Family Issues* 14 (1993): 484-509.

Martynowych, Orest. *Ukrainians in Canada: The Formative Period, 1891-1924*. Edmonton: Canadian Institute of Ukrainian Studies, 1991.

May, Elaine Tyler. *Great Expectations: Marriage and Divorce in Post-Victorian America*. Chicago and London: University of Chicago Press, 1980.

Memmi, Albert. *The Colonizer and the Colonized*. Boston: Beacon, 1965.

Mills, Allen. *Fools for Christ: The Political Thought of J.S. Woodsworth*. Toronto: University of Toronto Press, 1991.

Mills, Sara. *Discourses of Difference: An Analysis of Women's Travel Writing and Colonialism*. London: Routledge, 1991.

Mintz, Steven, and Susan Kellogg. *Domestic Revolutions: A Social History of American Family Life.* New York and London: Free Press, 1988.

Mitchinson, Wendy. *The Nature of Their Bodies: Women and Their Doctors in Victorian Canada.* Toronto: University of Toronto Press, 1991.

Moir, John S. "The Canadian Baptist and the Social Gospel Movement, 1879-1914." In *Baptists in Canada: Search for Identity amidst Diversity*, ed. Jarold K. Zeman, 147-60. Burlington, ON: Welch, 1980.

Morton, Suzanne. *Ideal Surroundings: Domestic Life in a Working-Class Suburb in the 1920s.* Toronto: University of Toronto Press, 1995.

______. "Separate Sphere in a Separate World: African-Nova Scotian Women in Late 19th Century Halifax County." *Acadiensis* 22, 2 (1993): 61-83.

Morton, W.L. *God's Galloping Girl: The Peace River Diaries of Monica Storrs, 1929-1931.* Vancouver: UBC Press, 1979.

Mouat, Jeremy. *Roaring Days: Rossland's Mines and the History of British Columbia.* Vancouver: UBC Press, 1995.

Moyles, R.G., and Doug Owram. *Imperial Dreams and Colonial Realities: British Views of Canada, 1880-1914.* Toronto: University of Toronto Press, 1988.

Mumford, Esther Hall. *Seattle's Black Victorians, 1852-1901.* Seattle: Ananse Press, 1980.

Murray, Peter. *The Devil and Mr. Duncan: The Tale of The Two Metlakatlas.* Victoria: Sono Nis, 1985.

Myers, Sandra. *Westering Women and the Frontier Experience, 1800-1915.* Albuquerque: University of New Mexico Press, 1982.

Nelson, Paula. *After the West Was Won: Homesteaders and Town-Builders in Western South Dakota, 1900-1917.* Iowa City: University of Iowa Press, 1986.

Nett, Emily N. *Canadian Families: Past and Present.* Toronto and Vancouver: Butterworths, 1988.

Newton, Janice. *The Feminist Challenge to the Canadian Left, 1900-1918.* Montreal and Kingston: McGill-Queen's University Press, 1995.

Ng, Roxana. "Immigrant Women: The Construction of a Labour Market Category." *Canadian Journal of Women and the Law* 4, 1 (1990): 96-112.

______. "The Social Construction of 'Immigrant Women' in Canada." In *The Politics of Diversity: Feminism, Marxism and Nationalism*, ed. Roberta Hamilton, and Michele Barrett, 269-86. London: New Left, 1986.

Norrie, Kenneth, and Douglas Owram. *A History of the Canadian Economy.* Toronto: Harcourt Brace Jovanovich, 1991.

Offen, Karen. "Defining Feminism: A Comparative Historical Approach." *Signs* 14, 1 (1988): 119-57.

Osterud, Nancy Grey. *Bonds of Community: The Lives of Farm Women in Nineteenth-Century New York.* Ithaca and London: Cornell University Press, 1991.

______. "Gender and the Transition to Capitalism in Rural America." *Agricultural History* 67, 2 (1993): 14-30.

Palmer, Howard. "Strangers and Stereotypes: The Rise of Nativism, 1880-1920." In *The Prairie West*, ed. Douglas Francis and Howard Palmer, 309-33. Edmonton: Pica Pica, 1985.

Palmer, Howard, and Tamara Palmer. *Alberta: A New History.* Edmonton: Hurtig, 1990.

Parr, Joy. "Gender History and Historical Practice." *Canadian Historical Review* 76, 3 (1995): 354-76.

______. *The Gender of Breadwinners: Women, Men, and Change in Two Industrial Towns, 1880-1950.* Toronto: University of Toronto Press, 1990.

Parr, Joy, and Mark Rosenfeld. *Gender and History in Canada.* Toronto: Copp Clark, 1996.

Parvez Wakil, S. *Marriage, Family and Society: Canadian Perspectives.* Toronto: Butterworths, 1975.

Pascoe, Peggy. "Ideologies of Women's Distinctiveness in Victorian and Postmodern Contexts." *Journal of Women's History* 7, 3 (1995): 137-45.

Pedersen, Diana. "'The Call to Service': The YWCA and the Canadian College Woman, 1886-1920." In *Youth, University and Canadian Society: Essays in the Social History of Higher Education*, ed. Paul Axelrod and John G. Reid, 187-215. Montreal and Kingston: McGill-Queen's University Press, 1989.

______. *Changing Women Changing History.* Ottawa: Carleton University Press, 1996.

Perkins, Joan. *Victorian Women.* London: John Murray, 1993.

Pilton, James. "Early Negro Settlement in Victoria." BA Thesis, University of British Columbia, 1949.

______. "Negro Settlement in British Columbia 1858-1871." MA thesis, University of British Columbia, 1951.

Pinkerton, Kathrene. *Three's a Crew*. Ganges, BC: Horsdal and Schubart, 1991.

Pomeroy, Earl. *In Search of the Golden West: The Tourist in Western America*. Lincoln and London: University of Nebraska Press, 1957.

Poovey, Mary. "Feminism and Deconstruction." *Feminist Studies* 14, 1 (1988): 51-65.

Prasch, Thomas J. "Orientalism's Other, Other Orientalisms: Women in the Scheme of Empire." *Journal of Women's History* 7, 4 (1995): 174-88.

Prentice, Alison et al., eds. *Canadian Women: A History*. Toronto: Harcourt Brace Jovanovich, 1988.

Prentice, Alison, and Susan Mann Trofimenkoff. *The Neglected Majority: Essays in Canadian Women's History*. Toronto: McClelland and Stewart, 1977.

Purvis, Jane. "Women's History and Poststructuralism." *Women's History Review* 5, 1 (1996): 5-7.

Ralston, H. Keith. "John Sullivan Deas: A Black Entrepreneur in British Columbia Salmon Canning." *BC Studies*, 32 (Winter 1976-7): 64-78.

Rauschenbusch, Walter. *Christianity and the Social Crisis*. New York and London: Association, 1907.

Rawlyk, G.A., A.L. McCrimmon, H.P. Widden, and T.T. Shields. "Christian Higher Education, and McMaster University." In *Canadian Baptists and Christian Higher Education*, ed. George A. Rawlyk, 31-62. Montreal: McGill-Queen's University Press, 1988.

Reid, John G. "Writing about Regions." In *Writing about Canada: A Handbook for Modern Canadian History*, ed. John Schultz, 71-96. Scarborough: Prentice-Hall, 1990.

Rendall, Jane. "Introduction." In *Equal or Different: Women's Politics 1800-1914*, ed. Jane Rendall. Oxford: Blackwell, 1987.

Richards, Jeffrey. "'Passing the Love of Women': Manly Love and Victorian Society." *In Manliness and Morality: Middle-Class Masculinity in Britain and America, 1800-1940*, ed. J.A. Mangan and James Walvin, 92-122. New York: St. Martin's Press, 1987.

Riley, Denise. *"Am I That Name?": Feminism and the Category of Women in History*. Minneapolis: University of Minnesota, 1988.

Roach Pierson, Ruth. "Experience, Difference, Dominance and Voice in the Writing of Canadian Women's History." In *Writing Women's History: International Perspectives*, ed. Karen Offen, Ruth Roach Pierson, and Jane Rendall, 79-106. Bloomington: Indiana University Press, 1991.

______. *"They're Still Women After All": The Second World War and Canadian Womanhood.* Toronto: McClelland and Stewart, 1986.

Roberts, Barbara. "Sex, Politics, and Religion: Controversies in Female Immigration Work in Montreal, 1881-1919." *Atlantis* 6, 1 (1980): 25-38.

______. "'They Drove Him to Drink': Donald Creighton's Macdonald and His Wives." *Canada: An Historical Magazine* 3, 2 (December 1975): 51-64.

______. "A Work of Empire: Canadian Reformers and the British Female Immigration." In *A Not Unreasonable Claim: Women and Reform in Canada, 1880s-1920s*, ed. Linda Kealey, 148-86. Toronto: Women's Press, 1979.

Roberts, Sarah. *Of Us and the Oxen*. Saskatoon: Modern, 1968.

Roberts, Wayne. "'Rocking the Cradle for the World': The New Woman and Maternal Feminism, Toronto, 1877-1914." In *A Not Unreasonable Claim: Women and Reform in Canada, 1880s-1920s*, ed. Linda Kealey, 15-46. Toronto: Women's Press, 1979.

Robin, Martin. *The Rush for Spoils: The Company Province, 1871-1933*. Toronto: McClelland and Stewart, 1972.

Robinson, Gregory. "British-Canadian Justice in the Ukrainian Colony: Crime and Law Enforcement in East Central Alberta, 1915-1929." MA thesis, University of Alberta, 1992.

______. "Rougher Than Any Other Nationality? Ukrainian Canadians and Crime in Alberta, 1915-29." *Journal of Ukrainian Studies* 16, 1-2 (1991): 147-79.

Rodgers, Roy H., and Gail Witney. "The Family Cycle in Twentieth Century Canada." *Journal of Marriage and the Family* 43, 3 (1981): 727-40.

Rolf, Knight. *Indians at Work: An Informal History of Native Indian Labour in British Columbia, 1858-1930*. Vancouver: New Star, 1978.

Rolph, William Kirby. *Henry Wise Wood of Alberta*. Toronto: University of Toronto Press, 1950.

Roome, Patricia. "Amelia Turner and Calgary Labour Women, 1919-1935." In *Beyond the Vote:*

Canadian Women and Politics, ed. Linda Kealey and Joan Sangster, 98-117. Toronto: University of Toronto Press, 1989.

Rose, H. *The Stump Farm*. Boston: Little Brown, 1928.

Ross, H. Miriam. *Shaping a Vision of Mission: Early Influences on the United Baptist Woman's Missionary Union*. Hantsport, NS: Lancelot, 1988.

Rothman, Ellen K. *Hands and Hearts: A History of Courtship in America*. New York: Basic, 1984.

Rotundo, E. Anthony. "American Fatherhood: A Historical Perspective." *American Behavioral Scientist* 29 (1985): 7-25.

Roy, Patricia E. *A White Man's Province: British Columbia Politicians and Chinese and Japanese Immigrants, 1858-1914*. Vancouver: UBC Press, 1989.

Rubinstein, David. *Before the Suffragettes: Women's Emancipation in the 1890s*. London: Harvester, 1986.

Sangster, Joan. "Beyond Dichotomies: Re-Assessing Gender History and Women's History in Canada." *Left History* 3, 1 (Spring/Summer 1995): 109-21.

______. "'Pardon Tales' from Magistrate's Court: Women, Crime, and the Court in Peterborough County, 1920-50." *Canadian Historical Review* 74, 2 (1993): 161-97.

______. "Reconsidering Dichotomies." *Left History* 3, 4 (Fall/Spring 1995/6): 238-48.

Sangster, Joan, ed. *Dreams of Equality: Women on the Canadian Left, 1920-1950*. Toronto: McClelland and Stewart, 1989.

Schlissel, Lillian, Vicki Ruiz, and Janice Monk. *Western Women: Their Land, Their Lives*. Albuquerque: University of New Mexico Press, 1988.

Scidmore, E. Ruhamah. *Alaska: Its Southern Coast and the Sitkan Archipelago*. Boston: Lothrop, 1885.

Segal, Lynne. *Why Feminism? Gender, Psychology, Politics*. New York: Columbia University Press, 1999.

Shorter, Edward. *A History of Women's Bodies*. New York: Basic, 1982.

Showalter, Elaine. *Sexual Anarchy: Gender and Culture at the Fin De Siècle*. New York: Viking, 1990.

Silverman, Eliane Leslau. "Women's Perceptions of Marriage on the Alberta Frontier." In *Building Beyond the Homestead: Rural History on the Prairies*, ed. David C. Jones and Ian MacPherson, 49-64. Calgary: University of Calgary Press, 1985.

Slattery, Brian, and Linda Charlton. *Canadian Native Law Cases, 1891-1910*. Saskatoon: Native Law Centre, 1985.

Sluman, Norma, and Jean Goodwill. *John Tootoosis: A Biography of a Cree Leader*. Ottawa: Golden Dog, 1982.

Smith, Erica. "'Gentlemen, This Is No Ordinary Trial': Sexual Narratives in the Trial of the Reverend Corbett, Red River, 1863." In *Reading Beyond Words: Contexts for Native History*, ed. Jennifer S.H. Brown and Elizabeth Vibert, 364-80. Peterborough, ON and Orchard Park, NY: Broadview, 1996.

Smith, Sherry L. "Single Women Homesteaders: The Perplexing Case of Elinore Pruitt Stewart." *Western Historical Quarterly*, 22 (1991): 163-83.

Smith-Rosenberg, Carroll. *Disorderly Conduct: Visions of Gender in Victorian America*. New York: Oxford University Press, 1985.

Snell, James G. *In the Shadow of the Law: Divorce in Canada, 1900-1939*. Toronto: University of Toronto Press, 1991.

Sprague, D.N. *Canada and the Métis, 1869-1885*. Waterloo, ON: Wilfrid Laurier University Press, 1988.

Stacey, Beverley A. "D.W. Davis: Whiskey Trader to Politician." *Alberta History* 38, 3 (1990): 1-11.

Stansell, Christine. *City of Women: Sex and Class in New York, 1789-1860*. New York: Knopf, 1986.

Stearns, Peter N. "Fatherhood in Historical Perspective: The Role of Social Change." In *Fatherhood and Families in Cultural Context*, ed. Frederick W. Bozett and Shirley M.H. Hanson, 28-52. New York: Springer, 1991.

Stoler, Ann Laura. "Carnal Knowledge and Imperial Power: Gender, Race and Morality in Colonial Asia." In *Gender at the Crossroads of Knowledge: Feminist Anthropology in the Postmodern Era*, ed. Micaela di Leonardo, 51-101. Berkeley: University of California Press, 1991.

______. *Race and the Education of Desire*. Durham and London: Duke University Press, 1995.

______. "Rethinking Colonial Categories: European Communities and the Boundaries of Rule." In *Colonialism and Culture*, ed. Nicholas B. Dirks, 319-52. Ann Arbor: University of Michigan Press, 1992.

Stone, Olive. "Canadian Women as Legal Persons." *Alberta Law Review* 17, 2 (1979): 357-82.

Strange, Carolyn. "Patriarchy Modified: The Criminal Prosecution of Rape in York County, Ontario, 1880-1930." In *Essays in the History of Canadian Law*, ed. Jim Phillips et al., 207-51. Toronto: University of Toronto Press, 1994.

______. "Wounded Womanhood and Dead Men: Chivalry and the Trials of Clara Ford and Carrie Davis." In *Gender Conflicts*, ed. Franca Iacovetta and Mariana Valverde, 149-88. Toronto: University of Toronto Press, 1992.

Strange, Kathleen. *With the West in Her Eyes: The Story of a Modern Pioneer*. New York: Dodge, 1937.

Strobel, Margaret. *European Women and the Second British Empire*. Bloomington and Indianapolis: Indiana University Press, 1991.

______. "Gender and Race in the Nineteenth- and Twentieth-Century British Empire." In *Becoming Visible: Women in European History*, ed. Renate Bridenthal et al. Boston: Houghton Mifflin, 1987.

Strong-Boag, Veronica. "Contested Space: The Politics of Canadian Memory." *Journal of the Canadian Historical Association* 5 (1994): 3-17.

______. *The New Day Recalled: Lives of Girls and Women in English Canada, 1919-1939*. Toronto: Copp Clark Pitman, 1988.

______. *The Parliament of Women: The National Council of Women of Canada, 1893-1929*. Ottawa: National Museums of Canada, 1976.

______. "Pulling in Double Harness or Hauling a Double Load: Women, Work and Feminism on the Canadian Prairie." *Journal of Canadian Studies* 21, 3 (1986): 32-52.

Sundberg, Sara Brooks. "Farm Women on the Canadian Prairie Frontier: The Helpmate Image." In *Rethinking Canada: The Promise of Women's History*, ed. Veronica Strong-Boag and Anita Fellman, 95-106. Toronto: Copp Clark Pitman, 1986.

Swyripa, Frances. *Wedded to the Cause: Ukrainian-Canadian Women and Ethnic Identity, 1891-1991*. Toronto: University of Toronto Press, 1993.

Szinovacz, Maximiliane E. "Family Power." In *Handbook of Marriage and the Family*, ed. Marvin B. Sussman and Suzanne K. Steinmetz, 651-93. New York: Plenum, 1987.

Taylor, Georgina. "Equals and Partners? An Examination of How Saskatchewan Women Reconciled Their Political Activities for the Co-operative Commonwealth Federation with Traditional Roles for Women." MA thesis, University of Saskatchewan, 1983.

______. "A Personal Tragedy Shapes the Future." *Western Producer* 10 (1991): 10.

______. "'The Women ... Shall Help to Lead the Way': Saskatchewan CCF-NDP Women Candidates in Provincial and Federal Elections, 1934-1965." In *Building the Co-Operative Commonwealth: Essays on the Democratic Socialist Tradition in Canada*, ed. J. William Brennan, 141-60. Regina: Canadian Plains Research Centre, University of Regina, 1984.

Taylor, Jeffrey M. "Dominant and Popular Ideologies in the Making of Rural Manitobans, 1890-1925." PhD thesis, University of Manitoba, 1988.

Thomas, Lewis H. "A History of Agriculture on the Prairies to 1914." In *The Prairie West*, ed. Douglas Francis and Howard Palmer, 221-36. Edmonton: Pica Pica, 1985.

Thompson, John Herd. *Forging the Prairie West*. Toronto and Oxford: Oxford University Press, 1998.

Tye, Diane. "Local Character Anecdotes: A Nova Scotia Case Study." *Western Folklore* 48 (July 1989): 181-99.

Valverde, Mariana. *The Age of Light, Soap, and Water: Moral Reform in English Canada, 1885-1925*. Toronto: McClelland and Stewart, 1991.

______. "Poststructural Gender Historians." *Labour/Le Travail* 25 (1990): 227-36.

______. "'When the Mother of the Race Is Free': Race, Reproduction, and Sexuality in First-Wave Feminism." In *Gender Conflicts*, ed. Franca Iacovetta and Mariana Valverde, 3-26. Toronto: University of Toronto Press, 1992.

Van Kirk, Sylvia. *"Many Tender Ties": Women in Fur Trade Society in Western Canada, 1670-1870*. Winnipeg: Watson and Dwyer, 1980.

______. "Tracing the Fortunes of Five Founding Families of Victoria." *BC Studies* 115/6 (Autumn/Winter 1997/8): 149-79.

______. "A Vital Presence: Women in the Cariboo Gold Rush, 1862-1875." In *British Columbia Reconsidered*, ed. Gillian Creese and Veronica Strong-Boag, 21-37. Vancouver: Press Gang Publishers, 1992.

Van Raaphorst, Donna L. *Union Maids Not Wanted: Organizing Domestic Workers, 1870-1940*. New York: Praeger, 1988.

Vicinus, Martha. *Independent Women: Work and Community for Single Women, 1850-1920*. Chicago: University of Chicago Press, 1985.

______. "Introduction: The Perfect Victorian Lady." In *Suffer and Be Still: Women in the Victorian Age*, ed. Martha Vicinus, vii-xv. Bloomington: Indiana University Press, 1972.

______. *A Widening Sphere*. Bloomington: Indiana University Press, 1977.

Voisey, Paul. "The Urbanization of the Canadian Prairies, 1871-1916." *Histoire Sociale/Social History*, 8 (1975): 77-101.

______. *Vulcan: The Making of a Prairie Community*. Toronto: University of Toronto Press, 1988.

Walker, James W. St. G. *The Black Loyalists: The Search for a Promised Land in Nova Scotia and Sierra Leone 1783-1870*. New York: Africana, 1976.

Ward, Peter. *Courtship, Love and Marriage in Nineteenth-Century English Canada*. Montreal and Kingston: McGill-Queen's University Press, 1990.

______. *White Canada Forever: Popular Attitudes and Public Policies toward Orientals in British Columbia*. Montreal and Kingston: McGill-Queen's University Press, 1990.

Ward, W. Peter. "Population Growth in Western Canada, 1901-71." In *The Developing West*, ed. John Foster, 155-77. Edmonton: University of Alberta Press, 1983.

Warne, Randi R. "Gender." In *Guide to the Study of Religion*, ed. Willi Braun and Russell T. McCutcheon. London and New York: Cassell, 1999.

Welter, Barbara. "The Feminization of American Religion: 1800-1860." In *Dimity Convictions: The American Woman in the Nineteenth Century*, ed. Barbara Welter, 83-102. Athens, OH: Ohio University Press, 1976.

West, Elliott. "Beyond Baby Doe: Child Rearing on the Mining Frontier." In *The Women's West*, ed. Susan Armitage and Elizabeth Jameson, 179-92. Norman and London: University of Oklahoma Press, 1987.

White, Margaret. "Restructuring the Domestic Sphere – Prairie Indian Women on Reserves: Image, Ideology and State Policy, 1880-1930." PhD thesis, McGill University, 1987.

Whitehead, Margaret. "'A Useful Christian Woman': First Nations Women and Protestant Missionary Work in British Columbia." *Atlantis* 18 (Fall/Summer 1992/3) 142-68.

______. "Women Were Made for Such Things: Women Missionaries in British Columbia, 1850s to 1940s." *Atlantis* 14 (1988): 141-50.

Winks, Robin. *The Blacks in Canada: A History*. London: Yale University Press, 1971.

Winthrop, Theodore. *The Canoe and the Saddle*. New York: Dodd, Mead and Company, 1862.

Withers Osmond, Marie, and Barrie Thorne. "Feminist Theories: The Social Construction of Gender in Families and Society." In *Sourcebook of Family Theories and Methods: A Contextual Approach*, ed. Pauline G. Boss et al., 591-623. New York and London: Plenum, 1993.

Worobec, Christine. "Temptress or Virgin? The Precarious Sexual Position of Women in Post-emancipation Ukrainian Peasant Society." In *Russian Peasant Women*, ed. Beatrice Farnsworth and Lynne Viola, 41-53. New York and Oxford: Oxford University Press, 1992.

Worsnop, Judith. "A Reevaluation of the Problem of Surplus Women in Nineteenth-Century England." *Women's Studies International Forum* 13, 1-2 (1990): 21-31.

Yee, Shirley J. "Gender Ideology and Black Women As Community-Builders in Ontario, 1850-1870." *Canadian Historical Review* 75, 1 (1994): 53-73.

Young, Robert J.C. *Colonial Desire: Hybridity in Theory, Culture and Race*. London and New York: Routledge, 1995.

Young, Walter D. *The Anatomy of a Party: The National CCF, 1932-61*. Toronto: University of Toronto Press, 1969.

Contributors

Beverly Boutilier is a graduate of Carleton University. She held a post-doctoral fellowship at the Ontario Institute for Studies in Education before taking up her current position advising Women's Studies programming in Ujung Pandang, Indonesia, as part of a gender equity and public sector reform project funded by CIDA. She is co-editor (with Alison Prentice) of *Creating Historical Memory: English-Canadian Women and the Work of History* (Vancouver: UBC Press, 1997).

Sarah Carter teaches history at the University of Calgary. In addition to her many articles she is author of *Capturing Women: The Manipulation of Cultural Imagery in Canada's Prairie West* (Montreal and Kingston: McGill-Queen's University Press, 1997); and *Lost Harvests: Prairie Indian Reserve Farmers and Government Policy* (Montreal and Kingston: McGill-Queen's University Press, 1990).

Catherine A. Cavanaugh teaches Women's Studies at Athabasca University. She co-edited (with Jeremy Mouat) *Making Western Canada: Essays on European Colonization and Settlement* (Toronto: Garamond, 1996) and (with Randi R. Warne) *Standing on New Ground: Women in Alberta* (Edmonton: University of Alberta Press, 1993). She is the recipient of the Joan Jensen-Darlis Miller Prize in western women's history (1998) and of the O.O. Winther Prize (1998).

Sherry Edmunds-Flett is a graduate of UCLA in African Studies. She is currently completing a PhD at Simon Fraser University, focusing on African-Canadian women in British Columbia. Sherry also teaches adult education in the BC prison system.

Frieda Esau Klippenstein is a historian with National Historic Sites, Canadian Heritage Department. Her work focuses on developing ethno-historical methods and approaches, including field research, oral histories, consultations, collaborations, and negotiated agreements in contemporary First Nations and immigrant cultural communities.

Nanci Langford teaches women's history at Athabasca University. She has published several articles on farm women and is the author of *Politics, Pitchforks and Pickle Jars: Seventy-Five Years of Organized Farm Women in Alberta* (Calgary: Detselig, 1997).

Ann Leger-Anderson teaches history in the Department of History, University of Regina. A pioneer in researching, writing, and teaching Prairie women's history, her article, "Canadian Prairie Women's History: An Uncertain Enterprise," appeared in *Journal of the West* 37 (January 1998), 47-59.

Sheila McManus is currently completing a PhD at York University. Her dissertation, "'The Line Which Separates': Race, Gender and the 49th Parallel in the Late Nineteenth Century," is a comparative study of race, gender, state formation, and borders in southern Alberta and northern Montana. Her article, "'Their Own Country': 'Race,' Gender, Landscape and Colonization around the 49th Parallel, 1862-1900," appeared in the Spring 1999 volume of *Agricultural History*, 168-82.

Nancy Pagh teaches at Western Washington University in Bellingham. She is a graduate of the University of British Columbia and has a PhD in Interdisciplinary Studies, combining the fields of English, History, Geography and Gender Studies. She has also published in such interdisciplinary journals as *Mosaic*, *ISLE*, and *Frontiers*. The ideas in her chapter are explored in depth in *At Home Afloat: Gender and Domesticity in Northwest Coast Marine Travel Accounts* (University of Calgary Press, forthcoming).

Myra Rutherdale teaches Women's Studies at Simon Fraser University in Vancouver. She is currently revising her dissertation, "Models of Grace and Boundaries of Culture: Anglican Women Missionaries on a Northern Frontier, 1860-1940," for publication. Her published articles can be found in *BC Studies* and *Canadian Woman Studies*.

Frances Swyripa teaches history at the University of Alberta, where she is also director of the Ukrainian-Canadian Programme in the Canadian Institute of Ukrainian Studies. In addition to being the author of numerous articles, she also wrote *Wedded to the Cause: Ukrainian-Canadian*

Women and Ethnic Identity, 1891-1991 (Toronto: University of Toronto Press, 1993).

Randi R. Warne teaches in Religious Studies at Mount St. Vincent University. Her publications include *Literature as Pulpit: The Christian Social Activism of Nellie L. McClung* (Waterloo: Wilfrid Laurier University Press, 1993); (with Catherine A. Cavanaugh) *Standing on New Ground: Women in Alberta* (Waterloo: Wilfrid Laurier University Press, 1993); and numerous publications in women/gender and religion, and Religious Studies method and theory.

Index

Set in Adobe Caslon by Brenda and Neil West, BN Typographics West

Printed and bound in Canada by Friesens

Copy editor: Joanne Richardson

Proofreader: Judy Phillips

Indexer: Christine Jacobs